PARIS

Christopher McIntosh

**Fourth
edition
of the
American
Express
Pocket
Guide**

Mitchell Beazley

The Author and Contributors

Christopher McIntosh is the author of many books and articles on subjects ranging from travel to biography. His other works include *The Swan King*, a biography of Ludwig II of Bavaria, and *The American Express Pocket Guide to Washington, DC*. Contributors to the original edition were Susan Heller Anderson (Nightlife, Shopping), Robert Barton-Clegg (Wines), Peter Graham (Eating in Paris, Cafés, Restaurants, Hotels) and William Green (Nightlife); and to this edition, Marie-Christine Viard (Shopping). This edition was revised in 1990 by Eileen Townsend Jones, who is a freelance writer and a travel editor for *The American Express Pocket Travel Guides*.

Acknowledgments

The authors and publishers would like to thank the following for their help and advice: Nicolle Roques and the staff of the Paris Tourist Office, Françoise Chabbert of Éditions Gallimard, Wendy and Jean-Pierre Richard, Elizabeth Dartiguenave, Chris and Mike Cowie, Naomi Jones and Keith Trodden, and Mike De Mello of Triptych Systems Ltd. The editor particularly wishes to thank Peter Graham, who acted as a consultant on Food and Drink for this edition.

The *American Express Pocket Travel Guide Series* was conceived under the direction of Susannah Read, Douglas Wilson, Hal Robinson and Eric Drewery. Fiona Duncan edited the original edition.

For the series

General Editor	David Townsend Jones
Managing Art Editor	Nigel O'Gorman
Art Editor	Christopher Howson
Map Editor	David Haslam
Indexer	Hilary Bird
Gazetteer	Sharon Charity

For this edition

Edited on desktop by	Eileen Townsend Jones
Illustrators	Jeremy Ford (David Lewis Artists), Illustra Design Ltd, Rodney Paull, Karen Cochrane
Jacket illustration	Pierre Marie Valat

Edited and designed by Mitchell Beazley International Limited, Artists House, 14-15 Manette Street, London W1V 5LB for the American Express (R) Pocket Travel Guide Series

Maps in 2-colour and 4-colour by Lovell Johns, Oxford, England.
Desktop layout in Ventura Publisher by Castle House Press, Llantrisant, Wales.
Typeset in Garamond and Univers.
Linotronic output through Microstar DTP Studio, Cardiff, Wales.
Produced by Mandarin Offset. Printed and bound in Malaysia.

Contents

How to use this book

The American Express Pocket Guide to Paris is an encyclopaedia of travel information, organized in the sections listed on the previous page. There is also a comprehensive *Index* (pages 208-219) and a *List of street names* (pages 220-224), and there are full-colour *Maps* at the end of the book.

For easy reference, all major sections (*Sights and places of interest, Hotels, Restaurants*), and other sections where possible, are arranged alphabetically. For the organization of the book as a whole, see *Contents*. For individual places that do not have separate entries in *Sights and places of interest*, see the *Index*.

Abbreviations   As a rule, only standard abbreviations are used, such as days of the week and months, points of the compass (N, S, E and W), street names (Av., Bd., Pl., Sq.), Saint and Sainte (St and Ste), rms (rooms), C (century), and measurements.

Bold type   **Bold type** is used mainly for emphasis, to draw attention to something of special interest or importance. It also picks out places — shops or minor museums, for example — that do not have full entries of their own. In such cases, it is usually followed in brackets by the address, telephone number, details of opening times, etc., which are printed in *italics*.

Cross-references   A special typeface, *sans serif italics*, is used for cross-references. Each time you see a place name, such as *Panthéon*, printed in this way, expect to find a full entry under that heading in the alphabetical *Sights and places of interest* (pages 45-128).

Similarly, when you see the title of a section of the book, such as *Hotels* or *Words and phrases*, printed in this way,

---

How entries are organized

Hood House

1411 Lincoln Ave., Lincoln Green, Sherwood Forest
☎ *426-5960 (house), 426-5961 (group tour reservations).*
Map 8J11 ☷ *Open Apr-Sept 9am-5pm, rest of year 9am-4pm. Closed Christmas, New Year's Day. Metro: Bow & Arrow.*

Robin Hood (?1149-1205) was the leading spokesman for the poor and downtrodden in their struggle for freedom and justice under the Plantagenets. He lectured and wrote books about his own early life as a serf, campaigned endlessly for human rights, helped recruit peasants to the Civil Service, and finally settled down to a distinguished old age in Sherwood Forest. He lived first in A St. (see *National Museum of Outlawed Art*), then bought Sheriff Villa, which he renamed Hood House, a handsome white dwelling on a height overlooking the Trent Valley. All the furnishings, except for curtains and wallpaper, are original. Hood's library and other belongings are still *in situ*, and the whole house is redolent of the spirit of a very remarkable man. In the **Visitors' Centre** at the foot of the hill you can see a film about Hood's life.

you can turn to that section for further information. (You will find a complete section-by-section breakdown of the book on the *Contents* page.)

For easy reference, use the headers printed at the top corner of each page (for example, **La Défense** on page 87, or **Restaurants** on page 140).

Map references   Each full-colour map at the end of the book is divided into a grid of squares, identified vertically by letters (A, B, C, D, etc.) and horizontally by numbers (1, 2, 3, 4, etc.). A map reference pinpoints the page (the first **bold** number) and position — thus *Arc de Triomphe* is located in Map **6**F3.

Price categories   Price categories for hotels and restaurants are represented by the symbols ☐ ☐☐ ☐☐☐ ☐☐☐☐ and ☐☐☐☐☐, which signify cheap, inexpensive, moderately priced, expensive and very expensive, respectively. These correspond approximately with the following actual prices, which give a guideline at the time of printing. Although actual prices will inevitably increase, as a rule the relative price category — for example, expensive or cheap — is likely to remain more or less the same.

Price categories	Corresponding to approximate prices	
	for **hotels**	for **restaurants**
	double room with bath + breakfast; singles are somewhat cheaper	*meal for one with service, taxes and house wine*
☐ cheap	under 250 francs	under 100 francs
☐☐ inexpensive	250-450 francs	100-170 francs
☐☐☐ moderate	450-650 francs	170-270 francs
☐☐☐☐ expensive	650-1,250 francs	270-500 francs
☐☐☐☐☐ very expensive	over 1,250 francs	over 500 francs

—— Bold blue type for entry headings.

—— Blue italics for address, practical information and symbols.
For list of symbols see page 6 or back flap of jacket.

—— Black text for description.

—— Sans serif italics used for cross-references to other entries or sections.

—— Bold type used for emphasis.

Entries for hotels, restaurants, shops, etc. follow the same organization, and are usually printed across a half column.
    In hotels, symbols indicating special facilities appear at the end of the entry, in black.——

Pullman
2600 Express Ave., Orient City 20037 ☎ *299-4450* ⓕ *299-4460.*
Map 2F4 ☐☐☐☐ *238 rms* ⇌ ☰ AE
CB ⊙ ⊙ VISA *Metro: High Standard.*
Location: On a height overlooking the Universal Trade Center. Part of a large conglomeration overlooking the seafront, this luxurious hotel is set in attractively landscaped grounds and is run with clockwork precision. Its restaurant, the **Simplon**, is highly regarded.
& ☙ ⫶ ⇌ ✠

Key to symbols

☎	Telephone	🚗	Secure garage
⊛	Telex	◠	Quiet hotel
ⓕ	Facsimile (fax)	⬆	Lift
★	Recommended sight	♿	Facilities for
☆	Worth a detour		disabled people
♣	Good value (in its	▢	TV in each room
	class)	☎	Telephone in each
i	Tourist information		room
←	Parking	▬	Mini-bar
⏟	Building of	🐕	Dogs not allowed
	architectural interest	☘	Garden
◉	Free entrance	◁€	Good view
▣	Entrance fee payable	≋	Swimming pool
✗	Photography forbidden	⌂	Sauna
𝑲	Guided tour available	⌁	Tennis
▬	Cafeteria	ᵼ	Gym/fitness
✷	Special interest for		facilities
	children	▥	Conference facilities
✧	Hotel	⊨	Restaurant
▬	Simple hotel	▬	Simple restaurant
▥	Luxury hotel	◁	Luxury restaurant
▢	Cheap	▬	Good wines
▥	Inexpensive	⊕	Open-air dining
▥	Moderately priced	⏁	Bar
▥	Expensive	●	Disco dancing
▥	Very expensive	▬	Nightclub
▤	Air conditioning	♫	Live music
AE	American Express	ᵛᵎ	Dancing
◉	Diners Club	▨	Revue

A note from the General Editor

No travel book can be completely free of errors and
totally up to date. Telephone numbers and opening
hours change without warning, and hotels and
restaurants come under new management, which can
affect standards. We make every effort to ensure that all
information is accurate at the time we go to press, but
are always delighted to receive corrections or
suggestions for improvements from our readers, which if
warranted will be incorporated in a future edition. We
are indebted to readers who wrote to us during the
preparation of this edition.

The publishers regret that they cannot accept any
consequences arising from the use of the book or from
the information it contains.

Paris: past, present & future

To go to Paris is not just to experience a beautiful city (some would say the most beautiful of all); it is to feel the pulse of a civilization that has held the admiration of the world for centuries — the civilization of France. The Parisian regards Paris not only as the capital of a great nation, but as the capital of all true culture. He can be forgiven if he feels he has no need to travel. Why should he go to the Himalayas when he can look at the Île de la Cité reflected in the waters of the Seine? Why should he learn other languages when his own is so perfect?

All Parisians are absolutely conscious of their heritage. They may seem arrogant — but they have much to be arrogant about. Think of the countless songs that have been written about Paris; the books that have been inspired by it; the millions of pilgrims who have beaten a path to the city over the centuries.

"Paris," wrote Henry James, "is the greatest temple ever built to material joys and the lust of the eyes." His words are as apt today as when they were written in the 1870s. Paris is indeed a temple, the doors of which are always open to anyone who is receptive to beauty, civilized values and delight of the senses. As a result, the visitor is almost inevitably transformed in some way by the experience. But it is not enough just to walk in and passively wait for the magic to work. You must become a little bit Parisian in the way you look at things and the way you react, understand something of the spirit of Paris and the history and traditions that have shaped it. Also you must avoid rigid preconceptions and expectations. Allow for the unexpected and elusive moments of pleasure that Paris so often gives.

People come here from all over the world and for a variety of reasons: to see the Paris of the travel brochures (the Eiffel Tower, Notre-Dame and Montmartre); to explore the great museums such as the Louvre; to enjoy the famous quality of Parisian food and wine; or to test Paris' reputation as the city of Eros. If you come for the last reason you may not find exactly what you had expected. Paris is not a particularly wicked city compared with many others in Europe, despite its red-light districts and the scarlet reputation that was established almost a century ago. What it does have is a subtle sensuality that bubbles over into the whole environment, giving zest to the very air of the city. You can see it in the easy flow of intimacy between young lovers strolling by the Seine or idling on the café terraces. It is impossible not to be affected by it, however imperceptibly.

Paris is a veritable ocean. Throw in the plumb line and you will never know the depth of it...

Balzac, *Père Goriot*

As for the inhabitants of Paris themselves, they can seem somewhat abrupt, even abrasive to the outsider, but this is usually a surface impression. Underneath you will find a good-humoured courtesy and friendliness that does them credit, considering the massive influx of visitors with whom they have to deal each year.

Remember that Paris is not just a vast museum for tourists. It is also a busy, thriving metropolis, and one that has coped superbly well with the problems that face all modern cities. While other capitals might crumble under the strain, Paris remains one of the smoothest-running urban machines in the world.

What might be called "Greater Paris", that is the whole metropolitan area, covers 479 square kilometers (185 square miles) and has a population of about 8½ million. But this guide focuses on the city proper. This area, cut in half by the Seine, and surrounded by the ring road known as the Périphérique, covers only 106 square kilometers (41 square miles) and has just under 2¼ million inhabitants. Although these are very tightly crammed into a small area, somehow, by a miraculous sleight of hand, Paris gives an impression of spaciousness. The Métro carries 4 million passengers a day — and does the job with the minimum of fuss and with subsidized fares at a very low cost. For the entertainment of its citizens and visitors, the city has some 10,000 restaurants, cafés and nightclubs, 80 municipal libraries, 2 city orchestras, 66 theatres, 27 café-theatres, 220 galleries, 465 cinemas, and 48 concert halls.

The smooth-running of the city is administered by a city council of 109 members who are elected for a 6-year term and meet in the palatial Hôtel de Ville. The council is headed by a mayor, who also sits for a 6-year term. For more than a century, the city had no mayor, and was controlled by the national government through a Prefect of Paris. This arrangement proved unsatisfactory because, as a result, the people of Paris had no direct influence over the running of their city. It was partly this state of affairs that enabled some grave planning errors of judgment to be made during President Pompidou's era. The building of the Tour Montparnasse, and the construction of a motorway along part of the riverside footpath, are now regarded as two such mistakes. In 1977, Paris was once again given a mayor in the person of the energetic Jacques Chirac, also twice prime minister, who has done much to improve the city's quality of life and environment.

Those who knew Paris more than 30 years ago, in the days before President de Gaulle came to power, will remember a city that seemed to be a symphony in shades of grey, the prevailing atmosphere one of picture-postcard scruffiness and exquisitely faded charm. The water was hazardous, plumbing was often antediluvian, and the franc was a precarious currency. Today all this has changed. Although there is still much poverty in evidence, Paris, along with the whole of France, has become much more buoyant. A massive cleaning programme has transformed the city centre, so that the boulevards and squares now gleam with pristine tones of cream and gold. Most houses now have modern plumbing, and old buildings are being restored district by district with grants from the city. The fall in the population, one of the great problems of recent years, has been stemmed by housing subsidies and by an attempt to attract light industries back into the city. The recent prosperity of Paris, and of France, and its desire to keep pace with modernization, is well illustrated by the construction of La Défense, the huge, gleaming "Manhattan-sur-Seine" complex of skyscrapers lying just outside the city limits.

Inevitably there has been a price to pay for progress. Charming old districts, such as Montparnasse, have been violated; fine buildings, such as the former market at Les Halles, have been pulled down. But Paris is riding on a prolonged wave of municipal confidence and general prosperity. The spirit of adventure is abroad, symbolized perhaps best of all in the astonishing pyramid that now stands proudly between the great wings of the Louvre. Clear-sighted political willpower is ensuring that Paris retains its old-fashioned charm while moving briskly forward towards the 21st century. The city deserves all the time that a visitor can possibly afford to give — for the rewards of that intimacy are without number.

Before you go

Documents required

Visitors to France, if they are citizens of the United Kingdom or
other EC countries, or if they are American, Canadian or Japanese
nationals, do not need a visa — a passport or identity card will
suffice. Vaccination certificates are not now normally required.
For stays of longer than three months, you will need to apply for
a *carte de séjour*, which can be obtained from the **French
Consulate** (*6A Conway Place, South Kensington, London SW7
2EW* ☎ *071-581-5292*).

If arriving by car, you need a valid driving licence (not
provisional) and must be 18 or over. An international driving
licence is not needed. You also need the vehicle registration
certificate (logbook), a national identity plate or sticker displayed
at the rear of the vehicle, and a certificate of insurance or
international green card proving that you have third-party
insurance.

Travel and medical insurance

It is advisable to travel with an insurance policy that covers loss
of deposits paid to airlines, hotels, tour operators, etc., and the
cost of dealing with emergency requirements, such as special
tickets home and extra nights in a hotel, as well as a medical
insurance policy. To obtain on-the-spot cover, contact your local
travel agent before departure.

There is a reciprocal agreement between EC countries whereby
visitors, who are entitled to full UK benefits, can obtain
emergency medical and dental treatment for the same cost as the
nationals themselves. To benefit from this you must have form
E111, which can now be obtained from any Post Office or Sub-
Post Office. Complete form CM1 (the application for form E111)
and your own E111 form, which will then be authorized at the
counter while you wait. Attached to the E111 is a leaflet, *Health
Care For Visitors to EC Countries*, which gives details on how to
claim. Keep your E111 when you return: it has no expiry date.
Study also the booklet T1, *The Traveller's Guide to Health*, which
gives comprehensive information on vaccinations and diseases
and provides useful health checklists. In France you are only
entitled to a refund of approximately 75 percent of the medical
services expenses you are charged, and about 70 percent of the
medicinal costs, so it is wise to take out private insurance.

There is a **British Hospital** (*Hôpital Franco-Britannique, 3
Rue Barbès, Levallois-Perret* ☎ *47-58-13-12*).The **American
Hospital** (*63 Bd. Victor-Hugo, Neuilly-sur-Seine* ☎ *47-47-
53-00*), accepts Blue Cross and Blue Shield medical insurance.

Money

The unit of currency is the franc (f), which consists of 100
centimes (c). There are coins for 5c, 10c, 20c and ½f, 1f, 2f, 5f and
10f, and notes for the following amounts: 20f, 50f, 100f and 500f.
There is no limit to the amount of currency you can bring into
France, but you can take out no more than 12,000f when you
leave, unless large sums are declared on entry. On days
preceding public holidays, banks are open only in the morning,
although exchange bureaux are open longer.

Travellers cheques issued by American Express, Thomas Cook,
Barclays and Citibank are widely recognized; make sure you read
the instructions included with your travellers cheques. It is
important to note separately the serial numbers of your cheques

Before you go

and the telephone number to call in case of loss. Specialist travellers cheque companies such as American Express provide extensive local refund facilities for lost cheques through their own offices or agents.

Major international credit cards such as American Express, Diners Club, Eurocard (MasterCard) and Carte Bleue (Visa) are widely accepted, the two latter cards being nowadays almost universal. In this book, acceptance of Mastercard and Visa cards is not shown, because most establishments accept most cards; establishments that accept American Express (**AE**) and Diners Club (**CB**) cards are marked thus; and if cards are not accepted, the words "no cards" appear. British citizens can take Eurocheques drawn on their bank account and a Eurocard, which works like a Visa card and can be used in cash dispensers.

American Express also has a **MoneyGram** (R) money transfer service that makes it possible to wire money worldwide in just minutes, from any American Express Travel Service Office. This service is available to all customers and is not limited to American Express Card members. See *Useful addresses* on page 18.

Customs

The completion of the European Single Market takes place at the end of 1992. No definite agreement has yet been reached on whether or not to retain the sale of goods at duty-free prices, although it seems likely that this will no longer apply. Information can be obtained from **HM Customs & Excise**, Single Market Unit ☎071-865-5426.

Duty- and tax-free shopping will still be available to travellers departing directly for countries outside the European Community.

Until Jan 1, 1993, the following is likely to remain the case. If you are visiting France for less than six months, you are entitled to bring, free of duty and tax, all personal effects, except tobacco goods, alcoholic drinks and perfume, which you intend to take with you when you leave. Make sure that you are carrying dated receipts for more valuable items such as cameras and watches, or you may be charged duty.

Duty-free allowances for import into France are given below. The figures in brackets show the increased allowances for goods obtained tax-paid in EC countries. Travellers under 17 are not entitled to the allowances on tobacco goods and alcoholic drinks.
Tobacco 200 (300) cigarettes *or* 100 (150) cigarillos *or* 50 (75) cigars *or* 250g (400g) tobacco.
Alcoholic drinks 1(1.5) litres spirits (more than 22 percent alcohol by volume) *or* 2(3) litres of alcoholic drink of 22 percent alcohol or less, or fortified wine or sparkling wine *plus* 2(5) litres of still table wine.
Perfume 50g/60cc/2fl oz(75g/90cc/3fl oz).
Other goods Commodities and articles to the value of 300f (2,400f); 150f (620f) for travellers under 15.

Prohibited and restricted goods include narcotics, gold and weapons. A more detailed list can be obtained from the French Government Tourist Office.

Visitors are exempt from paying Value Added Tax (TVA) on purchases above a certain amount, on completion of a simple form and presentation of a passport at the time of purchase (see *Shopping*). However, to validate the refund, which will be made to you at your home address, or through a credit card refund, you must present the paperwork and goods at a checkpoint before the passport control on leaving the country. Leave enough time to do this.

Getting there

By air   There are daily flights to Paris from many parts of the world, including many cities in the US, and an almost hourly shuttle service from London (Heathrow) run by British Airways and Air France, which both also fly from Gatwick. Stansted airport near London has flights to Paris run by Air France and Air UK, and London City Airport in London's Docklands is served by Brymon Airways/Air France and London City Airways. Other British cities including Aberdeen, Belfast, Birmingham, Bradford, Bristol, Edinburgh, Glasgow, Manchester, Newcastle and Southampton offer regular flights. Dublin is served by Aer Lingus and Air France. Paris has two passenger airports: Roissy/Charles de Gaulle to the N and Orly to the S.

By train   There is a regular train-and-boat service from London's Victoria Station, and a slightly more expensive but faster train-and-hovercraft service from Charing Cross and Victoria (most frequent in summer). The fastest, via Dover to Calais and on to Paris (Gare du Nord), takes about 7hrs.

By ferry or hovercraft   There are several routes across the Channel for both motorists and foot passengers. The major British ports with frequent ferry services are Dover, Folkestone, Portsmouth and Newhaven. From these ports you can sail direct to Dunkerque, Calais, Boulogne, Dieppe or Le Havre.

Hovercraft is the quickest way of crossing the Channel — 35mins from Dover to Calais in good weather — for those with or without cars. Hovercrafts operate between Dover and Calais or Boulogne. There are crossings several times a day throughout the year, these being more frequent in summer. The A26/A1 between Calais and Paris is a fast and direct route linking the capital to one of the Channel ports, so head for Calais if you are in a hurry.

By bus   Travelling by bus is the cheapest means of getting to Paris from England. From Victoria Coach Station in London, you can travel with **Eurolines UK** (☎ *(071) 730-0202*), which has two daily departures (noon and 9pm) throughout the year with an extra morning departure in high summer only, or with **Hoverspeed** (☎ *(0304) 240241*), which operates a daytime service all year round. Both have a journey time of about 9hrs. It is wise to book in advance, especially if you plan to travel during the summer.

Climate

In Aug the majority of Parisians evacuate the city, as Paris can be unpleasantly and surprisingly hot — temperatures average 23°C (75°F), and you might think you were much farther south. Autumn is often warm; spring brings clear blue skies, but can be chilly; and in winter it can be uncomfortably cold and damp.

Clothes

The famous Parisian *chic* is evident wherever you go; both men and women are beautifully turned out, rarely casually or scruffily dressed. The French are, however, tolerant of informality: you don't normally need to wear a tie to a smart restaurant, and women can feel free to wear trousers on virtually any occasion. Pack one warm garment even for spring, a light raincoat and an umbrella.

Poste restante

The central post office in Paris, at 52 Rue du Louvre, 75001 Paris (☎ *40-28-20-00*), will keep all mail marked *poste restante* unless specifically addressed to another Parisian post office. The addressee's name should be written clearly on the envelope. You will need identification when you collect your mail and may be charged a small fee. If the letter is addressed to two people, e.g., Mr and Mrs, addressees must collect the letter together. Travel companies such as American Express will also hold mail.

Getting around

From the airports to the city

Trains run every 15mins between 5.30am-11.30pm to the Gare du Nord from **Roissy/Charles de Gaulle** (☎ 48-62-22-80); the journey takes 35mins. Air France coaches (☎ 42-99-20-18 *recorded message*) take 25mins when traffic is clear, but up to 1hr at rush hours. They leave every 15-20mins, between 5.40am-11pm, for the Porte Maillot and Pl. Charles de Gaulle (*1 Av. Carnot*) terminals. Public buses are slow and relatively expensive.

From **Orly** Airport (☎ 48-84-32-10), s of Paris, trains take about 40mins and leave every 15mins for the Gare d'Austerlitz or Gare St-Michel. Air France coaches (☎ 43-23-97-10 *recorded message*) leave every 12-15mins between 5.40am-11pm; the journey takes about 40mins. Again, public buses can be very slow.

There are taxis at each airport, but a taxi ride to your destination will certainly be expensive and will not necessarily be any quicker. From Roissy/Charles de Gaulle Airport allow at least 30mins, or more in rush hour. Orly Airport is a cheaper, shorter journey, and should take only 20mins.

Public transport

Paris has one of the best public transport systems in the world, run by the **RATP** (*Réseau Autonome du Transport Parisien, 53ter Quai des Grands-Augustins, 6ᵉ*). Bus, Métro and inner RER systems use the same tickets, which are much cheaper if you buy a book (*carnet*) of ten, obtainable from bus or Métro stations, *tabacs* and, increasingly, from slot machines in the street. *Billets de tourisme* (tourist tickets) are also obtainable. New, money-saving schemes seem to be brought in each year, and it will be best to ask what is currently on offer. No ticket on any of the systems is valid until it has been punched or otherwise validated by passing through a machine, and frequent travelling bands of ticket inspectors can impose on-the-spot fines on anyone travelling without the correct ticket.

Métro

Unlike some underground systems, the Paris Métro is very clean, efficient and quite easy to understand. Each line is designated by a number, and by the names of the end stations. There are two classes, and smoking is prohibited. Inside Paris one ticket is valid no matter how far you go or how many changes you make, and you should retain your ticket until you reach your destination, as you may encounter a ticket-operated barrier when you leave. The Métro runs from 5.30am-12.30am. Métro stations are a popular haunt for musicians of all kinds; as in many great cities, you may come across beggars and pickpockets.

RER (Réseau Express Régional)

This is a fast suburban service which consists of three lines. Line A goes from St-Germain-en-Laye, Poissy or Cergy to Boissy-St-Léger; line B goes from Robinson St-Rémy-les-Chevreuse to

Roissy and Mitry-Claye; and line C connects Versailles and
St-Quentin-en-Yvelines to Dourdan. Within the Métro area, the
Métro/Bus/RER standard ticket can be used. For travelling into
the suburbs, you will need a supplementary ticket; the cost varies
with the distance. The service runs from 5.30am-12.30am.

Buses

On the buses, one ticket is valid for up to two *sections* (fare
stages or zones) and two tickets are valid for three stages or more
within the city boundary. When you enter the bus you have to
composter (punch) your ticket by inserting it into the machine
behind the driver. Tickets can also be bought from the driver, but
they are more expensive. Buses run from 7am-8.30pm, except to
main line stations, where the service operates until 12.30am.

Night buses leave the Châtelet (Av. Victoria) from 1.30-5.30am,
serving nine suburban destinations, and returning again on the
hour from 2-5am. Look for stops with a black and yellow owl
symbol. For bus information in English ☎ 40-46-42-12.

Taxis

At the last count there were 15,000 taxis in the city. They can be
ordered by telephone (☎ 49-36-10-10) or hailed in the street.
Some drivers will accept an American Express card, but ask when
booking. Whenever possible, take a taxi from a rank, rather than
telephoning for one, as the meter starts to run once the taxi
leaves its base.

Cabs have two lights on the roof: both lit means free, one lit
means occupied, both off means the driver is on his way home.
All registered cabs are equipped with meters. There is a
surcharge on Sun and between 10pm-6.30am. You will also pay
more if you are carrying a lot of heavy or bulky objects or if you
are picked up at a station — but taxis can be hard to find once
you're away from the rank.

Taxis will theoretically hold up to four passengers, but most
drivers nowadays will only take three unless you offer them
financial inducement in advance. This can be awkward for
families or groups of four. Under normal circumstances the driver
expects a tip of 12-15 percent.

Beware of pirate drivers who offer to take you for a "first-class"
fare, which will be about five times the normal one.

For taxis equipped for handicapped people ♿ ☎ 48-37-85-85.

Getting around by car

If you value your bumpers it is wise to avoid driving in Paris —
the Parisian drives as if he were on the dodgems at a fairground,
and parks as though he were shoving a book into a tight shelf.
The parking problem is severe, and meters are ubiquitous —
they run from 9am-7pm and are watched there by blue-uniformed
ladies sometimes known as *pervanches* (periwinkles). There are
also a number of underground, multi-storey car parks. In *zones
bleues* (streets where blue parking signs are displayed), a *disque
de contrôle* (parking disc) must be shown. These are obtainable
from hotels, garages and tourist offices.

Speed limits are 60kph (37mph) in the city and in built-up
areas, 80kph (50mph) on the Périphérique, 90kph (56mph) on
country roads, 130kph (80mph) on toll autoroutes and 110kph
(68mph) on free autoroutes and dual carriageways. It is as well to
be aware of the following laws: cars coming from the right have
priority unless otherwise signed; seat-belts are compulsory;
children under ten must not travel in the front seat; and headlight

beams must be adjusted for right-hand-drive cars.

Information on autoroute travelling, including free maps and a hotel reservation service, can be obtained from **Renseignements d'Autoroutes**, (*3 Rue Edmond Valentin, 75007 Paris* ☎ *47-05-90-01, open Mon-Fri 9am-noon, 2-6pm*).

Renting a car

It is worth renting a car for trips out to the suburbs or out of the city, although within the central area rentals are expensive and garages are scarce.

Most international car rental companies have offices in Paris, and there are also many reliable and often cheaper Parisian firms. Payment by credit card avoids the need for a large cash deposit. A current driving licence is required, and the minimum age is usually 21, although some companies have raised it to 25. Make sure the car is fully insured, even if it means making separate arrangements for insurance against damage to other vehicles and injury to your passengers.

Various companies are represented at the airports, and you can make fly-drive arrangements before you leave your home country.

Getting around on foot

Paris is a city built on a human scale and is therefore easy and pleasant to walk in. If you are not in a hurry, this is the most enjoyable way of getting about. A combination of walking and use of the excellent public transport system is ideal for exploring Paris. Crossing busy roads, however, can be hazardous, even at *passages cloutés* (pedestrian crossings), where drivers are supposed to give way but often don't. The motto in Paris is *walk with confidence*, so follow their example. The only people dithering on the boulevards are the foreign visitors.

Railway services

France's railway services are run by the SNCF (Société Nationale de Chemins de Fer). When travelling by train, as with the Métro, RER and buses, you must validate your ticket at the machine at the platform entrance. If you fail to do this, you will be treated as if you are travelling without a ticket and will have to pay an on-the-spot fine or a surcharge.

The terminals for travel beyond Paris are: **Gare d'Austerlitz** (southwest), **Gare de L'Est** (east), **Gare de Lyon** (southeast), **Gare Montparnasse** (west), **Gare du Nord** (north), **Gare St-Lazare** (northwest). For general information and times of trains ☎ 45-82-50-50.

Domestic airlines

Air Inter is France's major internal airline. The central office is at 49 Av. des Champs-Élysées, 8ᵉ ☎ 42-89-38-88.

Bicycling

If you are prepared to brave the traffic, bicycling in Paris can be an excellent way of exploring the city. Bicycles can be rented from the following:

Bicyclub   8 Pl. de la Porte-de-Champerret, 17ᵉ ☎ 47-66-55-92
Paris-Vélo (Rent-A-Bike)   2 Rue du Fer-à-Moulin, 5ᵉ ☎ 43-37-59-22
La Maison du Vélo   8 Rue de Belzunce, 10ᵉ ☎ 42-81-24-72 does not hire bikes, but its English and American-speaking staff offer repairs and very friendly advice, as well as sales.

Paris Héliport
The main heliport is situated in the 15e (*business or pleasure inquiries* ☎ *45-54-04-44*). See also *Helicopter flights* in **Activities and sports**.

On-the-spot information

Public holidays
New Year's Day, Jan 1; Easter Monday; Labour Day, May 1; VE Day, May 8; Ascension Day (sixth Thurs after Easter); Whit Monday (second Mon after Ascension); Bastille Day, July 14; Assumption, Aug 15; All Saints' Day, Nov 1; Remembrance Day, Nov 11; Dec 25. Most museums close, but some shops and restaurants remain open.

Time zones
Like most Western European countries, France is 1hr ahead of GMT in the winter and 2hrs ahead in summer, i.e., 1hr ahead of the UK most of the year.

Banks and currency exchange
In general, banks are open Mon-Fri 9am-4.30pm, but there are no standardized banking hours. They all close on the afternoon before a public holiday. Bureaux de change at airports and in most stations stay open late and are often open at weekends. The **American Express Office** (*11 Rue Scribe, 9^e* ☎ *42-66-09-99*) is open Mon-Fri 9am-5pm.

Money can also be exchanged in larger hotels, but the rate will be less good than in banks. It is advisable to ask about exchange rates and commission, as these can vary considerably. Remember that you need your passport when changing money.
Eurocheques can be cashed up to a value of £100, at all banks displaying the Eurocard sign. The Eurocard will also give a similar amount through cash-dispensing machines, but note that on-street machines are much less common than in the UK.

An automatic exchange machine will convert various currencies into francs — if you have the right banknotes. There is one at **Banque Régionale d'Escompte et de Dépôt** (*66 Av. des Champs-Élysées, 8e* ☎ *42-89-10-99. Métro: Franklin-D-Roosevelt*).

Shopping hours
Department stores usually remain open from 9.30am-6.30pm without interruption from Mon-Sat, and some are open until 8pm on Wed. Smaller boutiques generally open from about 10am-7pm Mon-Sat, although they sometimes close for an hour at lunch.

While neighbourhood shops often observe the traditional Mon closing, shops in main shopping areas stay open. And, while Aug was once the universal holiday month, most of the larger shops now stay open all summer. See also **Shopping**.

Rush hours
Between 7.30-9am and 5-7pm, the Métro is packed with workers going to and from their offices. On Fri evenings the weekend traffic out of Paris is very heavy. It is also wise to avoid leaving Paris on the first and last days of July or Aug, when the entire population of Paris is either leaving for or returning from its holidays.

On-the-spot information

Postal and telephone services

Post offices are marked by a sign with a blue swallow on a white disc or by the letters **PTT**, and are open Mon-Fri 8am-7pm, Sat 8am-noon. The main post offices are at 48-52 Rue du Louvre, 1ᵉʳ (*open 24hrs*) and 71 Av. des Champs-Élysées, 8ᵉ (*open Mon-Sat 8am-10pm, Sun 10.30am-12.30pm, 2-8pm, but after 7pm service is restricted to simple postal and telephone transactions*).

Stamps can be bought in tobacconists (*tabacs*), hotels and newsagents, and in yellow vending machines. Postboxes are also yellow and are marked *boîte aux lettres*. Allow 7-10 days for mail to reach France, and for your letters to reach home.

Addresses in Paris must all include the postcode, which combines **750-** with the numbers of the arrondissements. Thus the postcode in the 1ᵉʳ is 75001, and so on, to the 20ᵉ, where the postcode is 75020. Usefully, the postcode shows at once the arrondissement in which any address is to be found.

Telegrams can be sent from any post office or by telephone (*in English* ☎ *42-33-21-11; in French* ☎ *42-33-44-11*). Public telephones are found in post offices and cafés as well as in the street. Most telephones now accept cards, not cash, and it can be quite difficult to find a paying telephone in stations and airports. When you find one, it will take 50c, 1f, 2f and 5f coins. Phonecards (*télécartes*) can be bought at post offices, and at shops displaying the sticker *Télécarte en vente ici* (phonecards sold here), but note that 40 units (32f) is the cheapest card available.

The ringing signal is a shrill intermittent tone, while the engaged signal is less shrill and more rapid. For international calls, look in the telephone directory for the direct dialling code. **19** gives an international connection, then wait for the tone and dial **44** for the United Kingdom or **1** for the United States or Canada, the area code (leave off any initial 0) and the number. For reverse charge calls (*appel pcv*), dial **19**, wait for the tone, then **33** for the international operator.

For directory inquiries within France, dial **12**. International directory inquiries are expensive (8f): dial **19-33-12**, then the dialling code for the country required.

Public lavatories

Those who knew Paris before modernization started in earnest will remember the abundance of quaint, perforated-iron kiosks known as *vespasiennes*. Now only about 100 remain. Modern public conveniences (*sanisettes*) are spreading around the city, and are clean and well looked after. You will find them in many Métro stations and public parks, and you can use the facilities of nearly every café. Often you will find a lady presiding, who will expect a nominal sum (1 or 2f); in cafés leave a small tip in the saucer at the bar, if you have not bought a drink.

Electric current

The electric current is 220V (50 cycles AC). Plugs are standard European, with two round pins. Adaptors (*transformateurs*) can be bought at any good electrical shop or department store in Paris, or before you leave home, and, usually, in the airport departure lounge duty-free shops.

Laws and regulations

There are no particularly surprising laws in France; laws against drug abuse are as strongly enforced as elsewhere, with greater penalties for the buying and selling of drugs. Hitch-hiking is forbidden on motorways, although it is tolerated on other roads. Smoking in such public places as post offices, banks and cinemas is forbidden, and can incur a fine.

Customs and etiquette

The French are among the most manner-conscious of all nations, and observe a rather rigid code of behaviour in personal relationships, which is, however, beginning to be broken down by the younger generation. This consciousness is exemplified by the *vous* and *tu* forms of address; the former applies to everyone except relations, close friends and children. Hand-shaking is common when greeting or saying goodbye among friends, as well as between acquaintances and strangers, and close friends kiss each other energetically on alternate cheeks at least twice and often three times. It is customary, when addressing someone, to say *Madame* or *Monsieur* without using a surname.

Tipping

Tipping is less widely practised in France today, as bars, restaurants and hotels all include 15 percent service and taxes in their prices (*service compris*, which can also be seen as *s. c.*). If the service has been particularly good, you can show your appreciation by leaving a small extra tip for the waiter.

Small tips of up to a few francs should be given to cloakroom attendants, tour guides, doormen, hairdressers and cinema usherettes. Airport and railway porters have a fixed charge per item, while taxi drivers will expect 10-15 percent.

Disabled travellers

Special facilities for the disabled are becoming more and more common in France. The **Comité National Français de Liaison pour la Réadaptation des Handicapés** (*38 Bd. Raspail, 75007 Paris* ☎ *45-48-90-13*) publish an excellent booklet in their series *Touristes quand même* (Tourists nonetheless...), which contains invaluable information for the handicapped visitor to Paris. They prefer requests in writing. **RADAR** (*25 Mortimer St., London W1N 8AB* ☎ *071-637-5400*) will also provide a factsheet on travel to France. They also publish *Holidays and Travel Abroad*. These organizations can recommend travel agents specializing in holidays for handicapped people, wheelchair and hand-controlled-car rental, etc. The Paris **Office du Tourisme** publishes comprehensive lists of hotels and sights that give full details of wheelchair accessibility.

A brief guide (in English) to facilities for disabled travellers at Roissy/Charles de Gaulle and Orly airports can be obtained, free of charge, from **Aéroports de Paris** (*291 Bd. Raspail, 75675 Paris* ☎ *43-35-70-00*). More than 300 railway stations have wheelchairs and mobile steps. The authorities are fairly lenient to disabled drivers, and tend to ignore parking offences, although law-breaking is not to be encouraged....

Local publications

Useful publications giving full details of current events, cinemas, theatres, shows, sports, etc., are the weekly *Pariscope* and *l'Officiel des Spectacles*, and *Paris Passion*, an English-language magazine that appears monthly except Jan and Aug. These publications can be bought at most newspaper stands.

Major English bookshops include: **Abbey Bookshop** (*29 Rue de la Parcheminerie, 5ᵉ*), **Attica** (*for literature, 34 Rue des Écoles, 5ᵉ; for language books, 84 Bd. St-Michel, 6ᵉ*), **Attica**

Useful addresses

Junior (*23 Rue St-Jean-de-Beauvais, 5ᵉ*), **Brentano's** (*37 Av. de l'Opéra, 2ᵉ*), **Galignani** (*224 Rue de Rivoli, 1ᵉʳ*), **Le Nouveau Quartier Latin** (*78 Bd. St-Michel, 6ᵉ*), **Shakespeare and Co**. (*37 Rue de la Bûcherie, 5ᵉ*), which also has regular poetry readings, **W.H. Smith** (*248 Rue de Rivoli, 1ᵉʳ*), and **The Village Voice** (*6 Rue Princesse, 6ᵉ*), The last one is not just a bookshop, but also a snug little café, where readings take place.

Useful addresses

Tourist information

The **Office du Tourisme et des Congrès** (convention and visitors bureau) (*127 Av. des Champs-Élysées, 8ᵉ* ☎ 47-23-61-72. *Métro: George-V*) is open all year round, 9am-8pm, but is closed on Dec 25, Jan 1 and May 1. There are branches at Gare de Lyon, Gare d'Austerlitz and Gare de l'Est (*open Mon-Sat 8am-10pm*). The Gare du Nord branch is also open Sun 1-8pm, and there is an office at the *Eiffel Tower*, open daily 11am-6pm.

American Express Travel Service (*11 Rue Scribe, 9ᵉ* ☎ 42-66-09-99. *Métro: Opéra*) is a valuable source of information for any traveller in need of help, advice or emergency services. A bilingual freephone tourist advice and information service is available (*Mar-Oct Mon-Fri 10am-6pm* ☎ 05-201-202).

Telephone services

Tourist events (in English)   ☎ 47-20-88-98
Speaking clock   ☎ 36-99
Traffic report   ☎ 48-99-33-33
Weather   ☎ 30-66-30-66 (Paris), 64-09-01-01 (France)

Post offices

See *Postal and telephone services* p16.
52 Rue du Louvre, 1ᵉʳ ☎ 40-28-20-00
71 Av. des Champs-Élysées, 8ᵉ ☎ 43-59-55-18

Tour operators

The following companies run bus tours around Paris:
American Express   11 Rue Scribe, 9ᵉ ☎ 42-66-09-99
Cityrama   4 Pl. des Pyramides, 1ᵉʳ ☎ 42-60-30-14
Panam 2002   (lunch/dinner on board) ☎ 42-25-64-39
Paris-Vision (France-Tourisme)   214 Rue de Rivoli, 1ᵉʳ
☎ 42-60-31-25
Guides and interpreters
Amicale Inter-Guides   ☎ 42-68-01-04
Contact Paris   ☎ 43-22-42-27
Espaces et contacts   ☎ 45-45-53-30
Guides-Interpreters and Speakers' Association
☎ 47-82-24-91
National Club of Guides and Messengers   ☎ 42-80-01-27
River and canal trips
Bateaux-Mouches   Pont de l' Alma, 8ᵉ ☎ 42-25-96-10
Bateaux Vedettes de Paris Île-de-France   Port de Suffren, 7ᵉ
☎ 47-05-71-29
Bateaux Vedettes Parisiens Tour Eiffel   Port de la
Bourdonnais, 7ᵉ ☎ 47-05-50-00
Bateaux Vedettes Pont-Neuf   Sq. du Vert-Galant, 1ᵉʳ
☎ 46-33-98-38
Canauxrama Canal St-Martin   Pont de l'Arsenal, 12ᵉ, to La
Villette, 19ᵉ ☎ 42-39-15-00

Paris Canal   Seine and Canal St-Martin, from Quai Anatole France, 7ᵉ, to La Villette, 19ᵉ ☎ 42-40-96-97

Airlines
Air France   119 Av. des Champs-Élysées, 8ᵉ ☎ 45-35-61-61
Air Inter   49 Av. des Champs-Élysées, 1ᵉʳ ☎ 42-89-38-88
British Airways   12 Rue de Castiglione, 1ᵉʳ ☎ 47-78-14-14
Pan Am   1 Rue Scribe, 9ᵉ ☎ 42-66-45-45

Places of worship
For information on all denominations of churches in the Paris area, contact the **Centre d'informations et documentations religieuses** at Notre-Dame cathedral ☎ 46-33-01-01.
American Cathedral   23 Av. George-V, 8ᵉ ☎ 47-20-17-92
American Church   65 Quai d'Orsay, 7ᵉ ☎ 47-05-07-99
St George's (Anglican)   7 Rue Auguste-Vacquerie, 16ᵉ ☎ 47-20-22-51
St Joseph's English-speaking Catholic Church   50 Av. Hoche, 8ᵉ ☎ 42-27-28-56
St Michael's English Church (Anglican)   5 Rue d'Aguesseau, 8ᵉ ☎ 47-42-70-88
Scots Kirk   17 Rue Bayard, 8ᵉ ☎ 48-78-47-94
Synagogue   44 Rue de la Victoire, 9ᵉ ☎ 45-26-02-56
Union Liberale Israelite de France Synagogue (English Rabbi)   24 Rue Copernic, 16ᵉ ☎ 47-04-37-27

Major libraries
American Library   10 Rue du Général-Camou, 7ᵉ ☎ 45-51-46-82
Bibliothèque Publique d'Informations   Centre National d'Art et de Culture Georges-Pompidou, Plateau Beaubourg, 4ᵉ ☎ 42-77-12-33
Bibliothèque Nationale   4 Rue Vivienne, 2ᵉ ☎ 47-03-81-26
British Council Library   11 Rue Constantine, 7ᵉ ☎ 45-55-95-95

Embassies and consulates
Always contact the consulate on general matters. The embassy will deal with higher-profile, diplomatic affairs only. Unless stated, embassy and consulate are at the same address.
Australia   4 Rue Jean-Rey, 15ᵉ ☎ 40-59-33-00
Canada   35 Av. Montaigne, 8ᵉ ☎ 47-23-01-01
Ireland   4 Rue Rude, 16ᵉ ☎ 45-00-20-87
Japan   7 Av. Hoche, 8ᵉ ☎ 47-66-02-22
New Zealand   7ter Rue Léonard-de-Vinci, 16ᵉ ☎ 45-00-24-11
United Kingdom (embassy)   35 Rue du Faubourg-St-Honoré, 8ᵉ ☎ 42-66-91-42
United Kingdom (consulate)   16 Rue d'Anjou, 8ᵉ ☎ 42-66-91-42
United States (embassy)   2 Av. Gabriel, 8ᵉ ☎ 42-96-12-02
United States (consulate)   2 Rue St-Florentin, 1ᵉʳ ☎ as embassy.

Youth organizations
L'Acceuil des Jeunes en France (*12 Rue des Barres, 4ᵉ* ☎ *42-72-72-09*) looks after hostel reservations for young visitors, and can provide useful general information. It has other branches around Paris (*Gare du Nord; 119 Rue St-Martin, 4ᵉ; 16, Rue du Pont Louis-Philippe, 4ᵉ; 139 Bd. St-Michel, 5ᵉ*).

Emergency information

Emergency services

Police ☎17
Fire (*Sapeurs pompiers*) ☎18
Ambulance ☎43-78-26-26

There is no unified ambulance service — the operator will offer you the numbers of several companies.

Hospitals

For information on *Assistance Publique* (National Health) hospitals ☎40-27-30-00. See also *English-speaking hospitals* on page 9.

Medical and dental emergencies

Medical service: 24hrs ☎45-67-50-50
Dental emergencies: 24hrs ☎47-07-33-68

Pharmacies

To find out the nearest *pharmacie de garde* (all-night chemist), call the *mairie* of your *arrondissement*
English-speaking pharmacies are at 1 Rue Auber, 9ᵉ and 6 Rue Castiglione, 1ᵉʳ.

Help lines

Samaritans (English-speaking) ☎47-23-80-80 (3-11pm)

Motoring accidents

- Do not admit liability or incriminate yourself.
- Ask any witness(es) to stay and give a statement.
- Contact the police.
- Exchange names, addresses, car details and insurance company details with any other drivers involved.
- In serious accidents, ask the police to contact the sheriff's clerk (*huissier*) to make out a legally acceptable account of the incident. In a dispute his report will be considered to be authoritative.

Car breakdowns

- Put on flashing hazard warning lights and place a warning triangle 50m(55yds) behind the car.
- If in a rented car, ring the number you have been given.

Lost passport

Contact the local police and your consulate immediately.

Lost travellers cheques

Notify the local police immediately, then follow the instructions provided with your travellers cheques, or contact the issuing company. Contact your consulate or American Express if you are stranded with no money.

Lost property

If you have lost something on the street or on public transport, go to the **Bureau des Objets Trouvés** (*36 Rue des Morillons, 15ᵉ. Open Mon-Fri 9am-6pm. No informaton given by telephone. Métro: Convention*). Report all losses to the police.

Emergency phrases

Help! *Au secours!*
There has been an accident. *Il y a eu un accident.*
Where is the nearest telephone/hospital? *Où se trouve le téléphone/l'hôpital le plus proche?*
Call a doctor/ambulance! *Appelez un médecin/une ambulance!*
Call the police! *Appelez la police!*

Time chart

The Gallic origins

3rdC BC
: The Parisii, a Gallic tribe, made the Île de la Cité their fortified capital. They prospered from the river trade and from fishing, hunting and gathering.

The Roman era

52BC-
c.AD486
: In 52BC Julius Caesar's Roman legions conquered the island, which they called Lutetia, and in due course it became an important Roman centre, with the governor's palace erected on the island, and the forum and arena on the Left Bank.

As early as the 2nd or 3rd decade AD, a society of mercantile watermen had established itself in Paris, and these boatmen were to play an important role in the history of the city. The symbol of Paris is a ship, and her motto is *fluctuat nec murgitur* (she is tossed but does not sink).

In AD250 St Denis came to Paris, introducing Christianity and becoming the city's first bishop. But Rome was still officially pagan, and St Denis was decapitated by an angry mob.

Several Roman emperors stayed at Lutetia, notably Constantius Chlorus, who made it his headquarters in AD292. His son, Constantine the Great (c.274-337), who made Christianity the official religion of the empire, also stayed there for a time, as did Julian the Apostate, who was proclaimed Emperor of Rome at the city in 360. In that year Lutetia was named Paris.

Early Middle Ages

5thC AD
: In the vacuum left by the departure of the Romans, Paris stood in danger of being engulfed by barbarians, but the morale of the city was restored by a religious young woman from Nanterre, named Geneviève, who, in 451, correctly assured the Parisians that Attila the Hun and his hordes would not attack the city. Ten years later, when the city was besieged by the Franks, she helped relieve the famine. She later became patron saint of Paris.

The Merovingians

508-752
: In 508 the Christianized King Clovis of the Frankish Merovingian line made Paris his capital, and it remained in Merovingian hands until 752, when the last of the dynasty, Childeric, was finally ousted by Pepin the Short, father of Charlemagne.

The Carolingians

752-987
: This was an uneasy period for Paris, with frequent raids by Norman pirates, culminating in a great siege in 885-86 which ended in defeat of the Normans by Count Eudes, who was elected King of France in 887.

The Capetians

987-996
: Hugues Capet elected King of France at Senlis; his territories were not extensive, however. His descendants reigned from father to son until 1328, establishing the principle of monarchy in France.

996-1108
: The reigns of Robert the Pious, Henri I and Philippe I. The building of Notre-Dame cathedral was begun in Philippe's reign.

1108-37
: Reign of Louis VI the Fat.

1137-80
: Louis VII the Young, husband of Eleanor of

Aquitaine. Having been divorced by Louis, in 1152 Eleanor married Henri Plantagenet, subsequently Henry II of England, who ruled both NW France and Aquitaine, far more land than the French king.

1180-1223 Philippe Auguste erected the fortress of the Louvre and constructed a great defensive wall around the city: the Philippe-Auguste girdle. His reign also laid the foundation of the University of Paris.

1223-85 The reigns of Louis VIII, Louis IX, who was canonized, and Philippe III. The Sorbonne was established in the reign of Louis IX. Pierre de Montreuil built Sainte Chapelle to house relics of the true cross, which Louis IX had bought for a vast sum, and he worked on the St-Denis basilica, prototype of the Gothic style.

1285-1314 Philippe IV the Fair. Fair only in looks, Philippe was a cruel and vicious king who crushed the Templars, persecuted the Jews and caused misery and poverty among the Parisians through high taxation, forced labour and debasement of the currency. It was he who built the Conciergerie.

1314-28 The reigns of Louis X the Quarrelsome, Jean I (a few months only), Philippe V the Tall, and Charles IV the Fair, the last of the Capetians.
The Valois

1328-50 Philippe VI, first of the Valois kings, whose reign marked the start of a chaotic period for France; the country was weakened by war with England.

1350-64 Reign of Jean II. In 1358, Étienne Marcel, provost of the merchants and mayor of the city, led a popular uprising.

1364-80 Charles V the Wise, who restored order to France, built the Bastille and erected a wall on the Right Bank beyond the Philippe-Auguste wall.

1380-1422 Charles VI the Well-Beloved. A weak king, under whose reign the English invaders, and with them chaos, returned. In 1420 Paris was captured by Henry V of England.

1422-61 Charles VII the Victorious. In 1429 Joan of Arc relieved Orléans, but tried in vain to recapture Paris, which remained in English hands until 1436, when Charles VII recaptured it. In 1431 Henry VI of England had himself crowned at Notre-Dame. In 1453 the English withdrew from all of France except Calais.

1461-83 Louis XI. A cunning, authoritarian, but enlightened king. Under his reign Paris prospered. The city's first school of medicine was opened and its first printing press was set up, at the Sorbonne.

1483-1515 The reigns of Charles VIII and Louis XII, each of whom married Anne of Brittany; her lands were ceded to France after her death in 1514.

1515-47 François I, great patron of the arts, who was with Leonardo da Vinci when he died near Amboise. François helped to introduce the Italian Renaissance to France and acquired the first masterpieces for the Louvre. He began the reconstruction of the Louvre, and under his rule many magnificent buildings grew up in Paris.

1547-59 Henry II was killed in a jousting accident. His wife, Catherine de Medici, began the Tuileries palace.

1559-89   The reigns of Henry II and Catherine de Medici's three sons, François II, Charles IX and Henry III. During this period Paris was the scene of many bloody conflicts between the Catholics and the Protestants, culminating in the St Bartholomew's Day massacre in 1572, when 3,000 Huguenots were murdered in Paris. Henry III was then forced to flee Paris when the Catholic league turned against him in 1588. He was murdered at St-Cloud while laying siege to Paris in 1589. During his reign the construction of the Pont-Neuf was begun.

The Bourbons

1589-1610   Henry IV *Le Vert Galant* allayed for a time the religious uprisings by converting from Protestantism to Catholicism, and issuing the Edict of Nantes, allowing Protestants some freedom of worship. In Paris, he extended the Louvre and the Tuileries, created the Place des Vosges and completed the Pont-Neuf. He was assassinated by a fanatic named Ravaillac.

1610-43   Louis XIII. The 17thC was known as "Le Grand Siècle". Paris was now growing more magnificent as each year passed. The Île St-Louis was developed, Marie de Medici built the Luxembourg palace, and Cardinal Richelieu, first minister and far more powerful than the young king, built the Palais Royal and founded the Académie Française. The arts flourished, but brutality was also much in evidence, and gruesome public executions were frequent. In 1622 Paris became a bishopric.

1643-1715   Louis XIV the "Sun King", under whom France reached its zenith of power and prestige. Versailles was built and became the royal court, and the capital acquired many splendid new buildings and institutions: Les Invalides, the Salpêtrière, Gobelins, the Louvre colonnade and the Comédie Française.

      In 1648, when Louis XIV was still too young to rule, Paris had been convulsed by the Fronde uprising, a bloody protest against the centralized power of the monarchy. When Louis XIV took the reigns of power in 1661, he tightened the grip, abolishing the municipal institutions and the office of mayor, so that Paris was ruled by the state. This was to remain the case until the Revolution. In 1685 the king ordered the Revocation of the Edict of Nantes, causing thousands of Protestants to flee.

1715-74   Louis XV's reign saw financial crisis, disastrous wars with England over Québec and West Indian colonies and the growing unpopularity of the crown. But Paris was further enriched architecturally by the Panthéon, the Palais-Bourbon and the Pl. de la Concorde. Another encircling wall, known as the Farmers General Wall, was erected as a customs barrier, and further added to popular discontent.

1774-92   Louis XVI. The government was now financially, politically and morally bankrupt. Discontent among all classes was rife. Louis XVI, an ineffectual king, was unable to stem the tide of revolution.

The Revolution

1789-99   One of the great turning points in the history of

23

France, and of the world. The Revolution began symbolically with the storming of the Bastille on July 14, 1789. In Oct of that year a mob invaded Versailles, and the king returned to Paris. At first he remained on the throne while various reforms were carried out, but by 1792 he was deposed and imprisoned, and the following year he and his queen, Marie-Antoinette, were executed. Extremists, including Danton, Marat and de Robespierre, instituted the Reign of Terror, in which 2,800 people in Paris alone were executed, and another 14,000 in the rest of the country.

The Reign of Terror finally ended with the fall and execution of de Robespierre in 1794. The Revolution itself could be said to have ended when, in 1799, Napoleon appointed himself First Consul — in effect, dictator of France.

The Consulate and First Empire

1799-1815 After a period of stagnation Paris began, under Napoleon, to enjoy a new period of expansion and prosperity. The Farmers General Wall was done away with, the office of Prefect of the Seine was created, and many of the exiled nobles returned. The foundations of large-scale industry were laid, and the arts flourished once more. On the negative side, the city was terrorized by Napoleon's police under the ruthless first Prefect of Police, Joseph Fouché.

In 1804 Napoleon had himself crowned Emperor in Notre-Dame. Under Napoleon, France was master of Europe until 1814, when Paris fell to the invading allied armies. Napoleon abdicated at Fontainebleau and was exiled to the island of Elba. In 1815 he escaped from Elba and returned to France for his final campaign, which ended, in June 1815, at Waterloo. He was sent again into exile, this time to St Helena, where he died in 1821.

The Restoration

1815-48 After Napoleon's defeat, the Bourbon monarchy was restored and Louis XVIII crowned king. He was succeeded in 1824 by Charles X, who himself was ousted during the short-lived July Revolution in Paris in favour of Louis-Philippe of the Orléans line.

These were years of modernization for Paris. Between 1812-15 the Ourcq, St-Denis and St-Martin canals were built, and 1837 saw the opening of the first French railway line, from Paris to St-Germain-en-Laye. Pleasure steamers plied the Seine; gas lighting was installed; and a new wall, the Thiers fortifications, was erected around the city in 1841-45. Although this has vanished, it marks the line of the present Périphérique boundary. In 1832, 19,000 Parisians perished in a cholera epidemic.

The Second Republic and Second Empire

1848-70 Louis-Philippe was ousted in the "Year of Revolutions" which swept through Europe in 1848; a Second Republic was declared, only to give way to a Second Empire under Napoleon III (Emperor 1852-70). This was a key period in the development of Paris. Baron Haussmann, Prefect of the Seine, drove his great boulevards through the city, which was divided into the present 20 *arrondissements*

Haussmann's idea behind the building of the boulevards was partly to create streets too wide for barricading in the event of further street fighting and revolution. Among other new buildings, the Opéra and Les Halles sprang up, as well as the main stations, the sewers (*égouts*) and the Bois de Boulogne and Vincennes. In 1855 and 1867 spectacular international exhibitions were held in the capital. This gay period was ended by the Franco-Prussian War.

The Third Republic

1870-1945 The Third Republic was declared in 1870. Napoleon III surrendered at Sedan. Paris was besieged by the Prussians and fell to them in early 1871. St-Cloud château was burned down, and Napoleon III fled to England. Paris was taken over by the revolutionary government, the Commune, between Mar and May 1871. Although this was finally suppressed, the city suffered terrible damage.

After Paris had recovered, a new period of expansion and prosperity set in, symbolized by the World Exhibition of 1889 and the building of the Eiffel Tower. The year 1900 saw the opening of the first Métro line in Paris, and the city then played host to another World Exhibition.

During World War I, Paris sustained little physical damage, and comparatively little during World War II, but the population suffered much under Nazi occupation. The city was liberated in 1944. General de Gaulle led the new provisional government, which held power for just over a year.

Since World War II

1946 The inauguration of the Fourth Republic. A new constitution. Government by coalition of Socialists, Communists, Radicals and Catholic Democrats.

1958 French army takes power in Algeria. Fourth Republic falls and de Gaulle forms Fifth Republic.

1959 EEC (Common Market) founded, with France included among the six members.

1962 Algeria granted independence.

1968 Student riots and demonstrations in the streets of Paris, reaching a peak in May.

1969 Electoral defeat of de Gaulle. Election of Georges Pompidou as President. Les Halles market transferred to Rungis, in the suburbs.

1970 De Gaulle's death.

1973 Montparnasse Tower and the ring road completed.

1974 Pompidou's death. Election of Valéry Giscard d'Estaing as President.

1977 Election of Jacques Chirac as the first mayor of Paris since 1871.

1981 Electoral defeat of Giscard d'Estaing. A socialist government elected under the leadership of François Mitterrand.

1986 Appointment of a conservative prime minister, Jacques Chirac, under the continued presidency of Mitterrand.

1988 Re-election of Mitterrand and appointment of a socialist prime minister, Michel Rocard.

1989 Bi-centenary of the French Revolution.

Biographies

A list of the famous whose names are linked with Paris would be endless. The following personal selection pays particular attention to those mentioned in this book.

de Balzac, Honoré *(1799-1850)*
Author of the great series of novels and stories called *La Comédie Humaine*. Many of these portray intimately the life of Paris, its inhabitants and their social mores.

Barrault, Jean-Louis *(born 1910)*
Author, outstanding mime artist and theatre director, who reached international fame with his performance in Marcel Carne's celebrated film *Les Enfants du Paradis* (1944).

Chevalier, Maurice *(1888-1972)*
Actor, dancer and singer, who often appeared in English-speaking films as the embodiment of urbane Parisian charm.

Clemenceau, Georges *(1841-1929)*
Politician and journalist. Known as "the tiger" because of his tough belligerence. Clemenceau was Premier in 1906-09 and 1917-20.

Cocteau, Jean *(1889-1963)*
A flamboyant genius who achieved fame as an artist, novelist (*Les Enfants Terribles*), screenwriter and film director (*La Belle et la Bête*), and playwright (*Orphée*).

Colbert, Jean-Baptiste *(1619-83)*
Most effective of Louis XIV's ministers. His wise financial policies greatly enriched the state.

Colette *(1873-1954)*
Author of vividly sensual and perceptive novels, such as *Chéri* and *La Chatte*. She lived for a time in the Palais-Royal.

De Gaulle, Charles *(1890-1970)*
Soldier and statesman. After leading the Free French during the war, he headed a provisional government from 1944-46. In 1958 he came out of retirement to lead France again and draw up a new constitution. He resigned in 1969.

Dreyfus, Alfred *(1859-1935)*
Jewish army officer imprisoned in 1894 on a false charge of treason. The subsequent attempts by Zola and others to exonerate him split France into bitterly opposed factions and exposed an ugly streak of anti-Semitism.

Gambetta, Léon Michel *(1838-82)*
French leader during the Franco-Prussian War of 1870-71. He is famous for his daring escape from Paris by balloon when the city was under siege.

Geneviève, Sainte *(c.422-512)*
Patron saint of Paris. She calmed the Parisians by correctly predicting that Attila the Hun would not attack the city in AD451. Ten years later, she smuggled in food when Paris was besieged by the Franks.

Giscard d'Estaing, Valéry *(born 1926)*
Finance minister under de Gaulle. Leader of Independent Republican Party from 1967. President of France 1974-81.

Haussmann, Georges Eugène *(1809-91)*
As Prefect of the Seine under Napoleon III, he re-shaped large areas of Paris, creating boulevards, squares, parks and bridges. His grand, triumphal style is still an integral part of the city's personality.

Hugo, Victor *(1802-85)*
A towering figure in French literature and the leader of the

Romantic movement in France. Author of *Notre-Dame de Paris* (The Hunchback of Notre-Dame) and *Les Misérables*, he was also a member of parliament. As writer and politician he was a fierce champion of liberty and justice.

de Lafayette, Marquis *(1757-1834)*
A dashing and glamorous figure who fought against Britain in the American War of Independence, commanded the Paris National Guard after the fall of the Bastille, and was the main author of the Declaration of Rights.

Malraux, André *(1901-76)*
Novelist, art historian, revolutionary fighter, resistance hero and de Gaulle's Minister of Culture from 1958-69.

Mansart, François *(1598-1668)*
Architect who created the Classical style in French architecture, (e.g., the Hôtel Carnavalet), and gave his name to the steeply pitched Mansard roof.

Mansart, Jules Hardouin- *(1645-1708)*
Great nephew of François and chief architect to Louis XIV. His designs include the Grand Trianon and the Dôme church.

Mazarin, Jules *(1602-61)*
Cardinal and statesman. Chief Minister of France during the regency of Anne of Austria, mother of Louis XIV.

Mitterrand, François *(born 1916)*
Leader of the Socialist Party and President of the Republic since 1981.

Piaf, Edith *(1915-63)*
Singer, actress and cabaret performer, whose small size and lively personality won her the nickname "*La Môme*" (the sparrow), and whose inspired rendering of such songs as *La vie en rose*, *Milord* and *Je ne regrette rien* seemed to epitomize the spirit of Paris.

de Pompadour, Marquise *(1721-64)*
Mistress of Louis XV and a ruthless political intriguer. For 20yrs she unofficially controlled the French government. A lavish patron of the arts, she also helped to lead France into financial, political and military disaster.

Pompidou, Georges *(1911-74)*
De Gaulle's successor as president, he remained in office until his death. Many of the new building developments in Paris have resulted from his campaign to "modernize" the city.

Proust, Marcel *(1871-1922)*
One of the most influential novelists of all time. His fame rests on a seven-part work, *À la Recherche du Temps Perdu* (Remembrance of Things Past), a minutely detailed and searching autobiographical work. Proust was born in Paris and lived there for most of his life.

de Richelieu, Armand-Jean du Plessis *(1585-1642)*
Cardinal and effective ruler of France under Louis XIII, he greatly increased the power of France and of the crown. He was an energetic patron of literature and founded the Académie Française.

de Robespierre, Maximilien *(1758-94)*
Revolutionary leader and architect of the Reign of Terror, he was, in his turn, executed on the guillotine.

Sartre, Jean-Paul *(1886-1980)*
Novelist, playwright, existentialist philosopher, left-wing polemicist and doyen of the Left Bank intelligentsia, with his lifetime companion Simone de Beauvoir. He expounded his ideas in philosophical works such as *L'Être et le Néant* (Being and Nothingness) and in novels such as *Les Chemins de la Liberté* (Roads to Freedom).

Architecture

Perhaps the most striking element of Paris as a whole is its visual harmony. Although there are samples of many different periods and styles, each blends with the other in such a way as to create an environment that is both diverse and unified. Only in the past thirty years have any really disruptive elements been introduced, and even these have not destroyed the overall sense of unity. Most of the great architectural styles are represented in Paris, from Roman to ultra-modern.

Roman *(1st-4thC AD)*

The only examples of the Roman era still visible are the Thermal Baths in the Cluny museum and the restored Arènes de Lutèce. Both are evidence of the heavy, grandiose and colossal elements typical of Roman concrete and brick architecture, with massive walls, barrel vaults and big rounded arches. France has comparatively few Gallo-Roman remains, although some traces are evident in the foundations of Paris' St-Denis basilica.

Romanesque *(11th and 12thC)*

Skilful use was made of vaulting and pillars to create a striking

The **Thermal Baths**, reminder of Paris' Roman heritage, show the typical use of brickwork and rounded arches.

The **crypt of St-Denis** is a mixture of Romanesque and early Gothic styles.

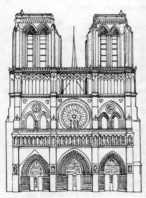

Notre-Dame cathedral. France is rich in superb Gothic cathedrals, and this is one of the most exquisite examples.

Sainte Chapelle shows perfectly the Gothic architect's desire to free space for light and stained glass.

sense of space. The style is characterized by rounded arches and monumental simplicity, the columns smooth except perhaps for a flourish of carving at the top. There are few examples of the Romanesque in Paris, but those that there are include the bell tower and small chancel columns of St-Germain-des-Prés, the capitals in St-Pierre, Montmartre, the belfry abutting the apse in St-Germain l'Auxerrois and part of St-Denis basilica crypt.

Early Gothic *(12th and 13thC)*

In place of the rounded arches and plainness of the Romanesque style, the Gothic builders used pointed arches and made great play with stained glass, sculptural decoration and vertical emphasis. It was pre-eminently an ecclesiastical style, with the ideal of liberating as much space as possible, creating a sense of void over solid and, by using verticals rather than horizontals, of producing a soaring, aspiring quality.

The precursor of Gothic architecture in Europe was the St-Denis basilica, designed by architect Abbot Suger, on the outskirts of Paris. But the outstanding example to be seen in Paris is the magnificent cathedral of Notre-Dame, the construction of which began in 1163 and was completed in 1330. In the early

The Flamboyant Gothic style of the late-15thC **Hôtel de Sens** is seen to good effect in the highly decorated turrets and battlements.

The **Dôme church** is Jules Hardouin-Mansart's classically proportioned Baroque masterpiece.

The courtyard of the **Hôtel Carnavalet** is a clear example of the influence of the Italian Renaissance.

Architecture

Gothic churches, windows were small and decoration comparatively restrained.

Mid-Gothic (13th and 14thC)

As the Gothic builders became more skilful at distributing weight through the use of buttresses, they were able to liberate larger areas of wall for stained-glass windows. The Sainte Chapelle in Paris is one of the finest examples of this period to be found anywhere. The chapel, designed by Pierre de Montreuil, is on two storeys, with the walls of the upper storey completely filled by stained-glass windows. The cathedral of Notre-Dame at Chartres is one of the most renowned examples of the High Gothic architectural style, and served as the experiment which opened the way for the later and even more spectacular architectural developments.

Late or Flamboyant Gothic (15thC)

In the late phase of the Gothic period, builders abandoned themselves to exuberant decoration characterized by Flamboyant (literally "flame-like") window tracery and columns rising into fan-vaulting, as in the ambulatory of St-Séverin. Other buildings that illustrate this style in Paris are the Hôtel de Sens, Hôtel de

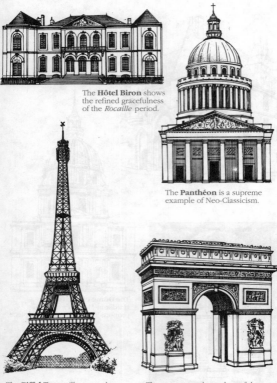

The **Hôtel Biron** shows the refined gracefulness of the *Rocaille* period.

The **Panthéon** is a supreme example of Neo-Classicism.

The **Eiffel Tower** illustrates the late-19thC interest in engineering, and the diversity of its architectural styles.

The monumental grandeur of the **Arc de Triomphe**, with its relief statues and friezes, displays an elaborate form of Classicism.

Cluny, the Tour St-Jacques and the Billettes Cloister. The church of St-Maclou at Rouen is also an outstanding example of this exotic phase.

Renaissance (16thC)

Military campaigns in Italy led the French to a gradual understanding of the Renaissance. In architecture it was marked by a return to Greek and Roman forms and motifs: allegorical sculptures, Classical columns, balustrades, pediments and rounded arches. François I, who reigned from 1515-47, was a patron of the arts who did much to introduce Renaissance architecture to France. One of its leading exponents was Pierre Lescot, who designed part of the Cour Carrée in the Louvre. Other examples are the courtyard of the Hôtel Carnavalet, the Porte Dorée (golden gate) at Fontainebleau, built by Gilles Le Breton, the Fontaine des Innocents at Les Halles and, in interior decoration, the rood-screen at St-Étienne-du-Mont.

French Baroque and Classicism (17thC)

In essence, the Baroque style is a more ornate version of Renaissance Classicism. Versailles is a striking instance; another is the E wing of the Louvre. In ecclesiastical architecture, Baroque

The **Opéra**, Charles Garnier's Second Empire extravaganza.

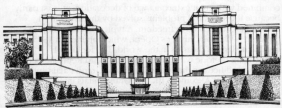

The **Palais de Chaillot** marries functionalism with more traditional elements of style.

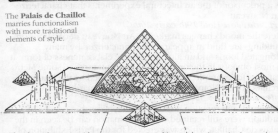

The clear-glass pyramid entrance to the **Louvre** shows the degree of confidence currently given to architectural projects. Ancient and modern sit side by side in joint majesty.

31

includes the so-called "Jesuit" style (based on the church of Gésu in Rome). Paris has many churches of this kind: the Sorbonne church (by Jacques Le Mercier), Val-de-Grâce, St-Paul-St-Louis, all featuring the Baroque predilection for domes. One of the outstanding architects of this period was François Mansart, who also gave his name to the high-pitched Mansard roof, as on the Val-de-Grâce cloister. His relative, Jules Hardouin-Mansart, married Baroque with the simple lines of Classicism in many superb secular buildings, notably Pl. Vendôme, and the Dôme church at Les Invalides.

Rococo *(18thC)*

After the death of Louis XIV, and with a child king on the throne, a new, lighter style made its appearance, which was characterized by elaborate but graceful ornamentation. This was Rococo (*Rocaille*), which was more restrained than elsewhere and mainly a feature of interior decoration — for example, in Paris, the Oval Salon of the Hôtel de Soubise by Germain Boffrand. The Hôtel Biron, now the Rodin museum, is an example of the refined elegance of the Rococo age. The 18thC Classical, monumental architecture reached its peak in Paris with such buildings as the Louvre Colonnade, the École Militaire and Pl. de la Concorde.

Neo-Classicism *(late 18th-early 19thC)*

Between the 1780s and 1830s, interest in Classical antiquity was revived in contrast to the ornate Rococo style. Once again, order, balance and clarity became the keynotes. The Madeleine illustrates the style, and Paris has the supreme examples of Neo-Classicism in the Panthéon and the chapel at Versailles.

Consulate, Empire and Restoration *(early 19thC)*

Buildings of this period are unimaginative, a heavier version of the Classical style, as in the Arc de Triomphe and La Madeleine.

Second Empire/early Third Republic *(mid-19th to early 20thC)*

Uniformity went by the board and was replaced by a great mixture of styles, drawing on many periods. Advanced engineering, exemplified by the Eiffel Tower, was often combined with great extravagance of decoration, at least partly because the structural problems solved by the use of iron allowed great decorative freedom. A typical Second-Empire building is Charles Garnier's Opéra, which opened in 1875 and is one of the largest theatres in the world. The feeling of extravagant rhetoric was carried into the Third Republic period with such edifices as the Sacré-Coeur, the Grand Palais and Petit Palais, and Pont Alexandre III. The Grand Palais interior illustrates particularly well the combination of practicality and decorativeness, and its use of stylized natural forms can be seen as a precursor of the architectural experiments that characterize Art Nouveau.

Art Nouveau *(late 19th-early 20thC)*

Here the mood changes markedly. Art Nouveau decorations on buildings are fluid in appearance, characterized by many elongated loops and an almost Baroque elaborateness of form. It is most obvious in the original cast-iron entrances to some Métro stations (for example, at the Louvre), designed by the leading architect of Art Nouveau in Paris, Hector Guimard.

Inter-war *(1918-39)*

Modernity and functionalism are the keynotes, but echoes of tradition were still retained. The combination can be seen in the Palais de Chaillot, which was erected for the Paris Exhibition of 1937, and the Palais de Tokyo, where full use is made of reinforced stone and concrete.

Postwar (1945-present day)

Le Corbusier was the most famous exponent of modern architecture in France, but Paris has little of his work. Some bleak expanses of glass, steel and concrete dating from the 1960s can be seen, particularly in the Tour Montparnasse, La Défense and the Palais des Congrès. Both praised and criticized for its innovative design in its heyday, Rogers and Piano's Pompidou Centre has not stood the test of time and is seen by many as waywardly ugly. But Paris under Jacques Chirac changed its planning policies in the mid-1970s. No more skyscraper developments have been permitted, and the city is committed to maintaining its glorious and much admired unity while allowing a developing dialogue with the world's leading architects.

I.M. Pei's glass and steel pyramid merges the 20thC with the stately buildings of the Louvre in a breathtaking way. The marble-clad grand arch at La Défense, by von Spreckelsen, completed in 1989, adds another landmark on the precise axes laid out 200yrs earlier. These, and Jean Nouvel's innovative Institut du Monde Arabe, are probably the best developments of the 1980s. For the 1990s, things augur well.

The arts in Paris

It is hard to pinpoint the beginning of Paris' greatness as a centre of culture and the arts. Its cultural roots can be traced back as far as the Gallo-Roman period, but in more recent times a point of origin can be seen in François Villon (born 1431), who is widely considered to be France's (and Paris') first great poet, and who combined the writing of brilliant verse with living as a thief among the maze of tiny streets and taverns of the Latin Quarter.

Villon was a forerunner of the great cultural outburst that came when Italian Renaissance art and architecture reached France under the influence of François I. François also stimulated a new interest in music, particularly songs accompanied by the lute, which were often heard in his court, and brought important Italian masterpieces — among them the *Mona Lisa* — to Paris. Literature also flourished, and it was at this time that François Rabelais (c.1494-c.1553) wrote his roistering and satirical stories of *Gargantua* and *Pantagruel*. The same period saw the emergence of the *Pléiade*, a group of seven poets who broke with medieval traditions, introduced Italian Renaissance forms and established the alexandrine (line of 12 syllables) as the basic metre of French verse. One of the group was Jean Antoine de Baïf, who in 1571 established an Academy of Music and Poetry in Paris.

The 17thC, known as "Le Grand Siècle", was culturally even richer. Drama was dominated by the tragedians Corneille (1606-84) and Racine (1639-99), and by Molière (1622-73), an actor and writer of sparkling comedies. The fondness at this time for strict rules of form in literature and drama found its most extreme expression in the Académie Française, founded by Cardinal Richelieu in 1635.

More stimulating and less conservative as a milieu for writers and thinkers were the *salons*, which began to flourish at about the same time, and provided a forum for philosophers and literati to exchange ideas and sharpen their wits on one another. When Louis XIV began to rule in 1661, he proved to be the greatest patron of the arts since François I. He founded the Comédie Française, the Royal Academy of Painting and

The arts

Sculpture, which was later reborn as the École des Beaux Arts, and the Royal Academy of Music, appointing as its operatic director the versatile composer Jean-Baptiste Lully. The literary arts also reached a new peak in the trenchant compositions of Madame de Sévigné, Madame de Lafayette's novel *La Princesse de Clèves*, and Pascal's anonymously published *Lettres Provinciales*.

While France declined politically under Louis XV and XVI, the nation's artistic and literary life remained vigorous. Painting was dominated by Jean-Antoine Watteau, who was one of the greatest Rococo artists, then later Jean-Honoré Fragonard with his delicate eroticism, and the court painter François Boucher, who became famous for his portraits of Louis XV's mistress, Madame de Pompadour. In music, operas were composed by Rameau and the German, Gluck, who had his greatest successes in Paris. And the world of letters resounded to the philosophy and wit of Voltaire, Rousseau, Montesquieu, Diderot and d'Alembert. In such company, the *salons* enjoyed their heyday under the patronage of some of the most fashionable hostesses, among them Madame de Lambert, Madame de Deffand, Madame Geoffrin and Madame de Pompadour herself. Despite revolution and war, the early half of the 19thC saw the flowering of great artists in all fields: Eugène Delacroix in painting, Hector Berlioz in music, Honoré de Balzac and Victor Hugo in literature.

Under the Second Empire, Parisian life once again became a glorious party, dancing to the tunes of Offenbach and captured in the caricatures of Daumier. But it was in the late 19thC, after Paris had recovered from the Franco-Prussian war, that the period of greatest cultural efflorescence began.

The artistic world felt itself alienated from bourgeois society and had carved out its own territory, "Bohemia", the world so vividly portrayed by Henri Murger in his novel *Scènes de la Vie de Bohème*. In the Second Empire, one of the favourite hostelries had been the Brasserie des Martyrs in the Rue des Martyrs, where Murger rubbed shoulders with the poet Baudelaire and the painter Gustave Courbet. Later the scene shifted to other cafés such as the Guerbois and the Nouvelle Athènes, where could be found a remarkable mixture of artistic rebels, drop-outs and failures, and a handful who became famous, among them writers like Zola and painters labelled "Impressionists": Monet, Pissarro, Renoir and Degas.

The late 19th-early 20thC, and particularly the Belle Époque (1900-14), brought forth many schools in the various branches of the arts. On the stage, Sarah Bernhardt was the toast of Paris. There were the "Symbolist" poets and painters, with their interest in the strange, the surreal, the mythological: Gustave Moreau in painting, Villiers de l'Isle Adam in literature; and there was Marcel Proust with his odyssey *À la Recherche du Temps Perdu*, which shows that even in the early decades of the 20thC the tradition of the *salon* was still alive. At the same time, the foundations of modern art were being laid. Picasso, for example, was already at work in Paris in 1901. He lived and worked in a remarkable artists' and writers' lodging house in Montmartre called the Bateau-Lavoir, in the company of other avant-garde painters like Van Dongen, Braque and Juan Gris, and writers such as Max Jacob and Guillaume Apollinaire.

Montmartre continued to be an artistic centre until well into this century — Utrillo, for example, lived there, and its streets appear in many of his paintings. But between World Wars I and II most of the artists and writers preferred Montparnasse, and it was here that James Joyce, Henry Miller, Ernest Hemingway, F. Scott Fitzgerald and Gertrude Stein sought inspiration. Miller's *Tropic of Cancer* and Hemingway's *A Moveable Feast* both vividly describe the Paris they knew.

In the interwar period, Paris gave birth to Surrealism, one of the most influential artistic and literary movements of modern times. Its founder was a poet, André Breton, but its best-known exponents were painters: René Magritte, André Masson, Salvador Dalí and Max Ernst. Literature also flourished in Paris in the interwar and postwar years under the hands of such renowned writers as Gide, Colette, Cocteau, Simenon, Queneau, Camus, Sartre and Simone de Beauvoir.

After 1945 the focus of intellectual life moved once again, this time to the St-Germain-des-Prés quarter, where the cafés were frequented by Sartre and his circle. The postwar years are also strongly associated with the cabaret singer, Edith Piaf, whose compelling voice and passionate lifestyle made her a legend both in her lifetime and beyond her untimely death in 1963.

Today the cultural life of Paris is as lively as ever, with the theatre of Jean-Louis Barrault and the music of the Paris Symphony Orchestra, with established filmmakers such as Alain Resnais and brilliant newcomers like Luc Besson, with an upsurge of interest in the highest standards of contemporary dance, and with the ever-increasing numbers of street poets, musicians and mime-artists who perform with such verve and imagination at busy spots such as the Pompidou Centre, the Musée d'Orsay, the Forum des Halles and the Bd. St-Germain.

When and where to go

The city of Paris is at its most hectic and crowded during the months of Apr and May and then once again during the months of Sept and Oct. Aug is still the quietest month of the year, but no longer dead as it used to be when most Parisians went on their annual holiday and half the city closed down. Nowadays Aug is a relaxing and pleasant time to visit Paris, and only a few of the museums are closed.

Paris is a compact city bounded by a ring road, the Périphérique, and divided into 20 districts (*arrondissements*) which spiral outwards from the centre. Each *arrondissement* has its own style and character — say the word "*seizième*" to a Parisian, and he will conjure up an image of a certain urban ambience and lifestyle; he will even hear a special accent. Within the *arrondissements*, and often overlapping them, are *quartiers* (quarters), such as **Montparnasse**, **Montmartre** and the **Latin Quarter**.

The **Seine** divides the city into **Rive Droite** (Right Bank) and **Rive Gauche** (Left Bank) with the two islands, **Île de la Cité** and **Île St-Louis**, in the middle. The Right Bank is conspicuous by its affluence and smartness and its high concentration of imposing buildings, large shops, museums and theatres. The districts of bright lights (and red ones) are also mostly concentrated on the Right Bank. The Left Bank has its share of fine buildings and some dazzle, but on the whole its charm is more subtle, romantic and Bohemian.

From a visitor's point of view the districts of greatest interest are the 1er to the 9e, with a few pockets in outlying places. Much of this is superb walking territory. The areas outside the Périphérique do not belong to Paris proper, except for the *Bois de Boulogne* and *Bois de Vincennes*, but there are places of interest on the outskirts, such as *La Défense*, the *Flea Market* and *St-Denis* basilica.

Calendar of events

See also *Activities and sports* and *Public holidays* in *Basic information*.

January
‡ **Fashion shows** (summer collections): see *Haute couture* in *Shopping* for addresses. ‡ End Jan: **Prix d'Amérique** at Vincennes racecourse.

February
‡ End Feb: **Five Nations Trophy** Rugby International at Parc des Princes, 16ᵉ.

March
‡ End Mar or early Apr: **Prix du Président de la République** at Auteuil racecourse, Bois de Boulogne. ‡ Palm Sunday-May: **Throne Fair**, Vincennes. ‡ Mid-Mar to mid-May: **Spring flower shows** at the Bagatelle and Floral gardens, Bois de Boulogne. ‡ Mid-Mar: **Les 25km de Paris**: marathon race, 13ᵉ. ‡ Easter week: **Foire aux Pains d'Épice** (Gingerbread Fair) in Pl. de la Nation.

April
‡ End Apr-early May: **Paris Fair** (commercial leisure exhibition) at Parc des Expositions, 15ᵉ. ‡ Apr-end Oct: **Son et Lumière** at Les Invalides (separate versions in English and French).

May
‡ Early May-end June: **Paris Festival**, featuring opera, concerts, dance performances. ‡ May-Sept (Sun only): **Grandes Eaux Musicales**, a display of illuminated fountains at Versailles. ‡ Mid-May: **Paris international marathon**, from Pl. de la Concorde to Château de Vincennes. ‡ Mid-May to end June: **Versailles music and drama festival. Festival de St-Denis** — recitals and sacred music at St-Denis basilica. ‡ End May: **French Rugby Championship final** at Parc des Princes, 16ᵉ. ‡ End May-early June: **French Open Tennis Championships** at Roland Garros stadium, 16ᵉ. **Boulogne-Billancourt Jazz Festival.** ‡ End May-Sept: **Rose flower show** at the Bagatelle gardens, Bois de Boulogne. ‡ End May or early June: **football Cup Final** at Parc des Princes, 16ᵉ.

June
‡ Early June (odd years only): **Paris Air Show**, a display of old and new planes, at Le Bourget Airport. ‡ Early June to mid-July: **Marais festival** with music, plays and exhibitions. ‡ Early June-end Sept: **rose display** at l'Häy-les-Roses. ‡ Mid-June: **Grand Steeplechase de Paris** at Auteuil racecourse, Bois de Boulogne. ‡ June 24: **Feux de la St-Jean** (fireworks) at Sacré-Coeur. ‡ End June: **Grand Prix de Paris** at Longchamp racecourse, Bois de Boulogne. ‡ One day in last week June: **Paris-Villages** — popular neighbourhood events and processions.

July
‡ **Fashion shows** (winter collections): see *Haute couture* in *Shopping* for addresses. ‡ Early July-end Aug: **Festival Musique en l'Île** — orchestral chamber music at the church of St-Louis en l'Île. ‡ July 14: **Bastille Day**, a national holiday, celebrated with fireworks, dancing, and a huge military parade along Av. des Champs-Élysées. ‡ Mid-July: the **Tour de France** cycle race finishes in Av. des Champs-Élysées. ‡ July-Aug: **Festival Estival de Paris**. Classical music concerts and recitals in all parts of the city.

September
‡ **Festival de Montmartre**. ‡ Early Sept: start of the **Tour de France des Grands-mères Automobiles** (cars built between 1905 and 1932) at Pl. de la Concorde (tour ends there also, mid-Sept). ‡ Mid-Sept to end Dec: **Festival d'Automne** — concerts, plays, dance and exhibitions, all over Paris.

October
‡ First Sun: **Prix de l'Arc de**

Triomphe at Longchamp racecourse, Bois de Boulogne. ‡ Early Oct: **Montmartre wine festival**. ‡ Early Oct (even years only): **Paris motor show** at Parc des Expositions. ‡ Oct-Dec: **Festival d'Art Sacré** — concerts in churches all over town. ‡ End Oct-early Nov: **Paris Jazz Festival**. **Paris Tennis Open** at Bercy, 12e.

November
‡ Nov 11: national public holiday

and **Armistice Day ceremony** at Arc de Triomphe. ‡ Mid-Nov: **Paris International Dance Festival** — classical and contemporary dance competitions. ‡ Mid-Nov to Mid-Dec: **Paris Guitar Festival**.

December
‡ During Dec: **Christmas decorations and illuminations** throughout Paris. ‡ New's Year's Eve: **street celebrations**, particularly in the Latin Quarter.

Area planners and visits

The following list outlines the most significant areas, with their corresponding *arrondissements* (shown in French by the superior letter ^{e} or ^{er} — short for *ième* or *ier* — following the number). The areas are listed in an order that starts at the centre of the city and works out in a spiral.

Opéra quarter (*part of 1er, 2e and 9e; maps 8 & 9*). An area of grand architecture, smart shops and highbrow culture. Glossy and expensive, but somewhat fraying at the edges.

Les Halles (*part of 1er; map 10 H9*). An exhilaratingly revitalized area following massive redevelopment.

Le Marais (*3e and part of 4e; maps 10 & 11*). An old, quiet, gracious district, with many museums, narrow rambling streets, and a strong flavour of the past.

Île de la Cité and Île St-Louis (*part of 1er and 4e; maps 10 & 11*). The former is the historic heart of Paris containing the *Conciergerie, Palais de Justice, Sainte Chapelle* and *Notre-Dame*. Busy and administrative. The Île St-Louis, by contrast, is charming, quiet and residential.

Latin Quarter (*5e; map 15*). This area was originally known as the Université, and has remained the learned quarter of Paris. Youthful, cosmopolitan, colourful, Bohemian, with a large student population.

St-Germain (*6e and part of 7e; maps 8 & 9 and 14 & 15*). A quarter with a wide boulevard, tiny side streets, old buildings, and a thriving café life. Intellectual, artistic and elegant.

Eiffel Tower and Les Invalides and environs (*remainder of 7e; maps 12 & 13*). Quiet, mainly residential area dominated by the axes of the *Champ-de-Mars* and *Les Invalides* complex.

Av. des Champs-Élysées and Rue du Faubourg-St-Honoré (*8e; maps 6 & 7*). Busy, expensive, grandiose.

Parc de Monceau and environs (*straddling 8e and 17e; map 2*). Stolid and residential. The world described by Proust.

Montparnasse (*straddling 14e and 15e; map 14*). Cosmopolitan, former Bohemian colony, torn apart by redevelopment, but retaining some of its old character.

Palais de Chaillot and environs (*16e; map 12*). Cluster of museums set in an opulently residential *arrondissement*.

Montmartre (*18e; map 4*). Often referred to by the locals as the "Butte". Rambling, picture-postcard quaintness, side by side with neon-lit yet shabby razzle-dazzle.

Belleville/Ménilmontant (*straddling 19e and 20e*). Its former dilapidated charm is now largely eroded by redevelopment. Strong North African flavour.

Orientation map

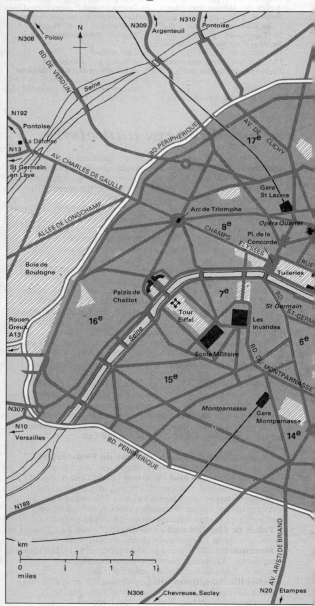

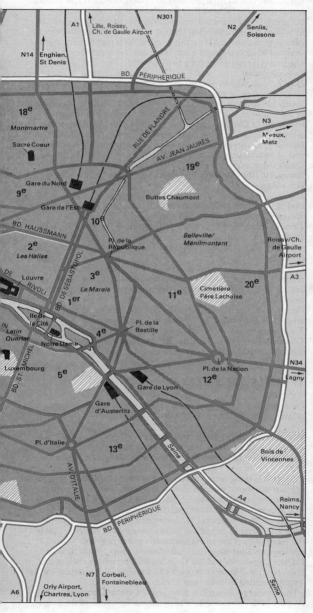

Organizing your time

On a short visit to Paris, the way to avoid frustration and cultural indigestion is to be selective. Remember that Paris has the advantage of being small and well-organized for the pedestrian, as well as having a superb Métro system, and it is a good idea to plan your sightseeing with this in mind. You may already have decided what you want to see, but if not, here are some suggested programmes for a two-day and a four-day visit.

Two-day visit

Day 1　In the morning go to the *Carnavalet* museum to get a bird's-eye view of the history of Paris. Then walk through the lovely old *Marais* district to the *Pompidou Centre* for a glimpse of the ultra-modern face of Paris. Go across the *Seine* through the *Île de la Cité* and have lunch in the *Latin Quarter*. In the afternoon take a boat trip on the Seine from the *Pont-Neuf.*

Day 2　Go up the *Eiffel Tower* and perhaps have lunch in one of its restaurants. Then take the Métro from Bir-Hakeim to Charles-de-Gaulle-Étoile and walk from the *Arc de Triomphe* down *Av. des Champs-Élysées* to *Pl. de la Concorde*.

Four-day visit

Day 1　Do *Walk 1: Getting to know Paris* (see below).

Day 2　Return to the *Île de la Cité* for a closer look at *Notre-Dame* and *Sainte Chapelle* and perhaps the *Conciergerie* and *Crypte Archéologique*. Have lunch on the *Île St-Louis*. In the afternoon either take *Walk 2: A riverside walk* (see page 41) or return to the Right Bank and spend some hours in the *Louvre*.

Day 3　Take the Métro to Trocadéro and admire the magnificent view from the *Palais de Chaillot*. Cross the river and climb the *Eiffel Tower*. In the afternoon take a river trip from the Pont d'Iéna.

Day 4　In the morning visit the *Sacré-Coeur* and wander around *Montmartre*. In the afternoon walk through the *Tuileries* gardens to *Pl. de la Concorde* along *Av. des Champs-Élysées* to *Pl. Charles de Gaulle* and see Paris from the top of the *Arc de Triomphe*.

Walks in Paris

Paris is a wonderful city for walking, and the fine texture of its urban landscape is best appreciated on foot.

Walk 1: Getting to know Paris

Walks 1 and 2 can be traced on the map opposite. Allow at least half a day. Maps 8,9&10. Métro: Opéra (1), Louvre (13).

This walk is designed to introduce the visitor to Paris, taking a spiral route round its heart. It encompasses many well-known landmarks, and contrasts the great boulevards and the rambling side streets, the Right Bank and the Left.

Begin at Pl. de l'Opéra (**1**), dominated by the ornate *Opéra* itself and forming one of the main crossroads of the city. This is the heart of the Paris of Haussmann, creator of grand townscapes, and the area is full of smart shops. Walk sw down Bd. des Capucines and Bd. de la Madeleine, which ends at the church of the *Madeleine* itself (**2**), looking, as it is meant to, like a stray building from ancient Rome.

From here, go down Rue Royale to *Pl. de la Concorde* (**3**), passing between two splendid matching buildings of the Louis

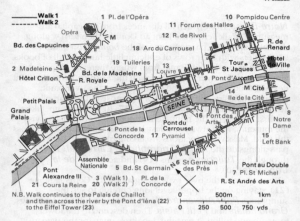

XV period, the one on the right housing the famous Hôtel de Crillon (see *Hotels*). Cross the river by the Pont de la Concorde (**4**), opposite the *Assemblée Nationale*, and walk down the great artery of the Left Bank, Bd. St-Germain (**5**), perhaps pausing for coffee at one of its host of famous cafés (see *Cafés*).

At the church of *St-Germain-des-Prés* (**6**), turn left to browse in the charming maze of old streets between the boulevard and the Seine, with their many little book and antique shops, art galleries and food stalls. Then take Rue St-André-des-Arts and follow it E to Pl. St-Michel (**7**), focal point of the *Latin Quarter*. This would be an ideal place to stop for lunch, as the area is full of good restaurants.

From here, cross by the Pont au Double to the *Île de la Cité* and *Notre-Dame* cathedral (**8**) and return to the Right Bank by the Pont d'Arcole (**9**), walking N with the *Hôtel de Ville* on the right and the Gothic eminence of the *Tour St-Jacques* to the left. Rue de Renard and Rue Beaubourg lead to the E side of the *Pompidou Centre* (**10**), Paris' lively cultural complex. To reach the main entrance, walk round the lively piazza in front of the building. Having seen the Centre, turn W, passing the *Forum des Halles* (**11**), a shopping complex that has taken the place of the old food market. Now turn left down to the elegant *Rue de Rivoli* (**12**), with its colonnade and luxurious shops, and turn right toward the *Louvre* (**13**). Whether or not you visit the museum (see *Walk 2* and entry in *Sights and places of interest*), set off for home from the Louvre Métro, which, with its low reliefs and statues, is Paris' most attractive Métro station.

Walk 2: A riverside walk
*Allow 3hrs. Maps 9,8,7&6. Métro: Cité (**14**), Trocadéro (**23**).*
Most of the great capitals of Europe have their equivalents of the Seine, but few have as intimate a relationship with their rivers as Paris does. History and romance flow thickly in its waters, and Parisians love it tenderly. This walk, beginning and ending at Paris' two greatest landmarks, does not stay on the river banks all the time, since the main roads run along much of them, but the Seine, with its ever-changing vistas, will never be far away.

The beginning is where Paris itself began: on the *Île de la Cité* (**14**). And what could be a more appropriate starting point than the brass compass marker set into the ground by the W door of

Notre-Dame, from which all distances from the capital are measured? Walk across the Pont au Double, then turn w along the Left Bank (**15**), passing some of the *bouquinistes*, the booksellers with their rows of enticing little hutches full of books. Continue along the Left Bank, from where there are magnificent views across the river, until level with the *Louvre*. Cross the Pont des Arts footbridge (**16**), and turn left along the river bank, walking alongside the Louvre. For a glimpse of the marvellously adventurous glass pyramid entrance (**17**) to the museum, take the first turning on the right. Remember that if you wish to visit the museum, it is unwise to allow less than half a day. Then cross the road. Massive excavations are taking place here, but you can pass alongside the *Arc de Triomphe du Carrousel* (**18**), through the *Tuileries* gardens (**19**) and across *Pl. de la Concorde* (**20**).

Now return to the river by walking along the Cours la Reine (**21**), staying on the upper level long enough to see the sumptuous *Pont Alexandre III* and the two exhibition buildings, *Grand Palais* and *Petit Palais*. Then descend to the lower footpath and follow it past the departure quay for the Bateaux-Mouches near Pont de l'Alma. The lower walkway is not continuous from here, so return at certain points to the road above. Continue in this way until you reach the gardens of the *Palais de Chaillot*. Cross the river by the Pont d'Iéna (**22**) to arrive at the foot of the *Eiffel Tower* (**23**), one of the great symbols of Paris and a suitable place to end the walk.

Walk 3: The literary Left Bank
Allow 3hrs. Maps 14,15,8&9. Métro: Raspail (1), St-Michel (14).

Almost any walk in Paris would be a "literary" walk, since there is hardly a corner that does not have some link with a writer or poet; but this one is particularly rich in literary associations.

Start at *Montparnasse* cemetery (**1**), which contains the graves of many literary figures including Maupassant, Huysmans and Baudelaire. Walk to the crossroads of Bd. du Montparnasse and Bd. Raspail. Close by are the Dôme, Coupole, Select and Rotonde, cafés that were the haunts of Hemingway, Fitzgerald, Miller and other expatriate writers of the interwar years. By the Rotonde on Bd. Raspail stands a cast of Rodin's famous *Balzac*. Turn right along Bd. du. Montparnasse. At the corner of this Bd. and Av. de l'Observatoire is La Closerie des Lilas, another old haunt of the American literary set, and still much favoured by Parisian *literati*.

Walk down the Av. de l'Observatoire (**2**) into the *Luxembourg* gardens, where you will find memorials to many writers, including (on the E side) Murger, author of *La Bohème*, Flaubert, Stendhal, George Sand and Lecomte de L'Isle. On the W side is a particularly striking memorial to the poet Paul Verlaine. Leave the gardens on the W side by Rue Fleurus (**3**), passing no. 27, where Gertrude Stein lived.

Turn right into Rue d'Assas. Now follow for a while the walk taken one night by d'Artagnan, in Dumas' *Three Musketeers*, while dreaming of his beloved, as he was "passing along a lane on the spot where Rue d'Assas is now situated." Turning into what must have been Rue de Vaugirard, d'Artagnan made for the house of his fellow musketeer Aramis, "situated between Rue Cassette and Rue Servandoni" (still in existence). "The hero passed Rue Cassette and caught sight of the door of his friend's house, shaded by a mass of sycamore and clematis, which

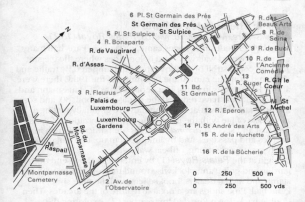

formed a vast arch above it." This must have been somewhere near where Rue Bonaparte begins. Walk down this street (**4**), full of antiquarian bookshops, to Pl. St-Sulpice (**5**), described so evocatively by Henry Miller in *Tropic of Cancer*. "St-Sulpice! The fat belfries, the garish posters over the door, the candles flaming inside. The Square so beloved of Anatole France with that drone and buzz from the altar, the splash of the fountain, the pigeons cooing...."

Continue down Rue Bonaparte to Pl. St-Germain-des-Prés (**6**). Here is the heart of **St-Germain**, once known as the "Capitale des Lettres" thanks to the presence of poets such as Apollinaire (who lived at 202 Bd. St-Germain) and later of Jean-Paul Sartre, Simone de Beauvoir, Raymond Queneau and Albert Camus. It was in the cafés here — Les Deux Magots, for example — that the Existentialist philosophy was nurtured. Continue N on Rue Bonaparte, then turn right into Rue des Beaux-Arts (**7**). "I am dying beyond my means," declared Oscar Wilde, who died at no. 13 in 1900. Even so, he would not recognize the contemporary luxury of l'Hôtel, as this building is now simply known (see *Hotels*).

Turn right into Rue de Seine (**8**), where at no. 21 there is the house once inhabited by George Sand. Turn left into Rue de Buci (**9**), right into Rue de l'Ancienne-Comédie (**10**), and walk s to Le Procope (*no.13*), which has been a literary haunt since it was founded in 1686 (see *Restaurants*). Molière and Racine came here when the *Comédie Française* was at no.14 in the same street. Later it was patronized by Balzac, Hugo, Verlaine and many others.

Back on Bd. St-Germain (**11**), continue your journey E past the Carrefour de l'Odéon and then turn left down Rue Éperon (**12**) and right into Rue Suger (**13**), where J.K. Huysmans was born at no. 11 in 1848. This road leads to Pl. St-André-des-Arts (**14**), where there is a café called Gentilhomme, described by Jack Kerouac in his *Satori in Paris*. Just around the corner in Rue Gît-le-Coeur is the Hôtel Vieux Paris where he, Allen Ginsberg and others of the "Beat Generation" used to stay when they were in town. From here turn left into Bd. St-Michel, and before the Seine turn right along Rue de la Huchette (**15**) and on into Rue de la Bûcherie (**16**), to find the famous bookshop, Shakespeare and Co., at no. 37. The shop is as full of atmosphere as it is of books, and continues the splendid literary tradition of this part of Paris in the lively poetry readings attended by young literati.

Walk 4: The arcades of Paris
Allow 3-4hrs. Maps 9&10. Métro: Palais-Royal (1&21).

Long before pedestrian zones came into vogue, Paris had many
arcades, covered walkways and colonnades where the elegant
flâneur could stroll or window-shop, unhampered by traffic and
sheltered from the rain. At the beginning of the 19thC there were
about 140 arcades in Paris. The depredations of Haussmann and
later developers have reduced the number to about 30, and some
are now rather down-at-heel, but they are gradually getting a
new lease of life with the increasing pedestrianization of Paris.
The first and second *arrondissements* are particularly rich in
arcades and passages, and by linking them up, one can quite
easily create a charming, offbeat walk.

Begin at the *Palais-Royal* (1) by entering at the SE end of the
garden and going anti-clockwise round the colonnade, with its
stamp and medal dealers, booksellers, and the pipe shop, À
l'Oriental. Pipe shops are a notable feature of the arcades. Then
double back down Rue de Montpensier (2), exploring the
following four covered passages, de Richelieu, Potier, Hulot and
de Beaujolais, which link this street with Rue de Richelieu. Then
turn right along Rue de Beaujolais (3) and go through Passage des
Deux Pavillons.

Across Rue des Petits-Champs are the entrances to the Galerie
Colbert and the Galerie Vivienne (4). Return to Rue des Petits-
Champs and turn right, walking past Rue Ste-Anne, and turning
right up Passage Choiseul (5), full of smart boutiques, leading to
Rue St-Augustin (6).

Carry on northwards along Rue de Choiseul to Bd. des Italiens
(7). Turn right, continuing until you arrive at Passage des Princes
(8), which links with Rue de Richelieu. Here you will find

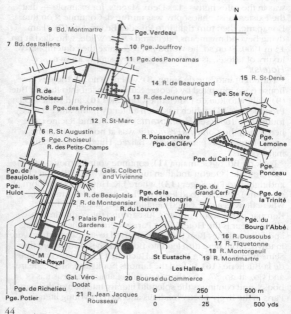

44

another old pipe shop, that of J. Sommer, specialist in meerschaums, many with the heads of notable figures such as J.F.Kennedy or de Gaulle carved around the bowl. The workshop where the pipes are made is visible from the window. Having emerged into Rue de Richelieu, turn left towards Bd. Montmartre (**9**) and continue travelling E past Rue Vivienne to the point where the two arcades lead off the boulevard. To the N, Passage Jouffroy (**10**) extends into Passage Verdeau. To the S, Passage des Panoramas (**11**) links up with a small rabbit warren of arcades, with a curious mixture of shops and restaurants.

Exit at the S side of the galleries into Rue St-Marc (**12**), then head E, walking via Rue des Jeûneurs (**13**), Rue Poissonnière and Rue de Beauregard (**14**) (off which runs the short Passage de Cléry) to the corner of Bd. de Bonne-Nouvelle and Rue St-Denis (**15**). From here walk S down Rue St-Denis, exploring in turn each of the seven covered passages that lead off it, to right and left: Lemoine, Ste-Foy, Ponceau, du Caire, de la Trinité, du Bourg-l'Abbé and du Grand-Cerf. These once-fashionable walkways have come down in the world, but still possess a faded charm. Passage du Caire has a cornice decorated with Egyptian reliefs and supported by sphinx-like heads. Passage du Grand-Cerf leads out into Rue Dussoubs (**16**).

Turn right into Rue Tiquetonne (**17**) and left again into Rue Montorgueil (**18**) to visit Passage de la Reine de Hongrie, one of the few with no shops. The alley got its name when a woman who ran a stall there gave a petition to Marie-Antoinette. The queen told her that she looked very like the Queen of Hungary, and the name stuck, both to the woman and the place where she worked. Emerge into Rue Montmartre (**19**) and skirt round *Les Halles* by the lovely *St-Eustache* church. Walk through the colonnade surrounding the *Bourse du Commerce* (**20**), then cross Rue du Louvre and turn left down Rue Jean-Jacques Rousseau (**21**) to the lovely Galerie Véro-Dodat. This arcade, with its gracefully proportioned shop fronts and carved mahogany panelling, brings you back to near the Palais-Royal.

Sights and places of interest

The sights of Paris are as diverse as they are many; do try to visit at least a few of the lesser-known ones as well as the great monuments and treasures. Opening times tend to alter with each new season, but in most cases, places will have extended rather than shortened their hours. Many museums in Paris are closed on Tues, and some are free or cheaper on Sun. The vast majority are closed on public holidays. Rules on photography vary, but often only flash is prohibited: look for the ⬛ symbol.

Each year, new ticket incentive schemes for visitors are introduced. If you plan to visit a number of museums, buy a *Carte Inter-Musée*, on sale at museums and monuments, Métro stations and tourist offices. This card, costing between 50-150f for 1, 3 or 5 days, allows you access to more than 60 sights, without the need to pay anything further — and without queueing for tickets.

The entries in this section have to be selective, but you should find just about anything you could possibly wish to visit during an average stay — and a great deal more besides. If you only know the name of a museum in English and cannot find it in the *A-Z*, try looking it up in the *Index*. Other sights that do not have their

Sights and places of interest

Major sights classified by type

Churches (all ▥)
Dôme ★
Madeleine ★
Notre-Dame de
  Paris ★ ◀€
Panthéon ★
Sacré-Coeur, Basilique
  du ★ ◀€
St-Denis, Basilique
St-Étienne-du-Mont
St-Eustache
St-Germain l'Auxerrois
St-Germain-des-Prés
St-Joseph-des-Carmes
St-Julien-le-Pauvre
St-Nicolas-des-Champs
St-Roch
St-Séverin
St-Sulpice
Sainte-Chapelle ★
Val-de-Grâce
Districts and streets
Champs-Élysées ★
Charles-de-Gaulle, Pl.
Concorde, Pl. de la ★
La Défense ▥ ◀€
Rue du Faubourg-St-
  Honoré
Île de la Cité ★
Latin Quarter ★
Marais ★
Montmartre ★
Montparnasse
Opéra Quarter
St-Germain Quarter
Pl. Vendôme ▥ ★
Pl. des Vosges ▥
Famous homes
Balzac, Maison de
Bourdelle, Musée
  Antoine
Le Corbusier
  Foundation
Delacroix, Musée
  Eugène
d'Ennery, Musée d'
Maison Victor Hugo ▥
Gustave Moreau, Musée
Pasteur, Musée
Zadkine, Musée
General interest
Arènes de Lutèce
Automobile, Centre
  International de l' ❀
Bastille, Pl. de la
Bourse des Valeurs ▥
Bourse du Commerce
Canal St-Martin
Catacombes
Cousteau, Parc
  Océanique ❀
Cristalleries, Musée des
Égouts (Sewers)
Entrepôts de Bercy
Flea Markets
Gobelins
Grévin, Musée ❀
Historial de Montmartre
Hôtel des Ventes
Père Lachaise, Cimetière
Publicité, Musée de la

Radio-France, Musée
  de ▥
Transports Urbains,
  Musée des
**Historic buildings
(all ▥)**
Assemblée Nationale
Beaux-Arts, École des
Bibliothèque Nationale
Collège de France
Comédie Française
Conciergerie ★
Hôtel de Ville
Institut de France
Les Invalides ★
Luxembourg Palais du
Observatoire
Opéra ★
Palais de l'Élysée
Palais de Justice
Palais-Royal
Panthéon ★
Vincennes, Château de
**Modern buildings
(all ▥)**
Le Corbusier Fondation
La Défense ◀€
Forum des Halles ★
Institut du Monde Arabe
Opéra Bastille
Palais de Chaillot
Palais des Congrès
Pompidou Centre ★ ❀
Radio-France, Maison
Tour Montparnasse ◀€
UNESCO Building
Monuments
Arc de Triomphe ▥
  ★ ◀€
Arc de Triomphe du
  Carrousel
Grande Arche de la
  Défense ▥ ◀€
Tour Eiffel ▥ ★ ◀€
**Museums and
galleries**
Armée
Arménien
Art Moderne
Art Moderne de la Ville
  de Paris
Arts Africains et
  Océaniens
Arts Décoratifs
Arts et Métiers
Arts de la Mode
Arts et Traditions
  Populaires
Arts Asiatiques Guimet
Balzac
Beaux-Arts
Bourdelle
Camondo, Nissim de ▥
Carnavalet ▥
Cernuschi
Chasse et nature ▥
Cinéma Henri-
  Langlois ▥
Clemenceau
Cluny ▥
Cognacq-Jay

Le Corbusier
Crypte Archéologique
  de Notre-Dame
Delacroix
d'Ennery
Grand Orient de France
Grand Palais ▥
Grévin
Guerres Mondiales,
  Deux
Gustave Moreau
Hébert ▥
Henner
en Herbe ❀
Histoire de France
Histoire Naturelle ❀
  l'Homme
Hugo, Victor
Institut du Monde
  Arabe
Jacquemart-André
Jeu de Paume ▥
Légion d'Honneur ▥
Louvre ▥ ★
Marine ▥
Marmottan ▥
Mode et Costume ▥
Monde Arabe ▥
Monnaie
Monuments
  Français ▥
Moreau, Gustave
Orangerie ▥
Orsay ▥ ★
Ordre de la Libération
Palais de la
  Découverte ▥
Pasteur
Petit Palais ▥
Picasso
Plans-Reliefs
Police
Pompidou Centre
Poste
Radio-France ▥
Renan-Scheffer
Rodin ▥ ★
Sculpture en Plein
  Air
Transports Urbains
Zadkine
Parks and gardens
Bois de Boulogne ★ ❀
Buttes Chaumont ❀ ◀€
Champ-de-Mars
Jardin des Plantes ❀
Jardin du
  Luxembourg ❀
Monceau ❀
Montsouris
Tuileries ❀
La Villette ★ ❀
Vincennes, Bois
  de ★ ❀
**Science &
technology**
Cité des Sciences et de
  l'Industrie ★ ❀
CNIT
Techniques, Musée
  des ❀

own entries may well be included in a district entry; look these up in the *Index* too.

Look for the ★ symbol against the most important sights and 血 for buildings of great architectural interest. Good views (≪) and places of special interest for children (✱) are also indicated.

Arc de Triomphe 血
Pl. Charles-de-Gaulle, 8ᵉ ☎ *43-80-31-31. Map 6F3* ▨ ≪
Open Apr 1–Sept 30 10am–5.30pm, winter 10am–4.30pm.
Closed public holidays. Métro: Charles-de-Gaulle-Étoile.
As much a symbol of Paris as the *Eiffel Tower* or *Notre-Dame*, the Arc de Triomphe is the largest structure of its kind in the world — 50m (164ft) high and 45m (148ft) wide — and its massive bulk dominates the *Pl. Charles-de-Gaulle*, formerly the Pl. de l'Étoile. It is surely one of the biggest "white elephants" ever created. The term is curiously appropriate, for an earlier plan for the site was to erect a vast stone elephant containing an amphitheatre, banqueting hall and other apartments.

The present arch was begun in 1806, on the orders of Napoleon, who wanted a monument to French military victories, but it remained unfinished at the time of his downfall. Under the restored monarchy, work on the arch continued spasmodically, and it was finally completed in 1836. Many artists worked on the decoration of the exterior, which includes four huge relief sculptures at the bases of the pillars: *The Triumph of 1810* by Cortot; *Resistance* and *Peace* by Etex; and *The Departure of the Volunteers* (commonly called *The Marseillaise*) by Rude, which is generally considered the best of the four.

Higher up are reliefs of battles and a crowded frieze, and engraved around the top are the names of major victories won during the Revolutionary and Napoleonic periods. On the inside walls appear the names of lesser victories and of 558 generals.

Set into the ground under the arch is the **Tomb of the Unknown Soldier**, commemorating the dead of World Wars I and II, whose memory is kept alight by an eternal flame — a few years ago, an irreverent person cooked an omelet over it. The arch seems to invite such disrespectful gestures: in 1919 the aviator Godefroy flew under it in an aeroplane, defying a police ban.

Inside the cross-piece of the building is a **museum of the arch's history**, which runs a continuous audiovisual programme in French and English recounting the monument's great moments.

Like many other disproportionately large and grandiose monuments in Paris, the arch has merged comfortably into the townscape, settling down to an almost homely, comfortable existence, like a retired general. But no trip to Paris would be complete without a visit, and from the top there is an excellent view over the city of Paris.

Arc de Triomphe du Carrousel
Pl. du Carrousel, 1ᵉʳ. Map 8H7. Métro: Palais-Royal.
This graceful arch, with its rose-coloured marble columns, is linked with the greater *Arc de Triomphe* by the splendid axis formed by the *Champs-Élysées* and the *Tuileries*. Completed in 1809, it commemorates Napoleon's victories in 1805 (including Austerlitz and Ulm), which are depicted on six marble low reliefs. It was formerly surmounted by the four gilded bronze horses from St Mark's in Venice. When these were returned to Italy in 1815 they were replaced by a bronze group, representing the Restoration, riding in a chariot drawn by four horses. The arch

once formed the gateway to the Tuileries Palace, burned down in
1871, and it now floats in the gardens between the great jaws of
the *Louvre* like a dainty morsel about to be swallowed by a
whale. Massive excavation and rebuilding works between this
area and the *Louvre* will continue during 1991, with the
eventual establishment of the **Palais de la Mode** (see *Tuileries*).

Arcades
Of interest as much for their architectural
qualities as for the shopping opportunities, Paris' many arcades
are described in detail in *Walks* page 44.

Archives Nationales: Musée de l'Histoire de France
(National Archives: Museum of French History) Ⅲ
Hôtel de Soubise, 60 Rue des Francs-Bourgeois, 3ᵉ
☎ *40-27-60-00. Map* **11H11** 🔲 🎌 *Open 2-5pm. Closed
Tues. Métro: Rambuteau, Hôtel-de-Ville.*

How many tumultuous events have started with an innocent-
looking document? The Revocation of the Edict of Nantes by
Louis XIV removed freedom of worship, and drove thousands of
Protestants out of France. The Revocation and the original Edict
are both in the Historical Museum of France, and form part of a
collection of documents belonging to the National Archives and
housed in one of the great mansions of the *Marais* district, the
Hôtel de Soubise. Here also are the wills of Louis XIV and
Napoleon, the Concordat of 1802 between Napoleon and the
Holy See, the Declaration of the Rights of Man, letters of Joan of
Arc and Voltaire — snippets of history skilfully displayed and
carefully illustrated with the use of maps, photographs and
captions to create an intriguing scrapbook of the French nation.
The National Archives themselves, which take up 280km (175
miles) of shelving, have been housed in the Hôtel de Soubise
since 1808 and in the adjacent **Hôtel de Rohan** since 1927.

There is more to see than just the documents. The Hôtel de
Soubise itself, with its elegant, colonnaded **courtyard**, is worth
visiting on its own account. From 1553-1688 it was a residence of
the powerful Guise family. It then became the home of the Prince
and Princesse de Soubise, who had it sumptuously decorated by
some of the greatest artists and craftsmen of the era, including
Boucher, van Loo and Lemoyne. Leaving the main room of the
museum on the first floor, formerly the guardroom, one passes
through a series of **private apartments**. Notice particularly the
Princess' Oval Salon with its eight paintings of the loves of
Psyche by Charles Natoire, and also her small bedroom, which
now houses a permanent exhibition on the French Revolution.
There are also temporary exhibitions in the apartments.

The **Hôtel de Rohan** (*87 Rue Vieille-du-Temple*), officially
called the Hôtel de Strasbourg, as well as being part of the
National Archives, is now frequently used for temporary
exhibitions. It was lived in by four successive cardinals of
Strasbourg who decorated their **apartments** with rich
extravagance. One of the rooms, the **Monkey Cabinet**, retains
its original panels, decorated with animals by Christophe Huet in
1745. The remainder of the interior is the result of skilful
restoration. The courtyard has a fine relief by Robert le Lorrain,
The Horses of Apollo.

Arènes de Lutèce
Entrances in Rue Monge and Rue de Navarre, 5ᵉ. Map
16K10. *Open summer 10am-8.30pm, winter 10am-5.30pm*
&. *Métro: Monge, Jussieu, Cardinal-Lemoine.*

Turning off the street into what seems like an ordinary Parisian park, you walk down a stone corridor and suddenly emerge into a Gallo-Roman amphitheatre with terraces for spectators. It was rediscovered in 1869 when Rue Monge was being constructed, and was later restored. Now it is enjoying a second and quieter lease of life surrounded by greenery, and it makes an ideal place for playing *boules* or for simply sitting and imagining life in *Lutetia* — as Paris was known in the Roman era.

Armée, Musée de l'   See *Les Invalides*.

Arménien, Musée *(Armenian Museum)*
59 Av. Foch, 16ᵉ. Map 6F1 and see map on page 54 🖾
Open Thurs, Sun 2-6pm. Closed Aug. Métro: Dauphine.
This small museum of works of art, documents and domestic objects provides an intriguing view of 3,000yrs of Armenian history and culture. It is in the same building as the *Musée d'Ennery*, which houses the private collection of 19thC dramatist and librettist Adolphe d'Ennery and his wife.

Art Moderne, Musée National d'   See *Pompidou Centre*.

Art Moderne de la Ville de Paris, Musée d'
(Museum of Modern Art of the City of Paris) 🏛
Palais de Tokyo, 11 Av. du Président. Wilson, Paris 16ᵉ
☎ *47-23-61-27. Map 12G3* 🖾 ♿ ▣ ✳ *Open 10am-5.30pm*
(Wed until 8.30pm). Closed Mon. Métro: Iéna, Alma-Marceau.
This lively museum is housed in the w wing of the *Palais de Tokyo*. The whole building is a typical example of 1930s style, which, at the time, seemed so aggressively modern and now looks quaintly dated. Something of the same feeling is also present as you enter the museum, and it is helpful to see the paintings in the context of their periods: for example, Raoul Dufy's huge canvas *La Fée Électricité* (The Good Fairy Electricity). Other items in this very fine collection include Cubist paintings by Picasso and Braque, canvases of the Fauve school (Matisse, Derain) and works by the so-called Paris school (Modigliani, Soutine, Pascin). There are also temporary exhibitions.

In addition to the main galleries, the museum has two other sections. On the top floor is **ARC** (*Animation, Recherche, Confrontation*),an area devoted to off-beat contemporary exhibitions and to concerts, lectures and other cultural events. Down on the lowest level is the **Musée des Enfants** (*entrance at 14 Av. de New York*), where children are able to participate in various creative activities, from painting to dancing, under the guidance of teachers.

Arts Africains et Océaniens, Musée National des
(Museum of African and Oceanic Arts)
293 Av. Daumesnil, 12ᵉ ☎ *43-43-14-54. Map 19D5 and see map on page 127* 🖾 𝒦 *by prior arrangement* ✳ ♿ *Open Mon, Wed-Fri 10am-noon, 1.30-5.30pm, Sat, Sun 12.30-6pm. Métro: Porte-Dorée.*
This museum contains a superb collection of ethnic art: Benin bronzes, masks from New Guinea, Aboriginal bark paintings and a particularly fine display of North African Islamic art. Down in the basement is one of the best tropical aquariums in Europe, complete with crocodiles, where admission is free for under-18s.

Arts Asiatiques Guimet, Musée National d'
(formerly Musée Guimet)
6 Pl. d'Iéna, 16ᵉ ☎ 47-23-61-65. Map 6G3 ⬛ ✗ Open 9.45am-5pm. Closed Tues. Métro Iéna.

If the East holds any appeal for you then this treasurehouse of Asian art is a must. Its nucleus is a collection formed by the 19thC industrialist Émile Guimet, whose intention was to gather together objects illustrating the civilizations and religions of the Orient. Since the museum became a national one, it has been greatly enriched by the addition of other Oriental collections, and now houses a splendid, wide-ranging array of works of art from Afghanistan, Pakistan, India, Vietnam, Laos, Kampuchea, China, Korea, Japan, Thailand, Tibet and Nepal. The museum is particularly renowned for its Kampuchean sculptures, as well as for its magnificent Tibetan *tangkas* (devotional paintings used for meditation), and ritual instruments reflecting the richly colourful and highly symbolic world of Tantric Buddhism.

Scholars are welcome to visit the museum's research and study centre, housing a library, a photographic archive and an auditorium.

Arts Décoratifs, Musée des *(Museum of Decorative Arts)* ⬛
Pavillon de Marsan, 107 Rue de Rivoli, 1ᵉʳ ☎ 42-60-32-14. Map 8H7 ⬛ ✗ Open 12.30-6pm, Sun 11am-6pm. Closed Mon, Tues, public holidays. Métro: Palais-Royal, Tuileries.

Founded in the 1870s as part of an attempt to combat mediocrity in the applied arts, this museum presents a panorama of decorative art from the Middle Ages to the 20thC. Housed in the **Marsan pavilion** of the *Louvre*, exhibits are set out in a series of rooms furnished and decorated in the style of different eras. Here you can see medieval carvings, chests and tapestry work, Renaissance stained glass, elaborate marquetry furniture of the 17thC, Vincennes porcelain of the 18thC, and Art Nouveau woodwork of the 20thC. One of the most striking rooms is a complete **Italianate salon** of the Second Empire with richly painted and gilt wood panelling. A further series of displays show furniture and household objects from more recent decades, and the museum also houses a large and important **toy collection** (✳).

Frequent temporary exhibitions on design and decoration are held. In the same building is the *Musée des Arts de la Mode*.

Arts de la Mode, Musée des
109 Rue de Rivoli, 1ᵉʳ ☎ 42-60-32-14. Map 8H7 ⬛ ✸ Open 12.30-6pm, Sun 11am-6pm. Closed Mon, Tues, public holidays. Métro: Palais-Royal, Tuileries.

Not to be confused with the *Musée de la Mode*, this museum is more specifically oriented to the fashion industry and its history, providing a record by preserving examples of important collections and items of clothing and illustrating the development of style.

Massive works in the *Tuileries*, started in 1990, will eventually provide a major focus for the world of Paris fashion. Completion of a new **Palais de la Mode** is scheduled for 1993, when underground developments to rival those across the way at the *Louvre* will house permanent and temporary exhibitions on all aspects of fashion design, as well as becoming the new and much-needed venue for the twice-yearly Paris fashion shows.

The architect, Gérard Grandval, has planned a subterranean

complex that will be invisible from above, apart from a splendid granite staircase on the Rue de Castiglione/Pont Solférino axis.

Arts et Traditions Populaires, Musée des *(Museum of Popular Arts and Traditions)*
6 Av.du Mahatma Gandhi, Bois de Boulogne, 16ᵉ
☎ *40-67-90-00. Map 18C3 and see map on page 54* 🔳 ⟨& ✗ *by prior arrangement* ✻ *Open 9.45am-5.15pm. Closed Tues. Métro: Sablons.*

A cock from a church steeple, models of fishing boats, Breton peasant costumes, a blacksmith's forge, a clairvoyant's consulting room complete with crystal ball and tarot cards — these and many more curiosities are to be found in this colourful museum dealing with French folk art and culture from the beginning of the Iron Age to the 20thC. A visit adds another element to a pleasant excursion to the *Bois de Boulogne*.

Assemblée Nationale *(National Assembly)* 🏛
Palais-Bourbon, 33 Quai d'Orsay, 7ᵉ ☎ *40-63-60-00. Map 8H6* 🔲 ✺ ✗ *compulsory. In session: open Sat 9-11am, 2-4pm. Out of session: open Mon-Sat 9-11am, 2-5pm (4pm Sat). Métro: Assemblée Nationale, Invalides.*

The French lower house of parliament (called the National Assembly or Chamber of Deputies) meets in a mansion originally built by the Duchess of Bourbon, a daughter of Louis XIV, and later acquired by the state and extensively altered. Only the great courtyard facing s preserves most of its original features. The facade looking onto the Seine, with its heavy Greek-style portico, was constructed in the time of Napoleon.

The National Assembly jealously guards its independence from the Government and the State. No minister can be a deputy as well, and the president cannot enter the building, though he can be received in the adjacent house of the president of the Assembly, the **Hôtel de Lassay**.

The 577 deputies meet in an ornate, semicircular chamber of red, white and gold. The marble speaker's tribune was originally adorned with a Napoleonic eagle, tactfully changed into a cock when republicanism finally triumphed, but the room retains an aspect of imperial splendour.

During sessions you can watch from a public gallery, but seats are limited. The first ten people in the queue on any given day are admitted on showing a passport or identity card.

Other parts of the building to which visitors are given access include the **library**, a discreetly grand room with a Delacroix ceiling depicting a **history of civilization**.

The Palais-Bourbon has the atmosphere of an exclusive London club; the deputies even have their own barbershop.

Automobile, Centre International de l'
25 Rue d'Estienne d'Orves, Pantin ☎ *48-43-79-14. Map 19C5* ⟨& ✻ *Open 10.30am-6.30pm (Tues 10pm). Métro: Hoche.*

Anyone who has ever wanted to see below the bonnet of a Bugatti, or daydream over cars that have seen the Daytona track, should head for this newly-opened centre dedicated to the glory of the automobile, from the early days of its conception to first glimpses of things to come.

Different makes of car are on show, from many countries of origin, and the programme of exhibits changes every 3-4mths. Children are welcome at the centre, and there are organized activities for over-3s, audiovisual road-safety instruction, and, for older children, driving-simulation games.

The traditional base of the French motor industry is to the w of Paris. This centre provides an eastern counterbalance at Pantin, and has revitalized the former Motobécane works.

Balzac, Maison de

47 Rue Raynouard, 16ᵉ ☎ *42-24-56-38. Map 12I1* 🔄 *✗ Open 10am-5.40pm. Closed Mon, public holidays. Métro: Passy, La Muette.*

This house is the only survivor of the several Paris homes lived in by the author of the great series of novels entitled *La Comédie Humaine*. It would no doubt appeal to Balzac's sense of irony to find it being used as a museum to his memory, for he considered it somewhat degrading. He fled there from his creditors in 1840, renting it in the name of his housekeeper to avoid their attentions, and remained there for 7yrs. It was here that he wrote some of his last novels, including *La Rabouilleuse, Une Ténébreuse Affaire* and *La Cousine Bette*.

Whatever reservations Balzac may have had about it, to the modern visitor his house appears an idyllic place still possessing the flavour of his era and the stamp of his personality. It is approached from a terrace lying below the level of Rue Raynouard. Passing through a gate that seems to lead nowhere, one suddenly descends some steps into the hidden garden of a charming, rustic-looking building with pale turquoise shutters. It appears to be a single-storey cottage but is, in fact, the top floor of a large house, which has another entrance on a lower street.

The house is full of fascinating mementoes of Balzac, including a series of bills from tradesmen. One of them is from a glovemaker, and the caption reveals that Balzac once bought 60 pairs of gloves in a month. Personal effects on display include his coffee pot — he often drank 30 cups a day to sustain his prodigious output. There is also a library of books by and about Balzac.

Bastille, Place de la

4ᵉ. Map 17J12. Métro: Bastille.

Built between 1370-82, the Bastille served for four centuries as a fortress and prison — mainly for powerful people who had fallen foul of the king. On July 14, 1789 it was stormed by a Revolutionary mob and afterwards demolished, an event still annually celebrated with gusto in France. Now all that remains of the Bastille is a line of cobblestones at the w side of the square, marking out the ground plan of the once formidable building with its projecting towers.

Today Pl. de la Bastille is a huge, bustling, chaotic crossroads, bounded on the s side by the **Arsenal Basin**, now a boating marina, and surrounded by rather garish cinemas, cafés and shops. It is dominated by the **July column**, a massive bronze edifice surmounted by an allegorical figure of *Liberty*, which commemorates the Parisians killed in the street-fighting of 1830 (the fall of Charles X) and 1848 (the fall of Louis-Philippe).

The completion in 1990 of the new opera house, the *Opéra Bastille*, to the SE, came as a welcome relief not only to lovers of opera but to the inhabitants and to visitors to the area, which had been blighted by the years of building work in progress.

Beaubourg

Familiar name for Paris' vibrant cultural centre. See *Pompidou Centre*.

Beaux-Arts, École nationale supérieure des *(School of Fine Arts)* ▥
17 Quai Malaquais, 6ᵉ ☎ 46-60-34-57. Map 9I8. Open Mon-Fri 9am-6pm (courtyards). Closed Sat, Sun, Aug, public holidays. Métro: St-Germain-des-Prés.

In his *Paris Sketch Book*, 150yrs ago, William Thackeray wrote of this building: "With its light and elegant fabric, its pretty fountain, its archway of the Renaissance, and fragments of sculpture, you can hardly see, on a fine day, a place more *riant* and pleasing." His words apply equally well today.

Temporary exhibitions are held here several times a year, but it is a pleasure simply to wander through the courtyards and mingle with the students.

Beaux-Arts de la Ville de Paris, Musée des   See *Petit Palais*.

Bercy   See *Entrepôts de Bercy*.

Bibliothèque Nationale *(National Library)* ▥
58 Rue de Richelieu, 2ᵉ ☎ 47-03-81-26. Map 9G8 ▨ Medallions and Antiques Gallery open 1-5pm. Mansart and Mazarine Galleries open noon-6pm. Photography Gallery (in the Rotonde Colbert, entered from 2 Rue Vivienne) open noon-6.30pm. Closed Sun, public holidays. Métro: Bourse, Palais-Royal.

As befits one of the world's greatest collections of books, manuscripts, prints, maps, medallions and other treasures, the Bibliothèque is housed in a splendid mansion, the main entrance of which is in Rue de Richelieu, reached via a fine courtyard. The building was created by Cardinal Mazarin in the 17thC out of two adjacent houses, the Hôtel Tubeuf and the Hôtel Chivry, and the resulting complex covers an entire block. After Mazarin's death, the mansion was split between different owners.

Part of it, which had come into the hands of the crown, became the repository of the royal library, later the National Library, which ultimately took over the whole of Mazarin's mansion. Since 1537, a copy of every French book published has, by law, been kept there.

Accredited scholars have access to the library's service departments, and members of the public can view the **medallion collection** on the first floor, the temporary exhibitions in the ground floor **Mansart Gallery** and the superb **Mazarin Gallery** at the top of the imposing stairway, and those in the **Rotonde Colbert** photographic gallery. Through a glass door, the magnificent Second Empire reading room, with its domed ceiling and cast-iron columns, gives the impression of a Byzantine cathedral.

With the expected furore created in 1989 by the selection of a young French architect, Dominique Perrault, the national library has announced its relocation to the ambitious development at Tolbiac (*map 17L13*), to the E. Work began in 1990 on a project that echoes yet again a trend towards building underground. The reading rooms will be lit from the side, via a 12,000sq.m garden punched through the piazza from above, and four L-shaped glass and steel towers stand one at each corner of the piazza, in the shape of open books.

Present opinions estimate completion by 1995, but time alone will tell. The future use of that beautiful but cramped building in the Rue de Richelieu has yet to be decided.

Bois de Boulogne
Map 18C3.

"I will not describe the Bois de Boulogne. It is simply a beautiful, cultivated, endless, wonderful wilderness." This was Mark Twain's reaction in *The Innocents Abroad* to the 900ha (2,224 acre) park on the western outskirts of Paris, which was once a royal hunting forest. Today, the Bois could no longer be described as a wilderness — there are too many roads. Furthermore, it is, in places, rather monotonous, and much of it is haunted by libidinous characters, especially at night.

However, there are many spots of great beauty, and you must be prepared to seek these out. The most delightful of all must surely be the **Bagatelle** (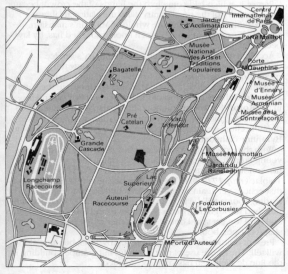 *open daily*) — a relatively small park within a park where in the 18thC the Count of Artois, the future King Charles X, built himself an enchanting little villa (constructed in less than 70 days on a bet with Marie-Antoinette) surrounded by a romantic and picturesque garden with artificial waterfalls, grottoes, Gothic ruins and other follies. Later, a second building, the Trianon, was added near the villa. Today the Bagatelle (the word means trifle) is a place of potent magic, with a renowned flower garden. There is also an elegant restaurant, **La Roseraie de la Bagatelle**, where you can sip afternoon tea languidly and dream.

Another appealing oasis in the Bois is the **Pré Catelan** () also a self-contained park. Its attractions include a majestic copper beech with a wider span of branches than any other tree in Paris. In addition, the Pré has a **Shakespeare Garden** () containing plants mentioned in the master's works.

If you have children with you, the spot to head for is the **Jardin d'Acclimatation** (), an amusement park on the N side of the Bois (*open daily*). Here you will find a zoo, a go-kart track, merry-go-rounds, a miniature golf course and a café, **La Ferme du Golf**, where youngsters can sit in a farmyard and eat an ice cream or pizza, while goats, sheep and ducks mill around their tables. Within the Jardin d'Acclimatation is the **Musée en Herbe** (☎ 40-67-97-66 ✉ ♿ ✿ *open Sun-Fri 10am-6pm, Sat 2-6pm*), which exists "to enable children to discover art while having fun." Lively temporary exhibitions are mounted, and there is a supervised studio in which children can paint or draw impressions of what they want seen. The *Musée des Arts et Traditions Populaires* is also nearby.

Other attractions in the Bois include lakes (the **Lac Inférieur** has boating facilities), two racecourses (**Auteuil** and **Longchamp**) and the **Municipal Floral Garden** of Paris.

Perhaps one of the best and most enjoyable methods of travelling about in the Bois is on two wheels. However, you may prefer, like the Englishman who broke the bank at Monte Carlo, to "walk along the Bois de Boulogne with an independent air."

Bourdelle, Musée Antoine
16 Rue Antoine-Bourdelle, 15ᵉ ☎ 45-48-67-27. Map 14K6 ✉ ⚇ on Sun ♿ ✗ Open 10am-5.40pm. Closed Mon, public holidays. Métro: Falguière, Montparnasse-Bienvenue.
This charming oasis in *Montparnasse* was for 45yrs the home and studio of Antoine Bourdelle (1861-1929), a sculptor of genius who, along with his friend Rodin, helped to give sculpture a new lease of life. Where Rodin's work has the fluidity of emotion, Bourdelle's is characterized by the thrusting, harnessed power of the will, seen in such creations as his *Héracles Archer* and *Tête d'Apollon*. These and other works are displayed in a series of light, spacious rooms and leafy courtyards. Part of the museum is used for temporary exhibitions by other sculptors.

Bourse des Valeurs (Stock Exchange) 🏛
4 Pl. de la Bourse, 2ᵉ ☎ 42-33-99-83. Map 9F8 ✉ ✉ Open Mon-Fri 11am-1pm. Métro: Bourse.
Outwardly a serene, 19thC Classical building surrounded by Corinthian columns, inwardly a scene of apparent bedlam with brokers in the main dealing room gesticulating wildly and yelling "*J'ai!*" or "*Je prends!*". To enable visitors to make sense of this puzzling spectacle, which they can witness from a gallery, they are first given a series of film shows and lectures on the workings of the Bourse and the stock market. It's all very slick and well organized — just what you would expect, in fact, from one of the bastions of French capitalism. Take some ID.

Bourse du Commerce (Commercial Exchange)
2 Rue de Viarmes, 1ᵉʳ. Map 10H9. Métro: Châtelet-Les-Halles, Les Halles.
Victor Hugo compared this drum-shaped building to a jockey's cap without the peak. Built in the 18thC and modified in the 19th, it once served as a corn exchange. Now the majestic domed hall is the scene of a busy commodity market for such products as sugar, coffee, cocoa and grain.

The building's site has had a varied history. Louis XII had a mansion there which he lost at a game of cribbage with his chamberlain, who proceeded to convert it into a convent for repentant girls — postulants had to prove that they had lived a life of prostitution. In 1572 Catherine de Medici dislodged the girls to make way for a magnificent palace constructed by Delorme and Bullant. All that remains today, at this western boundary of *Les Halles*, is the curious column on the s side of the present building, said to have been used as an observatory by the queen's astrologer, Ruggieri.

Bricard, Musée
This lock and metalwork museum is now closed. There are no known plans to re-open it elsewhere.

Buttes Chaumont, Parc des
Rue Manin, 19ᵉ. Map 19C5 ⟨⟨ ■ ✱ *Open daily. Métro: Buttes-Chaumont.*

This park is totally unlike any other in Paris and has a strongly romantic appeal. Brilliantly landscaped by Haussmann on a disused quarry site, it has steeply undulating wooded contours and a lake with a rocky island rising dramatically from the centre, spanned by two high bridges. On the island one path leads up a flight of steps through a grotto-like tunnel to the summit, which is crowned by a small Classical temple with an open colonnade. From here there is a superb view over the city to the N, E and W, with *Montmartre* and the *Sacré-Coeur* standing out against the horizon.

This is one of the few Parisian parks where one can actually sit on the grass. There are rides in a donkey cart for children, a boating lake, and, on the W side, an inviting restaurant, the **Pavillon du Lac** (☎ *42-02-08-97, open lunch and tea*) with tables overlooking the lake.

Camondo, Musée Nissim de ▥
63 Rue de Monceau, 8ᵉ ☎ *45-63-26-32. Map 7E5* ▨ ✗ *Open 10am-noon, 2-5pm. Closed Mon, Tues. Métro: Villiers, Monceau.*

Like the nearby *Cernuschi* museum, this is a private house and contents bequeathed to the nation. Its creator, Count Moïse de Camondo, was a rich collector with a passion for 18thC decorative art. In 1910 he built a house in the style of the Petit Trianon at Versailles, where he set out to re-create the atmosphere of an 18thC interior. Thanks to his discrimination and finely tuned visual sense, the effect is one of harmony combined with the highest quality. The furniture is by such master cabinet-makers as Jacob, Riesener and Saunier, and the tapestries come from the great workshops of *Gobelins*, Beauvais and Aubusson — one particularly fine set depicts the famous fables of LaFontaine.

The museum is sumptuous, although it is hard to imagine such objects ever being approached other than on tiptoe.

A school of bookbinding (*Centre des Arts du Livre* ☎ *45-63-37-39*) has recently been set up within the building. All aspects of binding, gilding and decoration are covered here, and anyone connected with books — librarians, typographers, illustrators or printers — are welcome. Plans are afoot to stage exhibitions open to the general public.

Canal St-Martin
19ᵉ and 10ᵉ. Maps 5&11. Métro: Jaurès, J. Bonsergent, Goncourt.

Built in the early 19thC, the Canal St-Martin links the Seine with the Canal de l'Ourcq and runs through a tunnel for about half its length. It is a working canal, plied by many barges and lined by warehouses and depots, but it has its picturesque moments, when it shakes off the dust and stops work for a pause. Particularly romantic is the stretch between Sq. Frédéric Lemaître and Rue Bichat, with its tree-lined banks and hump-backed bridges. Here the atmosphere is not unlike Amsterdam. Recently the canal has undergone some improvements, such as the construction of a new boating marina in the Bassin Arsénal, s of

Pl. de la Bastille. You can take a boat trip up the canal with
Quiztour (*19 Rue d'Athènes, 9ᵉ* ☎ *45-26-16-59*). Other canal
trips are listed on pages 18-19.

Carnavalet, Hôtel et Musée ⅢⅢ
23 Rue de Sévigné, 3ᵉ ☎ *42-72-21-13. Map* **11/11** 🔲 🔲 *on
Sun* ⚅ ✗ *Open 10am-5.40pm. Closed Mon. Métro: St-Paul,
Chemin-Vert, Bastille, Hôtel-de-Ville.*

If you visited no other building in Paris but this one, you would
still come away with a good understanding of the spirit of the
city. Every phase of Parisian history, from the early Renaissance
onwards, is illustrated, in painting, sculpture, models, furniture
and decoration — all on view in a series of splendid rooms. One
of the most pleasing displays is of old tradesmen's signs,
including the entire front of a druggist's shop. Another section
deals with the Revolution, and here you will find models of the
guillotines, portraits of Revolutionary leaders, placards, and
pictures of the royal family in captivity. A programme of
temporary exhibitions provides added interest. Some of the
museum's exhibits are on show at *Maison Renan-Scheffer*,
alongside memorabilia of George Sand.

The building itself, situated at the heart of the *Marais*, tells its
own part of the story. Built in the 1540s and later modified by
Mansart, it possesses a gracious entrance courtyard with
allegorical reliefs of the four seasons and a contemporary statue
of Louis XIV by Coysevox, anachronistically dressed as a Roman
general wearing a wig. From 1677-96 the house was occupied by
Mme de Sévigné, who immortalized herself by a series of lively
and witty letters, and who played hostess to distinguished writers
and thinkers of her time. Her apartments are preserved as part of
the museum, and she still casts her benign spell over the building.

Catacombes *(Catacombs)*
1 Pl. Denfert-Rochereau, 14ᵉ ☎ *43-22-47-63. Map* **14M7** 🔲
*Open Tues-Fri 2-4pm, Sat, Sun 9-11am, 2-4pm. Closed
Mon, public holidays. Métro: Denfert-Rochereau.*

Here is a creepy experience: a walk of three-quarters of an hour
through a subterranean necropolis. These are not ancient
catacombs like the ones in Rome, but former stone quarries that
were filled with the bones cleared from many Parisian cemeteries
during the 18th and 19thC. They have been open to the public
since 1874. The tunnels leading to the ossuary pass a
representation of a fort, carved out of the rock by an 18thC
tunnel worker in his leisure time. Then a chamber with black and
white painted pillars leads off to a doorway over which are the
words: "*Arrête! C'est ici l'empire de la mort.*" ("Stop! This is the
empire of death".) Beyond it stretches tunnel after tunnel, lined
on each side with neatly-piled bones interspersed with rows of
grinning skulls and enlivened by plaques bearing inscriptions of
death. There are 5-6 million skeletons here. The whole place is a
memento mori of the most dramatic kind.

The visitor sees only a small part of the 300km (187 miles) of
tunnels created by stone-quarrying.

Cernuschi, Musée
7 Av. Velazquez, 8ᵉ ☎ *45-63-50-75 Map* **2D5** 🔲 🔲 *on Sun
⚅ Open 10am-5.40pm. Closed Mon, public holidays.
Métro: Villiers, Monceau.*

Paris possesses this interesting museum of Chinese art, situated in
a fine house just near the E gate of the *Monceau* park, thanks to

a colourful Milanese financier named Cernuschi. A disciple of Garibaldi, Cernuschi was once condemned to death for his Revolutionary activities, but was reprieved by Napoleon III and later became a French citizen. Before his death in 1896 he bequeathed his house and magnificent collection of Chinese objects to the city of Paris. Not as large or as impressive as the collection in the *Guimet* museum, this exhibition still gives a very informative picture of the development of Chinese art from prehistoric times. It includes a selection of paintings by modern Chinese artists, but perhaps the most evocative picture is a 13thC ink-and-brush drawing of a bird on a twig, which combines humour and simplicity with sophistication.

Champ-de-Mars

7ᵉ. Map 12l3. Métro: Trocadéro, École-Militaire.
The Champ-de-Mars is the back garden of the *Eiffel Tower*. It was originally laid out in the 1760s as a parade ground for the *École Militaire*, hence its name, after Mars, the god of war. These days it is anything but martial — just a typically tranquil Parisian park with a symmetrical pattern of tree-lined avenues and numerous pleasant and secluded little corners in which to sit and read or contemplate the wonders of Eiffel's engineering. A fine new series of statues was erected here in 1989. Sculptor Yvan Theimer, commissioned for the bicentenary of the French Revolution, has created a composition depicting bronze figures of man, woman and child, in his *Monument to the Rights of Man.*

Champs-Élysées, Avenue des ★

8ᵉ. Maps 6&7. Métro: Charles-de-Gaulle-Étoile, George-V, Franklin-D-Roosevelt, Champs-Élysées-Clemenceau, Concorde.
If there is one Parisian street that is known throughout the world it is this one. It forms a great triumphal tree-lined sweep from *Pl. de la Concorde* to the *Arc de Triomphe*. At its lower end, as far as the crossroads known as the **Rond-Point**, it is bounded by strips of park. Then, along the stretch that climbs in a shallow ramp towards the Arc de Triomphe, it is lined by imposing buildings: offices, smart shops, cinemas, airline offices, restaurants and pavement cafés. The tone of this part of the avenue has been deteriorating in the past 10yrs and this problem is now being taken in hand. Mayor Chirac's 5yr refurbishment plan, with clampdowns on parking, street signs etc., was begun in 1990.

The lower part of the avenue was laid out by Louis XIV's gardener, Le Nôtre, in 1670, and the upper part some 40yrs later. However, the road remained a muddy and insalubrious thoroughfare until it acquired an element of fashion and style in the 18thC with the building of the grand houses in *Rue du Faubourg-St-Honoré*. From very early in its history it was frequented by ladies of pleasure. In 1778, for example, a Swiss guard apprehended a priest there, in the company of a young black woman to whom he claimed to be giving religious instruction. Half a century later, Balzac wrote of the "dark-eyed houris" who frequented the avenue. Their successors are still operating here today.

The street is an obvious route for processions. It was down the Champs-Élysées that the victorious German troops marched in 1940, and 4yrs later, the same street witnessed the triumphant return of de Gaulle. Walk down it and you will feel a swell of exultation, but curiously, despite its many cafés, it is not the most inviting place to linger. The ghosts of all those marchers seem to hurry you on.

Charles-de-Gaulle, Place *(Place de l'Étoile)*
8ᵉ. Map 6F3. Métro: Charles-de-Gaulle-Étoile.
The great crossroads encircling the **Arc de Triomphe** was given its present name after de Gaulle's death in 1970, but most Parisians still call it by its apt former name, the Pl. de l'Étoile (star). The Arc de Triomphe was built between 1806-36, but it was not until 1854 that Haussmann was commissioned by Napoleon III to create the grand townscape that we see there today.

Twelve great avenues radiate from l'Étoile. They include **Av. des Champs-Élysées**, which plunges down to **Pl. de la Concorde**, gracious, park-lined **Av. Foch** with its luxurious buildings stretching towards the **Bois de Boulogne**, and **Av. de la Grande Armée**, which points to Neuilly and **La Défense**.

Pl. Charles-de-Gaulle is one of the most photographed parts of Paris — especially from the air, where its layout looks particularly dramatic.

Chasse et de la Nature, Musée de la *(Museum of Hunting and Nature)* ▥
Hôtel Guénégaud, 60 Rue des Archives, 3ᵉ ☎ 42-72-86-43. Map 11H11 ▨ ✕ ✱ Open 10am-12.30pm, 1.30-5.30pm. Closed Tues. Métro: Rambuteau, Arts-et-Métiers, Hôtel-de-Ville.
Everything you ever needed to know about hunting is assembled in an attractive old **Marais** mansion: hunting weapons of all kinds, stuffed animals, paintings of famous hunters and huntresses such as *Diana* by Breughel and Rubens, and *St-Eustache* by Cranach.

The building, the **Hôtel Guénégaud**, with its well-mannered courtyard and dignified design, was built by François Mansart between 1648-51 and was in a dilapidated condition when François Sommer took it over in the early 1960s: his own big-game trophies are among those on display. Now the building stands beautifully restored, to delight architectural as well as hunting enthusiasts.

Cinéma Henri-Langlois, Musée du ▥
Palais de Chaillot, Pl. du Trocadéro, 16ᵉ ☎ 45-53-21-86. Map 12H2 ▨ ✿ ▣ ✱ ✕ at 10am, 11am, 2pm, 3pm, 4pm. Closed Tues, public holidays. Métro: Trocadéro.
The modest entrance to this museum (allied to the **Cinémathèque Française)** at the bottom of a flight of steps in the **Palais de Chaillot** does not prepare the visitor for the riches within. The museum staff take visitors first through the early technology of cinematography, dating back to 1895, then through a series of galleries full of the trappings that have enabled film-makers to create a world of make-believe. There are sets from famous films such as *The Cabinet of Doctor Caligari*, costumes such as the tunic worn by Rudolph Valentino in *The Sheik*, Garbo's robes, papier-mâché monsters, a robot from Fritz Lang's *Metropolis...* and much more. The conducted visit takes about an hour and a quarter.

Cinémathèque Française
Palais de Chaillot, Jardin du Trocadéro, Av. Albert-de-Mun, 16ᵉ ☎ 47-04-24-24. Map 12H2 ▨ Métro: Trocadéro.

Cité des Sciences et de l'Industrie

The film library in the *Palais de Chaillot* is a national institution for the screening of distinguished films from all periods of cinema history. See also *Nightlife and the performing arts*.

Cité des Sciences et de l'Industrie *(City of Science and Industry)*   See *La Villette, Parc de.*

Cité Universitaire
Bd. Jourdan, 14ᵉ. Map 19D4. Métro: Cité-Universitaire.
This sprawling student community on the s perimeter of Paris, with its pavilions for different nations, is an excellent place to study contrasting styles of architecture. Each building reflects some aspect of its country's architecture: the Greek pavilion is a Hellenic temple, and the Indo-Chinese building resembles a pagoda. Admirers of Le Corbusier will be interested in the Swiss and Brazilian halls which he designed. Inaugurated in 1925.

Clemenceau, Musée
8 Rue Franklin, 16ᵉ ☎ 45-20-53-41. Map 12H2 🖼 𝒳 Open Tues, Thurs, Sat, Sun 2-5pm. Métro: Passy, Trocadéro.
The apartment where the statesman Georges Clemenceau lived from 1895 until his death in 1929 is preserved exactly as he left it, down to the quill pen with which he wrote. The environment has the stamp of an exceptionally powerful and many-faceted personality.

Cluny, Musée de 🏛
6 Pl. Paul-Painlevé, 5ᵉ ☎ 43-25-62-00. Map 10J9 🖼 Open 9.45am-12.30pm, 2-5.15pm. Closed Tues, public holidays. Métro: Cluny-la-Sorbonne, Odéon.
This outstanding museum (full name: **Musée National des Thermes et de l'Hôtel de Cluny**) in the *Latin Quarter* is a remarkable archaeological site housing a great collection of ancient and medieval objects. It comprises two buildings: the remains of the Gallo-Roman baths, the **Thermes de Lutèce** (c.AD200); and the medieval **Hôtel de Cluny**, constructed in the 14th and 15thC for the rich abbots of Cluny as their Parisian residence.

The museum owns one of the finest collections of medieval tapestry work in existence. Its most famous exhibit is the set of six late 15thC tapestries known as the *Lady with the Unicorn* (★), woven in lively detail, in lovely muted colours. Five of the tapestries symbolically illustrate the five senses, and the sixth is thought to illustrate mastery of them.

The museum contains many other treasures, including everyday objects from the Middle Ages. On the first floor is a small chapel containing some impressive Gothic tracery. Passing into the Roman building, where a number of Roman artifacts are on show, one is overwhelmed by the vast room of the thermal baths, with its great vaulted roof.

Another gallery contains a sizeable array of early medieval ecclesiastical and votive items such as reliquary boxes, patens, chalices and candle holders, some of them in Limoges enamelwork. One light-filled room contains sculpture from the cathedral of *Notre-Dame de Paris*.

Cognacq-Jay, Musée
8 Rue Elzévir, 3ᵉ ☎ 42-61-94-54. Map 8F7 🖼 🔳 on Sun 𝒳 Open 10am-5.40pm. Closed Mon. Métro: St-Paul.
Ernest Cognacq, creator of the Samaritaine chain of shops, and

his wife, Louise Jay, opened to the public their collection of 18thC art in the 1920s. Paradoxically, Cognacq was no art-lover — he boasted that he had never entered the Louvre — and he became a collector purely for status reasons. However, with expert advice he succeeded in acquiring many works of the highest rank, such as Boucher's *Le Retour de Chasse de Diane*, Tiepolo's *Le Festin de Cléopatre* and Reynolds' portrait of Lord Northington. Watteau, Fragonard, Rembrandt and Gainsborough are among other artists represented. There is also a remarkable collection of porcelain ornaments, gold and silver boxes and other small *objets d'art*. Formerly in the **Opéra** quarter, the museum relocated to the **Hôtel Dinon** in 1990.

Collège de France
Rue des Écoles, 5ᵉ. Map 15J9. Métro: Maubert-Mutualité.
This great institute of learning in the **Latin Quarter** was founded in 1529 by François I at the instigation of the scholar Guillaume Budé, whose statue now stands in the w courtyard. The college was founded to counteract the hidebound dogmatism of the neighbouring **Sorbonne** and was for a time known as the "Three-Language College" because Hebrew, Greek and Latin were taught there. Subsequently, its syllabus expanded to include many other academic disciplines from Arabic to physics, and today it maintains a high reputation, as well as a liberal admissions policy.

Smaller and less bombastic in architecture than the Sorbonne, it has something of the intimate atmosphere of a small Oxford or Cambridge college.

La Comédie Française Ⅲ
2 Rue de Richelieu, 1ᵉʳ ☎ 42-96-10-24. Map 9H8 ▨ ✗ on 1st Sun of month 10am (call Mon-Fri to reserve ahead). Métro: Palais-Royal.
After it was founded in 1680 by Louis XIV, this famous company of actors moved house several times and finally settled on the present site at the end of the 18thC. The theatre, which has evolved over the years into the grand colonnaded building that we see today, is set in a prime position next to the **Palais-Royal**.

Despite its name, the company does not necessarily perform comedies. Traditionally the repertoire has emphasized classical French dramatists such as Molière, Corneille and Racine, but lately it has been widened to include modern and foreign playwrights.

La Conciergerie
1 Quai de l'Horloge, Île de la Cité, 4ᵉ ☎ 43-54-30-06. Map 10I9 ▨ ✗ Open June-Aug 9.30am-6.30pm, Sept, Apr, May 9.30am-6pm, Oct-Mar 10am-4.30pm. Closed most public holidays. Métro: Cité, Châtelet, St-Michel.
The Conciergerie has a gloomy atmosphere that matches its gloomy history as a place of imprisonment, death and torture. Part of the great palace built on the N side of the **Île de la Cité** by King Philippe le Bel (1284-1314), it is now incorporated into the **Palais de Justice** complex. The name is derived from the title of the royal officer called the Concierge ("*Comte des Cierges*" or Count of the Candles). He was superintendent of the palace and was empowered to administer justice in its environs. Increasingly the Conciergerie took on the functions of a prison, especially after the building became for a time the seat of parliament, which was also the country's supreme court.

Concorde, Place de la

It was here that such malefactors as Ravaillac, assassin of Henry IV, and Damiens, who attempted to kill Louis XV, were brought and hideously tortured before being executed. However, it was during the Revolution that the Conciergerie received its real baptism of blood. Its most famous prisoner was Marie-Antoinette, who was kept here before being taken to the guillotine. Her cell is now a chapel to her memory, but her name is only one of a list of many who passed through on their way to execution. The Revolutionary leader Danton condemned 22 Girondins, de Robespierre condemned Danton, the Thermidor Convention condemned de Robespierre... In all, nearly 2,600 prisoners were sent for execution from the Conciergerie between the winter of 1793 and summer of 1794. You can still see the grim little room where they were shaved and relieved of their possessions before being taken to the tumbrils. In 1792, 288 prisoners were murdered in the prison itself.

Despite the unpleasant vibrations created by this history, the building does, in fact, possess some beautiful features: the **Salle des Gardes**, the first room you enter, with its elegant vaulting and carved bosses; the magnificent **Salle des Gens d'Armes**, 69m (226ft) long and 27m (88ft) wide, with three rows of eight pillars, which is sometimes used as a setting for concerts; and the **kitchen**, with its four fireplaces, each big enough to roast an entire ox, which, in the 14thC, provided food for 5,000 people. The chapel, which housed the 22 condemned Girondin deputies, now contains a depressing but intriguing little collection of mementoes, including a guillotine blade, Marie-Antoinette's crucifix and two portraits of her from life.

Concorde, Place de la ★
8ᵉ. Map 8G6. Métro: Concorde.

The largest square in Paris is also arguably the most striking and beautiful townscape in the world, but to appreciate the square fully you must brave the whirling blizzard of traffic and cross the road to the centre. It is advisable to use the two official crossings.

This vantage point provides stately vistas in all directions: w up *Av. des Champs-Élysées* to the *Arc de Triomphe*, with the **Grande Arche** at *La Défense* just visible through it; E through the *Tuileries* to the *Louvre*, with the *Jeu de Paume* museum and the *Orangerie* on either side; S across the **Pont de la Concorde** to the *Palais-Bourbon* and N up **Rue Royale** to the *Madeleine* between the matching colonnaded facades of the **Hôtel de Crillon** (see *Hotels*) on the left and the **Hôtel de la Marine** on the right.

There once stood in the middle an equestrian statue of Louis XV, in whose reign the square was laid out. This was removed during the Revolution and replaced briefly by an allegorical statue of Liberty. Now the site is occupied by the 3,300yr-old **obelisk of Luxor**, given to King Louis-Philippe by Mohammed Ali, Viceroy of Egypt, and erected in 1836. A few metres from this spot stood the guillotine which, during the Revolution, claimed over a thousand victims including Louis XVI and Marie-Antoinette. Two **fountains** resplendent with water nymphs and sea-gods stand to the N and S of the obelisk.

Marking the octagonal perimeter of the original square are eight **statues** allegorically representing the towns of Lyon, Marseille, Bordeaux, Nantes, Lille, Strasbourg, Rouen and Brest. The curious pavilions on which they rest were once let out as tiny dwelling houses with just two rooms, one above the other. Other statues of note are the **Marly horses**, sculpted by Guillaume

Coustou in the 1740s, which flank the E end of Av. des Champs-Élysées, and the **statues** of Fame and Mercury on winged horses by Coysevox, which stand on either side of the entrance to the Tuileries.

Pl. de la Concorde is the magnificent pulsating heart of Paris, as breathtaking by day as it is by night, when floodlights transform its buildings, obelisks, fountains and statues into a stunning *tableau vivant.*

Conservatoire National de Musique   See *La Villette, Parc de.*

Corbusier, Fondation Le
Villa La Roche, 10 Sq. du Docteur-Blanche, 16ᵉ ☎ 42-88-41-53. Map 18D3 and see map on p54 ☜ Open 9am-12.30pm, 1-6pm. Closed Sat, Sun, Aug, public holidays. Métro: Jasmin, Ranelagh, Porte d'Auteuil.

The name Le Corbusier is synonymous with modern French architecture. This foundation, the purpose of which is to present Le Corbusier's work to the public, occupies two villas designed by the master himself in the 1920s. It encompasses a library, a photographic archive and a collection of paintings and sculptures by the architect. Temporary exhibitions are also held on various aspects of his work.

Crypte Archéologique   See *Notre-Dame.*

Cousteau, Parc Océanique Jacques
Forum des Halles, 1ᵉʳ ☎ 40-28-98-98. Map 10H9 ☜ & ✷ Open noon-7pm. Closed Mon. Métro: Châtelet, Les Halles, Louvre-Rivoli.

The sea has come to the heart of Paris. If the idea of a stroll through the belly of a blue whale appeals to you, then so will all the other revelations of the mysteries of the deep, explored with dedication and enthusiasm by Jacques-Yves and Jean-Michel Cousteau and assembled into an experience that covers every aspect of life under the sea. Visitors can explore shipwrecks, come face-to-face with a giant squid, and steer well clear of the sharks, as well as learning about modern diving and filming techniques. The centre also aims to improve general understanding of conservation issues.

La Défense
Map 18C3. RER: La Défense.

This vast commercial and residential complex, lying beyond the river to the W of Paris, has been nicknamed "Manhattan-sur-Seine". Certainly it has the brutality but arguably less style than "Manhattan-sur-Hudson". Begun in the 1960s, it dominates the western horizon of the city with its growing cluster of skyscrapers.

The main zone of La Défense focuses on a 1.2km-long podium running approximately W-E and descending towards the Seine in a series of terraces laid out with trees. On the S side, the prospect is hardly enhanced by *Les Deux Personnages*, an ugly Joan Miró sculpture painted in primary colours. Opposite stands Calder's giant red mobile.

The forest of glass, steel and concrete surrounding the podium includes such buildings as the spectacular **CNIT**, a vast three-cornered hall that forms a flamboyant showcase for new technologies and includes the **World Trade Center**, and **Les Quatre Temps**, the largest shopping centre in Europe with a floor space twice the area of all the shops in ***Av. des Champs-Élysées***. Soaring skyscrapers rise on every side, many of them the headquarters of French multinational companies.

From the western end of the podium there is a view of the outlying town of **Nanterre** and its bizarre apartment buildings painted in splotches of grey, blue, brown and green as though they had been camouflaged.

La Défense is a symbol of the aggressive prosperity that has overtaken France in the past 25yrs. Despite its multitude of amenities, many find it a place that dwarfs and crushes the spirit, although others are inspired by its vast scale and commercial drama. Crucially, in Paris, modern man's desire to build such structures has been concentrated into one area well away from the centre.

La Grande Arche de la Défense 🏛

Take the Grande Arche exit from RER ☎ 49-07-26-26 ⪤ ⇕ to roof ▭ Open Mon-Sat 9am-6pm, Sun, hols 9am-8pm. Last admission 1hr earlier.

The newest great arch in a city of arches, the awesome, monolithic Grande Arche, designed by Danish architect J.O. von Spreckelsen, focuses all eyes on the western end of La Défense.

From the cavernous space beneath it — as wide as Av. des Champs-Élysées — can be seen the dramatic W-E alignment of La Défense with the Arc de Triomphe and along Av. des Champs-Élysées to the Louvre. Above soars the vast marble-covered cube of the arch, 90m high and lined with office windows: a space large enough to shelter Notre-Dame.

Panoramic lifts rise and fall, carrying visitors into the roof. From here, another startling alignment is revealed: that of the arch, the Eiffel Tower and the Tour Montparnasse. The immense roof also houses an exhibition gallery, a bookshop and a conference centre.

Delacroix, Musée National Eugène

*6 Rue de Furstemberg, 6e ☎ 43-54-04-87. Map **9I8** ▭ ✗ Open 9.45am-12.30pm, 2-5.15pm. Closed Tues. Métro: St-Germain-des-Prés.*

Eugène Delacroix (1798-1863) was one of the great romantic painters of the 19thC, a Wagner among artists. His vivid canvases of battle scenes, lion hunts and other stirring subjects have a controlled fire to them, like Delacroix himself, whom Baudelaire described as "a volcanic crater artistically concealed beneath bouquets of flowers."

In his last years, Delacroix lived a life of almost monastic seclusion, in a charming Left Bank apartment with a studio overlooking a little garden. This apartment is now preserved as a museum, and is full of photographs, letters, portraits and other mementoes of the artist.

Dôme church

See *Les Invalides*.

École Militaire

*Pl. Joffre, 7e. Map **13J4**. Not open to public except by special arrangement. Write to: La Direction Générale, École Militaire, 1 Pl. Joffre, 75007. Métro: École-Militaire.*

Where its neighbour, ***Les Invalides***, is an officer in ceremonial dress, the École Militaire is a sergeant major bawling out across the ***Champ-de-Mars*** to the ***Eiffel Tower***. The long Classical facade has a great central-domed portico, and the vast courtyard facing Pl. de Fontenoy is imposing. It still serves as a military academy, for which purpose it was built by Gabriel in the reign of Louis XV. Napoleon was sent there at age 15 in 1784 — when he passed out he was told he would go far, given the right circumstances!

Égouts *(Sewers)*
*Entrance at corner of Quai d'Orsay and Pl. de la Résistance, 7ᵉ ☎ 47-05-10-29. Map **13**H4 ☒ ៤ Open Wed-Sun 3-8pm. Closed Mon, Tues. Métro: Alma-Marceau.*

"Below Paris," wrote Victor Hugo in *Les Misérables*, "is another city." He was referring to the sewer network, the existence of which is vital to the gracious city above. Laid end-to-end, its tunnels would stretch as far as Istanbul, and a small section of this labyrinth has been equipped for public viewing. Visitors are shown an exhibition of documents on the history of the sewers, followed by an audiovisual display about the workings of the system. A guided tour takes visitors through dripping tunnels, past waste-collection pits and along the edge of a murky grey river. Instructive but smelly. Once you know the odour of the sewers, you will occasionally catch whiffs of it from gratings as you walk through the city.

Ennery, Musée National d'
*59 Av. Foch, 16ᵉ ☎ 45-53-57-97. Map **6**F1 and see map on page 54 ☒ ✗ Open Thurs and Sun only 2-5pm. Closed Aug. Métro: Dauphine.*

Ming vases, *netsuke*, images of Buddha, porcelain dogs, Chinese furniture — these and other Oriental objects collected by the 19thC dramatist Adolphe d'Ennery and his wife are displayed in part of their opulent house. He bought indiscriminately, and perhaps one in ten of the objects have any real value. However, the museum has a curious, musty charm. The house is shared with the *Arménien* museum.

Entrepôts de Bercy *(Cité du Vin et de l'Alimentation)*
*Quai de Bercy, 12ᵉ. Map **17**M13. Métro: Bercy (other new stations being built).*

This run-down docklands quarter has been receiving total renovation treatment since 1989. By 1993, the transformation into a centre of wines and gastronomy will be complete, but some parts will be open to the public well before that date. The new Parc de Bercy will extend from the **Palais Omnisports**, covering what was once an area of old wine warehouses. The **Pavillons de Bercy**, warehouses that are now listed buildings, will accommodate major exhibitions, a conference centre and a **museum of wines and gastronomy**. The area will incorporate two hotels, a new **American Center** (due to open in 1992, in time to celebrate the 500th anniversary of Christopher Columbus' voyage of discovery), a number of brasseries, restaurants and wine-bars, and a park with lakes and mini-vineyards.

First of the new developments in Bercy/Tolbiac was the Ministry of Finance, which relocated in 1989 from its offices in a wing of the *Louvre* to a bold and often-criticized new building that straddles the road. The new *Bibliothèque Nationale*, due for completion in 1995, will also be located at this point on the Right Bank.

A new bridge across the Seine is to be constructed, as well as two new Métro stations.

l'Étoile, Place de See *Charles-de-Gaulle, Place.*

Faubourg-St-Honoré, Rue du

*8ᵉ. Maps 7&8. Métro: Ternes, St-Philippe-du-Roule,
Madeleine.*

The Parisian equivalent of Fifth Avenue or Knightsbridge, or the
Via Tornabuoni, this glossy shopping thoroughfare runs parallel
to *Av. des Champs-Élysées*. It is full of gracious houses once
occupied by the aristocracy, when the district took over from the
Marais as the fashionable place to live.

Today few people, apart from the president (see *Palais de
l'Élysée*), actually live here, and the old mansions have found
new uses. No. **35** houses the **British Embassy** and no. **96** the
Ministry of the Interior. Another mansion, at no. **112**,
disappeared in the 1920s to make way for the discreetly opulent
Hôtel Bristol (see *Hotels*). For the rest, the street is mostly
occupied by smart shops with such famous names as Heim,
Hermès, Lanvin, Yves-St-Laurent, Courrèges and Helena
Rubinstein. Beside the window of the Hermès shop is a jet
spurting clouds of perfume at the passers- by, filling the air with
the aroma of high living.

Flea Market   See *Marché aux Puces*.

Forum des Halles

1ᵉʳ. Map 10H9. Métro: Châtelet-Les-Halles, Les Halles.

Opened in 1979 as part of *Les Halles* redevelopment, this
complex is a commercial counterpart of the *Pompidou Centre*.
But, where the latter boldly thrusts up, the Forum plummets
down. Built on four descending levels, it has concave glass-and-
aluminium-walls that descend to a sunken courtyard, frequently
used by open-air performers, where there is a curiously stirring
sculpture by Julio Silva entitled *Pygmalion*, consisting of a group
of dream-like mythological figures.

With rare commercial insight, the centre combines architectural
excitement, and artistic and historical points of interest, with
diverse shopping. The overall design has a spare, crisp elegance
and avoids the harsh, plastic colours that mar so many modern
shopping precincts. There are some 200 shops (including fashion
boutiques, jewellers, booksellers and furniture shops), ten
cinemas and 12 restaurants, one with a terrace overlooking the
courtyard.

The Forum des Halles also houses a branch of the *Grévin*
waxworks museum (☎ *42-26-28-50, open Mon-Sat 10.30am-
6.45pm, Sun, bols 1-7.15pm* 🎬 ⓖ ✱), which contains an
imaginary reconstruction of a Parisian street of 1885, and the
Musée de l'Holographie (☎ *42-96-96-83, open Mon-Sat 10am-
7pm, Sun, bols 1-7pm* 🎬 𝒦).

From the lowest level there is access to the Métro and RER, and
there are two large underground car parks. At the N side of the
Forum is the **Pavillon des Arts** (☎ *42-33-82-50, open Tues-Sun
11.30am-6.30pm, closed Mon, bols*), a striking steel-and-glass
building in which temporary exhibitions are held.

At the western end of the Forum, an exciting new below-
ground complex was created beneath the new park and
children's playground in front of the *Bourse du Commerce*.
Here is located the **Vidéothèque de Paris** (*2 Grande Galerie,
Porte St-Eustache, 1ᵉʳ* ☎ *40-26-34-30, open Sun, Tues-Fri 12.30-
9pm, Sat 10am-9pm, closed Mon*), an archive of film material of
all eras relating to Paris. The Vidéothèque has three projection
rooms where films from a collection of 2,500 titles are shown,
with a different theme each week. There are facilities for

individual viewing. Here too is the *Parc Océanique Jacques Cousteau*.

Adult Parisians avoid the Forum at weekends, when the RER disgorges swarms of young people from the suburbs.

Gobelins, Manufacture Nationale des *(Tapestry Factories)*
*42 Av. des Gobelins, 13ᵉ ☎ 43-37-12-60. Map **16**M10 ▨ Open Tues, Wed, Thurs 2-4.30pm ✗ compulsory, lasting 75mins. Métro: Gobelins.*

If you have ever struggled with a home tapestry kit and found that it tried your patience, you should visit the Gobelins factory to find out what patience really means. Here, skilled weavers, carefully chosen and trained from the age of 16, work their way millimetre by millimetre across huge upright looms at the rate of as little as one square metre a year. Thus it can take 3-4yrs to complete a single tapestry with two or three people working on it full time.

The techniques used are essentially the same as when the Gobelins was founded as a royal factory under Louis XIV, but the tapestries are now worked in a far wider range of colours (14,920 altogether), and the subjects are no longer scenes of royal occasions and the like, but copies of modern paintings or designs.

The Gobelins is a state enterprise, and its products are never sold. They are either made use of by the government or given as gifts. The atmosphere of the factory complex in the SE of Paris is rather like an old university college, with a cobbled quadrangle, garden, and apartments for the employees.

A guided tour of the factory is given, which incorporates the two other state workshops of **Savonnerie** (carpets) and **Beauvais** (tapestries made on a horizontal loom). In an era of mass-production, here is craftsmanship of the highest standard.

Grand Orient de France, Musée du *(Freemasonry Museum)*
*16 Rue Cadet, 9ᵉ ☎ 45-23-20-92. Map **4**E9 ▱ ▨ ✗ Open 2-6pm. Closed Sun, public holidays. Métro: Cadet, Rue Montmartre.*

What did Lafayette, Garibaldi and Franklin D. Roosevelt have in common? Answer: they were all Freemasons, as you will discover from this intriguing museum of Masonic documents, mementos and regalia, related to European Freemasonry. L'Hôtel Cadet is the headquarters of Freemasonry in France.

Grand Palais, Galeries Nationales du ⅢI
*Av. Winston Churchill, 8ᵉ ☎ 42-89-54-10. Map **7**G5 ▨ ▣ Open 10am-8pm, Wed 10am-10pm. Closed Tues. Métro: Champs-Élysées-Clemenceau.*

The Grand Palais and the *Petit Palais*, built for the Universal Exhibition of 1900, echo each other like two thunderous fanfares across Av. Winston-Churchill, which runs from *Av. des Champs-Élysées* to the *Pont Alexandre III*. Some people would call them fussy and pompous, but it would be fairer to call them joyous and exuberant pieces of architectural rhetoric, although the Grand Palais oversteps the mark perhaps with its gargantuan porticoes, its frescoes and its mass of *cartouches* and swags of carved stonework.

The western part of the building is now given over to the *Palais de la Découverte*, a science museum. The rest is used for temporary art exhibitions and other large-scale shows. The interior is as imposing as the exterior, particularly the main hall, with its domed and vaulted roof in glass and iron. The N section of the building, fronted by a pleasing little garden with a fountain, contains a good self-service restaurant and a cinema showing free films on subjects related to the arts.

Grands Boulevards

9ᵉ and 10ᵉ. Maps 8F7-11G11. Métro: Madeleine, Opéra, Rue Montmartre, Bonne-Nouvelle, Strasbourg-St-Denis, République.

This is the name given to the string of boulevards extending roughly from the *Madeleine* to Pl. de la République — Bds. Capucines, Italiens, Montmartre, Poissonnière, Bonne-Nouvelle, St-Denis and St-Martin. They were constructed under Louis XIV to replace an obsolete line of fortifications, and soon became known just as "the Boulevards". In the mid-18thC, the Boulevards became elegant and fashionable, but the main stretch from Bd. Montmartre to Pl. de la République has long since become rather tawdry.

Grévin, Musée

10 Bd. Montmartre, 9ᵉ ☎ 47-70-85-05. Map 9F9 ☒ ☒ ✷ Open 1-7pm, longer during school holidays. Métro: Richelieu-Drouot, Rue Montmartre.

Cabinet fantastique are the words over the doorway, and fantasy is certainly what one experiences on entering this museum. As an appetizer, the visitor passes through a grotto with distorting mirrors, then through a series of ornate rooms filled with waxworks of contemporary personalities. Down in the basement are more waxworks, arranged in a sequence of fascinating historical tableaux. There are more than 500 wax figures in total. Upstairs, in a *spectacle d'illusion* in the *palais de mirages*, visitors are miraculously transported into a variety of exotic environments, including a jungle. Founded in 1882 by the caricaturist Grévin: another branch in the *Forum des Halles*.

Guimet, Musée   See *Arts Asiatiques, Musée*

Halles, Les

1ᵉʳ. Map 10H9. Métro: Châtelet-Les-Halles, Les Halles.

This area of the city is bounded roughly by Rue Étienne-Marcel and *Rue de Rivoli* to the N and S, with the *Bourse du Commerce* and the *Pompidou Centre* marking the W and E boundaries. During the 12thC it became a bustling food market (Zola called it "the belly of Paris") and it remained so until 1979, when the traders all moved to a huge new site at Rungis, near Orly Airport, taking the atmosphere with them and leaving the city of Paris with the problem of deciding what to do with the area.

The years since then have seen a total transformation. The graceful old glass-and-iron market hall, built under Napoleon III, was torn down and replaced by a commercial complex, the *Forum des Halles*. The changes were radical, but Les Halles adjusted to a new role as a centre of entertainment, shopping and culture, and has now emerged as one of the liveliest districts in Paris. Some of the old buildings have been renovated; the 16thC **Fontaine des Innocents** (*Sq. des Innocents*) has been restored, and much of the area has been pedestrianized.

The old market has mostly, although not completely, disappeared. There remain a few food merchants, and a number

of restaurants and bars of character: a particularly striking
example is the **Les Halles Bar** (*15 Rue Montmartre*), with its tiles
depicting scenes of the market in its heyday.

Hébert, Musée National Ernest 𝗺

Hôtel de Montmorency, 85 Rue du Cherche-Midi, 6ᵉ
☎ *42-22-23-82. Map 14K6 ⬛ ✗ Open 2-6pm. Closed Tues,*
public holidays. Métro: St-Placide, Sèvres-Babylone.
Housed in a small and gracious 18thC mansion on the Left Bank,
this museum is devoted mainly to temporary exhibitions of the
works of society painter Ernest Hébert (1817-1908) and his
contemporaries.

Henner, Musée National Jean-Jacques

43 Av. de Villiers, 17ᵉ ☎ 47-63-42-73. Map 2D4 ⬛ ✗ Open
10am-noon, 2-5pm. Closed Mon. Métro: Malesherbes,
Wagram.
This collection contains about 700 paintings, drawings and
sketches by the Alsatian artist Jean-Jacques Henner (1829-1905),
who was one of the great individualists among painters.
Following no school, but inspired by the old masters, he created
canvases of a delicate luminosity and haunting grace.

En Herbe, Musée   See *Bois de Boulogne*.

Histoire de France, Musée de l'   See *Archives Nationales*.

Histoire Naturelle, Muséum National d'   See
Jardin des Plantes.

Homme, Musée de l' *(Museum of Mankind)*

Palais de Chaillot, Pl. du Trocadéro 16ᵉ ☎ 45-53-70-60. Map
12H2 ⬛ ✗ ⇌ Open 9.45am-5.15pm. Closed Tues, public
holidays. Métro: Trocadéro.
Occupying the w wing of the *Palais de Chaillot*, this museum
contains one of the world's most important collections devoted
to anthropology, ethnology and prehistory. The objects are, for
the most part, arranged according to geographical region, and
include all manner of intriguing objects, from a Navajo sand-
painting to Japanese costumes. The excellent South American
section includes a shrivelled Inca mummy in a fetal position,
which inspired Munch's painting *The Scream*. There is an area
devoted to the arts and technologies of different world regions,
and another to anthropology, dealing with the biological and
physical characteristics of man.
  There is a fine restaurant with superb views of the *Eiffel Tower*.

Monnaie, Musée de la

Hôtel des Monnaies, 11 Quai de Conti, 6ᵉ ☎ 40-46-55-26.
Map 9I8 ⬛ ✗ Open 1-6pm. Closed Mon, public
holidays. Visits to workshops Tues, Fri at 2.15pm. Métro:
Pont-Neuf, Odéon, St-Michel.
This simple but dignified mansion, which overlooks the Seine,
was once the home of the Princess de Conti, but was taken over
by Louis XV in the 18thC and remodelled by Jacques Denis
Antoine to serve as the Royal Mint. There is a permanent
museum of coins and medallions and equipment for making
them. In addition, the Hôtel des Monnaies mounts temporary
exhibitions on related subjects. As the making of coins has been

transferred elsewhere, the workshops in the building now concentrate on the manufacture of medallions of all kinds. There is a **sales gallery** in the building (*accessible from 2 Rue Guénégaud, 6ᵉ*) where a selection of these are available. The medallions are not necessarily solemn objects — one has the cancan as its theme and shows a high-kicking leg. The Mint will even make you your own medallion — if you can afford it.

Hôtel de Rohan   18thC mansion built for the bishops of

Strasbourg. See *Archives Nationales*.

Hôtel des Archevêques de Sens ▥

1 Rue du Figuier, 4ᵉ ☎ 42-78-14-60. Map 11I11. Forney Library open Tues-Fri 1.30-8.30pm, Sat 10am-8.30pm. Closed Sun, Mon. Métro: Pont-Marie, St-Paul.

This mansion at the s edge of the *Marais* is such a perfect specimen of medieval architecture, with its pepper-pot turrets and pointed arches, that if you came upon it without prior knowledge you might think it was 19thC imitation Gothic, or perhaps a stray building from a Hollywood film set in the Middle Ages.

In fact it is one of the oldest houses in Paris and was built by Tristan de Salazar, Archbishop of Sens, between 1475-1507. It was an anachronism for its day, since the archbishop, who came from a military family, could not resist adding a few touches to create the illusion of a fortified castle: a dungeon, watch-tower and watchwalk. The building was a late burst of Gothic feudalism at the dawn of the French Renaissance. It is now owned by the City of Paris and houses the Forney Library, a library of science, technology, arts and crafts. Make a point of seeing the building's fine **courtyard**.

Hôtel de Soubise   18thC mansion with superb

courtyard. See *Archives Nationales*.

Hôtel des Ventes *(Auction rooms)*

Hôtel Drouot-Richelieu, 9 Rue Drouot, 9ᵉ ☎ 48-00-20-20. Map 4F8 ▣ Open Mon-Sat 11am-6pm. Closed Sun, Aug. Métro: Richelieu-Drouot. Hôtel Drouot-Montaigne, 15 Av. Montaigne, 8ᵉ ☎ 48-00-20-80. Map 7G4 ▣ Hours as above. Métro: Alma-Marceau.

The Parisian equivalent of Christie's, or Sotheby's or Parke Bernet, the Hôtel des Ventes has, like auction rooms everywhere, an atmosphere of glamour and excitement. In France, auctioneering is a more strictly regulated business than in most countries, and is controlled by the Compagnie des Commissaires Priseurs, the auctioneers' professional body, whose members can display a gold plaque outside their door.

The old Hôtel des Ventes, which stood on the site of the Hôtel Drouot-Richelieu, was demolished in the 1970s. However, in 1980 the new Hôtel Drouot was completed — a stylish building of steel, dark-tinted glass and concrete, with traditional touches such as a steep, vaulted roof and dormer windows.

In recent years, operations have diversified and the most prestigious sales now take place in the well-heeled Av. Montaigne showroom. Both auction houses have various rooms, where all kinds of objects — French tapestries, Italian drawings, autographed letters, Chinese vases — change hands under the eye of a *commissaire priseur* perched behind a high desk.

An amusing place to visit even if you are not bidding.

Hôtel de Ville *(Town Hall)* 🏛

Pl. de l'Hôtel-de-Ville, 4ᵉ ☎ 42-76-40-40. Map 10I10.
Building open Mon-Fri 9am-6.30pm, Sat 9am-6pm
✗ to salons, Mon only 10.30am (📷). Métro: Hôtel-de-Ville.

There has been a town hall on this site since 1357, when one of
the earliest mayors of Paris, Étienne Marcel, moved the city
council there. His equestrian statue now stands facing the river
by the s side of the building.

The first town hall was replaced by a more imposing one in
Renaissance style, which was burned down by the *Communards*
in 1871. The present edifice (1874-82) is a fairly convincing copy
of its Renaissance predecessor, but has a ponderous 19thC touch
to the ornate facade, in its numerous statues of Parisian
dignitaries ensconced in niches. Before 1830, the **Pl. de l'Hôtel-
de-Ville** formed part of the riverside and was called Pl. de Grève
(meaning foreshore). It was there that unemployed Parisians
gathered — hence the term *faire la grève* (to strike). It was also
the scene of numerous executions over the centuries.

For many years Paris had no mayor and was governed by a
prefect of the city. But in 1977 the office of mayor was
re-established, and the Hôtel de Ville is his headquarters. The 109
councillors meet in a spacious, wood-panelled chamber, which
can be viewed during sessions, from a public gallery. Other
rooms can be visted by conducted tour on Mon mornings.

A feast of visual extravagance, Paris must have kept an army of
artists and craftsmen employed here for many years. For those
interested in *fin-de-siècle* decor and painting, they are, perhaps,
of particular interest.

The public relations department of the Hôtel de Ville (*29 Rue
de Rivoli*) can give information relating to the municipality, and
exhibitions on Paris are also held here.

Hugo, Maison de Victor 🏛

6 Pl. des Vosges, 4ᵉ ☎ 42-72-16-65. Map 11I12 🚇 📷 on
Sun ✗ Open 10am-5.40pm. Closed Mon. Métro: St-Paul,
Chemin-Vert, Bastille.

This is the house where Victor Hugo, author of *Notre-Dame de
Paris* (The Hunchback of Notre-Dame) and other famous novels,
lived from 1832-48. By the time of his death, Hugo had attained
the status of national hero. He was given a spectacular public
funeral and was buried in the *Panthéon*. Many people do not
realise that Hugo, as well as being a great writer and
distinguished public figure, was also an artist of genius, and the
house is full of his drawings, paintings and lithographs — mostly
dream-like or surrealistic works depicting eerie landscapes with
curious vegetation and sombre castles. There are also many
portraits, documents and other mementoes of Hugo's public and
private life.

One room is devoted to illustrations of *Notre-Dame de Paris* by
various artists and also contains Rodin's powerful bust of Hugo.

Île de la Cité and Île St-Louis ★

1ᵉʳ and 4ᵉ. Maps 10&11. Métro: Cité.

The Île de la Cité floats in the Seine like a graceful galleon
carrying more than 2,000yrs of history as its cargo, for it was here
that Paris began, when the tribe known as the Parisii settled on
the island in the 3rdC. Trailing behind it is the smaller and less
heavily laden Île St-Louis.

A visit to the *Crypte Archéologique* in the square in front of

Notre-Dame takes the visitor back to the Île de la Cité's earliest times, and the different stages of settlement can be seen in layers. Another good place to begin is the little garden on a spit of land at the N end of the Îles, approached by a stairway from the *Pont-Neuf*. On the other side of the bridge, where the island begins to widen out, is a charming little triangular square, **Pl. Dauphine**, which André Breton describes in his novel *Nadja* as "one of the most profoundly secluded places I know." Farther on, straddling the width of the island and bounded by Bd. du Palais, is the vast historic complex containing the *Palais de Justice*, the *Sainte Chapelle* and the *Conciergerie*. Across Bd. du Palais is the rather forbidding Préfecture de Police, headquarters of the immortal Inspector Clouseau, offset by the **flower market** in Pl. Louis Lépine, which is, on Sun, a colourful **bird market**.

The focal point of the island is the **Pl. du Parvis-Notre-Dame**, crowned by Notre-Dame cathedral and bounded on the N side by the Hôtel-Dieu hospital, the foundations of which date from the 7thC. A riverside walk leads round the S side of the cathedral to the garden of **Sq. de l'Île de France**, at the E tip of the island. At the very end is the **Mémorial de la Déportation**, an underground vault commemorating the French victims of Nazi concentration camps. Its stark simplicity conveys solemnity, dignity and compassion.

Immediately to the N of the cathedral lies a cluster of streets, including **Rue Chanoinesse**. The name of this street derives from the canons of Notre-Dame whose houses used to line the street. Only two of these, nos. 22 and 24, remain, dating from the 16thC, but there are many fine facades belonging to later periods.

Off Rue Chanoinesse is **Rue de la Colombe**, where the line of the old Gallo-Roman wall is traced in the cobblestones. Continue N to **Quai aux Fleurs**; there are no flowers here, but of interest are two **stone heads** over the doorways of nos. 9 and 11. These represent the ill-fated lovers Abelard and Héloïse, who lived in a house on the spot in the 12thC. The Quai aux Fleurs leads E from here to the **Pont St-Louis**, linking the two islands. From the bridge there is a fine view of the lacework of flying buttresses and spires at the eastern end of Notre-Dame.

The Île St-Louis, named after Louis IX of France, has a different and quieter atmosphere from its neighbour, being more private and picturesque. Many of the fine houses have remained intact. Two of the finest are the **Hôtel de Lausun** (*17 Quai d'Anjou*) — note the magnificent drainpipes — and the **Hôtel Lambert** (*1-3 Quai d'Anjou*), both designed by Louis XIV's architect Le Vau. The former can be visited by application to the Town Hall (**☎** *42-77-40-40*).

The island is an architectural feast and also the town's first real-estate development, built as a unit in the 17thC. All along the river-front are houses with stately porticos and interesting stone carving, many of them also bearing plaques commemorating the distinguished men who lived there — aristocrats, politicians, artists, poets. The poet Baudelaire lived at 22 Quai de Béthune. The scientist Marie Curie lived at 36 Quai d'Orléans from 1912 until her death in 1934. In the 19thC, 6 Quai d'Orléans was a meeting place for expatriate Polish artists and writers and today is the **Adam Mickiewicz Museum** (**▣** *open Thurs 3-6pm, closed July 14-Sept 15*), named after the man who is considered to be the Polish Dante. It contains the mementoes of his life and of other famous Poles such as Chopin. There is also a library and a fine collection of pictures by French as well as Polish artists.

The spine of the island is **Rue St-Louis-en-l'Île**, with its

church of the same name, built between 1664-1725 and marked by a curious pierced spire and an ornate wrought-iron clock. The street is full of little shops and restaurants, many with old and interesting frontages. At no. 35 is the tiny bookshop **Librairie Ulysse**, which specializes in rare secondhand as well as new travel books. Two doors away, at no. 31, is **Berthillon**, one of the best ice-cream shops in Europe, with a constant queue outside to prove it. (A newer branch, **La Flore en L'Île** (*2 Rue Jean du Bellay*) is at the western tip opposite the Pont St-Louis.) For those who prefer a cup of tea, there is the **Salon de Thé St-Louis** at no. 81, where no fewer than 54 varieties are served. Devotees of beer might be interested in the **Brasserie de l'Île St-Louis**, beside the Pont St-Louis. It is much frequented by rugby-playing types, especially Englishmen, and has the boisterously convivial atmosphere of an Alsatian beer hall.

But the Île St-Louis is mostly a peaceful place, with its quiet streets, and a tree-lined riverside walk runs around most of the island. Its little park, **Sq. Barye**, at the E end, has a tiny play area for small children where parents can sit and read peacefully (take buckets, spades etc).

The **quays** that line the banks of the Seine on either side of the Île de la Cité and Île St-Louis afford some superb views of the islands and of Notre-Dame. Particularly magnificent are the views from Pont des Arts, Sq. René Viviani, Pont de l'Archevêché, Pont de la Tournelle and Pont de Sully on the Left Bank, and Quai de la Mégisserie and Quai des Celestins on the Right Bank. The parapets of the quays are lined with stalls selling second-hand books (*bouquinistes*), especially along the Left Bank.

Institut de France
21-25 Quai de Conti, 6ᵉ. Map 9I8. Not open to public except cultural groups by arrangement. Métro: Pont-Neuf, St-Germain-des-Prés.

"There is no venerable forest," wrote Zola in *L'Oeuvre*, "no mountain road, no prairie or plain where the sun sets so triumphally as behind the dome of the Institut. This is Paris going to sleep in her glory." The institute is indeed a majestic building, with a concave semi-circular facade facing the Seine. It was founded as a college and library with money bequeathed by Cardinal Mazarin, and was built by the ubiquitous architect Le Vau in 1663-4 on the site of the Nêsle gate and tower, which had formed part of the medieval city wall.

The college was suppressed after the Revolution, and in 1805 the building became the seat of the recently created Institut de France, which it remains to this day. Of the five learned academies that make up the institute, the best known is the **Académie Française**. This comprises 40 distinguished literary figures, approved by the head of state, whose main task is to protect the interests of the French language.

Zola, even though he wrote with such reverence of the building, was one of many famous Frenchmen, including Balzac, Maupassant, Proust and Molière, who were refused admission to the Académie Française. Most of its honoured members have attained total obscurity.

Invalides, Les 🏛
7ᵉ ☎ 45-55-92-30. Map 13I5. Métro: Invalides, Latour-Maubourg, École-Militaire.

When Louis XIV's architects designed this building in the 1670s as a home for his invalided soldiers, they poured into it all the architectural rhetoric of the Sun King's era. The 196m/645ft-long **facade** overlooks a wide **esplanade** stretching down to the Seine; the great portico is guarded by statues of Mars and Minerva; the dormer windows in the roof are framed by huge stone suits of armour; the **courtyard**, with its double colonnade, is worth seeing; the **Dôme church** (opposite) dominates the whole edifice. Most of the building is the work of Libéral Bruand, but the Dôme church was designed by Jules Hardouin-Mansart and the esplanade by Robert de Cotte.

Once, this building housed nearly 6,000 old soldiers. Now the number has dwindled to around 100, and Les Invalides has taken on a new role as the home of four museums and as the resting place of Napoleon Bonaparte.

Musée de l'Armée *(Army Museum)*
☎ 45-55-37-68 ▨ *Tickets also valid for Musée des Plans-Reliefs and Musée des Deux Guerres Mondiales on two consecutive days. Open Apr 1-Sept 30, 10am-6pm, Oct 1-Mar 31, 10am-5pm.*
This collection of militaria, one of the largest in the world, is divided into two sections, housed on the E and W sides of the courtyard. The E side tells the story of the French Army, illustrated by pictures, models and military mementoes of all kinds. Two large rooms on the ground floor, the **Salle Turenne** and the **Salle Vauban**, were once refectories for the inmates of the building. Now the former contains a fine collection of flags and standards, including those from World War I, while the latter is devoted mainly to exhibits relating to the cavalry, among them a row of lifesize dummies of dashing uniformed men on horseback.

Upstairs is a series of rooms covering different periods of French military history, and dealing with defeat as well as victory. Predictably, Napoleon I features prominently. His death mask is here, as is a reconstruction of the room at Longwood House, St Helena, where he died in 1821.

On the third floor, where there were once craft workshops manned by the invalids, there are now exhibits relating to the Second Empire and the Franco-Prussian War.

On the W side of the courtyard are two more former refectories, the **Salle François I** and the **Salle Henri IV**, which look back to the era when suits of armour were worn.

Two rooms at the rear are filled with 15th-17thC weapons, and there are also displays of prehistoric and Oriental weaponry. Upstairs, the exhibits are from World War I and II. There is also a room filled with model artillery guns; look out of the window into the **Cour de la Victoire** and you will see an impressive collection of the real thing.

Musée des Plans-Reliefs *(Museum of Relief Maps and Plans)*
☎ 45-51-93-02 ▨ *Joint ticket (see Musée de l'Armée above). Open Apr 1-Sept 30, 10am-5.45pm; Oct 1-Mar 31, 10am-4.45pm.*
Housed on the fourth floor, this museum owes its origin to Louvois, Louis XIV's Secretary of State for War, who suggested to the king that scale-models be made of French fortified frontier and maritime towns. This was done, and the practice was continued by subsequent regimes up to the end of the 19thC. Here are finely-detailed miniature versions of many towns, including Mont Saint-Michel, Neuf-Brisach, Metz and Strasbourg.

Musée des Deux Guerres Mondiales *(Museum of the Two World Wars)*
☎ 45-51-93-02 ▨ *Joint ticket (see Musée de l'Armée above). Open summer 10am-6pm, winter 9am-5pm. Closed Sun, Mon.*
This museum has a small collection of posters, documents and

relics from World Wars I and II, and holds temporary exhibitions on related subjects. The entrance is in the NW corner of the **Cour d'Honneur**.

Musée de l'Ordre de la Libération *(Museum of the Order of Liberation)*
51bis Bd. de LaTour-Maubourg ☎ *47-05-35-15* ▨ *Open 2-5pm. Closed Sun.*

The Order of Liberation was created by de Gaulle to honour those who gave outstanding service in the liberation of France. The museum, not linked with the Musée de l'Armée, has photographs, documents and mementoes of the Free French, the Resistance, the Deportation and the Liberation.

St-Louis-des-Invalides
This church, with its cool, light, barrel-vaulted interior, was where soldiers of Les Invalides worshipped. Its main entrance faces the Cour d'Honneur. When the Dôme church was added, the two opened into one another and shared a common altar. A glass barrier now separates them. Berlioz's *Requiem* received its first public performance in 1837 on the superb 17thC organ.

Dôme church ▥ ★
▨ *Joint ticket (see Musée de l'Armée above).*

When the rest of Les Invalides had been completed, Louis XIV decided that it needed an added touch of splendour, so he commissioned Hardouin-Mansart to add the Dôme church to the S side of the building. It was begun in 1677 and completed by Robert de Cotte after Mansart's death in 1708. With its high, slender, gilded **dome** and its **portico** with two rows of columns (Doric below, Corinthian above), it is considered one of the great masterpieces of its era.

However, the church is less visited for its architecture than for the fact that it contains one of the most prestigious graves in the world, the **tomb of Napoleon Bonaparte**. His body was brought here from St Helena in 1840 and was entombed amid lavish funeral celebrations. The Emperor now lies encased in six coffins, one inside the other, which in turn are placed in a red porphyry sarcophagus. This rests in an open circular **crypt** surrounded by a gallery in which are reliefs commemorating his achievements. His son, the King of Rome, also lies here.

Stop to appreciate the rest of the interior: the altar with its elaborate *baldachin* supported on twisted columns; the **cupola** with its vivid paintings by La Fosse; and the side-chapels containing the tombs of Maréchal Foch and other military heroes.

Napoleon would have been pleased with his final resting place. "I wish my remains," he said, "to repose on the banks of the Seine among the people of France whom I have loved so much."

Jacquemart-André, Musée
158 Bd. Haussmann, 8ᵉ ☎ *45-62-39-94. Map 7E5* ▨ ✗ *ᛕ Open 1-6pm. Closed Tues, Aug. Métro: St-Philippe-du-Roule, Miromesnil.*

Like the *Musée Marmottan* and the *Musée Nissim de Camondo*, this was originally a private house and collection. It was created by the Banker Edouard André and his wife, the portraitist Nélie Jacquemart, who continued to add to the collection after André's death in 1881. She bequeathed it to the *Institut de France*, along with the grand Neo-Classical house that her husband had built in 1875. Its opulent interior forms a pleasing setting for these 18thC and Italian Renaissance works, collected voraciously yet discerningly by the Andrés.

Among the collection you will find sculpture by Donatello,

paintings by Botticelli, Titian and Uccello, including the magnificent *St George Slaying the Dragon*. French 18thC painters are represented by Watteau, Fragonard, Greuze and Boucher, and foreign schools by Rembrandt, Reynolds, Murillo and others. There are frescoes by Tiepolo, a Savonnerie carpet, four *Gobelins* tapestries depicting the seasons, and a wealth of furniture and *objets d'art*. Notice too, the Boucicault *Book of Hours*, which once belonged to Diane de Poitiers.

Jardin des Plantes/Muséum National d'Histoire Naturelle *(Botanical Gardens/Natural History Museum)*

5ᵉ ☎ 40-79-30-00. Map **16**K11 🔲 ✗ ⬛ ✱ *Open 10am-5pm. Closed Tues, public holidays. Métro: Gare d'Austerlitz, Jussieu.*

"This morning," writes Henry Miller in *Tropic of Cancer*, "having nothing better to do, I visited the Jardin des Plantes. Marvellous pelicans here from Chapultepec and peacocks with studded fans that look at you with silly eyes." He might have added that there are llamas, bison, tigers, bears, baboons, a round animal house, built under Napoleon in the shape of a Legion of Honour cross, an open-air café and more.

The Jardin des Plantes is much more than a park and encompasses not only a botanical garden but also a **menagerie** and a **Natural History Museum**. The menagerie, the oldest public zoo in the country and dating back to the Revolution, is very popular despite some rather antiquated installations. A long-running building programme is underway at the museum, with all-round improvements likely by 1992.

Near the menagerie, the **botanical garden**, which was established in the 17thC as a medicinal herb garden, contains a wide variety of European and tropical plants, as well as a **maze** and a tunnel-like avenue of plane trees.

Along the SE side of the garden is a row of buildings housing four departments of the Natural History Museum. These are:

Palaeontology: passing the skeleton of a mammoth, you enter a room full of bones and pickled organs, human and animal; upstairs there are more skeletons, as well as casts of prehistoric monsters. **Palaeobotany**: a small collection of plant fossils, petrified tree trunks and other such recondite objects. A museum for the specialist. **Mineralogy**: fossils, crystalline growths and precious stones. **Entomology**: a tiny yet worldwide collection of brightly coloured beetles and other fascinating insects.

Jeu de Paume, Musée du 🏛

Pl. de la Concorde, 1ᵉʳ ☎ 42-60-12-07. Map **8**G6 🔲 *Open 10am-5.15pm. Métro: Concorde, Tuileries.*

This Second-Empire pavilion matches its twin, in which is housed the Musée de l'Orangerie, across the *Tuileries* gardens. It was known for many years as the home of one of the world's greatest collections of Impressionist paintings. This entire collection has now been rehoused in the *Musée d'Orsay*, and the Musée du Jeu de Paume, after substantial refurbishment, reopened as a gallery for contemporary art in 1990.

Latin Quarter ★

*5ᵉ. Map **15**. Métro: St-Michel, Cluny-La-Sorbonne, Maubert-Mutualité, Cardinal-Lemoine.*

The name *Quartier Latin* carries with it the image of a way of life: colourful, vibrant, intellectual, rebellious, Bohemian and,

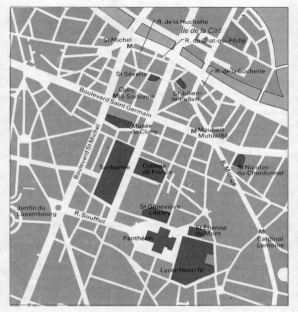

above all, cosmopolitan. It lies at the heart of the Left Bank and comprises most of the 5ᵉ and a sliver of the 6ᵉ districts, taking in the streets immediately to the w of the **Bd. St-Michel**.

Its name derives from the presence of the *Sorbonne* university and other colleges in the district, the scholars of which formerly spoke Latin. The area is still full of students, not only from the Sorbonne but also from the neighbouring *Collège de France*, the university of Jussieu a little farther to the E and the École Normale Supérieure to the S.

The term "Latin Quarter" is doubly appropriate, for the area now called the **Montagne Ste-Geneviève**, around the *Panthéon*, was once the focal point of the Roman colony. Although the governor had his palace on the *Île de la Cité*, it was here that the forum, temple and baths were built. Virtually the only Roman remains to be seen in Paris are the great thermal baths at the *Cluny* museum and in the *Arènes de Lutèce*.

The main artery of the Latin Quarter is Bd. St-Michel, or **Boul'Mich** as it is known by all. This busy tree-lined thoroughfare, full of bookshops and cafés, rises near the Luxembourg gardens and descends S towards the Seine into Pl. St-Michel, which is dominated by the huge St-Michel fountain.

The Boul'Mich is intersected by the other great artery of the Left Bank, **Bd. St-Germain**. At their junction is the *Cluny* museum, one of many architectural riches in the district. Here, too, is the refurbished Métro station of Cluny-La-Sorbonne, which at track level boasts the signatures of literary giants from across the centuries, spread across its vast mosaic-and-ceramic ceiling. Turn up Rue Soufflot and you will be confronted by the massive facade of the *Panthéon* standing on the Montagne Ste-

Geneviève. Nearby are the church of *St-Etienne-du-Mont*, the **Ste-Geneviève library**, built in the mid-19thC on the site of the medieval Montaigu college, and the **Lycée Henri IV**, the buildings of which incorporate the refectory and belfry of the old abbey of Ste-Geneviève.

There are three other important churches in the area: *St-Séverin*, *St-Julien-le-Pauvre* and **St-Nicolas-du-Chardonnet**. The last named is the stronghold of traditional Catholics, and mass is still said here in Latin.

The district's main attraction, however, lies not so much in its monuments as in the tortuous streets that twist around each other along the riverbank. The strongest impression of the cosmopolitan Bohemian life comes from the streets around St-Séverin and St-Julien-le-Pauvre. Here are restaurants of many nationalities, small bookshops, intimate little cafés, nightclubs and experimental cinemas. The pedestrian zone of **Rue de la Huchette** and its tributaries is particularly full of colour and atmosphere. Leading off Rue de la Huchette is the amusingly named **Rue du Chat-qui-Pêche** (Street of the Fishing Cat), said to be the smallest street in Paris.

A stone's throw to the E (*37 Rue de la Bûcherie*) is one of the most enticing bookshops in the city, **Shakespeare and Co**, which specializes in English-language material, both new and second-hand. Between the wars, Sylvia Beach owned the original Shakespeare and Co at 12 Rue de l'Odéon, which was the meeting place of expatriate literati such as Joyce, Pound, Miller and Hemingway. Eventually it was reincarnated in its present location by a genial American, George Whitman, who still runs the place with great verve, and accommodates penniless writers in rooms above the shop.

In the Latin Quarter one senses fewer barriers than in many other districts; the area seems to invite anyone who goes there, to participate in its life. No doubt this is because of the presence of so many nationalities and so many students.

Légion d'Honneur, Musée National de la ⌷

Hôtel de Salm, 2 Rue de Bellechasse, 7ᵉ ☎ 45-55-95-16. Map 8H6 ▨ ✗ by prior arrangement. Open 2-5pm. Closed Mon, public holidays. Métro: Solférino.

The museum is housed in the **Hôtel de Salm**, a fine 18thC mansion, built in Palladian style and resembling the White House in Washington, DC. Its occupants included the writer Mme de Staël, and Napoleon Bonaparte. The house was acquired by the Grand Chancellery of the Legion of Honour, soon after the Order's creation by Napoleon in 1802. It was burned down during the *Commune* but rebuilt in 1878.

The museum is devoted to the history of chivalric orders and other awards for distinction, including many from foreign countries, such as Britain's Victoria Cross and Order of the Bath. There is a rich selection of insignia, regalia and documents. In the section on the Legion of Honour itself, we learn that Rodin, Utrillo and Colette were among the recipients.

Louvre, Musée du ⌷ ★

*Palais du Louvre, 1ᵉʳ ☎ 40-20-51-51. Map 9H8 ▨
General ✗ for individuals (extra ▨), in English daily except Tues, Sun, at 10am, 11.30am, 2pm; register 15mins early. Groups should reserve up to 2mths in advance
☎ 40-20-51-77 ▣ ▭ Museum open 9am-6pm; Hall Napoléon (below pyramid: permanent exhibitions and all*

facilities) open 9am-10pm; Hall Napoléon (temporary exhibitions) open noon-10pm. All closed Tues. Métro: Palais-Royal-Musée du Louvre.

"I never knew what a palace was until I had a glimpse of the Louvre," wrote the 19thC American author Nathaniel Hawthorne. Today he would be surprised to find the main courtyard, the Cour Napoléon, dominated by a crisp glass-walled pyramid, flanked by three smaller pyramids and seven stretches of water, two with fountains, which mark the new entrance to the museum. The work of the American architect I.M. Pei, this pyramid is only one feature of a vast new development, which began in 1981 under the initiative of President Mitterrand, and is now complete, at a cost of 100 million francs.

It involved massive underground excavations to create new galleries, a centralized public reception area, and all the facilities that a museum handling 4 million visitors each year could need. The three wings of the vast palace now have a much-needed central focal point, and distances between the many galleries have been considerably shortened. The development also continues until 1993, the bicentenary of the Louvre first being opened to the public, and entails the conversion into galleries of the old Ministry of Finance offices in the N wing, the Pavillon Richelieu. The *Grand Louvre* is about to emerge in all its glory.

In the process of excavating the Cour Napoléon, some 20,000 artifacts were found, the relics of a *quartier* that was demolished in 1852. More exciting still was the discovery of the foundations of the original 12thC fortress, built by Philippe Auguste, renovated by Charles V as a residence and then demolished by François I in the 16thC in order to create a palace that was expanded piecemeal by every major French monarch up to Napoleon III.

Above these foundations is the **Cour Carrée (★)**, which was designed by Pierre Lescot for François I in the Renaissance style. In the 17thC Louis XIII commissioned Le Mercier to extend the W facade of the Cour Carrée in the same style, and the remainder was built by Louis XIV. Particularly noteworthy is the majestic **colonnade (★)** of 52 Corinthian columns along the outside of the court. This was the work of Claude Perrault, and is one of the outstanding examples of the Classical style in Paris. From the Cour Carrée, the Louvre grew haphazardly westwards in two gigantic wings as successive monarchs added pavilion after pavilion until it finally linked up with the now vanished Tuileries palace. Today the Louvre is so vast that it can only be encompassed in a single sweep of the eye if one observes it from the air or from a high vantage point.

The art collection grew in a similarly piecemeal way. Begun by François I, it was built up by his successors and continued to expand after the building was opened to the public in 1793. It was the fifth museum in the world to be opened in this way. The greatest leaders were the greatest collectors: François himself, then later Louis XIV and Napoleon. As the collection grew, more and more of the palace was opened up to accommodate it.

There are so many exhibits that if you were to spend half a minute in front of each one, it would take three months, night and day, to see the whole collection. So, clearly, anyone visiting the Louvre must ration their time carefully. If possible, try to make more than one visit. A good idea for the first-time visitor is to take one of the general guided tours. Then, having obtained a bird's-eye view of the museum, return later to explore individual parts in greater detail.

Louvre

What follows is a brief guide to the main sections and their highlights. Bear in mind that the locations of many exhibits will change, since the museum will continue its expansion and development programme over a number of years, taking best advantage of the increase in space given by the acquisition of the Richelieu wing.

It is not possible to give a detailed floor plan in this edition, as 80 percent of the total collection will be relocated between 1991-1993. However, the public information offered by the museum's management could not be better. A simple colour- and number-coding system (see illustration opposite) is now in operation, and a free orientation guide is available, in English and other languages. In the Hall Napoléon, a bank of video screens offers day-by-day information on all changeable elements; eight reception staff are on call to answer any specific questions about the museum or its exhibits; and a computer database is there to help them in their task. There are free programmes — even themed visits are offered, on such subjects as the birth of Christian art, and these encompass a number of different disciplines in various departments of the museum.

Reception area and underground galleries

The main entrance to the museum is through the pyramid. From the spacious underground reception area, the **Hall Napoléon**, there are striking views of the palace through the glass walls of the pyramid. Here are two restaurants and two cafeterias, a museum shop and bookshop, a post office and an auditorium. This is also the gathering point for anyone wishing to take a guided tour. A new display of chalcography (copper and brass engravings) is also here, along with temporary exhibition spaces that are well signposted. This area also boasts a display of the wealth of objects found during the excavation. Continue via the Gothic **Crypt of St-Louis** into the huge crypt under the Cour Carrée, which contains the massive, cyclopean remains of the ramparts and keep of the 12thC fortress. For a startling time-warp effect, go straight from here into the Egyptian galleries, where you will come face to face with an enormous sphinx.

The museum above ground has seven departments: Greek and Roman Antiquities, Oriental Antiquities, Egyptian Antiquities, Furniture, *Objets d'Art*, Painting and Drawing, and Sculpture.

Greek and Roman Antiquities

This heading encompasses every chapter in the history of Classical art, from early Hellenic times to the end of the Roman Empire. The department occupies ground-floor galleries in the Denon wing as well as part of the Sully wing, which includes the 16thC **Galerie des Caryatides**, once used as a ballroom, with its row of caryatids looking curiously like some of the exhibits. The armless *Venus de Milo* (★) was found in 1820 by a peasant on the Greek island of Milos and is one of the most prized items. Dating from the 3rd-2ndC BC, she embodies all the idealized beauty and dignity invested by the Greeks in their portrayals of the human form. Her face is rather masculine, a reminder that the Greeks of that time particularly exalted male physical beauty.

Another famous exhibit in this section is the headless *Winged Victory of Samothrace* (★ c.200BC). She dominates a grand staircase, which was rebuilt in the 1930s especially for her display. Remade from pieces found in 1863, the left wing entirely remade using the right wing as a model, the statue commemorates a naval victory and was once a ship's figurehead, symbolizing victory with far more impact than any triumphal arch.

Belonging to a much earlier period (6thC BC) is the *Hera of*

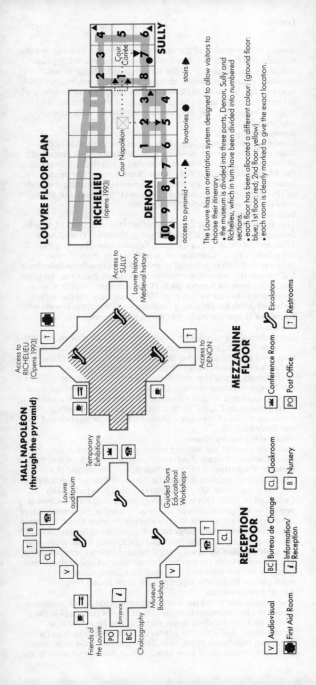

Samos. In this work and the other statues nearby, you can see the stiffness and frontal emphasis often found in ancient Egyptian statues — so different from the *Venus de Milo. Hera,* in her enclosed roundness, recalls statuary made from tree-trunks. Look out, too, for the *Rampin Horseman.* He has an archaic smile, and his beard and hair are stylized, geometrical approximations of reality. The bronze *Apollo of Piombino* (5thC BC) has superb copper inlay.

Oriental Antiquities

Currently occupying ground-floor rooms on the N side of the Sully wing, this section is devoted mainly to the civilizations of Mesopotamia, the Far Eastern section of the collection being in the *Musée National d'Arts Asiatiques.* Among the most impressive items here are the black basalt stele bearing the *Code of Law of King Hammurabi of Babylon* (1792-50BC), the *Stele of the Vultures* and the *Stele of Naram-Sim.*

Egyptian Antiquities

This is one of the finest Egyptian collections in the world, thanks to long-standing French prominence in this field. Founded in 1826, its first curator was the great Egyptologist Champollion, decipherer of the Rosetta stone, which is now in the British Museum in London. Situated in ground- and first-floor galleries in Sully wing, the collection contains such masterpieces as the great sandstone **bust of Amenophis IV** (Akhenaton), which was presented to France by Egypt in 1972. Look, too, for the superb **Gebel-el-Arak knife**, dating from about 3400BC, the **jewels of Rameses II** and the statue of Queen Karomama.

Sculpture

Housed on the ground floor of Denon wing, but moving in 1993 to the new Richelieu wing, this section encompasses the whole history of French sculpture, from its origins to the end of the 19thC, and includes works by foreign sculptors, such as Michelangelo's *Captives* and Benvenuto Cellini's bronze relief of the *Nymph of Fontainebleau.* The French sculptures range from austere medieval religious images, through Renaissance works such as German Pilon's *Three Graces,* to exuberant 19thC creations such as Carpeaux's *Dance,* which was reproduced on the *Opéra* facade.

Objets d'Art and Furniture

Currently located in a striking room on the N side of Sully wing, the collection of *objets d'art* and furniture can be found in the **Galerie d'Apollon**, which was luxuriously decorated in 1661. The murals by Le Brun feature the Sun God Apollo, symbolizing the Sun King, Louis XIV. The central ceiling was painted by Delacroix in 1848. This is an appropriate setting for the **Crown Jewels** — gorgeous crowns and regalia used at the coronation of the French kings, as well as priceless jewels such as the 137-carat diamond known as the **Regent**, purchased from England in 1717. The other galleries on the first floor of the Sully wing, known as the **Colonnade Galleries**, have beautiful ceilings and panelling, and present a wide panorama of decorative art and craftsmanship from the Middle Ages to the time of Napoleon. Some fine examples of *Gobelins* tapestries are to be found here.

Painting and Drawing

This department is the museum's greatest pride, and constitutes one of the most comprehensive collections of paintings in the world. By 1993, hardly a single painting will be found in its former place, and a further 2,000 will have been added to the 2,000 that were already on view. From the vast Salle Sully, you can catch a marvellous view along one of Paris' great axes: from

the pyramid and the *Arc de Triomphe du Carrousel* through
to *l'Etoile* and *La Défense*.

The collection was begun by François I, who acquired the
Louvre's most famous exhibit, Leonardo da Vinci's *Mona Lisa*
(★), along with other Italian masterpieces. Also called *La
Gioconda*, thanks to the most mysterious of smiles, she is now
displayed behind bullet-proof glass, and is the subject of major
security precautions. The Louvre undoubtedly has the richest
collection of Leonardos possessed by any museum in the world,
as it also includes *Bacchus*, a *John the Baptist*, the *Virgin of the
Rocks*, a small portrait of a lady, *La Belle Ferronnière*, and the
Virgin and Child with Ste-Anne. In each of Leonardo's paintings
you will see how he has suppressed two-dimensional line in
favour of mass and tone value, creating three-dimensional
illusion. This technique is called *chiaroscuro*, Italian for "light-
shadow". Further, by use of very thin coats of glaze, hard outlines
are obscured, giving the subject a hazy look. This technique is
called *sfumato*, Italian for haze. Leonardo also strove to reveal
the intention of the soul through gestures. In the *Virgin of the
Rocks* (★), the group is held together by various significant
gestures: pointing, praying, blessing and protecting. In the *Virgin
and the Child with Ste-Anne* (★), Mary is shown sitting on the
lap of her mother Ste-Anne and reaching out towards the baby
Jesus, who, in turn, reaches towards his future sacrifice for
mankind, which is symbolized by a lamb. The *Mona Lisa* is not
the only one smiling. That mysterious smile can be found
elsewhere, for instance in the *John the Baptist*.

In addition to the Leonardos, there is a wealth of paintings by
Titian, Raphael, Veronese, and other artists of the Italian
Renaissance, as well as earlier and later Italian works.

A small but distinguished Spanish collection includes such
masterpieces as El Greco's *Christ Crucified* and Murillo's *The
Young Beggar*, as well as works by Goya and Velázquez. English
works are also not numerous, but include portraits by
Gainsborough and Reynolds. The Flemish, Dutch and German
masters are well represented, and there is a series of Rembrandts.

French paintings form the bulk of the collection, and range
from the 14th-19thC. In Sully wing, around the Cour Carrée, there
are 12 newly-opened halls where the great collection of French
painters is now on view. You will find Poussin's limpid canvases
of mythological and allegorical subjects, La Tour's religious
paintings with their striking effects of light and shadow, and
Watteau's delicate scenes of gaiety touched with a nuance of
melancholy.

New spaces in the Richelieu wing are to be dedicated to the
museum's exceptional collection of 17thC French paintings. If it
is size and splendour you want, then move round into the 19thC
rooms where you will find David's vast painting *The Coronation
of Napoleon* and works by other 19thC painters such as Delacroix
and Corot.

In the past, only a small part of the drawings collection, mainly
pastels, was on permanent display. A much-expanded collection
is now on view, with works ranging across the centuries. In
addition, more drawings will be brought out for temporary
exhibitions on specific themes.

The 1990s will mark the end of a period of enormous upheaval
for this great museum. Every museum-goer in the civilized world
should offer congratulations on so fine a transformation — and
be thankful when it is at last possible to view the collections in an
uninterrupted way.

Luxembourg, Palais et Jardin du Ⅲ

Map 15J8 ■ ✱ Métro: Luxembourg.

The Palais du Luxembourg, which houses the French Senate, was built 1612-24 by Marie de Medici, widow of Henry IV. Finding the Louvre boring as a place of residence, she bought the house and grounds of the Duc de Piney-Luxembourg, then standing in a semi-rural position on the S edge of the city. Beside the duke's house (now known as the **Petit Luxembourg**) she built a grandiose mansion designed by Salomon de Brosse in the style of the Pitti Palace in Florence, but keeping the traditional French layout around a grand courtyard. However, her stay was short-lived, for in 1630, 5yrs after she had moved in, she was banished for life to Cologne.

During the Reign of Terror (1793-4) the palace became a prison, but after 1795 it housed the higher parliamentary assemblies, and the building underwent a series of alterations and enlargements. The Petit Luxembourg next door is now the residence of the Senate's president.

The gardens, like the palace, are French, with Italian touches such as the Baroque **Medici fountain**, which stands at the end of a long pool filled with goldfish and flanked by shaded walkways. The focal point of the gardens is a large octagonal pool, surrounded by formal terraces and *parterres* and usually filled with a fleet of toy sailing boats. The rest is an engaging mixture of formality and intimacy, with plenty of little secret corners as well as broad, straight avenues. One of the great delights of this park is its statues. Here you will find, among others, Delacroix, Verlaine, George Sand, Stendhal and Flaubert. In **Av. de l'Observatoire**, which forms an extension to the gardens, is an exuberant fountain with an armillary sphere held up by female figures representing the four quarters of the globe.

The gardens also have tennis courts, donkey rides, a marionette theatre (the **Théâtre du Luxembourg**), a school of bee-keeping and arboriculture, and an open-air café under the trees, which reminds one of a Renoir painting. In fact the Luxembourg Gardens have just about all the ingredients for a good day out, except that you cannot sit on the grass.

La Madeleine Ⅲ

Pl. de la Madeleine, 8ᵉ ☎ 42-65-52-17. Map 8F6 ✗ Open 7am-7pm, Sun 7.30am-1.30pm, 3.30-7pm. Métro: Madeleine.

Built to look like a Roman temple, this edifice, with its simple lines and colonnade of soaring Corinthian columns, stands at the hub of one of the most prosperous districts of Paris, confident of its architectural splendour, yet oddly uncertain of its role as a Christian church. Begun as a church in 1764, during the reign of Louis XV, it never seems to have quite thrown off the image of the bank that it nearly became in the early 19thC — other ideas included a theatre, a banqueting hall, a Temple of Glory to Napoleon's army, and a railway station. After much debate and many changes of design, it was finally consecrated as a church in 1842.

Contrasting with the rather austere exterior, the sensual beauty of the interior comes as something of a surprise — a feast of softly coloured marble, gilt Corinthian columns, rich murals, and some fine sculpture, including Rude's *Baptism of Christ* and the *Ascension of the Magdalen* by Marochetti, which dominates the high altar.

The church possesses a superb organ, and concerts are held

here several times a week, including free Sunday afternoon concerts twice a month during the academic year.

Le Marais ★
3ᵉ and 4ᵉ. Maps 10&11. Métro: Hôtel-de-Ville, St-Paul, Chemin-Vert, St-Sébastien-Froissart, Filles-du-Calvaire, Temple, Arts-et-Métiers, Rambuteau.

This fascinating district has a grave beauty that is haunting, powerful and peculiarly un-Parisian. The stamp of the Middle Ages is still firmly imprinted on the narrow, huddled streets, lined by venerable houses built in the 16th-18thC.

The name means "marshland", and this is what the area was, until in the 12thC it was drained by the Knights Templar. It became the site of many other religious communities, which have since disappeared but bequeathed their names to certain streets: Rue des Blancs-Manteaux, Rue des Filles-du-Calvaire, Rue Ste-Croix-de-la-Bretonnerie. The Knights' fortress, the Temple, became a prison during the Revolution, and it was here that the royal family was held. Today nothing remains of the building. The site, lying at the N of the Marais, is now a charming and secluded little park, the **Square du Temple**.

In the 15thC, the Marais had begun to be a fashionable residential district for the aristocracy, and by the 17thC it had reached its heyday, abounding in gracious mansions of the kind that became the model for the traditional French *hôtel*, with a courtyard at the front and formal garden at the back. There are still more mansions remaining in the Marais than in any other district of Paris. By the early 18thC, the nobility began to move w to the Faubourg-St-Germain. The Marais became less favoured and thereby began a gradual decline, which lasted until de

Le Marais

Gaulle's Minister of Culture, André Malraux, made it a conservation area in 1962, just in time to save it from wholesale redevelopment. Since then, a restoration programme has uncovered many treasures.

Not surprisingly, the Marais possesses what is claimed to be the oldest house in Paris, **3 Rue Volta**, built in about 1300, and also the second oldest, **51 Rue de Montmorency**, built in 1407 as a charitable lodging house. The house is now a restaurant. Near Rue Volta is the **Temple Quarter**, which includes the *Musée National des Techniques* (Technological Museum) and the church of *St-Nicolas-des-Champs*.

This northern part of the Marais also boasts, to the W, the *Archives Nationales*, housed in the outstanding **Hôtel de Soubise** and **Hôtel de Rohan**, and, to the E, the *Carnavalet* museum. Just to the N of the Archives Nationales, in Rue des Archives, is another notable feature, the **Hôtel Guénégaud**, now housing the *Chasse* museum, a quietly harmonious Mansart building. Around the *Carnavalet* are a wealth of beautiful *hôtels*. Best known are the **Hôtel Libéral-Bruand** in Rue de la Perle, and the **Hôtel Salé** in Rue de Thorigny, the home of the *Picasso* museum. Also worth seeing in nearby Rue de Turenne are the **Hôtel de Montrésor**, now a school, and the **Hôtel du Grand-Veneur**, former home of the master of the royal hunt. The facade is adorned with a boar's head and other symbols of hunting; inside, the impressive staircase is decorated with trophies (ask the caretaker if you wish to visit). Farther along the street is **St-Denys-du-Sacrement**, built in 1835 in the Roman style, which contains a *Deposition* by Delacroix.

Beginning at the Seine, a short itinerary takes in some of the southern part of the Marais' most interesting features. Just E of the *Hôtel de Ville* is the church of **St-Gervais-St-Protais**. A Gothic building with a superb Classical facade, it contains some fine works of art, including lovely stained glass, and, in the N transept, a Flemish *Passion* painted on wood. Walk down to the river and along to the *Hôtel des Archevêques de Sens*, one of the oldest mansions in the city. Continue E for a short distance, then turn up Rue des Jardins-St-Paul, leading into the **Village St-Paul** (*closed Tues, Wed*), a huddle of tiny craft studios and *bric-a-brac*-style antique shops.

Twisting N, turn left at Rue St-Antoine to visit the church of **St-Paul-St-Louis**, built in the Jesuit style in the 17thC. Return down Rue St-Antoine to the 17thC **Hôtel de Béthune Sully** at no.62, which is now the headquarters of the administration of national monuments and where temporary exhibitions on architecture and conservation are held. There is a particularly fine inner courtyard, and the interior contains panelling and painted ceilings (🕿 ✗ compulsory: *Wed, Sat, Sun 3pm*). Turn up Rue de Birague into the graceful red-brick expanse of *Pl. des Vosges*. Leave it by the NW corner and walk W down **Rue des Francs-Bourgeois** to the corner of Rue Pavée and the **Hôtel de Lamoignon**, now the Paris Historical Library, with its curious little corner tower jutting out over the pavement. The courtyard and building are of majestic proportions, the facade divided by tall Corinthian pilasters. Opposite is the *Carnavalet* museum and beyond it, up Rue Payenne, is **Sq. Georges-Cain**, a magical little oasis of a garden, full of intriguing fragments of sculpture. In the same street are two interesting buildings, the **Hôtel de Chatillon**, at no. 13, and the **Hôtel de Polastron-Polignac**, next door.

Returning to the Hôtel de Lamoignon, walk S down Rue Pavée

and immediately right into the area which for centuries has been a **Jewish quarter**. In this street, Rue des Rosiers, Rue des Écouffes, and in the nearby streets, synagogues, kosher food shops and Hebrew booksellers abound.

Not far away, in the street of the same name, is the graceful little church of **Notre-Dame-des-Blancs-Manteaux**, with its ornate Flemish wooden pulpit. Opposite is the attractive **Rue Aubriot**, dating from the Middle Ages, and, to the left, Rue des Guillemites, from which lead the tiny inner courts of the **Passage des Singes**. The passage leads to Rue Vieille-du-Temple, and to the left is the **Hôtel des Ambassadeurs de Hollande** (*not open to public*), one of the finest mansions in the Marais and once the home of Beaumarchais, who wrote the *Marriage of Figaro* there.

The lower half of Rue des Archives has the curious nickname of "the street where God was boiled". This dates from 1290, when a moneylender was said to have cut up a host (communion bread) with a knife. To his surprise the host began to bleed, whereupon he threw it into boiling water, which immediately turned red. The unfortunate man was apprehended and burned at the stake, and soon afterwards a church was built on the site of his house to commemorate the miracle. Around this the monastery of Carmes-Billettes grew up in the 14thC. The **Temple des Billettes** was rebuilt in the 18thC and is now Lutheran; the charming little **cloister** survives, the only complete medieval cloister in Paris.

A little distance to the w lies another interesting church, that of **St-Merri**, completed in 1612, but anachronistically built in the Flamboyant Gothic style. It has a richly decorated w front, and the oldest bell in Paris, made in 1331.

A block to the N of this church, up Rue St-Martin, lies the *Pompidou Centre*, taking the visitor with a jolt from some of the oldest architecture in Paris to a building that proclaims itself firmly in the 20thC.

Marché aux Puces (Flea Market)
Rue des Rosiers, St-Ouen. Map 19C4. Open Sat, Sun, Mon. Métro: Porte-de-Clignancourt.
There were once spectacular bargains to be had at this sprawling bazaar lying in a seedy area to the N of the Périphérique. Alas, this is no longer the case, and virtually the only cheap stalls are the ones selling tawdry modern goods. The market, now more than 2,000 stalls extending about 4 miles, consists of a maze of alleys lined with booths selling an intriguing variety of antiques and bric-à-brac, furniture and second-hand clothes. For prospective buyers it is frustrating, but it can be fun just to stroll and observe. See also *Markets* in *Shopping*.

Marine, Musée de la (Maritime Museum) ▥
Palais de Chaillot, Pl. du Trocadéro, 16ᵉ ☎ 45-53-31-70. Map 12H2 ☎ Open 10am-6pm. Closed Tues. Métro: Trocadéro.
The symbol of Paris is a ship, so it is appropriate that the city should possess a fine maritime museum. There is hardly anything relating to the French Navy and to seafaring in general that you will not find here, from old ship's cannons and figureheads to the bridge of a modern warship, from astrolabes to radar equipment. The museum is proud of its collection of model ships, which include Columbus' *Santa Maria*, and of its paintings on naval themes, among them Vernet's series on the ports of France. Another prized possession is a sumptuous barge made for Napoleon, in cream, green and gold, propelled by 28 oars.

Marmottan, Musée ▥
*2 Rue Louis-Boilly, 16ᵉ ☎ 42-24-07-02. Map **18**D3 and see map on page 54 ▨ ☜ ✗ Open 10am-5.30pm. Closed Mon. Métro: La Muette.*

This collection was begun by the 19thC industrialist Jules Marmottan and enlarged by his son Paul, who left it, along with his imposing house, to the *Institut de France*, which now administers it as a museum. Its appeal lies not so much in the value of the individual works as in the wayward charm of a private collection, comprising paintings, furniture and ornaments, displayed in a series of beautiful rooms.

Although there are works of many periods, there are three groups of items that are given pride of place: a series of rooms devoted to works of art and furniture of the Napoleonic era; a collection of medieval illuminated manuscripts; and a collection of works by Monet and his contemporaries. These include Monet's *Impression, Soleil Levant*, from which the term Impressionist is derived, and also many of his paintings of water lilies.

Mint   See *Musée de la Monnaie*.

Mode et du Costume, Musée de la *(Fashion Museum)* ▥
*Palais Galliéra, 10 Av. Pierre 1ᵉʳ-de-Serbie, 16ᵉ ☎ 47-20-85-23. Map **6**G3 ▨ ✗ Open 10am-5.40pm. Closed Mon. Métro: Iéna, Alma-Marceau.*

To many people, Paris and fashion are synonymous. Visit this stylish museum and you are sure to learn something new about the art of dressing. The museum has no permanent collection but plays host to a continuous series of well-mounted temporary exhibitions on various aspects of clothing and its history.

Even if fashion does not interest you, it is worth taking a look at the building. The **Palais Galliéra** was built in a striking Neo-Classical style by the Duchesse de Galliéra in the decade 1878-88. The s front gives onto a charming public **garden** where the sun splashes down onto the colonnaded facade and over the park with its fountains, statues and shaded benches, creating a truly Italian feel.

Monceau, Parc de
*Entrance in Bd. de Courcelles, 8ᵉ. Map **2**E4. Métro: Monceau.*

This is an unusual and rather poetic place. The entrance, through a gateway in a tall railing along Bd. de Courcelles, reveals a picturesque garden in the English style. Beside a little lake there is a semicircular Roman colonnade, and dotted about among the chestnuts, acacias and plane trees are curious objects: a pyramid, a stone archway, some Classical columns. These are all follies remaining from the garden designed for the Duke of Orléans by the writer and painter Carmontel in the late 18thC.

Monde Arabe, Musée de l'Institut du ▥
*Rue des Fossés-St-Bernard, 5ᵉ ☎ 40-51-38-38. Map **16**J10 ▨ ♿ ✗ ⇌ Open 1-8pm. Closed Mon. Métro: Jussieu, Cardinal-Lemoine, Sully-Morland.*

Islamic architecture for the space age is how one might describe the intended effect of architect Jean Nouvel's building, which houses this new institute. The s side of the building, for example, is shielded from the sun by metal screens based on Islamic patterns, but with light-sensitive apertures designed to open and close like the lens of a camera. The overall effect of the building can seem rather harsh and inhospitable, with its razor-sharp edges and dull grey tones. Don't be put off, because the museum inside contains a fine collection of art and artifacts illustrating the development of Islamic culture from its origins to the present day. The institute, often referred to by its acronym, IMA, is the result of a collaboration between France and 19 Muslim countries. Other facilities include a library, an audiovisual centre and a top-floor restaurant (see *Restaurants*) commanding a fine view over Paris.

Montagne Ste-Geneviève   See *Latin Quarter*.

Montmartre ★

18ᵉ. Map 4. Métro: Abbesses, Pigalle, Blanche, Anvers, Barbès-Rochechouart, Château-Rouge, Marcadet-Poissonniers, Jules-Joffrin, Lamarck-Caulaincourt.

In AD250 the martyred St-Denis is said to have picked up his severed head and walked up and over a hill to the N of the city. Since then millions of people have made the journey in more conventional style up through the winding streets of what is now called Montmartre or simply the **Butte** (hillock). Montmartre is a district full of contrasts. By turn quiet, raucous, quaint, sordid and hauntingly beautiful, it is a must on the itinerary of anyone wishing to absorb the spirit of Paris.

For centuries Montmartre was a country village, bristling with windmills that supplied flour to the city below. Then in the 19thC it became part of Paris, and its picturesque charm and atmosphere and low rents attracted painters, sculptors, writers and musicians. The late 19thC was the heyday of Bohemian Montmartre, when Toulouse-Lautrec drew the cancan girls at the **Moulin Rouge** in Pl. Blanche, when Picasso, Braque and others created Cubism at the **Bateau-Lavoir** studios (burned down in 1970 but since rebuilt) in Pl. Émile-Goudeau, and when artists' models hung about Pl. Pigalle looking for work. By 1914, most of the artists had migrated to the Left Bank, and the great tourist influx had begun.

Today Montmartre has a number of different faces. The garish nightlife that Toulouse-Lautrec loved to portray has now spread all along Bd. de Clichy and the surrounding streets. Pigalle today has become decidedly sleazy, the artists' models now replaced by numerous members of an older profession. This is the Montmartre of neon lights, strip clubs and cheap glitter. Farther up the hill in the area around the *Sacré-Coeur*, the ghost of the old Montmartre still lingers, but strictly for the tourists' benefit. Yet behind the facade of fake Bohemianism, Montmartre is still a village, an ordinary community with a strong sense of its own history. This aspect is most evident on the N side, an area of quiet residential streets.

One of the best ways to begin a visit to Montmartre is to take the Métro to Lamarck-Caulaincourt. Climb the stairs heading s and cross Rue Caulaincourt. Look at once for a sign directing you along **Rue St-Vincent** towards the **Cimetière St-Vincent** and the **Musée de Montmartre**. At the pretty, countrified crossroads with **Rue des Saules** is the café **Lapin Agile**, a famous meeting place in the Bohemian days. On the slope to the right is a little **vineyard**, the last survivor within the Parisian boundaries. Every year, on the first Sat in Oct, the vintage is celebrated by festivities and a procession.

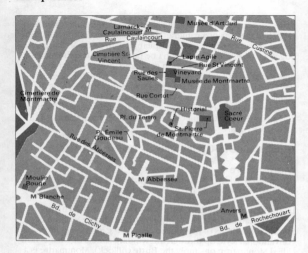

Head up Rue des Saules and turn left into the pretty **Rue Cortot**. Here is the entrance to the **Musée de Montparnasse** (☎ 46-06-61-11 ▧ ✗ *open Tues-Sat 2.30-6pm, Sun 11am-6pm, closed Mon*). A house with a terraced garden, inhabited by many artists in the past, it contains interesting mementoes of the district.

Within a short walk is the Butte's most prominent feature, the magnificent church of the *Sacré-Coeur*. Beside this landmark is the church of **St-Pierre de Montmartre**, a remnant of the great medieval abbey of Montmartre. Downhill to the W lies **Pl. du Tertre** with its cafés and cobbled, leafy square crammed with artists selling their pictures. Just off Pl. du Tertre is the **Historial de Montmartre** (*11 Rue Poulbot* ☎ 46-06-78-92 ▧ *open 10.30am-5.30pm*). A wax museum with tableaux on the history of Montmartre, it features Utrillo, Steinlen, Toulouse-Lautrec, Van Gogh, Victor Hugo and Chopin, among others.

Some of these people are buried in the Butte's two cemeteries, the small **Cimetière St-Vincent** and the much larger **Cimetière de Montmartre**. Beyond the smaller cemetery, to the N of Rue Caulaincourt, is a museum of Jewish art, the **Musée d'Art Juif** (*42 Rue des Saules* ☎ 42-57-84-15 ▧ ✗ *open Sun-Thurs 3-6pm, closed Fri, Sat, Aug, Jewish hols*).

The funicular at Montmartre had been in service for 55yrs, carrying up to 1,400 visitors an hour up the S slope of the Butte. Early in 1991, work was completed on a brand new system that operates the carriages as on an escalator. Now each of the two tracks can operate independently of the other, and will carry an estimated 4,500 visitors per hour.

Montparnasse

14ᵉ. Map 14. Métro: Montparnasse-Bienvenue.
Montparnasse, or "Mount Parnassus", was in Greek legend the mountain sacred to Apollo and the Muses. This was the nickname given to a grassy mound, formed from the debris of old quarries, which in the 17thC became a favourite haunt with student versifiers, who would gather to recite their poems. In the 18thC the mound was levelled off, but the name stuck, and so did the carefree, pleasure-loving image. By the time of the

Revolution, cafés and pleasure gardens had sprung up in Montparnasse, and it was here that the cancan was first performed.

In many ways Montparnasse is to the Left Bank what Montmartre is to the Right. Both are situated on hills, both, in their heyday, have been haunts of artists and literati, and both have since undergone a change of image. Montmartre now thrives on its picture-postcard quaintness, whereas Montparnasse became the victim of an uncharacteristically hard-nosed policy of redevelopment, exemplified by the *Tour Montparnasse* and a crop of mostly indifferent new buildings surrounding the redeveloped railway station: an exception is the opulently modern **Meridien Montparnasse** hotel (see *Hotels*). The once charming **Rue de la Gaîté**, some of whose little theatres are now down-at-heel, is swamped by ever more sex shops.

Yet the old Montparnasse struggles valiantly to survive, and there are still glimpses of it along Bd. du Montparnasse, once the centre of flourishing artistic endeavour. Among those drawn to the boulevard and its surrounding streets were artists Rousseau, Van Dongen, Modigliani, Chagall and Whistler, writers Rilke, Apollinaire, Max Jacob and Cocteau, musicians Satie and Stravinsky, and political exiles including Lenin and Trotsky. Between the wars, the district was particularly popular with American expatriates, most notably Ernest Hemingway.

The crowd of artists and intellectuals thronged the new cafés of the boulevard: La Coupole, Le Sélect, Le Dôme, La Rotonde and La Closerie des Lilas, which was one of Hemingway's favourite retreats. In *A Moveable Feast* the author recalls seeing the English occultist, Aleister Crowley, at the café, "a rather gaunt man wearing a cape." Crowley was another of the eccentric and colourful characters who used to frequent the district, and he appears pseudonymously as Oliver Haddo, the villain of Somerset Maugham's novel *The Magician*, in which a Montparnasse café scene is vividly described.

Those were the days when Montparnasse was one mad continuous party, a period that is vividly described by Georges-Michel in his novel *Les Montparnos* (1924). It was this writer who coined the word "Montparno" to refer to an inhabitant of the district.

Today the sparkling café life of Montparnasse has declined. Only La Coupole, Le Sélect and La Closerie des Lilas (see *Restaurants*) keep alive something of the atmosphere. The writers have dispersed, although there are still many artists' studios in the area.

Montparnasse enjoyed a brief moment of glory during the Liberation of Paris in 1944, when the **Gare Montparnasse** was used as the headquarters of General Leclerc. It was there that the German military governor signed his surrender. In 1967 it was demolished to make way for the present station complex, which incorporates huge blocks of offices and apartments. A new wave of modernization began again in 1989, bringing the station into the TGV age.

The station is the point of arrival from Brittany, so Montparnasse is traditionally a Breton area, especially Rue Montparnasse, where there are still excellent restaurants serving *crêpes* and Breton cider.

The streets to the NW of the station are relatively unspoiled. Here you will find the *Musée de la Poste* in Bd. de Vaugirard and the *Bourdelle* museum in the street named after the sculptor Antoine Bourdelle. The sculptor himself is buried in the tranquil **Montparnasse cemetery**, which also contains the graves of writers such as Baudelaire and Maupassant, composers César Franck and Saint-Saëns, and other distinguished figures. One of the graves has a bronze effigy of a couple sitting up in bed — no doubt very daring for its time. Another is decorated with Brancusi's sculpture, *The Kiss*, a tender and moving piece.

Montsouris, Parc de
Bd. Jourdan, 14ᵉ 💺 *Métro: Cité-Universitaire.*
The most striking feature of this appealing park, with its hills, lake and rambling paths, is a Moorish-looking building with onion domes, a replica of the Bey of Tunis' palace, given by the Bey for the Paris Exhibition of 1867.

The park also contains the Paris meteorological observatory and a tower marking the s bearing of the former Paris meridian.

Monuments Français, Musée National des 🏛
Palais de Chaillot, Pl. du Trocadéro, 16ᵉ ☎ *47-27-35-74. Map 12H2* 📷 *✗ ⛬ Open 9am-6pm. Closed Tues. Métro: Trocadéro.*
Try to imagine part of the facade of Chartres cathedral standing right next door to a tympanum from Reims, a pair of gargoyles from Nantes and some sculptures from Notre-Dame, and you will get some idea of what you will see when you enter this museum. You might well think for a moment that you had wandered by accident into the *Cinéma* museum, also housed in the *Palais de Chaillot*, and were looking at relics of a Hollywood film studio's props department — except that the replicas here are better made than on any film set. They are so well made in fact that, even close up, it is hard to tell that these are not stone- or wood-carvings but plaster copies. The same skill is seen in the department devoted to mural painting, where you may suddenly find yourself apparently inside a 12thC Romanesque church, painted with biblical scenes in flat ochres, browns and reds.

The original idea behind the museum was to restore French sculpture to its rightful place among the arts by showing casts of distinguished works. Formerly called the Museum of Comparative Sculpture, it was given its present title in 1937 and widened to include mural paintings and a small amount of stained glass. For the student of sculpture it is a treasure house, for the lay visitor an enjoyable feast of make-believe.

Moreau, Musée Gustave
14 Rue de la Rochefoucauld, 9ᵉ ☎ *48-74-38-50. Map 4E8* 📷 *✗ Open 10am-12.45pm, 2-5.15pm. Closed Tues. Métro: Trinité.*
"His sad and scholarly works," writes the novelist Huysmans about the symbolist painter Gustave Moreau (1826-98), "breathed a strange magic, an incantatory charm which stirred you to the depths of your being."

The artist's house and studio, located on the edge of *Montmartre*, where he lived a reclusive life, are now filled with a collection of his strange, dreamlike works.

Mouffetard, Rue
5ᵉ. Map 16K10. Métro: Monge.
This "wonderful, narrow, crowded market street", as Hemingway described it, begins at **Pl. de la Contrescarpe**, one of those little leafy village squares that bring a feeling of rusticity to so much of Paris. From here, Rue Mouffetard descends s in a haphazard

fashion. It is lined with charming old houses and shopfronts with interesting signs, such as at no. **122**, which reads "At the Sign of the Clear Spring" and has a well carved on the facade, and no. **134** with its swirling pattern of birds, foliage and wild boar. Nos. **101** and **104** mark the entrances to two tiny, undisturbed passages, **Pge. des Patriarches** and **Pge. des Postes**. The street itself remains a bustling shopping area, the food shops bursting with ripe cheeses, fruit and delicacies.

At its lower end is the little church of **St-Médard**. Here in the 1720s there grew up a curious cult in which groups of people assembled in the charnel house and took part in orgies of convulsion, hysteria and self-mortification in the hope of attaining miraculous cures or visions. These meetings of *convulsionnaires* were stopped by a royal order in 1732.

Rue Mouffetard and its tributaries constitute one of the few authentic Parisian "villages" that survive and flourish.

Notre-Dame de Paris, Cathédrale de ▥ ★
Pl. du Parvis-Notre-Dame 4ᵉ ☎ 43-26-07-39. Map **10**/J10. *Church* ▣ *✗ ◁€ Open 8am-7pm; for museum and towers see below. Métro: Cité.*

One of the world's great architectural masterpieces, the cathedral of Notre-Dame dominates the skyline of central Paris with its lacy facade and its two solid rectangular towers. It has fascinated artists and writers over the centuries, and was the setting for Victor Hugo's famous novel *Notre-Dame de Paris* (The Hunchback of Notre-Dame), whose hero, the bell-ringer Quasimodo, has become a figure of legend. "A vast symphony in stone" is how Hugo described it.

For 800yrs the history of Paris has unravelled around the cathedral. Its towers have looked down upon wars, revolutions, executions, pilgrimages and, today, a virtually unceasing stream of tourists. It is one of the symbols not only of Paris but of France itself, and appropriately, set into the ground just in front of the main doorway, is a brass plaque marking the zero point from which all distances from Paris are measured.

The site of Notre-Dame has been a place of worship since pagan times, when a temple to Jupiter stood there. Later came two adjacent Christian churches, one to the Virgin Mary and the other to St Stephen. These were removed in the 12thC, when the building of Notre-Dame began — a process that was to take nearly 200yrs. By 1330 the cathedral stood complete in its essential form, although in the 17th and 18thC sweeping internal alterations were carried out. During the Revolution, most of the statues of the portals and choir chapels were destroyed, the bells were melted down, the treasures were plundered, and the cathedral became a Temple of Reason. In the mid-19thC, a magnificent restoration was carried out by Viollet-le-Duc, who replaced hundreds of destroyed carvings. During the *Commune* of 1871 the whole cathedral very nearly perished when the *Communards* made a bonfire of chairs in the choir. Luckily the building was saved by the lack of air and the dampness of the walls.

An unusual feature of the cathedral is that its floor is absolutely level with the street, so that it seems to welcome passers-by to enter without formality.

Before going into the building, spend a while taking in the abundant sculptures on the **facade** (★), remembering that most are skilful copies or restorations by Viollet-le-Duc and his pupils. It was he who carved the 28 kings of Israel who stand in a row,

Notre-Dame de Paris, Cathédrale de

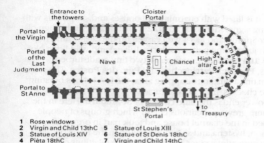

1 Rose windows
2 Virgin and Child 13thC
3 Statue of Louis XIV
4 Pièta 18thC
5 Statue of Louis XIII
6 Statue of St Denis 18thC
7 Virgin and Child 14thC

known as the **King's Gallery**, across the facade as ancestors of
Jesus Christ. The heads of the originals of these are now in the
Cluny museum. The three doorways are known as the **portals
of the Virgin Mary, of the Last Judgment** and **of St Anne**,
and the stonework is richly carved with appropriate figures, such
as Christ sitting in judgment (over the central doorway) flanked
by the Virgin Mary and St John as intercessors. Look for some of
the smaller carvings, such as the zodiacal signs on the left-hand
portal, and the curious medallions on the central one,
representing virtues and vices: purity is a salamander, and pride
is a man being thrown from a horse (these have also been given
an alchemical interpretation). The other facades also have some
fine carving; the most famous sculpture of all is that of the **Virgin**
by the door of the N transept, carved in the 13thC and unscathed
in the Revolution, except for the loss of the Child.

Go inside the cathedral and, before looking at individual
features, take in the majestic construction of the building, with its
walls rising in the traditional Gothic manner, through three tiers
of arches to a ribbed, vaulted ceiling that seems infinitely far
away. Stand in the centre of the transept and you will feel the full
impact of the architecture. From here you will also get a good
view of the **rose windows** — three great shimmering pools of
light and colour to the N, S and W. Only the N rose, made in 1270,
retains most of its original glass. The S window was extensively
restored in the 18thC and the W window in the 19thC. It is partly
hidden by the largest organ in France. Features of the transept
that are worth seeing include the lovely 14thC statue of the
Virgin and the Child against the S pillar flanking the entrance to
the chancel, and the 18thC statue of *St-Denis* against the
opposite pillar.

Around the nave is a series of chapels containing many fine
sculptures and paintings, mostly from the 17thC. In the St Peter
chapel on the S side there is some beautiful 14thC woodwork,
carved with representations of saints. In the ambulatory there are
more chapels, filled with the mausoleums of various bishops of
Paris.

The high altar in the chancel was made in the 19thC to a design
by Viollet-le-Duc. Behind it is an 18thC *Pièta*, to the right a statue
of Louis XIII, who in 1638 consecrated his kingdom to the Virgin.
To the left is a statue of Louis XIV.

On the S side of the ambulatory, a door leads to the **treasury**
(🕿 *open Mon-Sat 10am-6pm, Sun 2-6pm*), where a collection of
plate and other treasures, including a reliquary said to contain a
fragment of the Cross, can be seen.

No visit to Notre-Dame would be complete without climbing
the **towers** (☎ 43-54-22-63 🕿 ◄€ *open Apr-Sept 10am-6pm,*

Oct-Mar 10am-5pm). You ascend 387 steps via the N tower, then cross over to the S one, passing a series of splendid gargoyles and carved monsters, including the **striga** (a kind of vampire), who gazes, chin resting on his hands, over the city. In the S tower you can visit, with a guide, the belfry containing the great 13-ton bell that is rung only on special occasions.

The S tower can be climbed to the top, and on the descent you pass a room containing a **museum of the cathedral's history**. For a more detailed presentation of the building's history, cross the road to the **cathedral museum** (☎ 43-25-42-92☜ *open Wed, Sat, Sun 2.30-6pm*), which houses a small but fascinating collection of objects, pictures and documents that illustrate the cathedral's history.

Notre-Dame de Paris: Crypte Archéologique
Pl. du Parvis-Notre-Dame, 4ᵉ ☎ 43-29-83-51. Map 10/9 ☜ Open 10am-6pm Apr-Sept, 10am-5pm Oct-Mar. Closed public holidays. Métro: Cité.
This museum resulted from the discovery of an important archaeological site in front of *Notre-Dame*, and it was roofed over after the excavation finished. The resulting vault is the largest structure of its kind in the world. Descending a stairway from the square, one literally steps down into the Paris of an earlier age, finding an underground chamber where Gallo-Roman ramparts jostle the cellars of medieval houses. The remains are superbly presented, with information on the early history of Paris, illustrated by detailed models of the city at various stages.

Observatoire de Paris ▥
61 Av. de l'Observatoire, 14ᵉ. Map 15M8 ☒ ✗ compulsory. Open first Sat in month only, by arrangement: apply in writing to Secretariat at above address. RER: Port-Royal.
This chaste building, with its two-domed octagonal towers, was built between 1667-72. No iron was used in the construction because it might have affected the instruments, and wood was also avoided for fear of fire. The S wall of the building marks the latitude of Paris.

Today, the Observatory remains a major research centre for astronomy and related services. It is the headquarters of the Time and Frequences Laboratory, which sets the legal time for France, and also the headquarters of the International Earth Rotation Service, which contributes to setting universal time. In theory the building and its small museum can be visited by guided tour on the first Sat of every month, but there is usually a waiting list, sometimes to 2-3mths. However, the charming **garden** behind the Observatory, entered from Bd. Arago, is open to all, free of charge.

Opéra ▥
Pl. de l'Opéra, 9ᵉ ☎ 40-17-33-33, box office ☎ 47-42-57-50. Map 8F7 ☜ Foyer and amphitheatre open 11am-4.30pm except during afternoon performances, box office open 11am-7pm. Closed Sun. Métro: Opéra.
When Charles Garnier, architect of the Opéra, was asked by the Empress Eugénie whether the building was to be in the Greek or Roman style, he replied indignantly, "It is neither Greek nor Roman. It is in the Napoleon III style, Madame!"

In fact, no building epitomizes more strikingly the heavy opulence of that era. During its construction between 1862-75 the builders encountered an underground lake, which now lies beneath the cellars of the building, and where the "Phantom of the Opéra" had his dwelling. Above, however, all is brightness and gaiety.

The ornate facade, with its multitude of columns, friezes, winged figures and busts of famous composers, is the architectural equivalent of Offenbach's music: lighthearted and irresistible. Inside the building the tone changes. The richly coloured marble staircase, where caryatids hold elaborate candelabra, evokes the setting for Belshazzar's Feast.

As for the auditorium, it has all the right ingredients: red velvet, gold leaf and an abundance of plaster nymphs and cherubs. The only discordant element is the domed ceiling painted by Chagall — exquisite but out of key.

During the day you can walk around the building in return for a small fee, but really the only way to see the Opéra is to attend a performance there — always a great experience.

The removal of the major operatic performances to the new *Opéra Bastille* in 1990 has allowed the Opéra Garnier to expand its programme of ballet and contemporary dance, and concerts by visiting orchestras. (See *Nightlife and the performing arts*.)

Opéra Bastille

120 Rue de Lyon, 12ᵉ ☎ *40-01-17-89. Map* **17J12** 🔲 *Open 11am-6.30pm. Closed Sun* 🚾 💻 ⬥ *Métro: Bastille.*
Despite its splendour, the much-loved *Opéra* Garnier had been declared technically inadequate some years earlier, when the decision was taken in 1982 to build a new opera house on the site of the Bastille. No facilities to store large-scale scenery meant no repertoire of works; a limited seating capacity meant high ticket prices and an unquenchable demand. Poor rehearsal and studio space did not allow the Opéra to work as it should.

Architect Carlos Ott won the commission, in the face of competition from 750 contenders, and work began in 1985. The new opera house, its multi-faceted glass frontage dominating Pl. de la Bastille, was inaugurated during the Bicentenary celebrations in 1989, on a timetable running to plan despite 4yrs of delays and difficulties. Its formal opening in Mar 1990 launched a short season, following which a period of closure allowed various minor modifications to be made, both to the acoustics and to other technical aspects.

Its final reopening, in 1991, will reveal to the world Paris' first large prestigious opera house in its finished form. The modern glass ceiling echoes the lustres and decorated ceilings of the opera houses of an earlier age, reflecting the grey-blue granite of the walls and the oak block floor, as well as the giddying tiers of balconies that sweep up towards the roof.

As well as the main auditorium (2,700 seats), the Opéra Bastille houses a 450-seat amphitheatre, a 250-seat studio (see also *Nightlife and the performing arts*). A flexible hall seating 600-1,000 is also nearing completion and is scheduled to open in 1992.

The vast building welcomes visitors throughout the day, with bookstalls, a restaurant and cafeteria, and permanent and temporary exhibitions. Some say the period of its conception and birth was troubled. Others are not kind about the building's design. London's Barbican Centre overcame similar problems and achieved credibility very quickly. No doubt the Opéra Bastille will do the same.

Opéra Quarter

9ᵉ and 2ᵉ. Maps 8&9. Métro: Madeleine, Opéra, Havre-Caumartin, Chaussée-d'Antin-Lafayette, Richelieu-Drouot, Quatre-Septembre, Pyramides, Tuileries, Palais-Royal.

This distinctive area surrounding the magnificent old *Opéra* building falls roughly between Bd. Haussmann and *Rue de Rivoli* to the N and S, and Rue de Richelieu and the *Madeleine* to the E and W. More than any other district of Paris, it bears the stamp of Baron Haussmann, Napoleon III's energetic Prefect of the Seine, who replanned much of central Paris in the years 1853-70 and whose signature was the wide boulevard and spacious townscape. It was he who carved out **Pl. de l'Opéra**, which many considered unnecessarily large at the time, as well as **Av. de l'Opéra**, Rue Auber and Rue Halévy, which clasp the ornate Opéra buildings as in a forked stick.

Bd. des Italiens and its extensions were already a fashionable area for rich pleasure-seekers, but with Haussmann's developments and the Gare St-Lazare near at hand, the quarter also became a thriving commercial and financial centre. This transformation was accelerated by the building of the Métro at the beginning of the century.

The district today preserves both of these aspects. Everywhere you look there seem to be palatial banks, such as the frothy pile of the Crédit Lyonnais building in **Bd. des Italiens**, and huge shops — the renovated Trois Quartiers in **Bd. de la Madeleine**, Le Printemps and Galeries Lafayette in **Bd. Haussmann**. There are also many smaller but often more expensive shops, some bearing anglophile names like "Old England", others inimitably French, such as the couturiers in the elegant **Rue St-Honoré**, which becomes the even more elegant *Rue du Faubourg-St-Honoré*. The most luxurious street of all, however, is **Rue de la Paix**, leading from the Opéra to *Pl. Vendôme* and lined with sumptuous couturiers and jewellers, including **Cartier**.

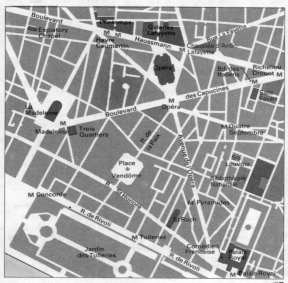

Orangerie, Musée de l'

Theatres in the district, apart from the Opéra itself, include the **Olympia** auditorium in Bd. des Capucines (mainly for pop concerts), the experimental **Salle Favart** (*Opéra Studio*) and the *Comédie Française*, the seat of Classical French drama. One of the Comédie's greatest (and funniest) dramatists, Molière (1622-73), is commemorated by the **Molière fountain**, near the site of his house in Rue de Richelieu. The fountain is a grand affair with a bronze statue of the playwright sitting on a pedestal supported by two languid female figures — a somewhat solemn monument for so humorous a writer.

Another appealing **fountain** lies a short distance farther up Rue de Richelieu in **Sq. Louvois**, a small park beside the *Bibliothèque Nationale*. Podgy cherubs on dolphins support a great bowl decorated with the signs of the zodiac, surmounted by four buxom women representing France's great rivers, the Seine, Saône, Loire and Garonne. The park, with its chestnut trees, is one of the few intimate little retreats in the district. Near the entrance is a *colonne Morris*, one of those charming onion-domed advertisement pillars that, alas, are disappearing almost as fast as the *pissotières*.

In the search for imposing architectural riches, you need only cross the road to the *Bibliothèque Nationale* or go w to *Pl. Vendôme* and the *Madeleine*, or s to the *Palais-Royal* or the church of *St-Roch*. One rather curious monument lies on the N fringes of the quarter. This is the **Expiatory Chapel**, built by order of Louis XVIII to the memory of his brother and sister-in-law, Louis XVI and Marie-Antoinette. It stands in **Sq. Louis XVI**, now another tranquil little garden off Bd. Haussmann, but formerly a cemetery where lie victims of the guillotine. Louis XVI and Marie-Antoinette were also buried here, until Louis XVIII had their bodies removed to *St-Denis*. The chapel itself looks rather like a glorified waterworks from the outside. Inside it is a frostily Classical mausoleum, like a miniature Panthéon, with statues of the unfortunate couple, and a gloomy little crypt below (**▨** *open 10am-noon, 2-5pm or 6pm*).

At no. 5 Rue Daunou is the famous American watering-hole, **Harry's New York Bar**. On the night before a US presidential election, a mock poll is held among the clientele — and more often than not predicts the winner.

Orangerie, Musée de l' ▥

Pl. de la Concorde, Jardin des Tuileries, 1ᵉʳ ☎ 42-97-48-16. Map 8G6. Open 9.45am-5.15pm. Closed Tues. Métro: Concorde.

Across the Tuileries from the *Jeu de Paume* is this matching pavilion housing the Walter-Guillaume collection of paintings. Exhibits cover the period from the end of the Impressionist era to 1930, and include works by Renoir, Cézanne, Soutine and Picasso. The gallery's other major possession is a collection of Monet's *Grandes Nymphéas* (Waterlilies), rivalling those displayed in the *Marmottan* museum.

Orsay, Musée d' ▥ ★

1 Rue de Bellechasse, 7ᵉ ☎ 40-49-48-14. General recorded information ☎ 45-49-11-11. Map 8H7 ▨ ✗ Open Tues, Wed, Fri, Sat 10am-6pm, Thurs 10am-9.45pm, Sun 9am-6pm (June 20-Sept 20 opens daily 9am). Closed Mon & ▭ ▣ Métro: Solférino. RER: Musée d'Orsay.

What better place for a major museum of the 19thC than the former Gare d'Orsay, a splendid example of *fin-de-siècle* grandeur, which has been beautifully restored and skilfully converted for museum purposes?

The site of the former Palais d'Orsay, occupied only by the strangely romantic ruins of the Cour des Comptes since the razing of the palace in the *Commune* of 1871, was bought by the Paris-Orléans railway company, which felt itself to be disadvantaged by the remoteness of its Gare d'Austerlitz. This became the location of a monumental yet modern new station, designed by Victor Laloux, which opened 2mths after the World Fair, in July 1900. Built around metal structures, the edifice was meant to be decorative as well as functional. In response to criticisms of the construction of such a large metal structure just across the river from the *Tuileries*, Laloux masked it with a stone facade along the quay and the front of the hotel on Rue de Bellechasse.

With its single hall, 32m (105ft) in height, 16 underground railway tracks and vast reception areas, the station was, for close on 40yrs, the terminus of the main line to the sw with about 200 departures each day.

But from being a symbol of progress, the station became the victim of progress. The electrification of the railway network produced the need for longer trains, and without the ability to extend its platforms, the station ended its long-distance service in 1939 and activities were restricted to suburban lines. Deprived of a large part of its lifeblood, the station quickly became too large. Its uses varied from a centre for the dispatch of packages destined for prisoners of war to a reception centre for those same returning prisoners, from the platform for de Gaulle's 1958 announcement of his plans to return to power to a film location for Orson Welles' production of Kafka's *The Trial* (1962) and Bertolucci's *Le Conformiste* (1970).

In 1961, the SNCF placed the building on the market. Many projects were proposed; all would result in the projected disappearance of the station, and the inclusion of a large modern hotel in the plans. This was the way of things in the years before Paris learned to recognize the value of its historic buildings (see *Architecture*). Yet the demolition of Laloux's work was prevented by the Minister for Cultural Affairs, Jacques Duhamel, in 1971, and it became a listed Historic Building in 1973. By 1978, the idea of a major national museum that would concentrate on the arts of the period 1848-1914 was formally agreed, architects were briefed, and work began in 1980.

The challenge of turning a space that had been designed for people to pass through into one where people would be encouraged to linger, of mastering the immense volume of space without breaking or enclosing it, was met in a concise and imaginative way. The existing glass panes, metal structures and decorative mouldings might have provoked imitation — yet the reshaping was done through contrast and simplicity, concentrating on the solid medium of stone.

Unlike in many vast buildings that have been adapted for museum use, a visitor to the d'Orsay can "see" the entire layout from the point of entry. The 1st- and 2nd-floor exhibits are arranged in hanging galleries, with the floor-to-ceiling drop always visible at the heart of the building. Galleries showing the permanent collection are kept apart from temporary exhibition areas, themed displays and information areas, and the museum's policy is to allow each work to speak for itself, in a neutral environment, rather than being shown in a period setting.

The entire collection now comprises 2,500 paintings and 250

pastel drawings, 1,500 sculptures, 1,100 *objets d'art* and 13,000 photographs, and is constantly being added to. Works have been imported from various collections, including those formerly housed in the *Jeu de Paume* museum, the **Palais de Tokyo**, the *Louvre*, the *Arts Décoratifs* museum, the châteaux of *Versailles* and *Fontainebleau*, as well as a number of private collections.

In painting, the period covered by the museum falls into two important phases: first, **from the late 1840s to the early 1870s**, marked by the birth of Impressionist painting; and second, **from Impressionism to the birth of Modern Art, around 1905**. While each of these phases had numerous influences, each has nevertheless two distinguishable and principal movements. In the **first phase**, these are: the movement arising from the heritage of the great **Neoclassicists** (Ingres and co.), and from the **Romanticists** (late works of Delacroix), which influenced such artists as Gustave Moreau, Puvis de Chavannes, and the first Degas; and the **Realists**, from Daumier and the Barbizon painters to the early **Impressionists**, by way of Millet, Courbet and Manet.

In the **second phase**, from 1870-1907/10, the two major movements are: the main **Impressionist** wave that began in 1870, and the **Post-Impressionists** that responded to the stimulus of Impressionism, namely Cézanne, Van Gogh, Lautrec, Redon and Seurat, and the **Neo-Impressionists**, Gauguin and the Pont-Aven school. Secondly, the diverse forms of painting that emerged from the *salons*, the official eclecticism of the Third Republic, which ranged from the **Second-Empire** Bourguereau to the **naturalists** Cormon and Bastien-Lepage, the brilliant end-of-century **portrait artists**, Boldini, Besnard and Blanche, **foreign influences** such as the American Homer and the Spaniard Sorolla, the *Bande Noire* painters such as Cottet, and, finally, the **symbolists**.

The museum also offers a perspective on **20thC art**, with works by Dufy, Klimt, Matisse, Munch, Rousseau and Van Dongen.

In the 60yrs of constant evolution and change in painting, the art of **sculpture** had remained closed to aesthetic innovations. With Rodin's *L'Age d'Airain* (1877), sculpture entered a grand new adventure, which would lead towards modernity. Exceptions in this field were perhaps, the small number of **painter/sculptors**, Daumier, Degas, Gauguin and Renoir, who were pioneers of the new paths that were opening up.

The creation of *objets d'art* and **furniture** was deeply influenced by the introduction of new manufacturing techniques. The English "**Arts and Crafts**" movement pioneered by William Morris, Rossetti and Burne-Jones was echoed in France by Viollet-le-Duc, who brought contemporary detail to works of architecture. **Art Nouveau** finally allowed the architect to take his contribution beyond that of structure, and examples can be seen of the urban furniture of Guimard and the furnishings of Lloyd Wright and Van de Velde.

The newborn art of **photography** was, meanwhile, exploring many different perspectives. Photographic journalism, social observation, fictional photography and "living paintings", landscape and aerial photography, all produced leading exponents over the period of 60yrs.

In **architecture**, the period covered by the museum spans Haussmann's urban planning, Garnier's *Opéra*, the construction of the *Tour Eiffel*, the classic styles of Duban and Viollet-le-Duc and the Baroque styles of Lefuel and Garnier. These led to the Art Nouveau explosion, which became the source of 20thC inspiration. The Musée d'Orsay's rich storehouse has gathered together entire collections of the graphic work of some architects, including Eiffel and Garnier.

No floor plan need be given here — the Musée d'Orsay is laid out in such a way that the visitor can follow the clear signs, and gauge the scale of the exhibition areas so easily, that a diagram would be superfluous. In any case, most museums, especially new ones, change the use of their spaces from time to time.

You begin on the ground floor, where you pass through the **Second Empire** collection. Here is the cool, formal Classicism of Ingres, the fluid, romantic canvases from Delacroix's later period, the calm, pastoral scenes of Millet and Corot, and the early work of the **Impressionists-to-be**: Manet, Monet and Renoir. There are also some striking sculptures in the centre aisle, as well as a broad-ranging architecture section and a large area devoted to the *Opéra*, with a model of the *Opéra Quarter* under a glass floor and a cut-away model of the *Opéra* building itself.

If you follow the recommended route, you then go straight to the upper level, where you find the great **Impressionist** collection, shown to best advantage in the natural light. Here you will see classics such as Monet's *Rouen Cathedral*, Van Gogh's *Self-Portrait*, Renoir's joyful *Moulin de la Galette*, and many more. Other works on this floor include the eerie scenes of Douanier Rousseau and the paintings of the Pont-Aven school: Gauguin, Bernard and Sérusier.

While on the top floor, you might wish to visit the café located behind the face of the enormous station clock — you can watch the hands moving as you sip your coffee.

Finally, descend to the middle level, to the glass-domed rooms overlooking the Seine. Among the paintings exhibited here are the uncanny visions of the **Symbolists** and, as a total contrast, the vivid canvases of Bonnard. The **decorative arts** are well represented on this floor. There is a series of rooms with superb **Art Nouveau** objects gathered from France and beyond (Charles Rennie Mackintosh, William Morris and Frank Lloyd Wright are to be found in company with Hector Guimard and René Lalique), and a section devoted to the **decorative arts of the Third Republic** is appropriately housed in one of the ornate public rooms of the old station hotel.

The elegant former restaurant of the hotel has sprung to life again as the **Restaurant du Musée d'Orsay** (*entrance at 62bis Rue de Lille* ☎ 45-49-42-33, *closed Sun eve, Mon* ━ AE ◉), a large, bright room, all white and gold, with chandeliers and an exquisitely painted ceiling — a dining ambience wholly in keeping with the spirit of the museum.

Palais-Bourbon   See *Assemblée Nationale*.

Palais de Chaillot Ⅲ
Pl. du Trocadéro, 16ᵉ. Map 12H2. Métro: Trocadéro.
The commanding height on the Right Bank of the Seine, known as the Chaillot, has been occupied by a series of buildings. It began as a country house built by Catherine de Medici in the 1580s. After the Restoration, Charles X wanted to build a monument to commemorate the French capture of the Trocadéro fort near Cadiz in Spain. This was never built, but the name stuck and was given to an elaborate palace created there for the Paris Exhibition of 1878. Its successor, built for the Exhibition of 1937,

was called the Palais de Chaillot, and the name
Trocadéro was kept for the square onto which the N side of the
building faces. The whole complex is aligned with the *Tour
Eiffel* and the *Champ-de-Mars* across the river, creating a
dramatic townscape.

With its simple lines, Neo-Classical colonnades and heroic
sculptures, the palace is reminiscent of the monumental Fascist
and Soviet architecture of the period. But it has aged well, and its
sandstone facade has a crisp elegance.

From a spacious piazza with a magnificent view of the Eiffel
Tower, two curving wings reach out, embracing a garden that
slopes down towards the Seine, the central axis of which is laid
out in a descending series of fountains and pools.

The Palais de Chaillot now houses the following museums:
du Cinéma, de l'Homme, de la Marine and *des Monuments
Français*. Also housed here are the film library of the
Cinémathèque Française and the **Théâtre National de
Chaillot**, with its two auditoriums.

Palais des Congrès: Centre International de Paris
Pl. de la Porte-Maillot, 17ᵉ ☎ *46-40-27-01. Map 6D2. Métro:
Porte-Maillot.*
A streamlined, multi-purpose building, opened in 1974,
dominates the chaotic spaghetti crossroads by the NE corner of
the *Bois de Boulogne*. It comprises the Palais des Congrès and
a vast hotel. The palais itself is a low-rise block, housing
exhibition halls, shops, restaurants, cinemas, conference rooms, a
discotheque, an air terminal and the huge and impressive **Main
Conference Hall**, home of the Paris Symphony Orchestra and
also used for conferences (*no admittance unless attending a
performance*).

Beside this is the high-rise **Hôtel Concorde- LaFayette**, with
1,000 rooms. The whole complex, known as the **Centre
International de Paris** (CIP), is a planners' dream, with every
facility — except, some feel, charm.

Palais de la Découverte *(Palace of Discovery)* 🏛
Av. Franklin-D-Roosevelt, 8ᵉ ☎ *40-74-80-00. Map 7G5* ▨
📧 *in Grand Palais. Open Tues-Sun 10am-6pm. Closed
Mon, public holidays. Planetarium lectures 4 or 5 times a
day. Métro: Champs-Élysées-Clemenceau, Franklin-D-
Roosevelt.*
The imposing W wing of the Grand Palais, with its huge domed
entrance hall, is a place in which to wonder at the properties of
the symbol Pi, the structure of the atom, the nature of laser
beams or the fundamentals of genetics. These and many other
branches of discovery are imaginatively presented and kept up to
date. What makes the Palais de la Découverte attractive is that
attendants are present in every room to explain and demonstrate
the exhibits.

The museum has a **planetarium** where different aspects of the
universe are projected onto a hemispherical dome. There are
regular temporary exhibitions, film shows and lectures.

Palais de l'Élysée
*55 Rue du Faubourg-St-Honoré, 8ᵉ. Map 7F5. Métro:
St-Philippe-du-Roule, Champs-Élysées-Clemenceau.*
Built in 1718 for the Comte d'Evreux and later lived in by
Madame de Pompadour and Napoleons I and III (Napoleon I
signed his abdication here), among others, this palace with its

extensive garden has since 1873 been the official residence of the French president and the meeting place of the Council of Ministers. The public is not allowed in, but can glimpse the elegant facade and courtyard beyond a heavily guarded gateway.

Palais Galliéra   See *Mode et du Costume, Musée de la*

Palais de Justice *(Law Courts)*
4 Bd. du Palais, 1ᵉʳ ☎ 43-29-12-55. Map 10|9 ⊙ ✕ Open Mon-Sat 10am-6pm (approximate times). Closed Sun. Métro: Cité, Châtelet, St-Michel.

Together with *Sainte-Chapelle* and the *Conciergerie*, the Palais de Justice forms a vast complex of buildings running the whole width of the *Île de la Cité*, with an imposing courtyard and entrance on Bd. du Palais. There was a palace here in Roman times, and later the site was occupied by a magnificent royal residence, which in the 14thC became the seat of parliament. Since the Revolution, the buildings have been occupied by civil and criminal law courts.

The most impressive room in the complex of courts and galleries is the **Lobby** (Salle de Pas-Perdus), formerly the great hall of the palace, which was twice destroyed by fire and was rebuilt in its present form in the 1870s. The royal courtiers are now replaced by lawyers and litigants scurrying about the "cathedral of chicanery", as Balzac called it. If you want to see them in action, you can drop into any except the juvenile court.

Palais de la Mode   See *Arts de la Mode, Musée des*.

Palais-Royal ▥
Pl. du Palais-Royal, 1ᵉʳ. Map 9H8. Métro: Palais-Royal.

Few buildings in Paris have played as many different roles as the Palais-Royal. Built by Cardinal Richelieu in the 17thC as his private palace, it later came into the hands of the Orléans family, one of whom was the dissolute regent Philippe II of Orléans, who turned the palace into a scene of frenzied orgies. His descendant, the so-called "Philippe Égalité," needing to raise money, built matching terraces of apartment houses around the garden, with an arcade at ground level in which there were premises for tradesmen. These buildings form the splendid quadrangle, the **Cour d'Honneur**, that one can enter to the N of the palace. A controversial addition to this courtyard consists of a series of black-and-white columns of unequal height, created by the artist Buren.

In the heated period before the Revolution, this quadrangle was the scene of rallies and demonstrations — the "nucleus of the Revolution," Marat called it. Then, after the execution of Philippe Égalité, the palace, its gardens and cafés, became a centre of gambling and prostitution.

Returned to the Orléans family at the Restoration, the palace was sacked during the Revolution of 1848 and set on fire by the mob during the *Commune* of 1871.

Now the office of the Council of State and closed to the public, the Palais-Royal seems content after its hectic past. The garden is a public park, with the buildings around it given over to apartments and small shops. A fountain plays lazily in the middle of the courtyard, and the sunlight filters through the trees.

Palais de Tokyo   Elegant 1930s building housing several museums. See *Art Moderne de la Ville de Paris, Musée d'*.

Panthéon 🏛 ★

*Pl. du Panthéon, 5ᵉ ☎ 43-54-34-51. Map **15K9*** 🚇
*✗ (compulsory for crypt) 📷 in crypt, fee elsewhere. Open
Apr-Sept 10am-6pm, Oct-Mar 10am-12.30pm, 2-5.30pm.
Métro: Jussieu, Cardinal-Lemoine.*

For half of its life this building has led a schizophrenic existence.
It was initiated by Louis XV in thanksgiving for his recovery from
an illness, and was intended as a more magnificent shrine to
Paris' patroness Ste-Geneviève than the old abbey church of that
name (later demolished). Situated in a commanding position on
the Montagne Ste-Geneviève, it was built in the form of a Greek
cross, with a **dome** at the intersection and a massive **portico**
with Corinthian columns.

Hardly had it been completed than the new Revolutionary
government decided to change it from a church into a
mausoleum for the bodies of great Frenchmen. For this purpose,
many of the windows were removed and blocked up, hence its
rather bald and forbidding appearance. Twice it was to revert to
its role as a church and then be changed back to a secular
mausoleum. The last occasion was in 1885 when it was finally
secularized to provide a suitable resting place for Victor Hugo.
Did they consider that there was not enough room for God
and Hugo?

When you enter the building it strikes a chill, with its pale,
diluted light that filters down from the high windows and
through the clerestory in the dome, seeming to freeze as it falls
on the chaste stonework and the great empty expanse of floor.
However, as you look around, there is much to please the eye,
particularly the series of **paintings** by the 19thC symbolist Puvis
de Chavannes, depicting scenes from the lives of Ste-Geneviève
and St-Germain-d'Auxerre. His deliberately flat, pale colours
harmonize well with the building. There is also a horrifying
painting showing the newly decapitated St-Denis reaching out to
pick up his head as an astonished executioner looks on.

The **crypt**, which runs in a series of vaulted corridors beneath
the whole building, holds the remains of countless illustrious
Frenchmen. The tombs are housed in gloomy little rooms that
look for all the world like prison cells. Hugo shares one with Zola
— a curious pair of cell-mates. Rousseau's tomb is like a dog
kennel, out of which reaches a hand holding a torch. Others
buried here include the building's architect, Soufflot, the chemist
Berthelot and the Resistance leader Jean Moulin. A distinguished
assembly but one that the visitor is glad to escape from into the
light of day.

Paradis, Rue de

*10ᵉ. Map **5E10**. Métro: Château-d'Eau, Poissonnière.*
Unexpectedly situated in the rather characterless hinterland
between the *Grands Boulevards* and the Gare du Nord, this
street is monopolized by retailers of glass and ceramic tableware.
The goods displayed in these shops range from the
breathtakingly vulgar to the stunningly beautiful. At no.30 is the
glassware museum, **Musée des Cristalleries** (☎ 47-70-64-30
📷 *open Mon-Fri 9am-6pm, Sat 9am-noon, 2-5pm; closed Sun,
public holidays*), run by the firm of Baccarat and containing a
dazzling collection of glass objects dating from the early 19thC to
the present day.

Another interesting museum is the **Musée de la Publicité**
(Poster Museum) (☎ 42-46-13-09 🚇 *open noon-6pm; closed
Tues*) at no.18. There is a frequently changing programme of

exhibitions of posters and publicity material drawn from its archive of more than 120,000 items, some dating as far back as the end of the 18thC. Housed in the former premises of a ceramics manufacturer, it has a superbly tiled entrance.

Pasteur, Musée

25 Rue du Dr-Roux, 15ᵉ ☎ 45-68-82-82. Map 13L5 🔲 🎏
✗ by prior arrangement. Open 2-5.30pm. Closed Sat, Sun, Aug, public holidays. Métro: Pasteur.

The name of Louis Pasteur (1822-95) has been immortalized in the word "pasteurization". His development of immunization and other disease-controlling methods has become legendary, and has saved innumerable lives. Pasteur's house, now surrounded by the buildings of the Pasteur Institute, is a museum affording an interesting glimpse of both the scientific and private life of this great man. His remains rest in a magnificent tomb in the basement, built in the form of a small Byzantine chapel, with rich mosaics illustrating different aspects of his work.

Père Lachaise, Cimetière

20ᵉ. Map 19D5. Open daily. Métro: Père-Lachaise.

Like many old cemeteries, this one, the largest in Paris, has a powerfully romantic appeal. Named after Louis XIV's confessor, this cemetery was originally the site of a Jesuit house of retreat, and its hilly ground was laid out in 1804. The closely huddled graves encompass a wide variety of sepulchral art. It is easy to lose one's way among the twisting, tree-lined lanes, but in return for a small tip, the custodian will provide a map that marks the graves of the many celebrities buried here. These include Molière, Balzac, Chopin, Rossini, Colette, Edith Piaf, Oscar Wilde and Jim Morrison. The monument to Wilde is a massive block by Jacob Epstein, adorned with a winged Egyptian figure. One of the most visited graves is that of the spiritualist Allan Kardec, whose followers can sometimes be seen communing with his spirit by passing their hands over his statue. The tomb of Abelard and Héloise, erected in 1779, was thoroughly restored in 1990.

Petit Palais 🏛

Av. Winston-Churchill, 8ᵉ ☎ 42-65-12-73. Map 7G5 🔲
✗ by prior arrangement. Open 10am-5.40pm (hours of temporary exhibitions vary). Closed Mon, public holidays. Métro: Champs-Élysées-Clemenceau.

Completed in 1900 along with the neighbouring *Grand Palais*, the Petit Palais has rather more harmonious proportions and a less obtrusive personality than the other. Lying a stone's throw from the *Champs-Élysées*, it houses the **Musée des Beaux Arts de la Ville de Paris**, whose galleries divide into two groups.

In the galleries facing the outside of the building, you will pass from ancient Egyptian and Classical sculptures, through medieval and Renaissance art, to paintings, furniture and porcelain of the 18thC. The inner galleries are devoted to French art of the 19th and early 20thC. This is a wonderfully rich collection including works by Delacroix, Courbet, Corot, Manet, Monet, Cézanne, Pissarro, Sisley, Redon and Bonnard. Among famous individual works are Courbet's painting of two sleeping women, *Le Sommeil*, and Bonnard's vibrant *Nu dans le Bain*. Bonnard's palette is here on display as well — a riot of colour like his paintings. The museum also offers a programme of changing exhibitions.

The galleries are surrounded by a courtyard, which, with its

Roman-style colonnade, pool and garden, is a charming place for a short break.

Picasso, Musée

Hôtel Salé, 5 Rue de Thorigny, 3ᵉ ☎ 42-71-25-21. Map 11H11 🖼 *𝒳 & ▣ Open 9.15am-5.15pm (10pm Wed). Closed Tues. Métro: Chemin-Vert, St-Paul.*

Picasso was rare among major artists in that all his life he kept a significant proportion of his own paintings and sculpture for his personal collection. Much of this collection passed to the French government in lieu of tax after Picasso's death, and it was decided to create a new museum to house it. The Hôtel Salé, a gracious 17thC *Marais* mansion, both emphasizes and complements the modernity of Picasso's work.

Although many of his famous paintings are already in other museums, this collection gives a unique personal view of the whole span of Picasso's long, creative life. The works range from his astonishing childhood creations such as *Girl with Bare Feet*, painted when he was only 14, through his blue, rose and Cubist periods, to the inimitable style of his later years. The joy, anguish and turbulence of his private life are brought out in these works, for Picasso was an extraordinarily self-revelatory artist.

The museum contains works by other artists from Picasso's collection, including paintings by Cézanne, Renoir, Matisse and Rousseau.

Pompidou Centre *(Centre National d'Art et de Culture Georges-Pompidou)* 🏛 ★

Plateau Beaubourg, 4ᵉ ☎ 42-77-12-33. Map 10H10 ▣ ⇥ ✱ 🖼 *for museums* 🖼 *on Sun. Day passes available 𝒳 daily at 3.30pm with English-speaking guides. Open Mon, Wed, Thurs, Fri noon-10pm; Sat, Sun, public holidays 10am-10pm. Closed Tues. Métro: Hôtel-de-Ville, Rambuteau, Châtelet.*

Like the Eiffel Tower nearly a century ago, the Centre Georges-Pompidou (or **Beaubourg** as it is informally called) has aroused both shock and admiration. It is now one of the major attractions of the city, and a place that pulsates with energy. Shaped like a giant matchbox on its side, brightly painted as though in a child's colouring book, and enveloped in a cat's cradle of gleaming steel girders, it looks like a crazy oil refinery. Even if you are a die-hard opponent of modern architecture, it will take your breath away, especially if you come upon it at night, when, confronted by its glittering expanse, you might think you had wandered onto the set of a science-fiction film.

It is one of the most revolutionary buildings of its age. Built on the initiative of President Georges Pompidou as part of the redevelopment of Les Halles and opened in 1977, it was designed by the British architect Richard Rogers and the Italian Renzo Piano. The building is turned, as it were, inside-out, so that its intestines — pipes, shafts, escalators, etc. — are festooned around the outside, thus liberating large areas of space within. The main escalator runs in a transparent tube up the front of the building, so that the visitor can see a changing panorama of the city while ascending the five storeys.

The Beaubourg radiates a sense of celebration that spills over into the surrounding area. As a foretaste of the building itself, the visitor crosses a huge sloping piazza, which is the scene of perpetual "happenings". Here one may come across a poet, a juggler, a fire-eater or a group of street actors.

The function of the Beaubourg is to provide a multi-media centre in which modern art and culture are made excitingly accessible. Its four main departments are listed here.

Musée National d'Art Moderne
Opening hours as for centre.

Housed on the third and fourth floors, this is the largest museum of its kind in the world, and one of the most stimulating. The third floor is devoted to frequently changing exhibitions of contemporary works, that is from about 1965 to the present, and these vary constantly. The fourth floor houses a permanent exhibition of works from 1905 onwards, starting with **Fauvism** (from the French *fauve*, meaning wild beast) and progressing through **Cubism**, **Abstract Expressionism**, **Dadaism**, **Surrealism**, and other movements right up to the present day.

Under Cubism, for example, you will find a number of painters who, in their different ways, shared the same tendencies: an interest in elementary forms, such as the cube and the cylinder, and a renunciation of colour in favour of light and shape. The works represented include Georges Braque's *Young Girl with a Guitar*, Picasso's *Seated Woman* and Fernand Léger's *La Noce*, which also anticipates Futurism in its suggestion of movement through repetition of shapes in a sequence. In a similar way, Surrealism is represented by artists as diverse as Salvador Dalí, Max Ernst and Joan Miró, all of whom subsequently developed in very different directions.

Progressing through the galleries, you will find that certain artists reappear as they pass through different phases. Picasso crops up at intervals as his style and subject matter change. We see him pass through a period of interest in Classical antiquity, exemplified by his *Minotaur*, then his work becomes increasingly abstract. Other painters — Kandinsky, Matisse, Braque, Léger — also manifest changing styles. Thus one perceives the dynamic way in which 20thC art has developed, with schools merging, overlapping and breaking away.

The works also include many sculptures, such as Constantin Brancusi's deliciously simple *Seal* in grey and white marble, and Raoul Haussmann's Dadaist work *The Spirit of our Times*, showing a dummy-like head with a tape-measure, purse, watch and other oddments stuck to the skull.

For a proper understanding of this museum and the way the paintings are presented, it is worth joining a guided tour (details above) with one of the centre's lively *animateurs*. Alternatively there is an excellent audio guide to the collection.

Bibliothèque Publique d'Information *(Public Information Library)*
This is essentially a library (**Ⓘ**) of the 20thC; it has some half a million books, and plans to reach a million.

Centre de Création Industrielle *(Industrial Design Centre)*
A gallery on the ground floor presents exhibitions on all aspects of our planned environment.

Institut de Recherches Contemporaines Acoustiques Musicales
(Institute for Contemporary Acoustic and Musical Research)
The underground studios are closed to the public, but lectures and demonstrations are held here. On the top floor there is a large gallery for temporary exhibitions.

Other features of the Beaubourg include a **library** and supervised **play centre** for children, a reconstruction of the **studio of the sculptor Brancusi**, a lively cinema (the **Salle Garance**), an **auditorium** for lectures, concerts and theatrical performances, and a top-floor self-service **restaurant**, with a superb view over Paris.

Pont Alexandre III

7ᵉ and 8ᵉ. Map 7H5. Métro: Champs-Élysées-Clemenceau, Invalides.

The broadest bridge in Paris and also one of the most beautiful, it forms part of a great triumphal way leading down Av. Winston-Churchill, past the *Grand Palais* and *Petit Palais*, across the Seine and down the esplanade to *Les Invalides*. It was built for the 1900 World Exhibition and named after Tsar Alexander III of Russia (1845-94).

The bridge is flanked by two massive pillars at each end, whose recently re-gilded decorations represent, on the Right Bank, medieval and modern France, and, on the Left, Renaissance France and the era of Louis XIV. All along the bridge are cast-iron lamp standards with the ornate, prosperous look that characterized the *Belle Époque*.

Pont-Neuf

1ᵉʳ. Map 9I8. Métro: Pont-Neuf.

"Of all the bridges which were ever built, the whole world who have passed over the Pont-Neuf must own that it is the noblest, the finest, the grandest, the lightest, the longest, the broadest that ever conjoined land and land together upon the face of the tremendous globe."

Thus wrote the 18thC English novelist Laurence Sterne of the bridge that spans the *Seine* in two sections, divided by the w spike of the *Île de la Cité*. He might have added that, despite its name, it is also the oldest.

Completed in 1607 under Henry IV, whose equestrian statue stands at the centre, it has 12 arches, all of slightly different sizes. The cornices overlooking the river are carved with a row of amusing faces caricaturing Henry IV's ministers and courtiers, and there are comic carvings of stall-holders, pickpockets and tooth-drawers.

The bridge, the two halves of which are not quite in line, was designed by Androuet du Cerceau. A 10yr improvement scheme will reach completion in 2001.

Porte St-Denis and Porte St-Martin

10ᵉ. Map 10F10. Métro: Strasbourg-St-Denis, St-Martin.

These two triumphal arches, situated close to one another on the *Grands Boulevards*, were built in the 1670s to commemorate Louis XIV's military victories. They replaced two fortified gates that had disappeared along with the old perimeter wall. Both bear reliefs glorifying the Sun King, but the Porte St-Denis is the grander and more elaborate of the two.

Poste, Musée de la

34 Bd. de Vaugirard, 15ᵉ ☎ 43-20-15-30. Map 13L5 ▩
✗ on request. Open 10am-5pm. Closed Sun, public holidays. Métro: Montparnasse-Bienvenue, Pasteur, Falguière.

Did you know that in 1870, during the Siege of Paris, microfilm messages were carried out of the city by pigeons whose wings were stamped with a postmark? This is one of many snippets of information to be gleaned here, in four floors of imaginative displays on philately and the history of worldwide postal communication — everything relating to the subject, from postmen's uniforms and mailboxes to modern sorting machines and stamp-making equipment. There are stamps galore and a ground-floor gallery showing postage-stamp art.

Préfecture de Police, Musée des collections historiques de la

4 Rue de la Montagne-Ste-Geneviève, 5ᵉ ☎ *43-29-21-57. Map 10J9* ▨ *Open Mon-Thurs 9am-5pm, Fri 9am-4.30pm. Métro: Maubert-Mutualité, St-Michel.*

A sober but fascinating collection of documents and objects is housed in this little museum in the heart of the *Latin Quarter*. It presents a panorama of police and criminal activity in Paris from the *ancien régime* to the 20thC.

It includes a frightening display of criminal tools and weapons, and documents such as the orders for the arrest of such prominent figures as Danton and Marat's assassin Charlotte Corday.

Quatre-Saisons, Fontaine des *(Four Seasons Fountain)*

57-59 Rue de Grenelle, 7ᵉ. Map 8I6. Métro: Rue-du-Bac.
When this fountain was built by Bouchardon in the 1730s, to supply water to the district, Voltaire complained that such a splendid monument should not have been erected in so narrow a street.

He had a point, for the two-tiered facade cannot be seen to best effect unless you are standing immediately in front of it. A central portico with a seated figure representing Paris is flanked by elegant reclining personifications of the Seine and Marne; and on either side are curved walls adorned with statues of the four seasons.

Radio-France, Musée de 🏛

116 Av. du Président Kennedy, 16ᵉ ☎ *42-30-21-80. Map 12I1* ▨ & ✻ *in museum* ✗ *compulsory, at 10.30am, 11.30am, 2.30pm, 3.30pm, 4.30pm. Closed Sun, public holidays. Métro: Ranelagh, Passy, Mirabeau.*

This huge glass-and-aluminium edifice, shaped like a giant cylinder, is the nerve centre of French radio. Built between 1953-63, it is a statistician's delight — 500m (800yds) in circumference, with 3,500 personnel, 58 studios and 1,000 offices.

Architecturally, though, it may leave the visitor cold. Its main attractions are the extensive **museum of the history of radio and television** and the concerts and shows held there on a regular basis.

Renan-Scheffer, Maison *(Musée de la Vie Romantique)*

16 Rue Chaptal, 9ᵉ ☎ *48-74-95-38. Map 4D8* ▨ ✗ *Open 10am-5.40pm. Closed Mon, public holidays. Métro: St-Georges, Blanche.*

From 1830 this secluded house in Montmartre was the home of the painter Ary Scheffer and the scene of Friday-evening salons attended by such celebrities as Delacroix, Liszt, George Sand and Chopin. Another guest was the writer Ernest Renan, who married Scheffer's niece. Their daughter later took over the house and continued to hold salons there.

It is now a branch of the *Carnavalet* Museum. The ground floor houses a permanent exhibition of portraits and memorabilia connected with George Sand. The first floor is reserved for temporary exhibitions periodically culled from the Carnavalet collections and relating to many aspects of the literary and artistic life of the 19thC.

Rivoli, Rue de

1er and 4e. Maps 8,9,10&11. Métro: Hôtel-de-Ville, Châtelet, Louvre, Palais-Royal, Tuileries, Concorde.

Like so many long Parisian thoroughfares, Rue de Rivoli begins with one personality and ends with another. It starts at *Pl. de la Concorde* and runs down beside the *Tuileries* and the *Louvre* in a long, uniform colonnade, with many smart shops and an elegant café or two — a place for promenading in style. This section was laid out between 1800-35.

Beyond the Louvre, the street becomes progressively less formal as it wends its way past the *Hôtel de Ville* and on into the *Marais*. It ends, however, not with a whimper but with a bang, with the marvellous facade of the church of **St-Paul-St-Louis**.

Rodin, Musée ▥ ★

Hôtel Biron, 77 Rue de Varenne, 7e ☎ 47-05-01-34. Map 13I5 ▨ & ▣ Open 10am-5.30pm (4.30pm in winter). Closed Mon. Métro: Varenne.

Auguste Rodin (1840-1917) is widely considered to be the greatest sculptor of the 19thC. You will see why when you visit this museum, housed in a splendid 18thC mansion near *Les Invalides*. It is impossible not to marvel at the way in which Rodin magically transformed stone, clay or bronze into the living tissue of human emotion and experience. Take, for example, his famous work, *Le Baiser* (The Kiss), which powerfully evokes in white marble the tenderness of love between man and woman; or his *Homme qui Marche* (Walking Man), which embodies all the urgency and thrust of human aspiration; or *La Cathédrale*, where a pair of hands speaks of piety and contemplation.

The delightful garden surrounding the museum makes an ideal setting for many of Rodin's works. Here we find, among others, casts of his *Balzac*, *Le Penseur* (The Thinker), *La Porte de l'Enfer* (The Gates of Hell) and *Les Bourgeois de Calais* (The Burghers of Calais). Temporary exhibitions of work by other artists are held in a building to the right of the entrance.

The lovely **Hôtel Biron** was built by Gabriel The Elder for a rich wig-maker in 1728, and was subsequently lived in by, among others, Marshal Biron, who was beheaded in 1793. Later the building became a convent, and much of the painted and gilt panelling was ripped out, although some has been restored.

At the beginning of this century the building was bought by the state and was made available for artists. Rodin himself occupied a ground-floor studio from 1907 until his death. A massive development of the museum will take place from 1991-94, allowing more of the collection to be displayed, together with the work of other sculptors. Plans submitted by architect Henri Gaudin include the relocation of the reception area and administrative offices into the old chapel, and the creation of an underground viewing gallery, linked to the basement of the existing building.

Sacré-Coeur, Basilique du ▥ ★

Pl. du Parvis-du-Sacré-Coeur, 18e ☎ 42-51-17-02. Map 4C9. Church ▣ & Open 6.45am-11pm. Dome and crypt ▨ & Open Apr-Sept 9.15am-7pm; Oct-Mar call for details. Métro: Abbesses, Anvers, Château-Rouge, Lamarck-Caulaincourt.

Subject of countless travel posters and paintings, the Sacré-Coeur has acquired the status of a visual cliché. However, seen afresh, in its superb setting on *Montmartre's* hill, the Butte, it has stunning impact and beauty, whether glimpsed from a train as it draws into one of the northern stations, or revealed suddenly as you turn a corner on one of the old streets nearby. (See also *Montmartre*)

The church rose, phoenix-like, from the ashes of the Franco-Prussian War of 1870. As a reaction to the despair aroused by France's defeat, parliament vowed, in 1873, to erect a church in Paris as a symbol of contrition and a manifestation of hope. A competition was held and there were 78 entries. The winner was an architect named Abadie, with a Romano-Byzantine design. The first stone was laid in 1875 and the cathedral was completed by 1914, but the World War delayed its consecration until 1919. Since 1885, worshippers have kept up perpetual adoration before the high altar, continuing night and day even through the German occupation.

The material used for the church was Château-Landon stone, which hardens and whitens with age — notice how much greyer the stonework of the interior is, compared with the gleaming exterior. The design is not to everyone's taste, but many find the outline of its five beehive-like domes pleasing.

Approach the church by the long flight of steps from the S (you can go part of the way by railway). This way you get the full impact of the main facade, with its great portico surmounted on each side by equestrian statues of St-Louis and Joan of Arc. The bell tower to the N, higher than the rest of the church, contains one of the largest bells in the world, weighing more than 17 tonnes.

The inside is light and elegantly proportioned. The eye follows the great rounded arching sweeps of stonework, up to the cupola with its clerestory and its two encircling balconies and down again to the nave, coming to rest on the natural focal point of the interior, the great mosaic in the alcove above the high altar. This **mosaic**, one of the largest in the world, depicts Christ with outstretched arms, exposing a golden heart, while grouped around him are worshippers, including the Virgin, St Michael and Joan of Arc.

The crypt, entered by a stairway from the W aisle, is somewhat gloomy and severe. It contains the church treasury and a number of chapels, the central one possessing a *Pièta* on the altar. By the same stairway one ascends to the dome, with vertiginous views down into the church and out over Paris.

St-Denis, Basilique 🏛

Pl. de l'Hôtel-de-Ville, St-Denis. Map 19B4 ☎ *Open Apr-Sept Mon-Sat 10am-7pm, Sun 1-7pm; Oct-Mar Mon-Sat 10am-5pm, Sun 1pm-5pm. Métro: St-Denis-Basilique.*
Visitors on their way to Paris from Charles-de-Gaulle Airport are often surprised to see an imposing cathedral rising out of grim industrial surroundings. It is the Basilique St-Denis, necropolis of the kings of France and precursor of the Gothic style of architecture that was soon to sweep over Europe.

It was in the 12thC that the learned Abbot Suger, friend of Louis VII, decided to rebuild his church dedicated to the Apostle of France, St-Denis. Having been beheaded in Montmartre by the ungrateful Gallo-Romans for trying to show them Christianity, St-Denis walked northwards with his head tucked under his arm until he fell down, on the spot where his church was later founded. The prestige of being buried near the relics of a saint made the church a natural choice for a royal necropolis for all but a handful of French kings and their queens, starting with

Dagobert in the 7thC. The **tombs and statuary** of the kings are as good a reason for visiting St-Denis as the church itself. The tombs are empty, however. During the Revolution, 800 royal bodies were pitched into a communal grave in the crypt under the N transept. Luckily the tombs were saved from destruction, the archaeologist Lenoir having had the foresight to remove them to safety some time earlier.

In the late 13thC, Louis IX (St-Louis) ordered purely symbolic effigies of all his ancestors back to the 7thC, but, from the death of Philippe The Bold in 1285, likenesses were taken from real portraits. Notice particularly the **Renaissance mausoleums** of François I and Henry II. Unfortunately, all the tombs are chained off, and close inspection is difficult.

The beginnings of lightness, harmony and rational disposition of the elements in the church itself, proclaim the spirit of a new age and the close of the Dark Ages. Elements that had been developed separately were now combined for the first time: the Latin cross plan with radiating pilgrimage chapels, the pointed arch, the ribbed groin vault. You can see these facets of Suger's original plan in the ambulatory, apse and facade. The latter has an air of dissymmetry, with its pointed Gothic and rounded Romanesque arches and its missing N tower. The facade boasts the first-ever **rose window**, a feature which was soon to become standard.

Within the church, a further progress towards lightness was made in the next century, when the architect Pierre de Montreuil gave the nave, side aisles and chancel an architectural lift that recalls his masterwork, *La Sainte-Chapelle*.

St-Étienne-du-Mont ▥
Pl. Ste-Geneviève, 5ᵉ. Map 15K9. Open daily. Métro: Cardinal-Lemoine.
Built between 1492-1626, the church is a mixture of styles that defy all the rules of architectural purity. The result is rather like a crazy composite photograph, amalgamating elements from contrasting buildings. Take the main **facade**, for example, with its three pediments piled one on top of the other, combining Classical motifs with a Gothic rose window stuck in the middle. The **belfry** is similarly eclectic, begun in the Medieval style and topped with a little Renaissance dome. Nevertheless, the whole effect is pleasing.

The interior, which preserves greater consistency of style, has some remarkable features, notably the 16thC **rood screen**, with its delicately pierced stonework and its two flanking spiral stairways. This is the only surviving rood screen in Paris. Notice also the flamboyant **vaulting** over the transept, the 5.5m(18ft) hanging **keystone**, the splendidly ornate **organ loft** (1630) and the richly carved wooden **pulpit** (1650). At the W end of the nave is a slab indicating where the Archbishop of Paris was assassinated by an unfrocked priest in 1857. Those buried in the church include the writers Pascal and Racine, both commemorated by plaques on either side of the entrance to the Lady Chapel.

There is also a **chapel to Ste-Geneviève**, created in 1803 and containing the stone on which her body had rested in the former abbey church of Ste-Geneviève before her remains were destroyed during the Revolution. All that is left of her body is a bone or two, now preserved in an elaborate reliquary.

Although the church was badly plundered and damaged during the Revolution, it was later skilfully restored and today contains

some valuable works of art. Particularly striking is the series of
stained-glass windows in the cloister.

St-Eustache ✠✠✠
2 Rue du Jour, 1ᵉʳ. Map 10H9. Open 9am-7pm. Métro: Les Halles.

This lovely church, the largest in Paris after *Notre-Dame*,
deserves to be better known than it is. For centuries it has stood
at the focal point of Parisian history and, until recently, was the
local church of Les Halles market. Now it surveys the new
Forum des Halles with the solid equanimity of the Middle Ages
confronting the transience of the present day. The site was
originally occupied by a small 13thC chapel to Ste-Agnes. This
was later rededicated to St-Eustache, the 2ndC Roman who, like
St-Hubert later on, is said to have seen a vision of the Cross
between the antlers of a stag. The building as we see it today,
with its elegant flying buttresses, took shape between 1532-1640
and is a curious mixture, the form being Gothic, the details
Classical.

Many famous names crop up in the history of the church.
Cardinal Richelieu, Mme de Pompadour and Molière were
baptized in it, and Louis XIV celebrated his first communion here.
During the Revolution, the church was pillaged, then made a
Temple of Agriculture. In 1844 it suffered a worse fate, when it
was devastated by a fire. It was completely restored by Baltard
and today stands as one of the finest of Paris' architectural
monuments.

The interior is thrilling, with its exhilarating vertical emphasis.
Everything thrusts upwards to the ceiling with its delicate
network of **ribbed vaulting** and elaborately **carved bosses**. The
stained glass is luxurious, and there are some important **works
of art** here, including an early Rubens, *Pilgrims at Emmaus*, and
Pigalle's sculpture of the Virgin, on the altar of the Lady Chapel.

One of the church's proudest possessions is its **organ**. This is
one of the finest in the city, and its restoration was completed in
1989. Concerts are held here periodically, carrying on a well-
established musical tradition. It was here in 1855 that Berlioz
conducted the first performance of his *Te Deum*.

St-Germain l'Auxerrois ✠✠✠
2 Pl. du Louvre, 1ᵉʳ. Map 9H9. Open daily. Métro: Louvre, Pont-Neuf.

Opposite the E end of the *Louvre* stands a church that embodies
a fascinating resumé of medieval architecture. There has been a
church on this site since the 6thC, when an oratory dedicated to
St-Germanus was built. The present building is the fourth on the
spot and is a combination of 500yrs of architectural design.

12thC: the oldest part of the building is the Romanesque
belfry behind the transept crossing. It played a sombre role
during the Wars of Religion when, in 1572, Catherine de Medici
ordered the bells to ring out to signal the start of the Massacre of
St-Bartholomew. Three thousand Huguenots, in town to
celebrate the marriage of Henri de Navarre to his cousin
Marguerite de Valois, were slaughtered in their beds and thrown
from the windows.

13thC: the Gothic **ambulatory** and **chancel**, the **Lady
Chapel** on the right and the **central portal** were all added.

14thC: St-Germain l'Auxerrois became the royal parish church
when Charles V transformed the Louvre from fortress to medieval
palace. The **nave** dates from this century.

15thC: the unusual and Flamboyant Gothic **porch** was built, with its lovely multi-ribbed vaulting.

16thC: the Renaissance came, leaving its mark on the **doorway** N of the choir. The late Gothic **transept portals** were added.

In the **17thC**, Versailles was built, the court abandoned the Louvre to the court artists, who made their studios there, and St-Germain became their parish church. Many artists, sculptors and poets are buried here. Even today artists and show people come here on Ash Wednesday to celebrate a special mass. Royalists have not been forgotten: every year on Jan 21, the anniversary of his execution in 1793, a mass is said for Louis XVI.

St-Germain-des-Prés Ⅲ
Pl. St-Germain-des-Prés, 6ᵉ. Map 9I8. Open daily. Métro: St-Germain-des-Prés.

The oldest church in Paris stands passively at the hub of the lively *St-Germain Quarter*. Its origin dates back to AD542, when the Merovingian King Childebert I, son of Clovis, brought back from Spain the tunic of St-Vincent, and a golden cross said to have been made by Solomon. To receive these relics he built a monastery and church which was at first called the Basilica of St-Vincent and St-Croix but later came to be named after St Germanus, the Bishop of Paris, who consecrated the church in AD558 and was buried there.

As the burial place of the Merovingian kings and a seat of the great Benedictine order, it became virtually a miniature state in its own right, possessing 17,000ha (42,000 acres) of land, its buildings fortified by towers and a moat fed from the Seine. For centuries it stood in meadows called the Pré aux Clercs (a curious thought, this, as you survey the contemporary city-centre scene).

The church was destroyed twice by the Normans, and its present form dates from the 11thC. During the Revolution, the abbey was dissolved and the property subjected to an orgy of vandalism in which the royal tombs and most of the buildings were destroyed, the church itself being turned into a saltpetre factory. Of the once-splendid complex, only the church, minus its transepts, and the abbot's palace on the NE side remain.

Except for a few capitals and columns, nothing that can be seen in the church is earlier than 11thC. The interior is an interesting mixture of different periods, with its **Romanesque arches**, Gothic **vaulting** and polychrome **wall painting** by the 19thC artist Hippolyte Flandrin. The **works of art** in the church include a 14thC Virgin and Child known as *Notre-Dame de Consolation*, and a number of fine **tombs**, including that of John Casimir, a 17thC Polish king who became abbot of St-Germain. There are also tombs of two Scottish noblemen, William and James Douglas, courtiers of Henry IV and Louis XIII respectively.

Beside the church, facing S, a little garden shaded by chestnut trees is a tranquil and secluded refuge from the busy Bd. St-Germain.

St-Germain Quarter
6ᵉ and 7ᵉ. Maps 8&9, 14&15. Métro: St-Germain-des-Prés, Rue-du-Bac, Solférino, Mabillon, Odéon.

The St-Germain district is really made up of two adjacent quarters: **St-Germain-des-Prés**, consisting roughly of the northern half of the 6ᵉ; and the **Faubourg-St-Germain**, comprising the NE section of the 7ᵉ. These two areas have their own distinct personalities, complementing each other well.

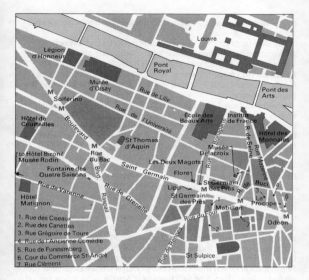

1. Rue des Ciseaux
2. Rue des Canettes
3. Rue Grégoire de Tours
4. Rue de l'Ancienne Comédie
5. Rue de Furstemberg
6. Cour du Commerce St-André
7. Rue Clément

The former community first grew up around the great medieval monastery and church of *St-Germain-des-Prés*, but for centuries it lay outside the Paris boundaries and remained cut off from the life of the city. Its only link with the Right Bank was a ferry (*bac*), which was reached by Rue du Bac. This remained the case until the 17thC, when Louis XIV began to extend the *Louvre*, for which purpose stone had to be brought from the quarries at Denfert-Rochereau in the s. The ferry was too slow a means of bringing it across the river, and so the **Pont-Royal** was built, ending the isolation of St-Germain.

It was also Louis XIV who established the *École des Beaux-Arts*, across the river from the Louvre. Later, after the Louvre had become a museum, the narrow footbridge known as the Passerelle des Arts (now **Pont des Arts**) was built, to allow the students to cross the river to look at the works of art. The construction of the Pont-Royal turned St-Germain-des-Prés into a thriving community, and it soon became a favourite haunt of writers and intellectuals.

The Faubourg- (suburb) St-Germain is, as the name implies, of more recent origin. During the reign of Louis XIV, the aristocracy had been concentrated around the court at Versailles, but under the more relaxed regime of Louis XV they felt able to take up residence in Paris again and chose the plain to the E of *Les Invalides* as the place to build their homes.

The result can be seen today in the gracious houses that line such streets as **Rue de Lille**, **Rue de l'Université**, **Rue de Grenelle** and **Rue de Varenne**. In recent years the majority of the larger ones have become government buildings or embassies. The **Hôtel de Matignon** (*57 Rue de Varenne*) is now the residence of the Prime Minister, while the **Hôtel de Courteilles** (*110 Rue de Grenelle*) has become the Ministry of Education. Rue de Grenelle is also the site of the lovely *Quatre-Saisons* fountain. A few well-heeled families still live in the area, and the atmosphere retains the privileged, inward-looking quality that it has always possessed, whether dominated by aristocrats or civil servants.

The buildings belong to a felicitous period when French architecture had thrown off the Italian influence and blossomed into a light but restrained elegance. This was typified by the **Hôtel Biron** (★) at the western end of Rue de Varenne. Now the **Rodin** museum, this is one of the few houses in the area that the public can enter.

Edward Bulwer-Lytton described the Faubourg-St-Germain vividly in his novel, *Pelham*: "I love that *quartier*! If ever I go to Paris again I shall reside there.... *There*, indeed, you are among the French, the fossilized remains of the old régime — the very houses have an air of desolate, yet venerable grandeur....You cross one of the numerous bridges, and you enter another time — you are inhaling the atmosphere of a past century; no flaunting *boutique*, French in its trumpery, English in its prices, stares you in the face....Vast hotels, with their gloomy frontals and magnificent contempt for comfort; shops, such as shops might have been in the aristocratic days of Louis Quatorze....all strike on the mind with a vague and nameless impression of antiquity; a something solemn even in gaiety, and faded in pomp, appears to linger over all you behold."

The link between these two areas is Bd. St-Germain, a great bow-shaped thoroughfare which touches the Seine at each end. Begin a stroll down the boulevard perhaps somewhere near the secluded little church of **St-Thomas d'Aquin**, which lies just off the route to the N. This is still the Faubourg-St-Germain, but, approaching the church of *St-Germain-des-Prés* itself, everything becomes busier, more colourful and more cosmopolitan. Turn right opposite the church into **Rue des Ciseaux**, a little Italian enclave with many pizzerias. This spills over into **Rue des Canettes** (Duckling St.), which runs up to *St-Sulpice* — notice the ducklings over the doorway of no.18. Farther E, **Rue Grégoire de Tours** is full of Greek restaurants. This street leads into **Rue de Buci**. Here and in the neighbouring **Rue de Seine** is one of the best outdoor food markets in the city of Paris. Sadly, the arched entrances to the **Marché St-Germain**, built in 1810, in **Rue Clément**, are under threat of demolition, to make way for a modern food market, offices and parking. It might be worth a look to see whether or not the forces of today prevailed.

Nearby is the church of *St-Germain-des-Prés*, dominating the crossroads of Bd. St-Germain, Rue de Rennes and Rue Bonaparte. This is the heart of the district that has come to be known as the "*Capitale des Lettres*" (Literary Capital), a role that it began to take on in the 17thC when the Comédie Française played in what is now Rue de l'Ancienne Comédie. **Le Procope** (see *Restaurants*) at no.**13**, was the haunt of Molière, Corneille, Racine and, in later centuries, Voltaire, Balzac, Verlaine and Anatole France.

Between the wars, the quarter was fuelled by an influx of writers from Montmartre and Montparnasse, who met habitually in the three great cafés in front of St-Germain-des-Prés: **Flore, Lipp** and **Les Deux Magots** (see *Cafés*). Publishers, booksellers, painters and art dealers also set up shop there in increasing numbers.

After World War II, St-Germain became the headquarters of a new generation of intelligentsia, revolving around Jean-Paul Sartre and the Existentialists. In those days they crowded into jazz cellars such as the Tabou in Rue Dauphine, and small bars such as the Bar Vert in Rue Jacob. The atmosphere of the district has changed since then, but the "*Germanopratins*", as the inhabitants are called, remain friendly and lively, and there is always plenty to do and see, especially around Pl. St-Germain-des-Prés by the church, where most evenings you will find street performers at work.

A gentler atmosphere of festivity is often to be found nearby in the quaint little tree-lined **Rue de Furstemberg**, where the glow of the old-fashioned street lamps attracts singers, guitarists and harpists. The great 19thC artist Delacroix had his studio here (now the *Delacroix* museum), and the Romantic spirit is still strongly felt, especially at night.

Apart from the Delacroix, there are few museums in this part of Paris. As well as the *Musée d'Orsay* and the *Rodin*, there is the *Musée de la Monnaie* and the *Légion d'Honneur*. However, the district makes up for this deficiency in the density of its small art galleries (mostly around Rue de Seine and Rue Mazarine) and its second-hand bookshops. If you like to drink coffee while you browse, you can try the bookshop-café **Un Moment... en Plus** (*1 Rue de Varenne, 7ᵉ* ☎ *42-22-23-45*).

There are many little pockets in St-Germain where history can be found. One of them is **Cour du Commerce-St-André**, an alley off Rue St-André-des-Arts. If you look through the windows of no.**4** you will see part of one of the towers of the medieval city wall. No.**9** was the site of the workshop of a German carpenter called Schmidt, who built the first guillotine and tested it out on unfortunate sheep.

Much of the attraction of St-Germain lies in unexpected moments of visual delight: an old shop front, a flourish of carved stonework above a well-proportioned doorway, the glimpse of a cobbled courtyard through an arch. It is an area to be seen at leisure if its many attractions are not to be missed.

St-Joseph-des-Carmes ▥
*70 Rue de Vaugirard, 6ᵉ. Map **14**J7. Métro: Rennes, St-Placide.*

This elegant little church forms part of the **Institut Catholique de Paris** complex, which stands on the site once occupied by a great Carmelite monastery with vast gardens, many treasures and a priceless library.

During the Revolution, the monastery was closed, its treasures confiscated and the buildings turned into a prison where, in September 1792, 115 priests and three bishops were massacred. Their bones are buried in the crypt of the church, which today possesses a gloomy atmosphere despite its fine works of art. These include, to the left of the transept, a marble *Virgin and Child* after a model by Bernini.

St-Julien-le-Pauvre ▥
*1 Rue St-Julien-le-Pauvre, 5ᵉ. Map **10**J9. Open daily. Métro: St-Michel, Cluny-La-Sorbonne.*

This enchanting little building, set in a charming garden, **Sq. René Viviani**, facing *Notre-Dame* from the Left Bank, is the oldest complete church in Paris, built between 1170-1240. Only parts of *St-Germain-des-Prés* are older. The beauty of the interior, with its elegantly foliated **capitals**, is all the more potent for its modesty. The **wooden screen** (iconostasis) across the choir is a reminder that this is now a church of the Melchite (Greek Catholic) rite. From the square there is also an attractive view across Rue St-Jacques to *St-Séverin*.

St-Michel, Boulevard

St-Michel, Boulevard   Called the **Boul 'Mich**, this is the main artery of the Left Bank. See *Latin Quarter*.

St-Nicolas-des-Champs ⅢⅢ
254 Rue St-Martin, 3ᵉ. Map 10G10. Open daily. Métro: Arts-et-Métiers.
Begun in the 12thC, this church boasts distinguished features from different periods: a Flamboyant Gothic **facade** and **belfry**, a fine Renaissance **doorway** on the S side and many paintings from the 17th-19thC. In the St-Michel chapel, a pudgy archangel steps daintily on a pitiful bald-headed devil. The high altar is curiously like a stone bath complete with lion's feet. In short, the church is a mixture of beauty and bathos.

St-Roch ⅢⅢ
296 Rue St-Honoré, 1ᵉʳ. Map 8G7. Open daily. Métro: Pyramides, Tuileries.
As Paris grew westward in the 17thC, the need arose for a new parish church in the vicinity of the *Palais-Royal*. St-Roch was created, and the author of the *Grand Siècle*, Louis XIV himself, laid the first stone in 1635. The interior is marked by some of the great creative personalities that make the 17thC alive to us today. There is the tomb of André Le Nôtre, a kind old man, friend to Louis XIV and the first gardener to make history, with the park of Versailles. He also created the nearby *Tuileries*. Other **tombs** include those of the playwright Corneille and the philosopher Diderot.

The church itself was designed by some of the most important architects of the 17thC, notably Jacques Lemercier, and work was prolonged into the 18thC, making for a combination of Classical and Baroque elements, with a Jesuit-style facade designed by de Cotte in 1736.

Unlike the Gothic churches of Paris, the church is not oriented E-W but N-S because of the terrain. It is also unusually long, with one chapel following another, beyond the chancel.

In the **nave**, one can admire the vaulting, which has penetrating arches. This part of the building was financed in 1719 by John Law, the Scottish wheeler-dealer of the Mississippi Bubble. Notice the **pulpit** in the highly theatrical Baroque style by Challe (1755). The round-domed room beyond the chancel, the **Lady Chapel**, was designed by Jules Hardouin-Mansart. Its ceiling portrays the cloudscape of the *Triumph of the Virgin* by J.B. Pierre (1750); and above the altar, with its nativity group, is a mass of clouds in gilded stucco. Behind the Lady Chapel is the small Holy Communion Chapel, and behind this a Calvary Chapel. The church has three organs and excellent acoustics, making it a splendid musical auditorium, and concerts take place regularly.

On leaving, one should pause by the bullet-riddled **facade**. These are a reminder of a terrible battle that took place in front of the church in 1795. The Republican Convention was under attack by royalists and anarchists, but thanks to the technical skill of the leader of the Republican forces, the Revolution was saved. The leader: a 27-year-old general, Napoleon Bonaparte.

St-Séverin ⅢⅢ
Rue des Prêtres St-Séverin, 5ᵉ. Map 10J9. Open daily. Métro: St-Michel.
Tucked away among the labyrinth of narrow streets in the *Latin Quarter* to the E of Bd. St-Michel, St-Séverin is one of the most

cherished medieval churches in the city, possessing a quiet magic all of its own. The church is named after two saints named Séverin: a hermit who once lived on the site in an oratory dedicated to St-Martin, and a namesake of the same era who was Abbot of Agaune.

The present building was begun in the early 13thC and was much altered and enlarged in the 15thC, when it was stamped with the so-called "Flamboyant" (flame-like) style to be seen in the shape of the stonework in the **stained-glass windows**. The double **ambulatory**, with its forest of columns, one of them with twisted veins, is particularly fine.

What the church lacks in size it makes up for in the perfection of its proportions and the delicacy of its decoration. Every arch, column, piece of ribbed vaulting and lozenge of stained glass sings out in joyful harmony. Perhaps this is why it is such a wonderful place for listening to music — don't miss a concert here if you get the chance. The only discordant note is the ungainly Baroque touch given to the chancel in the 18thC when part of the arcade was rounded and faced with false marble — the effect is comparable to that of a nun wearing an ostrich-feather hat.

Adjoining the church to the S is a little garden shaded by trees and bordered on two sides by the arcades of the former charnel house. Standing in the garden (possible during concerts), one feels one is in a time-warp, for beyond the cloistered calm stands the neon-lit front of a restaurant.

St-Sulpice ▥

Pl. St-Sulpice, 6°. Map 15J8. Open Mon-Sat. Closed Sun, except services. Métro: St-Sulpice.

Unlike many of the other great churches of Paris, this one does not form part of an imposing townscape. It looms unexpectedly out of the maze of narrow streets to the N of the *Palais de Luxembourg*.

Starting life as a modest medieval church dedicated to St Sulpicius, the 16thC Archbishop of Bourges, it was reconstructed in a piecemeal fashion between the years 1655-1788 by six different architects, the essential Classical form being the work of the Florentine Giovanni Servandoni. The result is not the hotchpotch that one might expect, but a grand and harmonious whole, apart from the unmatching towers over the portico with its two tiers of columns.

During the Revolutionary period the church became a Temple of Reason, then of Victory. In Nov 1799, it was the scene of a sumptuous banquet in honour of Napoleon Bonaparte.

The interior houses vast recesses of space, and the stillness seems trapped beneath a great weight of stone. There are many interesting objects in the church, including two enormous shells serving as **holy-water stoups**, with rock-like bases sculpted by Pigalle.

Another feature worth noticing is the bronze **meridian line** running from a plaque set into the floor of the S transept to a marble obelisk in the N transept. The sunlight, passing through a window in the S transept, strikes the line at different points to mark the equinoxes and solstices.

The **Lady Chapel**, at the E end of the church, is heavily ornate, with Pigalle's *Virgin and Child* floating above a cascade of plaster clouds. Don't miss the Delacroix **murals** in the side chapel immediately to the right of the main door. The one depicting Jacob struggling with the Angel is particularly compelling. The splendid **organ**, with its 6,588 pipes, is one of the largest in the world, and organ recitals are given here frequently.

Sainte-Chapelle ▥ ★
4 Bd. du Palais, 1ᵉʳ ☎ *43-54-30-09. Map 10|9* ▨ *ϗ Open Apr-Sept 9.30am-6.30pm, Oct-Mar 10am-5pm. Métro: Châtelet, St-Michel, Cité.*

It is hard to describe the beauty of this church without hyperbole; its interior is one of the most thrilling visual experiences that Paris affords. Formerly adjacent to a palace of the medieval kings, it now stands hidden away in a side courtyard of the *Palais de Justice* on the *Île de la Cité*. It was built by Louis IX (St-Louis) in the 1240s, to house relics believed to be the Crown of Thorns and a portion of the True Cross (which cost the king more than the church itself). They were kept in a tabernacle on a platform over the high altar, and on feast days, the king would take out the Crown of Thorns and hold it up before his courtiers and the public. The relics are now kept in *Notre-Dame*. When the Revolution came, the church suffered the indignity of being turned into a flour shop, then a club and finally a storage place for archives. Under the *Commune* in 1871 it narrowly escaped destruction by fire.

The building has an unusual "double-decker" construction with two chapels, one above the other. The upper one, dedicated to the Holy Crown and the Holy Cross, was intended only for the king and his retinue. The lower one, dedicated to the Virgin Mary, was for the staff of the chapel and certain officials of the court.

Entering by the rather dark **lower chapel**, note the low ceiling supported by columns painted in the 19thC. From here, mount a spiral staircase to the **upper chapel** (★) and emerge into a soaring chamber to be dazzled by the jewelled light that pours through the enormous **stained-glass windows** (★) on every side. The remarkable effect of lightness was achieved by what was then the revolutionary technique of supporting the roof on buttresses.

The **window** to the left of the entrance depicts scenes from Genesis. The remainder, taken clockwise, show more Old Testament events, as well as the story of Christ. The next-to-last window is devoted to Ste-Hélène and the True Cross, together with St-Louis and the relics of the Crucifixion. The **rose window** to the w shows scenes from the Apocalypse.

La Sainte-Chapelle and its neighbour, the *Conciergerie*, present a striking contrast. The latter represents the baseness and cruelty of the Middle Ages; the former embodies all that was God-seeking in the medieval world.

Salpêtrière, Hôpital
Bd. de l'Hôpital, 13ᵉ. Map 16L11. Métro: St-Marcel.

Les Invalides with a gentler voice could be the description of this sprawling hospital in se Paris. It stands on the site of a former gunpowder factory, and its name derives from the 75-percent saltpetre content of that substance. Built by Louis XIV as a refuge for beggars, to a design by Le Vau, it became a hospital, an asylum for the insane, a house of correction for prostitutes, and a prison. The inmates were often treated brutally, but towards the end of the 18thC, the Salpêtrière pioneered a more humane treatment of the insane, and today it has a justifiably distinguished reputation in the field of neurology and neuropsychiatry, as well as a general hospital. The main **facade**, with its central domed **St-Louis chapel** designed by Libéral Bruand, is one of the most majestic in Paris.

Sciences et de l'Industrie, Cité des *(City of Science and Industry)*   See *La Villette, Parc de*.

Sculpture de Plein Air, Musée de la *(Open Air Sculpture Museum)*
Quai St-Bernard, 5ᵉ ☎ 43-26-91-90. Map 16K11 ▣ Open daily. Métro: Jussieu, Gare d'Austerlitz.

If you are tired of the *Venus de Milo* and want to see postwar modern sculpture, you will find it at this open-air museum, which is situated in a riverside park near the *Jardin des Plantes*. There is a permanent display, and temporary exhibitions are also mounted.

La Seine
Lovers, painters and songwriters have for so long made the Seine their own that it is easy to forget the vital role played by the river in Paris' history, as an artery of trade and a strategic route since Roman times. In fact, without the Seine there would be no Paris. It is not for nothing that the badge of Paris depicts a boat, for the men who operated the river trade were for centuries the leading citizens of the town, and it was their corporation that formed the municipal administration in the Middle Ages.

Parisians often measure the level of the water by looking at the statue of the *Zouave* (an Algerian soldier of the Second Empire), which stands at the E side of the Pont de l'Alma. When the *Zouave* has his feet in the water it is a sign that the river is getting dangerously high. In the notorious floods of 1910, the water reached his chin.

The Seine provides some of the most beautiful riverscapes in the world. To get to know the river at close hand, walk along the riverside path (see *Planning and walks*), or take a trip on one of the many riverboats that now ply its waters.

Sewers   See *Égouts*.

La Sorbonne
Rue de la Sorbonne, 5ᵉ. Map 15J9. Métro: Cluny-La-Sorbonne, Maubert-Mutualité, Luxembourg.

The imposing buildings of the Sorbonne, which dominate the centre of the **Latin Quarter**, testify to the long and distinguished history of this world-famous university. Founded in 1253 by Robert de Sorbon, confessor to Louis IX, it began life as a college for 16 poor theological students, but grew rapidly into a powerful body with its own government, laws and jurisdiction — virtually a state-within-a-state.

In the 17thC, its chancellor, Cardinal Richelieu, commissioned the architect Jacques Lemercier to reconstruct the college buildings and added the magnificent domed Jesuit-style **church**, the interior of which can, unfortunately, be seen only during temporary exhibitions.

The university was closed during the Revolution, then reopened by Napoleon as the premier university of France. Alas, it no longer exists as a university in its own right. After the student riots of 1968, in which it played a key role, the Sorbonne became merely part of the University of Paris, with its multitude of buildings scattered over the city.

However, the glory of the past still clings to the buildings: the great courtyard with its superb **sundial**, surmounted by a relief of Apollo in his chariot; the Baroque **library** possessing more than 1.5 million volumes; and the ornate **lecture rooms**, with their numerous murals.

It is amusing to walk around and rub shoulders with the students. They no longer talk Latin, as they did in the days when the name "Latin Quarter" was born; but they are heirs to an illustrious tradition.

Techniques, Musée National des *(formerly Conservatoire des Arts et Métiers)* ▥
270 Rue St-Martin, Paris 3ᵉ ☎ 40-27-20-00. Map 10G10 ▦ Open Tues-Sat 1-5.30pm, Sun 10am-5.15pm. Closed Mon, public holidays. Métro: Réaumur-Sébastopol, Arts-et-Métiers.

This large technical museum, and a college of technology, are housed in the former priory of **St-Martin-des-Champs** in the NW corner of the *Marais*. The two most distinguished elements that remain from the medieval priory are the beautifully proportioned and vaulted **refectory**, now a library (*visits by prior arrangement only*), and the church of **St-Martin-des-Champs**, which is now part of the museum. The collection of more than 80,000 items, of which not more than one tenth is on display, records developments in the engineering sciences over the last half-millenium.

If archaeologists of the future ever discover this chapel and its contents, they might think that they have stumbled upon a bizarre temple dedicated to the worship of machinery. In the Gothic ambulatory, where the shrines of saints should be, there are engine components, car and airplane motors and similar objects, some of them placed in glass cases like holy relics, suggesting perhaps the cult of "Our Ford" in Huxley's *Brave New World*.

For the technically minded, the museum is fascinating. Here you can see models and displays demonstrating the technical progress of water power, the automobile, photography, television, musical instruments and more — all examples of man's inventiveness and skill.

Thermes, Musée National des   See *Cluny, Musée*.

Tour Eiffel *(Eiffel Tower)* ▥ ★
Champ-de-Mars, 7ᵉ ☎ 45-50-34-56. Map 12H3 ▦ ✗ for groups ⌂ ≠ Open Sept 24-Mar 10am-11pm, Apr-June 9.30am-11pm (Fri, Sat, hols, till midnight), July-Sept 9 9.30am-midnight, Sept 10-23 9.30am-11pm (Fri, Sat, till midnight). Métro: Bir-Hakeim, École-Militaire, Trocadéro.

The controversy that once raged over this world-famous tower has long since died down, and it has become universally accepted as the unofficial symbol of Paris. The reason for its construction in 1889 has been almost forgotten: to commemorate the centenary of the French Revolution. Those who think that Gustave Eiffel's design is bad enough should remember that it was one of 700 submitted for a competition in which rival proposals included a gigantic lighthouse capable of illuminating the entire city, and a tower shaped like a guillotine to honour the victims of the Reign of Terror. Fortunately Gustave Eiffel's design was unanimously accepted, and the iron tower was completed in time for the centenary and the World Exhibition. It rose 300m

(984ft) and was a miracle of engineering, comprising 9,700 tonnes of material. Today its height, including aerials, is 320.75m (1,052ft).

At first is was widely reviled. The writer Huysmans scornfully called it a "hollow candlestick", and a group of distinguished Parisians published a manifesto declaring it a "dishonour to Paris". Many advocated its demolition, but it was saved by World War I, when it became an important military centre for radio and telegraphic transmission. In 1964 it was classified as a national monument.

The journey to the summit is made in three stages. The first and second platforms of the tower, which can be reached by lift or stairs, support restaurants and souvenir shops. The first-class restaurant, the **Jules Verne** (see *Restaurants*), offers *nouvelle cuisine* and panoramic dining, but is heavily booked. The third and top platforms, which can be reached only by lift, have a bar, souvenir shops and the office, now restored, in which Eiffel worked. The superb **panorama** (★) over the city can be viewed from behind glass or from a balcony.

The tower has witnessed some strange scenes in its history. One man died trying to fly from it with artificial wings; in 1923 a daredevil journalist succeeded in riding a bicycle down from the first floor; and in 1954 it was scaled by a mountaineer. However, most people climb it for the view, or simply to be able to say that they have been to the top of the famous Eiffel Tower.

Tour Montparnasse *(Montparnasse Tower)*
Rue de l'Arrivée, 15e ☎ *45-38-52-56. Map 14L6* 🚇 ◄≡ ≡ 🖪
♈ *Open daily 10am-10pm. Métro: Montparnasse-Bienvenue.*

Opened in 1973, this 200m/656ft-high tower, with its adjacent shopping centre, dominates the whole quarter. Many regard it as one of the worst atrocities ever inflicted on Paris, a sad relic of Georges Pompidou's misguided attempts to "modernize" the French capital. It rises, like a vast black tombstone, from the centre of *Montparnasse*, dominating the skyline from almost every part of the city and introducing a discordant element into the otherwise human scale of central Paris (a trend that has since been halted — see *Architecture*).

It must be admitted, however, that the view from the top of the tower is spectacular, and interestingly different from the one afforded by the *Tour Eiffel*. The 56th floor has a rather shabby viewing gallery with a bar and a good restaurant (**IIⅢ**). You can also go right up onto the 59th-floor flat roof of the building via some hideous stairs.

The adjacent **Maine-Montparnasse** shopping centre is a multi-level complex containing shops, restaurants and squash courts. It is linked to the tower by a vast, bleak podium, which makes a good place for roller-skaters.

Tour St-Jacques
Sq. de la Tour St-Jacques, 4e. Map 10I9. Métro: Châtelet.
This curiously haunting edifice, rising out of a little park off *Rue de Rívoli*, is all that remains of the medieval church of St-Jacques-la-Boucherie, once a starting point for pilgrims setting out for the shrine of St James of Compostella in Spain. The church was demolished in 1802, but the bell tower was spared, to be used for dropping globules of molten lead in the manufacture of shot. It was later bought and restored by the City of Paris, and now serves as a meteorological station. At the base sits a statue of

Blaise Pascal who, in 1647, carried out the first meteorological experiment with a barometer at the summit.

Transports Urbains, Musée des *(Urban Transport Museum)*

60 Av. de Sainte-Marie, 94160 St Mandé ☎ 43-28-37-12. Map 19D5 and see map page 127 ◪ ✗ for groups. Open Apr 15-Oct 31, Sat, Sun 2-6pm; winter, 1st Sun in month only. Closed weekdays. Métro: Porte-Dorée.

What are a Glasgow corporation tram and a London trolley bus doing in a Paris suburb? Answer: they are part of an intriguing museum devoted to urban public transport vehicles, from horse-drawn buses to Métro carriages, housed in a former RATP bus depot and run entirely by an amateur association. Its members are very willing to share their enthusiasm with any visitor. You will find plenty here to stir nostalgia.

Tuileries

1ᵉʳ. Map 8H7 ◙ Métro: Tuileries.

If you want to see French formal gardening at its most elegant, you need go no farther than the Jardin des Tuileries, laid out by Louis XIV's gardener, Le Nôtre, and occupying a splendid site bounded by the **Louvre**, **Pl. de la Concorde** and **Rue de Rivoli**, with the **Jeu de Paume** and **Orangerie** museums on raised terraces at the western end. The central avenue, with its two ponds, is dramatically aligned with **Av. des Champs-Élysées** and the **Louvre**.

There seem to be almost as many statues in the gardens as there are trees: ancient gods and goddesses, allegorical figures of rivers and the seasons, and, near the Concorde entrance, a bust of Le Nôtre himself. There are many modern sculptures, forming a sort of extension of the reorganized Louvre. Although demonstrably popular with Parisians, the peacefulness of the Tuileries is striking. Birdsong stills the roar of traffic, which is muffled by massed trees. Children can play happily on old-fashioned merry-go-rounds, or hire toy wooden sailing boats.

There is not peace everywhere, though. A massive excavation project is taking place, between the **Arc de Triomphe du Carrousel** and the **Louvre**, which will result, by 1993, in a new centre of fashion design (see **Arts de la Mode, Musée des**). If the end result is as pleasing and as thoughtfully executed as the work in the **Cour Napoléon** at the **Louvre**, the gardens and surrounding areas will soon regain their lost beauty.

However, contrasted with the gaiety of the gardens and the dust of the excavations, is the tragic spectre of the vanished Tuileries palace, which once ran N-S between the two projecting western pavilions of the Louvre, with the **Arc de Triomphe du Carrousel** forming the entrance to its courtyard.

Queen Catherine de Medici built the palace in the 16thC but never lived there because her astrologer warned her against it, and subsequently an evil spell seemed to afflict the building. It witnessed violent and dramatic events, such as the escape of Louis XVI and his family across the gardens in 1792, the massacre of the Swiss Guards at the same date, and the riots which led to the departure of Charles X in 1830 and of Louis-Philippe in 1848. Finally, it was sacked and burned by the *Communards* in 1871.

UNESCO ⏛

7 Pl. de Fontenoy, 7ᵉ ☎ 45-68-10-00. Map 13J4 ▣ for exhibitions ◪ for performances ✗ for groups, by prior arrangement. Open 9.30am-12.30pm, 2-6pm. Closed public holidays 🐾 *Métro: Ségur.*

This Y-shaped structure must have seemed daringly modern when it was opened in 1958, but nowadays it has a rather old-fashioned look. In the grounds, the black metal Alexander Calder mobile and Henry Moore's *Figure in Repose* add to the period flavour, as does the Picasso mural in the interior. They are security-conscious here, so one cannot just walk in and look without making prior arrangements, but there are regular exhibitions that the public can attend, and the assembly chamber is used for spectacles ranging from circuses to piano recitals. The atmosphere is lively and international.

Val-de-Grâce 血血血

*1 Pl. Alphonse-Laveran, 5ᵉ. Map **15L9**. Open daily. Métro: Port-Royal.*

One of the great architectural treasures of Paris, the Val-de-Grâce hides its light under a bushel, tucked away as it is down Rue St-Jacques. In 1622, Anne of Austria, wife of Louis XIII, installed a Benedictine convent here, for use as a retreat. The buildings still remain, including the superbly proportioned **cloister**. Later she added the church, in thanksgiving for the birth of a son (the future Louis XIV) in 1638, after 23 childless years of marriage; the young king himself laid the first stone of the building in 1645.

The church, in the Jesuit style, has many beautiful features including a **cupola**, painted with frescoes by Mignard, an · unusual six-columned **baldachin** over the altar, and an attractive sculpted ceiling, whose pattern is reproduced in the floor tiles.

In the Revolution, the convent was turned into a military hospital, which it remains to this day. It houses a museum relating to the history of military medicine, but this is closed for alterations and is due to reopen in July 1993. The Val-de-Grâce stands in an area devoted to medicine, with its large hospital and various medical institutions.

Vendôme, Place 血血血 ★

*1ᵉʳ. Map **8G7**. Métro: Tuileries.*

Few squares in the world convey such an impression of effortless opulence and wealth as this one. Built under Louis XIV to a design by Jules Hardouin-Mansart (1645-1708), it presents a uniform facade of the utmost beauty of proportion: an arcade at ground level, then Corinthian pilasters rising through two storeys, topped by a roof with dormer windows. The keystones of the arches are carved with Bacchanalian faces, each with a different expression, like a ring of revellers at some expensive feast. This jolly throng has witnessed many dramatic events in the square. The statue of Louis XIV, which stood in the centre, was destroyed during the Revolution and later replaced by a bronze column constructed by Denon, Gondouin and Lepère from 1806-10, commemorating Napoleon's victories in Germany and modelled on Trajan's column in Rome. This monument was pulled down during the *Commune* but later re-erected. It is surmounted by a statue of Napoleon.

Besides numerous financiers and aristocrats, the square housed such colourful characters as the Austrian F.A. Mesmer, inventor of mesmerism, who held sessions of "animal magnetism" at no.**16**, and Chopin, who died at no.**12**.

Today the square is occupied mainly by offices and expensive shops. The **Ministry of Justice** is at nos.**11** and **13**, and the luxurious **Ritz** (see *Hotels*) is next door. You will also find here banks, jewellers and art dealers. Like a beautiful woman grown used to riches, Pl. Vendôme has an aloofness that does not invite closer acquaintance — unless you happen to be very well-heeled.

La Villette, Parc de ★

19ᵉ. Map 19C5 =≈ 🍴 ♣ Métro: Porte-de-la-Villette, Corentin-Cariou.

This is one of Paris's most exciting recent developments. La Villette is a former cattle market and abattoir district at the crossroads of the Canal de l'Ourcq and the Canal St-Denis, at the extreme NE corner of Paris. The area, including the Villette Basin, has undergone a vast redevelopment programme and has now emerged as a futuristic park and museum complex covering 55ha (136 acres). The **Cité des Sciences et de l'Industrie** (see below), established in the late 1980s, has been followed by the **Cité de la Musique** (City of Music), which was established in 1990. It now includes the **Conservatoire National de Musique**, which has relocated here from cramped surroundings in the 8ᵉ, and its **museum**, with its impressive collection of instruments, including some exquisite harpsichords and spinets.

Elsewhere in the park is **Le Zénith**, a pop and rock music auditorium; a gallery devoted to electronic games; the **Maison de la Villette**, a centre for the study of local history; and the **Théâtre Paris-Villette**.

Between these buildings, and flanking the canals, is a large area of attractively landscaped park with plenty of trees and grassy areas. There are also restaurants, bars and shops, as well as an excellent free play area for younger children. For scientifically minded adults and children, La Villette is an absorbing place for a day's outing.

Cité des Sciences et de l'Industrie *(City of Science and Industry) 30 Av. Corentin, Cariou, 19ᵉ ☎ 46-42-13-13 ⬛ ⚅ ♣ Open 10am-6pm. Closed Mon. Self-guided audio tours available in English.*

The Cité is already one of the largest and most imaginative scientific and technical centres in the world. Its permanent series of displays, called **Explora**, cover such themes as the nature of the earth and the universe, organic life, scientific laws, and language and communication. A brilliantly conceived series of installations, hands-on computers, videos, lasers and mathematical games enthralls even the non-technically-minded.

Elsewhere in the Cité is the **Médiathèque** resource and documentation centre, offering free consultation of books, periodicals and educational computer programs, and the **planétarium**, an amphitheatre where visitors can be whisked off into the universe thanks to an astronomical simulator and multisource projector. **L'Inventorium** takes children aged 3-6 and 6-12 into areas of scientific discovery in a play environment, while **La Géode**, a gleaming sphere of stainless steel, houses a movie theatre with a 1,000sq.m hemispherical screen, which gives spectators the impression of being enveloped in the image.

Vincennes, Château and Bois de

Château: Av. de Paris, 94300 Vincennes ☎ 43-28-15-48. Map 19D5 ⬛ ✗ compulsory for both keep and chapel. Open Oct-Mar 10am-4.15pm, Apr-Sept 9.30am-6.15pm (Sat, Sun 10am-4.15pm). Métro: Château-de-Vincennes. RER: Vincennes.

The Château de Vincennes is made up of a series of buildings of different periods, parts of which have served at various times as

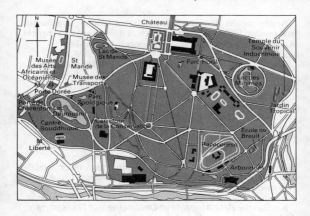

royal residence, prison, porcelain factory and arsenal. The main entrance is approached across a vast moat, now overgrown with grass, and the whole place has a rather forbidding aspect that mirrors its grim history. Henry V of England died of dysentery here in 1422, and in 1944 the Germans executed 26 members of the Resistance, who had blown up part of the castle and set fire to one of the pavilions. The **keep** (*donjon*) — the only medieval example near Paris — houses the **museum** of the château.

Opposite the keep is a Gothic chapel, the **Sainte-Chapelle**, which was founded by Charles V in 1379, and modelled on the one of the same name on the *Île de la Cité*. It has some fine stonework and magnificent **stained-glass windows**. Both chapel and keep can only be seen with a guide. To the S of the keep and chapel are two 17thC **pavilions** facing each other across a courtyard. Louis XIV spent his honeymoon in one of these buildings in 1660.

The restoration of the château was begun on the order of Napoleon III and continued spasmodically for a century. It is now complete.

Bois de Vincennes ★
=≡ ✱

This great open space of woodland lies to the SE of Paris at the opposite pole to the *Bois de Boulogne*. Flanking the city like lungs, these two great parks have provided generations of Parisians with easy access to greenery, open air and a variety of recreations.

Enclosed by Philippe Auguste in the 12thC as a royal hunting ground, it was made into a park for the citizens of Paris by Louis XV and was given to the town by Napoleon in 1860. Since then, many inroads have been made into it, and much of the greenery has been lost. In recent years, however, the municipality has started to reclaim some of the lost parkland; thousands of trees have been planted and new avenues laid out.

Although not as fashionable or well-known as the *Bois de Boulogne*, this park contains just as many features of beauty and interest. Starting at the château and travelling clockwise, you come first to the attractively laid out **floral garden** (Parc Floral) (*open daily*), which is planted with an interesting variety of flora. It includes a small lake, riding stables, a children's play area and a restaurant. Flower shows are held here throughout the year.

Nearby are the **Minimes Lake**, with three islands, a restaurant and boating facilities, and the garden of the **School of Tropical Agronomy**, with its Oriental touches and its **temple** commemorating the Indo-Chinese killed in World War I.

Turning s you come to the **Breuil School of Horticulture**, with more lovely gardens and an arboretum. Close by is the Vincennes **racecourse**.

A walk E through the woods will bring you to the **Daumesnil Lake**, a popular boating place with a plush café-restaurant on one of its two islands. Near the lakes is the **Buddhist Centre**, whose temple contains the largest effigy of Buddha in Europe, made of glass fibre and covered with gold leaf.

On the opposite side of the lake is the **zoological park**, the largest of the Paris zoos (*open daily*). Here you can see elephants, bison, kangaroos, peacocks, and many other animals and birds roaming in natural-looking surroundings. There are two cafés and a huge artificial rock from the top of which you have an excellent view over the Bois to the E and Paris to the w.

See also the *Arts Africains et Océaniens* and *Transports Urbains* museums, which are close by and merit a diversion.

Vosges, Pl. des ▥ ★
4ᵉ. Map 11I11. Métro: St-Paul, Chemin-Vert.

The oldest square in Paris is also arguably the most beautiful. It was built on the orders of Henry IV, who wished to create a square suitable for *fêtes* and ceremonial occasions, but it was not finished until 1612, 2yrs after his death. Planned as a single unit of matching facades, it was begun with the **King's Pavilion** on the s side, which is counterbalanced to the N by the **Queen's Pavilion**. The buildings are constructed of red brick and pale gold stone, with an arcade at ground level in which are a number of shops and cafés — try **Ma Bourgogne** (*no.19*) at the NW corner.

In its solid, quiet elegance, Pl. des Vosges, like the rest of the *Marais* in which it is situated, is rather uncharacteristic of the city of Paris. The poet Gérard de Nerval left behind him a vivid description of the houses in the square at sunset:

"When you see their high windows and brick facades, interspersed and framed with stone, at the moment when they are lit up by the splendid rays of the setting sun, you feel the same veneration as you do before a parliamentary court, assembled in red robes trimmed with ermine."

The square had many distinguished residents. Mme de Sévigné was born at no.**1bis**, Richelieu lived at no.**21**, and Victor Hugo at no.**6**, now a museum (see *Hugo, Musée Victor*).

In the garden enclosed by the square, where summer *fêtes* and duels once took place, children now play and lovers stroll. Fashionable Paris has long since moved westwards, but Pl. des Vosges retains an aristocratic patina.

Zadkine, Musée
100bis Rue d'Assas, 6ᵉ ☎ 43-26-91-90. Map 14K8 ▦ ✗
Open 10am-5.30pm. Closed Mon. Métro: Port-Royal, Vavin, Notre-Dame-des-Champs.

Here is a collection of works by the Russian-born painter Osip Zadkine, assembled in the home where he lived and worked from 1928 until his death in 1967. The house, studio and garden are all crammed with Zadkine's creations, which display a remarkable range of styles, from his early primitive and Cubist sculptures to the monumental work of later years.

Where to stay

Hotel life in Paris can be a mixed delight: like any other city it has its hazards, but on the whole it is full of pleasant surprises. Few cities have such a rich and varied choice of hotels, and many of them preserve an old-fashioned style of management that is rapidly dying out elsewhere: as well as cleanliness, they offer courtesy, a high ratio of staff to guests, and often a quintessentially French atmosphere. On the debit side, however, Paris has its share of sleazy hotels, and smallness of rooms is a common characteristic, so it is wise to choose carefully and book well in advance.

Reservations
Although Paris boasts some 1,400 hotels from the French grade of one star and up, there can be problems getting a room at short notice: it is best to book at least a month in advance (see *Sample reservation letter* on page 201). If booking at the last minute is unavoidable, you can use the services of the tourist offices at Orly and Roissy/Charles-de-Gaulle airports, the Gare du Nord, Gare d'Austerlitz, Gare de Lyon, Gare de l'Est and at the *Tour Eiffel*, as well as at the main **Tourist Office** (*127 Av. des Champs-Élysées, 8ᵉ*). July and Aug are two of the least heavily reserved months.

Price
The price categories quoted for each hotel in this book are a rough guide to what you can expect to pay. These are: cheap (☐), inexpensive (☐☐), moderate (☐☐☐), expensive (☐☐☐☐) and very expensive (☐☐☐☐☐). Approximate corresponding prices are given in *How to use this book* on page 5. In Paris, ☐☐☐☐☐ means some of the best hotels in the world, whereas ☐ signifies the civilized bare essentials, where cleanliness and general atmosphere are what count. Prices in the intervening categories are dependent on the lavishness of the fittings and amenities, the size of the room and the quality and quantity of the service. Nearly all the hotels listed here have the standard amenities of toilet, bath and/or shower, and bidet. In France, two people occupying one room will pay little more than one.

Tipping
Hotel prices now always include all service and taxes. If you are particularly pleased with the service you can always slip a few more francs to the chambermaid and/or receptionist.

Meals
French hotel breakfasts are the one blot on the nation's gastronomic copybook: too often cardboard croissants and individually packed portions of butter and jam are served up, except in top-notch establishments, which charge a fortune for good breakfasts. A breakfast is not usually included in the price of the room, and unless you give priority to breakfasting in bed, you may find better value round the corner from the hotel at a nearby café or *salon de thé*. Expect breakfast in your room only in hotels with 3 or more stars.

Choosing
Apart from price, a convenient location is usually the most important factor in choosing a hotel, so it is best to decide first on where you want to stay and then to pick the most

suitable hotel in that area (see list following). You can deduce the *arrondissement* in which the hotel is located from the last two numbers of the postcode.

The two most popular areas for hotels are **St-Germain** and the **Av. des Champs-Élysées**/Rue St-Honoré district. Both are central, and the former is one of the liveliest, yet most historic parts of the city, whereas the latter is the most sophisticated and business-oriented. Becoming increasingly popular since renovation began in the 1960s is the **Marais**, where the lovely old town houses make ideal small hotels. **Montparnasse**, once Bohemian, has attracted giant luxury hotels such as the **Meridien Montparnasse**.

If you are reserving at the last minute through the Tourist Office's reservation service, do not be too put off if all you are offered is hotels in one of the less central of the 20 *arrondissements*. The capital is small and compact (it can be easily walked across in about 2hrs), and has an excellent Métro and bus system.

The selection in this book has been made not only to give a wide choice of price and area, but also with other factors in mind: atmosphere, relative quiet and space. Addresses, telephone and fax numbers (and telex where appropriate) and nearest Métro stations are given, as well as symbols showing which hotels are particularly luxurious (🏨) or simple (■), and which represent good value (♣). Other symbols show price categories, and give a resumé of the facilities that are available. See **Key to symbols** on page 6, or the back jacket flap, for the full list of symbols. Refer to *Money* (pp9-10) for an explanation of our credit card listings.

L'Abbaye St-Germain

10 Rue Cassette, 75006 Paris
☎ 45-44-38-11. Map**14**J7 **III** to
IIII 44 rms ▱ No cards. Métro:
St-Sulpice.
*Location: In a short, quiet street
close to St-Germain-des-Prés and the
Luxembourg Gardens.* This
magnificent and extraordinary
converted 17thC convent shows just
what results can be obtained when
the ancient and modern are skilfully
combined. Contemporary sofas are
surrounded by 18thC antiques in the
downstairs lobby, while the rooms
themselves, some with original
beams and alcoves, are tastefully
decorated, with successfully unusual
colour schemes and fabrics. The
courtesy and helpfulness of the staff
are exemplary. With so much to
recommend it, however, it can be
extremely difficult to find a room
here in peak periods, and reserving
ahead is advised.
▱ ‡ ▱ ▱ ▱ Ψ

Bradford

*10 Rue St-Philippe-du-Roule,
75008 Paris* ☎ 43-59-24-20
▱ 45-63-20-07. Map **7**F4 **III** 48
rms. Métro: St-Philippe-du-
Roule, Franklin-D-Roosevelt.
*Location: Near Rue du Faubourg-St-
Honoré and Av. des Champs-
Élysées.* Friendliness is one of the
best features of this unassuming
hotel, and the rooms are large and
pleasantly furnished. Most welcome,
in an area blighted by heavy traffic,
is the almost total quiet and
seclusion of the little Rue St-
Philippe-du-Roule.
▱ ‡ ▱ & ▱

de la Bretonnerie

*22 Rue Ste-Croix-de-la-
Bretonnerie, 75004 Paris*
☎ 48-87-77-63 ▱ 42-77-26-78
▱ 305551. Map **10**I10 **III** 31 rms.
Métro: Hôtel-de-Ville.
*Location: In the fascinating Marais
district, between the Jewish Quarter
and the Pompidou Centre.* This
quiet hotel, housed in a 17thC
building, has a cosy atmosphere. It
combines modern comfort with
good use of the building's
traditional features, such as rough
stone walls and exposed wooden
beams. Furnishings and decoration
harmonize well.
▱ ‡ ▱ ▱ ▱

Le Bristol ▥

*112 Rue du Faubourg-St-
Honoré, 75008 Paris*
☎ 42-66-91-45 ▱ 42-66-68-68
▱ 280961. Map **7**F6 **IIII** 200 rms

▤ ▱ ▱ ▱ ▱ Métro:
Champs-Élysées-Clemenceau.
*Location: In one of the most
exclusive and expensive streets in
Paris.* Heads of government and
high-flying diplomats who have an
appointment with the President at
the Élysée Palace generally like to
stay at the Bristol, which is very
conveniently located just down the
road. It is also one of Paris' finest
hotels. Both traditional and
luxurious, it is richly decorated with
original oil paintings, antiques and
Oriental carpets. Bathrooms are
sumptuous, with several in Art Deco
style. There is a hairdressing salon
and massage parlour, conference
room, and an excellent restaurant.
The private car park and swimming
pool are marks of distinction shared
with few Paris hotels.
‡ □ ▱ ≈ ▱ Ψ

Chopin

46 Passage Jouffroy, 75009 Paris
☎ 47-70-58-10 ▱ 47-70-12-05
▱ 281085. Map **9**F9 **II** 37 rms.
Métro: Rue Montmartre.
*Location: In one of Paris' distinctive
arcades, close to the Opéra Quarter.*
It must have occurred to anyone
who has wandered through the area
of delightful arcades that branch
unobtrusively off the noisy Grands
Boulevards, that this would be an
ideally traffic-free place to stay in
Paris (or live, for that matter). The
charming mid-19thC Hôtel Chopin
fits the bill perfectly, even if the
majority of its rooms are small. This
is a relaxing and soothing place to
stay.
▱ ‡ □ ▱

de Crillon ▥

*10 Pl. de la Concorde, 75008
Paris* ☎ 42-65-24-24
▱ 47 2-72-10 ▱ 290204. Map
8G6 **IIII** 163 rms ▤ ▱ ▱ ▱
Métro: Concorde.
*Location: Overlooking one of the
most famous townscapes in the
world, at the hub of the Right Bank.*
The Crillon has long been
established as one of the great
classic hotels of the world. Its air of
quiet excellence is symbolized by
the fact that it displays no
ostentatious signs, only its name in
discreet letters over the entrance to
its magnificent 18thC premises. In
one of the best positions of any
hotel in Paris, and formerly an
aristocrat's mansion, it became a
hotel in 1907, and the sumptuous
decor and formal inner courtyard
were preserved. Its wood-panelled
reception rooms are now deservedly

131

classified as a national treasure.
Here you will find the last word in
elegance and controlled good taste,
along with a good restaurant, a
famous bar, and a clientele that
includes official guests of the French
government and the occasional film
star shunning the company of other
film stars.

≉ & ⎕ ⌷ ⊀ ♨ ⵌ

des Deux Îles

*59 Rue St-Louis-en-l'Île, 75004
Paris* ☎ 43-26-13-35
℗ 43-29-60-25. Map **10J10** ▥ 17
rms. Métro: Cité.
*Location: On the Île St-Louis, the
smaller and quieter of the Seine's
two islands, in the heart of Paris.*
The Hôtel des Deux Îles occupies a
17thC building in the quiet street
that runs the length of the Île St-
Louis. The rooms could not by any
stretch of the imagination be
described as large, but they do have
delightfully tiled bathrooms; the bar
in the cellar, with its open fire and
comfy sofas, is the ideal place for a
rendezvous galant on a cold
winter's evening.

⌂ ≉ ⎕ ⌷ ⵌ

des Ducs d'Anjou

*1 Rue Ste-Opportune, 75001
Paris* ☎ 42-36-92-24. Map **10H9**
▥ 38 rms ⒜ Métro: Les
Halles.
*Location: In the Halles/Beaubourg
area.* This hotel is a pleasant if
unremarkable base from which to
explore the vicinity, which includes
the Forum des Halles, that curious
cross between a mega-shopping
centre and a meeting place for
people of every description. The
rooms are very quiet, if somewhat
dark, and the hotel is located on the
very pretty Pl. Ste-Opportune.

⌂ ≉ ⎕ ⌷

Duc de St-Simon

14 Rue de St-Simon, 75007 Paris
☎ 45-48-35-66 ℗ 45-48-68-25
℗ 203277. Map **8I6** ▥ 34 rms. No
cards. Métro: Rue-du-Bac.
*Location: In a calm street just off
Bd. St-Germain.* Quiet, cosy,
intimate, welcoming, discreet and
lived-in are all adjectives that have
been liberally applied to this 19thC
hotel. The Duc de St-Simon,
remarkable for its period
furnishings, is run by a Swede, M.
Lindqvist, whose hobby is antiques.
New pieces have been gradually
added to the rooms, making it a
delightful and consequently
extremely popular hotel.

⌂ ≉ ⎕ ⌷ ⌘ ⵌ

132

Étoile ♣

3 Rue de l'Étoile, 75017 Paris
☎ 43-80-36-94 ℗ 44-40-49-19
℗ 642028. Map **6E3** ▥ 25 rms ⒜
⦿ Métro: Ternes.
*Location: Close to the Arc de
Triomphe.* A small, intimate hotel
where you can live like a prince,
almost for a song, with colour TV,
mini-bar, thick wall-to-wall carpets
and functional modern furniture in
your room, plus a bar and a mini-
library in the lobby.

⌂ ≉ ⎕ ⌷

Family Hôtel

35 Rue Cambon, 75001 Paris
☎ 42-61-54-84. Map **8G7** ▥ to
▥ 25 rms ⒜ Métro: Madeleine.
*Location: In the fashionable area
between Rue St-Honoré and La
Madeleine.* Surprisingly for such a
luxurious area, this hotel is just what
its Anglified name suggests — a
hôtel familial. Run by a very
friendly and courteous husband-
and-wife team, it has a tranquil air
and attractive bedrooms. Renovated
quite recently, the hotel has kept its
stylish 1930s look.

⌂ ≉ ⎕ ⌷

Fauconnier ⌂ ♣

*11 Rue du Fauconnier, 75004
Paris* ☎ 42-74-23-45
℗ 42-74-08-93. Map **11I11** ⎕ 100
beds. Métro: St-Paul.
*Location: In a small street by the
Seine, opposite the Île St-Louis.* Like
the nearby **Maubuisson** (see
below), this is a government-
subsidized hotel-hostel, in theory for
young people, in a superb 17thC
former private house, with beams,
original floor tiles, stone flagging
and antique furniture. Rooms have
anything from two to six beds in
them, and although there used to be
an upper age limit of 30, anyone
willing to share a room with a
stranger — or strangers — of the
same sex is now welcome. Spotless,
friendly, and assuredly very cheap.

⌂ ⵌ

France et Choiseul

239 Rue St-Honoré, 75001 Paris
☎ 42-61-54-60 ℗ 680959. Map
8G7 ▥ 120 rms ⦿ ▤ ⇌ ⒜ ⦿
Métro: Tuileries.
*Location: In the smart, fashionable
area of Rue St-Honoré and Pl.
Vendôme.* Although Ladbroke-
owned, an unhurried, timeless air
and a courtly, old-fashioned style of
management mark out this
traditional Paris hotel with its
upright Louis XV-style furniture. The
rooms are small, but have been

carefully modernized, each with its own up-to-date bathroom. There's a pretty patio at the rear.
✠ ❑ ☞ ❦ ♨

George-V 🏨
31 Av. George-V, 75008 Paris
☎ *47-23-54-00* Ⓢ *(reservations)*
47-20-06-49 Ⓢ *(management)*
47-20-40-00 Ⓢ *(reservations)*
650082. Map 7F4 ▓ *301 rms* ▤
☂ ⟶ Ⓐ Ⓔ *Métro: George-V.*
Location: Just off Av. des Champs-Élysées, in the city's principal business area. Unlike the equally luxurious **Crillon**, with its discreet elegance, the George-V is grand and unashamedly lavish. Flemish tapestries, sculptures, ormolu clocks and original paintings (including Renoir's *Le Vase des Roses*) complement the gracious 18thC-style furniture.

The hotel has a delightful bar and a lovely inner courtyard, where in summer meals are served amid red umbrellas and masses of potted plants as part of the excellent restaurant, **Les Princes**. A deluxe brasserie, **Le Grill**, has recently opened.
✠ ❧ ❑ ☞ ♨ Ⓨ

Grand Hôtel Inter-Continental 🏨
2 Rue Scribe, 75009 Paris
☎ *40-07-32-32* Ⓢ *42-66-12-51*
☎ *220875. Map 8F7* ▓ *551 rms*
▤ ⟶ Ⓐ Ⓔ *Métro: Opéra.*
Location: On Pl. de l'Opéra. Paris' largest old hotel was designed by Charles Garnier, architect of the *Opéra*, which dominates the view from the front windows. It was refurbished in 1989-90 and is now successfully aiming (although not exclusively) at the upper end of the business market. There are 17 daylit air-conditioned conference rooms. Air conditioning and soundproof double-glazing are now universal, and the rooms have received a luxury treatment, in a delightful range of pastel colours. A glass atrium has been added to the traditional winter garden, which opens onto a statue-lined courtyard. The next phase of this 400-million-franc refurbishment will see the restoration of the public areas to their original splendour. The celebrated **Café de la Paix** and the **Relais Capucines** front the street, the **Opéra** restaurant offers *haute gastronomie*, and business lunches are to be had in the patio garden. For good measure, guests can make use of a sauna, sun lounge and gymnasium.
✠ ❑ ☞ ♨ Ⓨ

Hilton International Paris 🏨
18 Av. de Suffren, 75015 Paris
☎ *42-73-92-00* Ⓢ *47-83-62-66*
☎ *200955. Map 12I3* ▓ *456 rms*
▤ ☂ ⟶ Ⓐ Ⓔ *Métro: Champ-de-Mars.*
Location: Close to the Seine and the Eiffel Tower. The Paris Hilton, considerably more luxurious and expensive than many others in the Hilton chain, was the first modern hotel built in Paris after the war. Excellent conference suites look out over the Eiffel Tower. One of the two restaurants, **Le Western**, provides all-American far-west catering. Indeed, in general, no expense is spared to provide home comforts for Americans in Paris.
⌂ ✠ ❧ ❑ ☞ ♨ Ⓨ

L'Hôtel 🏨
13 Rue des Beaux-Arts, 75006 Paris ☎ *43-25-27-22*
Ⓢ *43-25-64-81* ☎ *270870. Map 9I8*
▓ *to* ▓ *27 rms* ▤ ⟶ Ⓐ Ⓔ
Métro: St-Germain-des-Prés.
Location: In the heart of the St-Germain quarter. The ornate style of this hotel is not to everyone's taste — there are antiques everywhere, pink Venetian marble in the bathrooms, and velvet on virtually every surface, from the lift to the uniforms. The facilities include a winter garden with restaurant, and an intimate cellar bar. You may be given the room containing Mistinguett's own Art Deco furniture, the bedroom (and bed) that Oscar Wilde died in, or one of the two top-floor suites with flower-decked balconies and a view over the church of St-Germain-des-Prés. You might rub shoulders with any number of personalities (both real and aspiring) from showbiz, fashion or advertising. This extravaganza is the brainchild of Guy-Louis Duboucheron, who converted it, 25yrs ago, from the cheap, sleazy hotel that Oscar Wilde knew. Quite fittingly dubbed *Le Ritz du rive gauche*, L'Hôtel is a very small hotel that prides itself in offering a superb — but above all discreet — service.
⌂ ✠ ❑ ☞ ♨ Ⓨ

Inter-Continental Paris 🏨
3 Rue de Castiglione, 75001 Paris ☎ *42-60-37-80*
Ⓢ *42-61-14-03* ☎ *220114. Map 8G7* ▓ *500 rms* ▤ ☂ ⟶ Ⓐ Ⓔ
Métro: Tuileries.
Location: Close to Pl. Vendôme. The hotel was built in 1878 by Charles Garnier, architect of the Paris Opéra, and also of the **Grand Hôtel**.

Hotels

Several of its amazingly ornate *salons* are now listed as historic monuments. Completely and intelligently renovated while keeping its original atmosphere almost intact, the hotel has all the trappings of a modern luxury hotel: 24hr room service, a bar and discotheque, as well as a number of conference rooms, complete with secretaries, interpreters, and audiovisual facilities. The hotel also has a beautiful covered terrace, and its all-year restaurant, **La Terrasse Fleurie**, is a highly fashionable spot. The top-floor rooms afford a majestic view over the Tuileries Gardens.

≋ ⟁ ▢ ⊡ ⟨⟨ ⚰ ⊻ ⊙

Le Jardin des Plantes ✿
5 Rue Linné, 75005 Paris
☎ 47-07-06-20 ☏ 203684. Map **16K10** ⬚⬚⬚ *33 rms* ⇌ AE ☒
Métro: Jussieu.
Location: Opposite the tranquil Jardin des Plantes, a 5min walk from the Sorbonne and the student quarter. Comfortable, clean and colourful, this charming hotel appeals to individual travellers: organized groups are not welcomed. Americans particularly love the freedom to jog in the Jardin opposite. The well-appointed rooms are appropriately decorated, using floral themes, and art exhibitions enliven the vaulted basement lounge. There is a small sauna and a guests' ironing room. A delightful option is breakfast on the roof terrace, which has a fragrant rose garden.

≋ ⟁ ▢ ⊡ ▣

Lancaster ⌂
7 Rue de Berri, 75008 Paris
☎ 43-59-90-43. ☏ 42-89-22-71
☏ 640991. Map **7E4** ⬚⬚⬚⬚ *66 rms* ▤
⬆ ⇌ AE ☒ *Métro: St-Philippe-du-Roule.*
Location: In a fairly quiet street just off Av. des Champs-Élysées. This haunt of American film stars and big-time journalists looks and feels more like a smart private house than a hotel. Most of its rooms overlook a charming, flower-filled, statue-lined courtyard. The less fortunate ones on the street side have double-glazing, so a good night's sleep is guaranteed despite the proximity of the 24hr traffic on the Champs-Élysées.

⌂ ≋ ⟁ ▢ ⊡ ▣

Lenox ✿
9 Rue de l'Université, 75007 Paris ☎ 42-96-10-95

☏ 42-61-52-83 ☏ 260745. Map **8I7** ⬚⬚⬚ *34 rms* AE ☒ *Métro: Rue-du-Bac.*
Location: Three minutes' walk from Bd. St-Germain and the Seine. One of those rare hotels that stands out, not only in its class, but by any standards, because of a special thoroughbred quality. All the bedrooms and the reception area have been furnished and decorated with excellent taste, and the whole atmosphere has a warm elegance. What's more, the staff is extremely friendly, and the service is willing. Light meals can be provided in your room at any time of the day. Its sister hotel in Montparnasse (*15 Rue Delambre, 14ᵉ* ☎ 43-35-35-50) gives the same excellent value.

≋ ⟁ ▢ ⊡ ▣

Lotti ⌂
7 Rue de Castiglione, 75001 Paris ☎ 42-60-37-34
☏ 40-15-93-56 ☏ 240066. Map **8G7** ⬚⬚⬚ *133 rms* ▤▤ ⇌ AE ☒
Métro: Tuileries.
Location: Close to Pl. Vendôme and Rue St-Honoré. A luxury hotel of manageable proportions with a subdued but regal air, the Lotti caters for the high society of many countries, but particularly Britain, Italy and France. The decor is traditional and extremely tasteful, with no two bedrooms the same. The service is quick, efficient and unobtrusive, and an air of calm and sophistication pervades the whole establishment.

⌂ ≋ ⟁ ▢ ⚰

---

des Marronniers ✿
21 Rue Jacob, 75006 Paris
☎ 43-25-30-60 ☏ 40-46-83-56.
Map **9I8** ⬚⬚⬚ *37 rms. No cards.*
Métro: Mabillon.
Location: In the heart of the St-Germain quarter, on the Left Bank. Mother Nature has a strong hold on this tall hotel, from the profusion of leaves, flowers and birds on the wallpaper and carpets, the fruit on the crockery, and the flower-filled vases, to the delightful little garden at the back, with its veranda, white garden furniture, and chestnut trees (which give the hotel its name).

There are two cosy lounges in the ancient vaulted cellars. To top it all, the prices are as soothing as the service.

≋ ▢ ⊡ ☀ ⚰ ⊻

Maubuisson ◼ ✿
12 Rue des Barres, 75004 Paris
☎ 42-72-72-09 ☏ 40-27-08-71.

Map 10|10 □ 92 beds. Métro:
Hôtel-de-Ville.
*Location: In a tiny street behind
St-Gervais-St-Protais church by the
Hôtel-de-Ville.* This hotel-hostel with
dormitories is, in every respect, like
the **Fauconnier** (a couple of
minutes' walk away — see above),
from the 17thC building, original
flooring and quiet location, to the
rock-bottom prices.
🏠

Meridien Montparnasse Paris

*19 Rue du Cdt René-Mouchotte,
75014 Paris* ☎ 43-20-15-51
Ⓧ 43-20-61-03 ⊕ 200135. Map
14L6 ▥▥ to ▥▥ 950 rms ▤▤ ▦ ⇌
▣▣ ⊙ *Métro: Montparnasse-
Bienvenue.*
*Location: In the centre of
Montparnasse.* Formerly a member
of the worldwide Sheraton chain,
this hotel was built as part of the
Montparnasse redevelopment
scheme. The building itself, by
Pierre Dufau, who also designed
part of La Défense, is an elegant
white giant, rising 35 storeys and
contrasting strongly with its
unlovely surroundings.

With the benefit of the Gare
Montparnasse and Métro at its side,
the hotel caters with renowned
efficiency for its guests, which
include tour groups and business
executives. They appreciate the
many facilities, which include a
business suite with conference
rooms, and three restaurants,
including **Le Montparnasse**, which
serves a decent enough *cuisine
classique.*
✳ ♿ ▢ ▧ ⇜ ▦ Y

Meurice 🏨

228 Rue de Rivoli, 75001 Paris
☎ 42-60-38-60 Ⓧ 49-27-98-06
⊕ 230673. Map 8G7 ▥▥ 187 rms
▤▤ ⇌ ▣▣ ⊙ *Métro: Tuileries.*
*Location: Opposite the Tuileries
Gardens and within walking
distance to just about everywhere.*
Opened in 1816, the Meurice used
to receive almost all the crowned
heads of Europe. More recently the
hotel has been patronized by
Salvador Dalí, Gulf State Arabs, and
other members of the international
set. The splendid salons, with their
gilded panelling, tapestries and
huge chandeliers, have been added
to the list of historical monuments.
Like many of the best hotels, the
Meurice now has an excellent
Business Service centre, with the
availability of conference rooms and
secretarial services.
✳ ♿ ▢ ▧ ⇜ ▦ Y

Montana-Tuileries 🌸

12 Rue St-Roch, 75001 Paris
☎ 42-60-35-10 Ⓧ 42-61-12-28.
Map 8G7 ▥▥ 25 rms ▣▣ ⊙
Métro: Pyramides.
*Location: Just off Rue de Rivoli and
Rue St-Honoré.* If you feel like
giving yourself a treat but can't
afford the luxury hotels that line Rue
de Rivoli (**Meurice, St-James et
Albany, Inter-Continental**), take a
few steps down a side-street and try
this small but spacious hotel. The
Montana-Tuileries has almost all the
facilities of its more illustrious
neighbours, but it won't cost the
earth. Parts were renovated in 1990,
and there are now several rooms in
the ▥▥ price bracket.
🏠 ✳ ♿ ▢ ▧ ⇜ 🍴 Y

Nikko de Paris 🏨

61 Quai de Grenelle, 75015 Paris
☎ 40-58-20-00 Ⓧ 45-75-42-35
⊕ 260012. Map 12J1 ▥▥ 779 rms
▤▤ ⇜ ⇌ ▣▣ ⊙ *Métro: Bir-
Hakeim.*
*Location: On the quais overlooking
the Seine, opposite Maison de Radio-
France.* With admirable efficiency,
the Japanese moved into the Paris
hotel scene and in no time, the
Nikko's restaurant, **Les Célébrités**,
won accolades. There are all the
amenities of a smoothly run
international hotel, from streamlined
accommodation (with Japanese or
Western decor) to a clutch of bars, a
sauna, a swimming pool and a good
Japanese restaurant, the **Benkay**.
✳ ♿ ▢ ▧ ⇜ ⇌ ▦ Y

Nouvel Hôtel 🌸

24 Av. du Bel-Air, 75012 Paris
☎ 43-43-01-81 Ⓧ 43-44-64-13
⊕ 240139 □ 28 rms ▣▣ ⊙
*Location: Not much more than a
stone's throw from Pl. de la Nation.*
The tranquility of this little hotel is
astonishing. About the only thing
that will wake you is the sound of
the birds in the hotel's ivy-filled
garden, where you can take
breakfast on fine mornings. The
rooms are prettily decorated, each
with an individual touch. The
service is cheerful and courteous.
There is paying parking nearby, and
the proximity of the Nouvel Hôtel to
major roads makes it a good bet for
those passing through Paris.
Perhaps its old-world charm is what
makes it so popular with British and
American visitors.
🏠 ▢ ▧ ⇜ ⚘

Perreyve

63 Rue Madame, 75006 Paris
☎ 45-48-35-01 ⊕ 205080. Map

14J7 ◨ 30 rms AE ◉ Métro: Rennes.

Location: A quiet street near the Luxembourg Gardens. The Jardin du Luxembourg, a pocket of relaxing greenery among the hurly-burly of the Left Bank, is just round the corner from this charming hotel. The decor is in the best of taste, the rooms are comfortable, and the bathrooms, although small, are sparkling clean.

⌂ ≈ ☐ ⌐

Plaza-Athénée 🏰

25 Av. Montaigne, 75008 Paris
☎ 47-23-78-33 ⊗ 47-20-20-70
☎ 650092. Map **7**G4 ⅢⅢ 218 rms
▤ ▰ ⇌ AE ◉ Métro: Franklin-D-Roosevelt.

Location: Near the Seine and Av. des Champs-Élysées, but away from the noise and bustle. Perhaps the most glamorous and elegant hotel of all in Paris, attracting a galaxy of stars, this is a particular favourite of wealthy South Americans and Greeks. Afternoon tea can be taken in the elegant long gallery, and there is a beautiful inner patio. Gorgeous period-style suites and attractive bedrooms, superb service (albeit slightly cool towards mere mortals), two celebrity-studded bars and an excellent restaurant, the **Régence-Plaza**.

≈ & ☐ ⌐ ♠ Y

Pont-Royal

7 Rue Montalembert, 75007 Paris ☎ 45-44-38-27
⊗ 45-44-92-07 ☎ 270113. Map **8**I7
ⅢⅢ to ⅢⅢ 78 rms ⇌ AE ◉
Métro: Rue-du-Bac.

Location: In a small street between the river and Bd. St-Germain. Conveniently located for the restaurants and charms of the Left Bank, yet only a short walk to the river, Notre-Dame and the Louvre, this hotel, now part of the Best-Western group, provides a consistent standard of comfort and a good base for the tourist who wants a genuinely middle-of-the-road hotel. The rooms, if a little small, are pleasantly furnished and comfortable, and have a mini-bar and even a safe. The terrace restaurant, **Les Antiquaires**, is a safe bet for a business lunch, but there is plenty of competition close at hand. There is an underground car park nearby.

≈ ☐ ⌐ ♠

Quai Voltaire ✿

19 Quai Voltaire, 75007 Paris
☎ 42-61-50-91 ⊗ 42-61-62-26.

Map **8**H7 ◨ to ⅢⅢ 33 rms AE ◉
Métro: Solférino.

Location: On the Left Bank overlooking the Seine, opposite the Tuileries Gardens. Most rooms in this light, bright and unfortunately rather noisy little hotel afford a superb view over the Seine — a view enhanced by the tall French windows. The establishment has a literary past — it was patronized by Charles Baudelaire and Oscar Wilde in their time — and its small, unostentatious bar is a choice meeting place for the lions of modern French literature.

≈ & ☐ ⌐ ≪ Y

Raphael 🏰

17 Av. Kléber, 75016 Paris
☎ 45-02-16-00 ⊗ 45-01-21-50
☎ 610356. Map **6**F2 ⅢⅢ 89 rms ⇌
AE ◉ Métro: Kléber.

Location: On one of the avenues radiating from Pl. Charles-de-Gaulle and the Arc de Triomphe. The smallest of the Parisian *palaces* (luxury hotels), the Raphael has a curiously unreal atmosphere that is heightened by dark wood-panelling, heavy tapestries, thick carpets, and a huge seascape by Turner. This, and its discreet location, may be what appeals to the international film stars and producers who stay here regularly. It's also located conveniently close to the film-world's offices, which are clustered around Pl. Charles-de-Gaulle and Av. des Champs-Élysées.

≈ & ☐ ⌐ ♠ Y

Regent's Garden ✿

6 Rue Pierre-Demours, 75017 Paris ☎ 45-74-07-30
⊗ 40-55-01-42 ☎ 640127. Map **6**D3 ⅢⅢ 40 rms ▱ AE ◉ Métro: Ternes.

Location: A quiet street in a residential area. The Regent's Garden lives up to its name by possessing a real garden (as opposed to the courtyard found in so many Parisian hotels), complete with statues and fountains. The building itself is typical of the showy *grand bourgeois* architecture of the mid-19thC. Its cavernous rooms, whose lofty ceilings sport decorative mouldings, are furnished in appropriate style, with brass bedsteads and large mirrors. The bathrooms, on the other hand, are equipped with thoroughly 20thC conveniences. The 17e may seem a little far from the hub of things, but is in fact only a few minutes' walk from the Arc de Triomphe.

⌂ ≈ ☐ ⌐ ✿ ♠ Y

Relais Christine
3 Rue Christine, 75006 Paris
☎ 43-26-71-80 ⊗ 43-26-89-38
⊕ 202606. Map 9|8 ⅢⅢ. to ⅢⅢ 51
rms ▦▦ ⓢ *Métro:*
Mabillon, Odéon.
*Location: A tiny backwater in the
heart of the Latin Quarter, close to
Pl. St-Michel.* Rue Christine not only
boasts an excellent cinema and the
Photogalerie restaurant, but one of
the area's most distinguished hotels,
the Relais Christine. The 16thC
building, once a monastery,
became, among other things, a
publisher's book depot, before
being transformed into a hotel in
1979. Its comfortable, spacious and
tastefully decorated rooms, several
of which are split-level apartments,
are individually furnished with
period pieces. Those on the lower
floors are a trifle dim, although one
ground-floor room has a stone wall
and a fine carved door. Other
features include parking in the
tranquil hotel courtyard, and such
niceties as automatic shoe-cleaning
machines.
▨ ‡ ☐ ◪ ◪ ⚲ ⚱ ▦ ☒

Résidence Foch
10 Rue Marbeau, 75016 Paris
☎ 45-00-46-50 ⊗ 45-01-98-68
⊕ 630886 ⅢⅢ to ⅢⅢ 25 rms ▣▣ ⓢ
Métro: Porte-Maillot.
*Location: In the expensive
residential area of the 16ᵉ.* This
small and exclusive luxury hotel is
tucked away in the secluded calm of
a tiny street near Paris' millionaires'
row, Av. Foch, a minute or two's
stroll from the Bois de Boulogne,
and very near the excellent **Le Petit
Bedon** restaurant. Résidence Foch
is furnished with pleasant antiques,
has an intimate bar, and includes,
among its attractive rooms, a large
and brightly lit split-level suite on
the top floor.
▨ ‡ ☐ ◪ ⚲ ▦

Résidence Lord Byron
*5 Rue de Châteaubriand, 75008
Paris* ☎ 43-59-89-98
⊗ 42-89-46-04 ⊕ 649662. Map 7F4
ⅢⅢ to ⅢⅢ 31 rms. *Métro: Charles-
de-Gaulle-Étoile, George-V.*
*Location: Close to the Arc de
Triomphe and Av. des Champs-
Élysées.* One of the quietest and
most pleasant places to stay, within
a minute's walk from Av. des
Champs-Élysées, and a must for
anyone shunning the sometimes
over-fussy service of the area's
bigger hotels in the same high class.
The furniture and decor are discreet
and relaxing. Many of the rooms

overlook an attractive inner
courtyard with intricate trelliswork.
▨ ‡ ☐ ◪ ⚲ ▦

Ritz ▦
15 Pl. Vendôme, 75001 Paris
☎ 42-60-38-30 ⊗ 42-60-23-71
⊕ 220262. Map 8G7 ⅢⅢ 187 rms
▦▦ ▬ ⇌ ▣▣ ⓢ *Métro:*
Pyramides.
*Location: Superbly located in the
exclusive and beautiful Pl.
Vendôme.* Arguably the most
famous hotel in the world, the Ritz
lives up to its reputation, seeming to
exude luxury, attentiveness and just
the right amount of old-fashioned
charm. Nor has it rested on its
laurels like many other long-famous
hotels, but has been sensitively
renovated over a period of years:
the huge and splendid original baths
remained, while the telephones
were computerized.
   The benefits of staying at the Ritz
are many: kind and unobtrusive
service, beautiful period furnishings,
a lovely inner garden, several chic
bars, and an exceptionally good
restaurant, **L'Espadon**.
   New facilities include the Ritz
Health Club, which offers a spa,
swimming pool and beauty centre,
the Ritz-Escoffier School of
Gastronomy, and a private supper
club, the **Ritz Club**.
▨ ‡ ♿ ☐ ◪ ⚲ ‘Ψ’ ⇌ ▦

Royal Monceau ▦
35 Av. Hoche, 75008 Paris
☎ 45-61-98-00 ⊗ 45-63-28-93
⊕ 650361. Map 2E4 ⅢⅢ 220 rms
▦▦ ⇌ ▣▣ ⓢ *Métro: Courcelles.*
*Location: Between the Arc de
Triomphe and the attractive Parc
Monceau.* Not long ago this luxury
hotel came under new management
and was given a complete overhaul.
It is a favourite with international
business clients, but all who can
afford the Monceau would most
certainly enjoy its serene, pastel
charm and excellent features. In
addition to its lovely, very "unhotel-
like" rooms and attentive staff, the
Monceau also boasts two *haute
cuisine* restaurants, both of which
are favourites with many Parisians.
Offering Italian fare, there is the
well-known **Il Carpaccio**, situated
in the hotel's main building. In the
courtyard is the round, glass-
enclosed **Le Jardin**, offering
superb, imaginatively prepared
gourmet fare and white-gloved
service. In addition, there are also
two elegant cocktail bars. The hotel
also features **Les Thermes**, an
exclusive fitness club, which

Hotels

includes a swimming pool, a sauna and gym, massage, hydrotherapy, and its own separate health-conscious restaurant.

The Royal Monceau is also well equipped to cater for the corporate traveller, and has several fine rooms that are especially suitable for conference or banqueting functions, and a fully-equipped business centre.

≈ ‡ □ ◚ ♥ ≈ ♨ ☟

St-James et Albany
202 Rue de Rivoli, 75001 Paris
☎ 42-60-31-60 ® 40-15-92-21
● 213031. Map **8G7** ⅢⅢ 207 rms
⇒ ⇌ ⒜ ⊙ Métro: *Tuileries.*
Location: Overlooking the Tuileries Gardens. For years, the Hôtel St-James et Albany, parts of which date from the time of Louis XIV, chugged along in its old-fashioned way with its own select band of aristocratic habitués (as one would expect of a hotel with a name so wonderfully redolent of London's clubland).

With the inevitable refurbishment came an unusually successful combination of the old and the new in fittings and furniture. The refurbished and well-managed hotel, with its own excellent restaurant, is now giving its prestigious neighbours on Rue de Rivoli some stiff competition.
‡ & □ ◚ ⅘ ≪ ♨ ☟

de Seine ✿
52 Rue de Seine, 75006 Paris
☎ 46-34-22-80 ® 46-34-04-74.
Map **9I8** ⅢⅢ 30 rms ⒜ ⊙ Métro: St-Germain-des-Prés, Odéon, Mabillon.
Location: On the Left Bank, in an attractive, quiet, art gallery-filled street within the bustling St-Germain quarter. The Hôtel de Seine is one of Paris's best-kept secrets. Run by the multilingual Monsieur Edouard with friendliness and great efficiency, the hotel itself is not fancy, but is, however, well-maintained and secure. It is excellent value for money. An easy walk from the *quai*, the hotel is a fine base from which to explore all the nooks and crannies of the Latin Quarter or for that other favourite French pastime, eating and café-hopping, with a remarkable choice virtually outside your door. Rue de Seine also has a superb open-air food market.

As one might expect with all these advantages, the hotel is usually heavily booked.
⌂ ‡ ◚ □ ⅘

138

Solférino
91 Rue de Lille, 75007 Paris
☎ 47-05-85-54 ® 45-55-51-17
● 203865. Map **8H7** ⅢⅢ 33 rms.
Métro: *Solférino.*
Location: In St-Germain, tucked between the Seine and Bd. St-Germain. The Solférino is a charming, old-fashioned and modest hotel with prettily and tastefully decorated, high-ceilinged bedrooms, a delightful little *salon* and a veranda for breakfasting. The faithful, mainly English and American, clientele are especially appreciative of the warm welcome extended by the Solférino's friendly staff.
‡ □ ◚

Splendid Étoile
1 Av. Carnot, 75017 Paris
☎ 43-80-14-56 ® 47-64-05-09
● 280773. Map **6E3** ⅢⅢ 57 rms
⇌ ⊙ Métro: *Charles-de-Gaulle-Étoile.*
Location: Right on the bustling Pl. Charles-de-Gaulle. This fine 19thC mansion makes a comparatively small hotel, with 57 spacious and elegantly furnished bedrooms. Some of the rooms look directly onto the Arc de Triomphe, but the double-glazing allows you to enjoy the sensation of being at the hub of Paris without suffering the attendant noise. There are conference facilities, an "English" bar and a fashionable restaurant, **Le Pré Carré**, which is often frequented by well-known faces.
‡ & □ ◚ ♨ ☟

de Suède
31 Rue Vaneau, 75007 Paris
☎ 47-05-00-08 ® 47-05-69-27
● 200596. Map **14J6** ⅢⅢ to ⅢⅢ 41 rms ⒜ Métro: *Sèvres-Babylone.*
Location: In a plush area between Rue de Varenne and Rue de Babylone. Cool elegance distinguishes this hotel, and that is just as it should be, since it backs onto the gardens of the Prime Minister's official residence, the Hôtel Matignon. If you want to try to glimpse the man, or simply admire the towering plane trees that grow here, ask for a room on the second or third floor. The hotel also has a large, gently-lit lounge in the Directoire style, and a pretty little inner courtyard where morning or afternoon refreshment may be taken.
⌂ ‡ & □ ◚ ≪ ⅘

Terminus Nord ✿
12 Bd. de Denain, 75010 Paris
☎ 42-80-20-00 ® 42-80-63-89

☎ 660615. Map 5E10 ▮▮▯ 220 rms
▥ ▥ Métro: Gare du Nord.
Location: Opposite the Gare du Nord. Situated in an extremely convenient location for anyone in transit to or from the capital via the Gare du Nord, this hotel underwent its transformation a decade ago and is now firmly settled in the lower-middle range of respectable hotels that serve their purpose. Rooms facing the street are well insulated against street noise.

‡ & ▢ ▱ ⅍ ≛ ⴲ

Terrass

12 Rue Joseph-de-Maistre,
75018 Paris ☎ 46-06-72-85
☎ 42-52-29-11 ☎ 280830. Map 4C8
▮▮▮▮ 101 rms ═ ▥ ▥ Métro:
Blanche.
Location: On the edge of Montmartre. The best views from a hotel are undoubtedly to be found in this first-class establishment, perched on an outcrop of the Butte de Montmartre. From the hotel you can see the Panthéon, the surprisingly tall Opéra, Les Invalides, the Arc de Triomphe and the Eiffel Tower, and even La Défense can be glimpsed. Otherwise the Terrass, built in 1912 but modernized more than once since then, and being the only 4-star hotel in Montmartre, provides all the services one would expect — but manages to charge marginally less for them than its rivals located in other parts of the city.

‡ ▢ ▱ ⴷ ≛ ⴲ

---

des Tuileries

10 Rue St-Hyacinthe, 75001 Paris
☎ 42-61-04-17 ☎ 49-27-91-56
☎ 240744. Map 8G7 ▮▮▯ to ▮▮▮▮ 26
rms ▥ ▥ ▥ Métro: Pyramides.
Location: Close to Pl. Vendôme and within easy reach of Av. de l'Opéra and the Tuileries Gardens. You won't find a much quieter street in the centre of Paris than the tiny Rue St-Hyacinthe: it is scarcely used by vehicles except those looking for a parking space. The Hôtel des Tuileries occupies a late 18thC building with a superb carved wooden front door. Modernization has been carried out with care, and each room has a different decor. Plenty of warm, old-fashioned velvet still abounds. Lavish marble-clad bathrooms were recently installed.

▱ ‡ ▢ ▱ ⴲ ⴵ

Université

22 Rue de l'Université, 75007
Paris ☎ 42-61-09-39

☎ 42-60-40-84 ☎ 260717 quoting
OREM 310. Map 8/7 ▮▮▯ to ▮▮▮▮ 28
rms. No cards. Métro:
Rue-du-Bac.
Location: On the Left Bank, between Bd. St-Germain and the Seine. This hotel is reserved well ahead by people who want to stay in style at the antique-dealing and publishing end of the St-Germain quarter. The establishment, which occupies a 17thC *hôtel particulier* (private house), has been completely refurbished, and is filled with antiques and tapestries. The rooms are decorated with individual style and the breakfast lounge, hall, and tiny courtyard are charming.

‡ ▢ ▱ ⅍ ⴲ

---

du Vieux Marais ✿

8 Rue du Plâtre, 75004 Paris
☎ 42-78-47-22 ☎ 42-78-34-32.
Map 10H10 ▮▮▯ to ▮▮▯ 30 rms.
Métro: Rambuteau.
Location: On one of the less picturesque streets in the Marais. This charming quarter was a virtual slum a quarter of a century ago. Now almost completely renovated, it contains some of the priciest property in town, but perhaps still does not have its fair share of hotels. The Hôtel du Vieux Marais dates back to the 16thC, and every part of the 5-floor building is simply but brightly decorated. The rooms overlooking the courtyard are particularly attractive.

▱ ‡ ▢ ▱ ⅍ ⴲ

La Villa

29 Rue Jacob, 75006 Paris
☎ 43-26-60-00 ☎ 46-34-63-63
☎ 202437. Map 9/8 ▮▮▮▮ to ▮▮▮▮ 32
rms ▤▤ ═ ▥ Métro: Mabillon,
St-Germain-des-Prés.
Location: Between Bd. St-Germain and the Seine. In his search to create an *avant-garde* mood with the ultimate in designer chic, owner Vincent Darnaud took the gamble of entrusting his new hotel's entire design to the young but highly-regarded Marie-Christine Dorner. The result, startling in its simplicity, is a seductively balanced design that blends anthracite-coloured marble, burnished metal, plane wood, leather, and sanded and engraved glass, with a thrilling sense of colour throughout. Halogen-spotlit door-numbers pinpoint each superbly-appointed room. A split-level bar/jazz-cellar and roof terrace add further spice. Reserve well ahead: La Villa is *très à la mode* among architects and design folk.

▱ ‡ ▢ ▱ ≛ ⴲ ▦ ♫

Eating in Paris

French cuisine is renowned as the finest in the world; the superb standard of cooking in the average French household is matched by the unequalled quality of France's restaurants. Whereas provincial restaurants reflect local produce and traditions, those in Paris act as a focus for the rest of the country, bringing together the individual and varied regional cuisines. They seem continually interested in change and innovation, and are constantly striving for new limits of perfection. In Paris, with a little judicious choosing, you can quite simply have the gastronomic experience of a lifetime, whether it is a perfectly smoked Auvergne ham in a crowded wine bar, or a 5-course extravaganza in one of the city's revered establishments.

Cooking in France is regarded not as a necessity but as an art, and its leading exponents, such as Paul Bocuse, Michel Guérard, Joël Robuchon and Roger Vergé, are held in god-like esteem. They are the modern-day successors of the immortalized 19th and early 20thC chefs Carême and Escoffier, masters of *grande* or *haute cuisine*; but whereas Escoffier, for all his technical brilliance, put many strictures on French cuisine, many of today's great chefs have broken free from his rules and sought entirely new directions.

This style of cooking, pioneered in France since the war by such chefs as Alexandre Dumaine, André Pic and Fernand Point, is termed just that: *nouvelle cuisine*. (The term *nouvelle cuisine* had in fact been used previously in the 1740s during a similar culinary seachange.) In keeping with the modern trend away from rich, heavy food, and with the emphasis on absolute freshness, *nouvelle cuisine* at its best is lighter and tastier than traditional French cuisine, and is often characterized by unusual combinations of high-quality ingredients, and carefully presented, smaller and more manageable portions. *Nouvelle cuisine* is not a total culinary revolution, because although the ideas are different, the methods remain the same, but it is a far-reaching adaptation of classic French cooking to the requirements of the late 20thC.

It must not be thought, however, that *nouvelle cuisine* has entirely swept traditional French cookery aside. On the contrary, the classic dishes will always remain, as will the excellent and more than ever popular *cuisine bourgeoise* that is the root of all French cooking. Regional cookery still flourishes, as a visit to Normandy or Nice, Alsace or the Auvergne or to many of the regionally-inspired restaurants in Paris will tell you.

Of course, it's not just French cuisine that can be sampled in Paris. Like all major capital cities, Paris is cosmopolitan, and although in our selection of the city's restaurants we have, for reasons of space, concentrated almost solely on French cooking, the food of many different nations is also to be found. Some parts of Paris have a remarkably ethnic flavour, such as the Marais, which is packed with Jewish restaurants.

Choosing a place to eat
There is little doubt that in Paris practically any mood or gastronomic whim can be catered for. Apart from the restaurants proper, upon which the selection on the following pages concentrates, there are many other types of eating houses providing snacks and lighter meals. Since few people can even eat, let alone enjoy, two full-blooded French meals a day, it is a good idea to try a place of this sort for lunch, and

visit a restaurant in the evening, or vice versa.

Brasseries are restaurants-cum-cafés, often with a long bar, which serve both large and light meals, and some of the best are included in our selection of restaurants. Choosing somewhere for a pleasant snack is unlikely to prove problematic or disappointing, but taking pot-luck with restaurants is more hazardous, although it can just as easily

---

A resumé of cooking styles in Paris restaurants
Grande cuisine
Although the simpler classic dishes will survive no matter what, *grande cuisine* (also known as *haute cuisine*) on a grand scale has gone into irreversible decline, as labour costs have risen and people have become fussier about their digestions and waistlines. The cooking may necessitate 50 or more scullions in the kitchen, preparing rich and complicated dishes. Definitely food for a treat rather than for every day.

Nouvelle cuisine
The four main tenets of France's most recent school of cookery are that produce should be: fresh and of the highest quality; under- rather than over-cooked whenever possible; undisguised by rich, indigestible sauces; and often imaginatively combined with other ingredients. Particularly in Paris, however, one must beware of chefs who have exploited the cult of *nouvelle cuisine* by serving badly thought-out and often outlandish combinations of ingredients in amounts so tiny that they do not even cover the centres of the basketweave-patterned crockery that in such places seems to be *de rigueur*. Less unscrupulous and more dedicated chefs tend to re-interpret the well-established favourites of *cuisine bourgeoise* while retaining the better elements of *nouvelle cuisine*.

Cuisine bourgeoise
This can be classical, traditional or mainstream cooking, often with a regional flavour. It is the alchemy that turns a tough old bird or gristly cut of meat into a dish that melts in your mouth. *Cuisine bourgeoise* has never been more popular. An increasing number of Paris restaurants that once served nothing but *grande cuisine*, then tried pure *nouvelle cuisine*, now offer lighter versions of such stalwarts as *coq au vin, blanquette de veau, civet de lièvre*, and so on.

Regional cookery
One of the great fountainheads of mainstream French cooking, regional dishes have as their keynotes extraordinary variety and the ingenious use of mundane ingredients. Languedoc's *cassoulet* is an example, being made from white haricot beans, sausages, pork and preserved goose. Regional cookery lends an added dimension to some of Paris' best restaurants.

Ethnic cookery
Chinese (usually Vietnamese in disguise), unashamed Vietnamese, Italian, Russian and Jewish are the main non-French cuisines to be found in Paris, as well as North African food, from the former French colonies of Morocco, Tunisia and Algeria.

turn out to be a real find as a disaster. Look carefully at the menu in the window of the restaurant. If the chef takes any trouble, there will be a few *plats du jour*, *specialités* or unusual dishes; a drab list of easily refrigerated *escalopes*, chops and steaks bodes ill.

A packed restaurant is always a good sign, but this is no golden rule, as some good and less expensive restaurants are half-empty in the evening, while fashionable establishments do not fill up until 9pm. Bear in mind that it is always worth making a reservation, particularly if the restaurant you have chosen is a well-established one.

Our selection of restaurants has been made not only to give a good choice of price and area, but also with consideration to atmosphere, and style of cuisine. Addresses, telephone numbers and nearest Métro stations are given, as well as symbols showing particularly luxurious (⌂) or simple (⌷) restaurants, and those that represent good value (♣). Other symbols show price categories, and other noteworthy points. See *Key to symbols* on page 6, or the back jacket flap, for the full list of symbols. Refer to *Money* on pages 9-10 for an explanation of our credit card listings.

For those in a hurry...
The **Drugstores** (little like their American originals) are popular too and, like *brasseries*, provide continuous service throughout the day. The ordinary café, always close at hand, is an excellent place for anything from a *croque-monsieur* (ham-and-cheese sandwich fried in egg batter) to a midday *plat du jour*, often scrawled in whitewash on the window. Ask for *un sandwich mixte* to get one of those huge pieces of *baguette* that come stuffed with cheese and ham. People eat these quite happily on the street, too.

The more prestigious *salons de thé* and their recent offshoots, sometimes called *tarteries*, specialize in tarts, quiches and pizzas. The **Tarte Julie** chain give guaranteed quality. Hamburger chains are firmly established in Paris, and the ubiquitous **McDonald's** prove a good bargain for family meals if the kids are feeling unadventurous. A more indigenous and imaginative version of fast food is the *croissant* in various unorthodox guises (stuffed with anything from cheese to raspberries and bananas). *Crêpes*, too, make delicious take-away food.

Perhaps the very best place for a gourmet snack, however, is one of the cafés that serve a very wide range of excellent wines by the glass, with sandwiches of equally high quality. The **L'Écluse** group are worth looking out for, as well as an ever-increasing number of winebars, such as **Willi's**.

The menu
At first sight, a French menu can be a mystifying document. But, particularly if you are trying to estimate the likely cost, there are several things for which you should look. Does the set menu (*menu à prix fixe* or *menu conseillé*), if available, include drink (*boisson comprise* or *b.c.*, *vin compris* or *v.c.*), and is it free of *suppléments* on the dishes you want? If not, you may find yourself paying substantially more than the basic price. Fortunately the service charge now has to be included, by law.

The set menu is often very good value at more expensive restaurants. The choice of dishes may be rather limited, but the difference in price compared with the same fare *à la carte* is often considerable, even if portions are occasionally smaller.

The menu at a restaurant that offers only *à la carte* fare needs careful scrutiny too, because sometimes normally inexpensive dishes such as salads may be offered at a disproportionately high price.

Restaurants that offer both set-price and *à la carte* menus often keep the former on a separate card, and you may find you have to ask specifically for this.

A full 5-course meal in France begins with hors-d'oeuvre, then continues with an *entrée* (often a fish dish), main course (often a *plat du jour*) and sometimes salad, before cheese, and finally a dessert. A true feast, but if all that sounds too much for your palate to cope with, you can order a main course with either a starter or dessert from the *à la carte* menu. See *Menu decoder* in **Words and phrases**, p205.

As you are handed the menu, you will probably be asked if you want an aperitif. The French prefer not to knock out their taste buds with a whisky or dry Martini (the properly mixed version of which is unknown outside a few deluxe hotel bars). Instead they might order a *kir* (blackcurrant liqueur — *cassis* — with white wine) or a *kir royal* (with champagne).

Wines in Paris

The wine you choose when eating out depends very much on your choice of restaurant, and in Paris you can find the richest variety in the world. Among these you will also find differing degrees of seriousness about wine, ranging from the establishments that push the wine with the highest profit margin, to some, like **L'Écluse**, where their primary interest is in featuring 15 Bordeaux and offering light meals to match.

Although there is much talk about asking the advice of a wine-waiter (*sommelier*), in fact there are hardly two dozen Paris restaurants that have one who is properly qualified.

A restaurant need not have a *sommelier* to keep a good wine list, however. Try asking advice from the owner, who is not infrequently the person who greets and seats the customers, and is probably also the one who buys the wines.

You should always look at the wine list for an idea of the price range and qualities offered *before* asking advice. There are invariably some bargains, but they are not always easy to find. On average the mark-up is about three times higher than the price you will pay in a wine shop.

French wines are classified into *Appellation Contrôlée*, *VDQS* (*Vin Délimité de Qualité Supérieure*), *Vin de Pays* or *Vin de Table*, which is not a guarantee of quality. They simply mean that each category must conform to certain criteria of origin, vinification and grape variety. The criteria are more strict for *Appellation Contrôlée* than *VDQS*, and so on down the scale, and prices reflect this. Good value, however, can be found in each category. *Vin de Pays*, literally "country wine", offers the best value in many restaurants. These wines are from lesser regions, but are made according to strict rules. Often they are labelled by their grape variety — Cabernet Sauvignon, Chardonnay etc. — which is not usually the case with *Appellation Contrôlée* wines.

The reputation of the grower, château or *négociant* is another extremely important criterion, particularly with

Burgundies. If a name is not familiar, it is often wiser to choose according to the year, because a good vintage *VDQS* can often be better quality, and value, than a mediocre vintage of an *Appellation Contrôlée*. Most wine in the lower categories is blended by the shippers and does not carry vintage dates. *Vin de Table* is commonly served in carafes or jugs called *pichets*. *VDQS* is being slowly phased out, leaving *AC* and *Vin de Pays* as the two categories. In choosing wines, the so-called *Réserve du Patron* should generally be avoided. In nearly all Paris restaurants it is of very poor quality and simply not worth the risk.

It is now rare to find old wines on Parisian lists, the French taste being more inclined towards the more recent vintages.

An important consideration when choosing wine is the type of cuisine. The more thoughtful restaurateurs will pick their wine list with their cooking in mind; thus a *nouvelle cuisine* establishment will favour lighter, more elegant wines than one serving robust regional cooking. Unfortunately in many restaurants, fashion, ignorance or sheer laziness dictate the choice. It is hard to create adventurous wine and food matches when the wine list features only the old standbys.

Wine and food

Choosing wine to go with food is primarily a matter of common sense. A meal is a progression of tastes, and for this reason a dry wine is often chosen at the beginning of a meal to accompany the more simple-tasting first course. This progression may also be a cause of difficulties with cheese: some are too fatty or strong-tasting for the delicate old red that was drunk with the main course. Ordering a white or young red would be an anticlimax and, consequently, it is rare that a wine is specifically ordered to go with the cheese.

But you can always be adventurous and try following the guidance of your palate. And to this end it is interesting that the Lyonnais sometimes drink a light chilled Beaujolais with oysters; and one of Paris' best wine waiters dispels the myth than no wine goes with salad vinaigrette, suggesting that a young Chinon or Beaujolais agree perfectly well.

When eating regional food, it pays to pick a wine from the same area. Some partnerships are enshrined in gastronomic legend: red Bordeaux with lamb, Muscadet with shellfish. Others are less obvious but equally enjoyable: in the Loire Valley they enjoy salmon with a light red, such as Chinon or Saumur Champigny. Dishes from Provence, with their emphasis on strong olive oil, tomato and herb flavours, are well matched by Provençal and Rhône wines. The cuisine of the Lot and Dordogne, built around rich foods such as preserved duck, goose and truffles, is complemented by the red wines of Bergerac, Cahors and Duras.

It is risky, even in Paris, to order very fine wines in a restaurant: too much depends on unknowable factors such as skill of the cellarman and the sense of the *sommelier*.

Restaurants listed by arrondissement

2ᵉ
Chez Pierrot *▯* to *▯▯*
Delmonico *▯▯▯*
Le Vaudeville *▯▯* to *▯▯▯*
3ᵉ
L'Ambassade d'Auvergne *▯▯*
La Taverne des Templiers *▯▯* to *▯▯▯*
4ᵉ
L'Ambroisie *▯▯▯* △
Esther Street *▯▯*
La Taverne du Sergent Recruteur
▯▯
5ᵉ
Atelier Maître Albert *▯▯* ✿
Le Balzar *▯▯*
Bistrot de la Nouvelle Mairie *▯▯* ☗
La Bûcherie *▯▯* to *▯▯▯*
Chez Toutoune *▯▯* ✿
Dodin Bouffant *▯▯▯* ✿
Institut du Monde Arabe *▯▯* to *▯▯▯*
Au Pactole *▯▯* to *▯▯▯*
La Tour d'Argent *▯▯▯* △
6ᵉ
L'Assiette au Boeuf-I *▯* to *▯▯*
L'Attrape-Coeur *▯▯* ✿
Bistro de la Gare-II *▯▯*
Le Chat Grippé *▯▯*
Le Cherche Midi *▯▯*
Chez Claude Sainlouis *▯* ✿
La Closerie des Lilas *▯▯▯*
L'Écluse *▯▯*
La Hulotte *▯▯* ✿
Lapérouse *▯▯▯*
Lipp *▯▯*
La Méditerranée *▯▯▯* to *▯▯▯*
Le Muniche *▯▯*
Le Petit Zinc *▯▯*
Polidor *▯▯* ☗ ✿
Le Procope *▯▯* to *▯▯▯*
7ᵉ
Bistrot de Paris *▯▯▯*
Chez Françoise *▯▯*
Chez Ribe *▯▯*
Aux Fins Gourmets *▯▯*
Le Jardin *▯▯*
Jules Verne *▯▯▯*
La Petite Chaise *▯* to *▯▯*
Relais Saint-Germain *▯▯* ✿
Le Sancerrois *▯▯* ☗
Thoumieux *▯▯*
Le Télégraphe *▯▯* to *▯▯▯*
8ᵉ
Bateaux-Mouches *▯▯▯* ✿
Baumann-Marbeuf *▯▯*
Baumann-Napoléon *▯▯▯*
Bistro de la Gare III *▯▯*
Boulangerie St-Philippe *▯* to
▯▯ ☗

La Boutique à Sandwichs *▯* to
▯ ☗ ☗
Le Bristol *▯▯▯* △
Chez Edgard *▯▯▯*
Daru *▯▯*
L'Écluse *▯▯*
La Fermette Marbeuf *▯▯*
Lasserre *▯▯▯* △
Laurent *▯▯▯* △
Le Lord Gourmand *▯▯* to *▯▯▯*
La Marcande *▯▯▯*
Maxim's *▯▯▯* △
Le Moulin du Village *▯▯*
Au Petit Montmorency *▯▯*
to *▯▯▯*
Les Princes *▯▯▯* △
Régence-Plaza *▯▯▯* △
Taillevent *▯▯▯* △
Le Val d'Or *▯▯* ✿
Au Vieux Berlin *▯* to *▯▯*
9ᵉ
Bistro de la Gare-IV *▯▯*
Chartier *▯* ☗ ✿
L'Écluse *▯▯*
Le Grand Café *▯▯*
Au Petit Riche *▯▯*
10ᵉ
Brasserie Flo *▯▯*
Julien *▯▯*
Terminus Nord *▯▯*
12ᵉ
Le Trou Gascon *▯▯* to *▯▯▯*
14ᵉ
L'Auberge de l'Argoat *▯▯* ✿
La Coupole *▯▯*
Le Duc *▯▯* to *▯▯▯*
Hawai *▯* ✿
Pavillon Montsouris *▯▯*
to *▯▯▯* △
Le Pouilly *▯▯*
15ᵉ
L'Aquitaine *▯▯▯*
Le Clos Morillons *▯▯* to *▯▯▯*
Morot-Gaudry *▯▯▯*
Pierre Vedel *▯▯* ✿
16ᵉ
Au Clocher du Village *▯▯*
to *▯▯*
Le Pré Catelan *▯▯▯* △
Robuchon (Jamin) *▯▯▯*
Le Vivarois *▯▯▯* △
17ᵉ
Chez Gorisse *▯▯* ✿
Chez Fred *▯▯*
Au Relais Pereire *▯▯*
18ᵉ
A. Beauvilliers *▯▯▯* △
Le Maquis *▯▯* to *▯▯*

L'Ambassade d'Auvergne
22 Rue du Grenier-St-Lazare, 3ᵉ
☎ 42-72-31-22. Map **10**H10 *▯▯* ⒶⒺ
🍴 Last orders 11.30pm. Métro:
Arts-et-Métiers, Rambuteau.
The vast majority of café-owners in
Paris hail from the Auvergne. When
they have something to celebrate,
they will, as often as not, head for
this invitingly rustic "embassy" of

Auvergnat tradition to savour the
dishes of their — or their parents' —
childhood. Only here can they find
such specialities as *mourtayrol* and
estofinado. The Auvergne cheeses,
which owner Joseph Petrucci obtains
from his wife's relations, are quite
superb. The welcome, the family
atmosphere... and the food, are
delightful.

Restaurants

L'Ambroisie ⌂
9 Pl. des Vosges, 4ᵉ
☎ 42-78-51-45. Map 11❚11 ▥
▣ ▬ ⊶ Last orders 10.15pm.
Closed Mon, 1st 3wks in
Aug. Métro: Bastille.
Awarded a Michelin 3-star rating
most recently, master chef Bernard
Pacaud's L'Ambroisie is now rightly
placed among the highest ranks of
Paris restaurants. Built towards the
end of the 16thC, this fine house
was refashioned in 1984 by top
gastronome decorator François-
Joseph Graf, who brought to its
high-ceilinged main dining room the
elegance of a Venetian villa. An
immense tapestry dominates the
tranquil, flower-decorated space.
Pacaud's cooking is imaginatively
nouvelle. A relatively short menu
seems to be the model of sobriety,
yet there are wondrous subtleties to
be experienced in every dish. This is
a small establishment (40 places), so
best book at least 2wks ahead.

André Faure ♣
40 Rue du Mont-Thabor, 1ᵉʳ
☎ 42-60-74-28. Map 8G7 □ Last
orders 10pm. Closed Sun, Aug.
Métro: Concorde.
This conveniently located restaurant
(just by Pl. de la Concorde) offers
nourishing fare and generous
portions at very modest prices. The
emphasis is on straightforward
cuisine bourgeoise rather than on
great subtlety.

L'Aquitaine
54 Rue de Dantzig, 15ᵉ
☎ 48-28-67-38 ▥ 🍴 ▣AE ▣ Last
orders 11.30pm. Closed Sun,
Mon. Métro: Convention.
There are few pleasures greater than
eating on the first-floor terrace of
L'Aquitaine, overlooking La Ruche,
the "*cité des artistes*" where Soutine,
Modigliani and Chagall worked.
Sample the superb cuisine of
Christiane Massia, who, with the
help of an all-female team of
assistant cooks — and her husband
Michel, for the fine selection of
wines and Armagnacs — treats
typically southwestern ingredients
with an idiosyncratically light touch.
Confits come with sorrel purée; a
discreet Roquefort sauce is served
with steamed turbot.

Armand au Palais-Royal
6 Rue de Beaujolais, 1ᵉʳ
☎ 42-60-05-11. Map 9G8 ▥ ▣AE
▣ Last orders 1am. Closed Sat
lunch, Sun, four days over
Christmas. Métro: Bourse,
Palais-Royal.

Elegant and subtle lighting over the
royal blue carpet and Louis XIII
chairs help to create a beautiful
dining experience in the shadow of
the colonnades of the Palais-Royal,
glimpsed through picture windows.
A skilfully handled *nouvelle cuisine*
bill of fare is highly regarded and
the fixed-price menu at lunch is
excellent value.

L'Assiette au Boeuf
22 Rue Guillaume-Apollinaire, 6ᵉ
☎ 42-60-88-44. Map 8I7 □ to I□
Last orders 1am. Métro: St-
Germain-des-Prés.
A jolly place to dine: always
crowded with all kinds of folk who
appreciate a standard "safe" menu
that can be relied on for quality, at a
very reasonable price, and in a
richly-mirrored Art Nouveau setting
that remains delightfully unspoiled.

Atelier Maître Albert ♣
1-5 Rue Maître-Albert, 5ᵉ
☎ 46-33-13-78. Map 10J10 ▥□ ▬
Last orders midnight. Closed for
lunch and Sun. Métro: Maubert-
Mutualité.
When a formula works, it's a good
idea to stick to it, and that's how
things are at this maze-like, low-lit
restaurant. For years, contented Left
Bankers have flocked back for the
very reasonably-priced set dinner
(no lunch) offering plenty of choice:
five starters, seven main dishes, two
cheeses and seven desserts, washed
down by, perhaps, a well-chosen
Gamay de Touraine. In winter the
superb old fireplace springs to life
with a blaze of logs.

L'Attrape-Coeur ♣
9 Rue Christine, 6ᵉ ☎ 43-54-
43-42. Map 9I8 I□ ▣ Last
orders 11pm (midnight Sat).
Closed Sat lunch, Sun, Mon,
1wk at Christmas, Easter, 3wks
in Aug. Métro: Odéon, Mabillon.
The quietness and gentility of Rue
Christine provide a contrast to the
bustling charm of this excellent little
restaurant. Ancient stone walls,
bronzed mirrors and an abundance
of fresh flowers; charmingly efficient
staff serving *cuisine bourgeoise*
prepared with a light touch, to the
Latin Quarter crowds. Plenty of
French people in there along with
visitors from afar.

L'Auberge de l'Argoat ♣
27 Av. Reille, 14ᵉ ☎ 45-89-17-05.
I□ ▬ 🍴 Last orders 10pm.
Closed Sun, Mon, 3wks in Aug.
Métro: Porte-d'Orléans.
A warm atmosphere prevails in this

unjustly little-known restaurant.
Jeanine Gaulon, who presides over
the kitchen, has brought her own
style while still giving the traditional
pride of place to fish, marrying it
with recondite combinations such as
raw fish with fresh ginger. This
family restaurant goes from strength
to strength. Good value.

Le Balzar
49 Rue des Écoles, 5ᵉ
☎ 43-54-13-67. Map 15J9 ▥▯ Æ
*Last orders 12.30am. Closed
Aug. Métro: Maubert-Mutualité.*
Solid, traditional fare (grilled pigs'
trotters, fillet of beef) is served here
by expert waiters in waistcoats and
long aprons. But people eat at this
old-fashioned Latin Quarter
brasserie (or have a drink in its
small café section) not so much for
the food as to watch famous actors
and actresses, television
personalities, talent-spotters and
members of the literary world.
Perennially popular — long may
they keep the sawdust-strewn floor.

Bateaux-Mouches ✿
Pont de l'Alma, 8ᵉ
☎ 42-25-96-10. Map 7G4 ▥▯
children ▥▯ 📞 ▦ ▦ ▣ For
dinner open every day, but
closed Mon Nov 1-Mar 5. Lunch
Sat, Sun only, Nov 1-Mar 5.
Métro: Alma-Marceau.
Eating on a Bateaux-Mouches
cruiser as it chugs up and down the
River Seine may not appeal to
everyone, but it is a romantic and
remarkably neat way to combine
traffic-free sightseeing with good
classical food. The two options
available — a moderately priced
lunch trip and a more expensive
and lavish dinner outing (jacket and
tie required) — are both very good
value, considering that they include
the price of the very pleasant river
trip. You could even spend tea-time
on board: one-week reservation
(*Tues, Thurs, Sat 3.30-5.45pm*).

Baumann-Marbeuf
15 Rue Marbeuf, 8ᵉ
☎ 47-20-11-11. Map 7F4 ▥▯ ▤
📞 ▣ Last orders 1am.
Closed Aug. Métro: Franklin-
D-Roosevelt.
One of the best brasseries around —
complete with a butcher who cuts
his meat from a vantage point in the
middle of the room. They offer a
wide choice of red meats, and the
house speciality is *choucroute*, for
which Baumann is justly famed.
Good wines, too, and all-round
cheerful service, which go a long

way towards making this a very
popular place. Extraordinary Louis
XV chandeliers and mirrors
everywhere give a Hollywood feel.

Baumann-Napoléon
38 Av. de Friedland, 8ᵉ
☎ 42-27-99-50. Map 7E4 ▥▯ ▤
▦ ▣ Last orders 10.30pm.
Closed Aug. Métro: Charles-de-
Gaulle-Étoile.
This restaurant, and the **Marbeuf**,
(above) are owned by Guy-Pierre
Baumann, and serve a cuisine that is
predominantly Alsatian. These days,
the Napoléon is exclusively a fish
restaurant, and strikes a balance
between *nouvelle* and *classique
cuisine*. Many types of sauerkraut
are featured, plus a good selection
of wines and Alsatian *alcools blancs*
(fruit spirits). Chef Eric Lassauce
works wonders with centuries-old
recipes — as well as up-to-the-
minute dishes.

A. Beauvilliers ◭
52 Rue Lamarck, 18ᵉ
☎ 42-54-19-50. Map 4C8 ▥▯ ▤
📞 ▣ Last orders 10.30pm.
Closed Sun, Mon lunch, Sept.
Métro: Lamarck-Caulaincourt.
One has the sense, when dining
here, of being a guest in a calm and
beautiful private house, and that is
precisely the effect that owner
Edouard Carlier has striven to
create. The restaurant is filled with
lovely things: antique silver,
porcelain, flowers, and Carlier's
own superb collection of prints. The
house itself stands on the hillside of
Montmartre and has a delightful
terrace. The food, served either
indoors or on the terrace, matches
the surroundings — Carlier aims for
top quality, and always seems to
achieve it.

Bistro de la Gare-I
30 Rue St-Denis, 1ᵉʳ ☎ 40-26-82-
80. Map 9H9 ▯ Last orders
1am. Métro: Châtelet-Les-Halles.
Bistro de la Gare-II
59 Bd. du Montparnasse, 6ᵉ
☎ 45-48-38-01. Map 14K7 ▯
Last orders 1am. Métro:
Montparnasse-Bienvenue.
Bistro de la Gare-III
73 Av. des Champs-Élysées, 8ᵉ
☎ 43-59-67-83. Map 7F4 ▯ Last
orders 1am. Métro: George-V.
Bistro de la Gare-IV
38 Bd. des Italiens, 9ᵉ ☎ 48-24-
49-61. Map 9F8 ▯ Last orders
1am. Métro: Richelieu-Drouot.
The Bistro de la Gare group have
proved to be among Paris' best
stand-bys for people who want a

reliable, quick meal when going to a show or film. They provide — every day of the year till the early hours — limited but carefully balanced set menus at a reasonable price. The simplest *formule* (formula) menu — just main course and a salad — is ideal at lunchtime, while for a little more, you have a wide choice of starters and main dishes. Look out, too, for the option to eat *à volonté* (all you can eat for one price).

The Montparnasse branch, formerly the Restaurant Rougeot, boasts one of the finest Art Nouveau decors in Paris, with mini-landscapes in *faïence*, mirrors, and a stained-glass ceiling.

Bistrot de la Nouvelle Mairie ≡
19 Rue des Fossés-St-Jacques, 5ᵉ ☎ 43-26-80-18. Map 15K9 □ ≡ Last orders midnight. Closed Sat, Sun, Aug. Métro: Luxembourg.
A few minutes' walk from the Luxembourg Gardens is this attractive prewar café. The small selection of good hot snacks and sandwiches is really only a pretext for cracking open a bottle (or two) from their succinct but excellent range of Beaujolais and Loire wines, or for trying the proprietor's superb old rum.

Bistrot de Paris
33 Rue de Lille, 7ᵉ ☎ 42-61-16-83. Map 8H7 ■■■ Last orders 11pm. Closed Sat lunch, Sun. Métro: Solférino.
The fashionable gastronomic meeting place, the Bistrot de Paris, is the jewel in the crown of restaurant supremo Michel Oliver. Tables are packed, the conversation animated, the Art Nouveau decor ravishing, and the food first class. The bill undoubtedly reflects not only the food, but the famous faces to be found eating there.

Boulangerie St-Philippe ≡
73 Av. Franklin-D-Roosevelt, 8ᵉ ☎ 43-59-78-76. Map 7G5 □ to ■■ Closed for dinner and Sat. Métro: Franklin-D-Roosevelt.
Elbow your way through the crowds of gourmet shoppers and office workers buying snacks in this busy bakery, and you'll find a pleasant little lunch restaurant serving surprisingly sophisticated *plats du jour*. The butter and cream used in these dishes, and in the delicious desserts and pastries, comes from Echiré, which has an *appellation*, like a wine-producing area.

La Boutique à Sandwichs ≡ ✿
12 Rue du Colisée, 8ᵉ ☎ 43-59-56-69. Map 2F5 □ to ■■ Last orders 1am. Closed Sun, Aug. Métro: Franklin-D-Roosevelt.
There is hidden treasure behind the rather modest name and exterior. Two Alsatian brothers, Claude and Hubert Schick, run the place with great dash, flair and friendliness. On the ground-floor is a sandwich boutique, but an unusually good one, selling some 40 different varieties, all made to order. Upstairs is a cosy dining room where you can count on the kind of wholesome cooking, lovingly prepared, for which Alsace is famous. Especially delicious are the *pickelfleisch* (salt beef) and *raclette valaisanne* (fondu cheese with potatoes, pickles and charcuterie). Hearty portions at bargain prices. Located just off the Champs-Élysées and open late, this is a useful stand-by for film-goers.

Brasserie Flo
7 Cour des Petites-Écuries, 10ᵉ ☎ 47-70-13-59. Map 5F10 ■■ ▣ Last orders 10.30pm. Métro: Château-d'Eau.
One of Jean-Paul Bucher's six Paris restaurants (see also **La Coupole**, **Julien**, **Terminus Nord** and **Le Vaudeville**), Brasserie Flo reflects his Alsatian origins in its food and drink, and there is beer drawn from the barrel, a rarity in Paris. The turn-of-the-century decor, with its old brass luggage racks and hat-stands, is equally reminiscent of France's most Germanic province. Despite, or because of, the brasserie's cramped seating and reasonable prices, it attracts a lot of well-known faces.

Le Bristol ⌂
112 Rue du Faubourg-St-Honoré, 8ᵉ ☎ 42-66-91-45. Map 7F6 ■■■ ▣ ▣ Last orders 10.30pm. Métro: Champs-Élysées-Clemenceau.
It's the decor and the clientele that are most distinctive and distinguished here (see also *Hotels*). The dining room, gently lit from above and lined with *Régence* wood panelling, is one of the most elegant to be found in any luxury Parisian hotel. Your neighbours at the next table are likely to be members of the more staid international jet-set (politicians, chief executives, elderly heiresses). If you don't care about the setting or the company, you can always fall

back on Émile Tabourdiau's excellent cuisine, which is best described as discreetly *nouvelle*.

La Bûcherie
41 Rue de la Bûcherie, 5ᵉ
☎ 43-54-78-06. Map **19J9** ⬛ to
⬛⬛ ⬛ ⬛ ⬛ *Last orders 12.30am. Open as salon de thé 3-7.30pm. Métro: Maubert-Mutualité.*
This restaurant can be a bit cramped, but on a cold winter's evening, with the logs crackling in the grate and lots of convivial neighbours, few would object. Amiable, bear-like Bernard Bosque is an inventive cook: witness his interpretation of fish *à l'oseille*, in which he replaces sorrel with the equally tart but distinctive rhubarb. He delights when game is in season and contents himself with specializing in fish for the rest of the year.

His desserts are light and delicious, and his wine list strong, featuring both well-known and less familiar vintages.

Chartier 🍴 ♣
7 Rue du Faubourg-Montmartre, 9ᵉ ☎ 47-70-86-29. Map **9F9** ⬜
Last orders 9.30pm. Métro: Rue-Montmartre.
Hurry to get a last glimpse of Paris' sole surviving mid-19thC *bouillon* decor (*bouillons* were popular restaurants, or soup kitchens) before it becomes transmogrified, with taste of course, into a chic "eatery". The atmosphere is very much the same as it must have been 100yrs ago, and prices don't seem to have risen much either. The Bohemian atmosphere, and not the food, is what going to Chartier's is all about.

Le Châtelet Gourmand ♣
13 Rue des Lavandières-Ste-Opportune, 1ᵉʳ ☎ 40-26-45-00.
Map **9H9** ⬛ to ⬛⬛ ⬛ *Closed Sun, Mon, 1st 2wks in Feb, 1st 3wks in Aug. Last orders 10.30pm. Métro: Châtelet.*
Guy Girard, who used to run **Le Petit Coin de la Bourse**, has bounced back to Paris after a spell in the provinces and a recovery from a serious illness. Now 60, he got his first Michelin star at 23 and has been known for many years for his unusual approach. His encyclopaedic knowledge of the history of cooking shows in the dishes on offer at this attractive but unpretentious restaurant. He is particularly interested in medieval spit-roasting techniques and will

spit-roast anything, from spiny lobsters and monkfish to venison and lamb. 19thC dishes have been skilfully brought up to date: try sweetbreads in *sauce financière*, or a magical fusion of duck with orange in the *magret Grand Marnier*. The set menus are a real bargain, and you can eat fabulous food here, for little more than a song.

Le Chat Grippé
87 Rue d'Assas, 6ᵉ
☎ 43-54-70-00. Map **15K8** ⬛
Last orders 10.30pm. Closed Sat lunch, Easter, Aug. Métro: Vavin.
A small, elegant and well-regarded establishment in the hinterland of the Luxembourg Gardens, an area not over-endowed with restaurants. The proprietor, Marc Prunières, provides a broad-based menu, geared to seasonal availability. Strong points in his repertoire include *foie gras au ratafia de champagne*, and some mouthwatering desserts such as *"pastis" quercynois avec sorbet à la pomme.*

Le Cherche Midi
22 Rue du Cherche Midi, 6ᵉ
☎ 45-48-27-44. Map **14J7** ⬛
Last orders midnight. Métro: Sèvres-Babylone.
If you want a change from French cuisine and like the idea of an Italian meal, this friendly, informal restaurant would be a good choice. There is a small but consistently good-quality menu offering a variety of fresh pastas, as well as such dishes as Parma ham, and *carpaccio* made with mushrooms, celery and parmesan.

The decor has a homely touch, with large primitive paintings of country scenes. It is advisable to reserve in advance.

Chez Claude Sainlouis ♣
27 Rue du Dragon, 6ᵉ
☎ 45-48-29-68. Map **8I7** ⬜ *Last orders 11pm. Closed Sun, Aug, Easter, Christmas, New Year. Métro: St-Germain-des-Prés.*
When owner Claude Sainlouis (real name, Claude Piau) gave up his job as a stuntman and took up catering, he decided he wasn't going to take any more risks. For the last 25yrs or so, he has been serving an immutable menu of salad, expertly grilled steak and chocolate mousse for (almost) a song. His caution paid off: the place is permanently packed with people out for an evening in St-Germain-des-Prés.

Restaurants

Chez Edgard
4 Rue Marbeuf, 8ᵉ
☎ 47-20-51-15. Map 7F4 ▥▥ AE
◉ 🦞 Last orders 12.30am.
Closed Sun. Métro: Franklin-D-Roosevelt.

Perhaps the most startling thing about this excellent if rather noisy restaurant, which is located in the plush business quarter of Av. George-V and constantly bulges at the seams with personalities from politics, the cinema, and commercial radio, is its wide spectrum of prices. The food is not the bargain it once was, but you can still eat a 3-course meal for a reasonable price. The fare is simple but imaginative, and the sweet whiff of the sea, as you walk in, bears witness to the freshness of the shellfish displayed outside.

Chez Françoise
Aérogare des Invalides, 7ᵉ
☎ 47-05-49-03. Map 13H5 ▥▥ AE
◉ Last orders midnight. Closed Sun evening and Aug. Métro: Invalides.

Conveniently tucked away in the Invalides Air Terminal, this is a rather old-fashioned-looking buffet, with skylight and potted plants. However, it provides reliable and far from dull dishes, as well as inexpensive wines, for the air traveller wishing to leave the capital with a pleasant taste in the mouth.

Chez Fred
190bis, Bd. Pereire, 17ᵉ
☎ 45-74-20-48. ▥▥ AE ◉ Closed Sat lunch, Sun. Last orders 10.30pm. Métro: Ternes.

A cosy bistro serving good, solid traditional fare (terrines, coq au vin etc.) in an area where such places do not lie thick on the ground. Chez Fred is a great favourite with television and showbiz personalities. Its relaxed atmosphere is generated by the patron, Robert Marc, who is banteringly chatty without being obtrusive.

Chez Gorisse ♥
84 Rue Nollet, 17ᵉ
☎ 46-27-43-05. Map 3C6 ▥▥ 🍴
Last orders 10pm. Closed Sun. Métro: La Fourche.

Here you will find a cosy and old-fashioned atmosphere and reasonable prices. The cooking is a mixture of such down-to-earth dishes as navarin d'agneau and pot-au-feu, and more inventive ones such as brioche à la moelle. But the fare, although simple, is always excellent. A good little place for people in the know.

Chez Pierrot ♥
18 Rue Étienne-Marcel, 2ᵉ
☎ 45-08-05-48. Map 10G9 ▥ to
▥▥ No cards. Métro: Étienne-Marcel.

No fancy decor, no pretensions — a straightforward style that belies the gastronomic treat in store. Cuisine bourgeoise cooked with the lightest and surest of touches is served with considerable charm in a warm, family atmosphere.

Chez Ribe
15 Av. de Suffren, 7ᵉ
☎ 45-66-53-79. Map 12I3 ▥ AE
◉ 🦞 Last orders 10.30pm.
Closed Sun, last 2wks Aug, week of Christmas and New Year.
Métro: Champ-de-Mars.

Radio and TV people working in the area like this well-redecorated former bougnat (coal merchant's shop and café). Owner Antoine Pérès cooks most of the dishes, which are generously served, while his diet-conscious wife Mireille is in charge of starters and desserts. The style is fairly traditional, with regional touches, although there are also more modern dishes such as raw marinated scallops (when in season) and veal with limes.

Chez Toutoune ♥
5 Rue de Pontoise, 5ᵉ
☎ 43-26-56-81. Map 10J10 ▥▥
AE Last orders 10.45pm. Closed Sun, Mon lunch, Aug 15-Sept 15. Métro: Maubert-Mutualité.

Good food cuts across class divisions (in France at least), which probably explains Chez Toutoune's wide spectrum of customers, from casually-dressed students to elderly bourgeois couples complete with pearls and Légion d'honneur rosettes. The friendly atmosphere is effortlessly created by the blonde Toutoune herself.

The formula is a lavish 5-course set menu chalked up each day on a blackboard: a soup, a good choice of entrées and main dishes, two cheeses in peak condition, and a battery of desserts. The cuisine is sophisticated provincial — like the best of grandmother's recipes. Toutoune's fame through her TV presentations brought even more business to an already popular restaurant, so reservations are advisable.

Au Clocher du Village ♥
8bis Rue Verderet, 16ᵉ
☎ 42-88-35-87. ▥ to ▥▥ Last orders 10.30pm. Closed Sat,

Sun, Aug. Métro: Église d'Auteuil.

A picture-postcard place with the atmosphere of an old *auberge*, located in a charming little village square. Lace curtains, old posters on the walls, wine presses hanging from the ceiling, the place positively oozes charm. The food is excellent — well-prepared, classic French cuisine, leaving you glad to have had a taste of the "real France".

Le Clos Morillons
50 Rue des Morillons, 15ᵉ
☎ 48-28-04-37 〔 〕 to 〔〕〕 ▬ *Last orders 10.15pm. Closed Sat lunch, Sun. Métro: Convention.*
Located in rather a backwater of the 15ᵉ, this restaurant nevertheless has a good track record. Brothers Philippe and Marc Delacourcelle offer a fine selection of *nouvelle cuisine* that changes with the seasons. It tends to lightness and is prepared with great finesse. They specialize in Loire wines.

La Closerie des Lilas
171 Bd. du Montparnasse, 6ᵉ
☎ 43-26-70-50. Map **15L8**. 〔〕〕 〔AE〕
〔CB〕 ▬ 🏠 *Last orders 12.30am. Métro: Vavin.*
La Closerie has always been, and is still, the haunt of literati, artists and plain hacks. Nowadays they tend to congregate in the bar and brasserie section, whose prices are lower than in the restaurant proper, where a pleasant terrace accommodates an altogether more *bourgeois* crowd, and the food is appropriately classical.

La Coupole
102 Bd. du Montparnasse, 14ᵉ
☎ 43-20-14-20. Map **14K7** 〔〕〕
Open noon-2am. Closed Aug. Métro: Vavin.
La Coupole is Paris' largest brasserie, and an institution. It probably serves the most motley crowd of customers to be found in any Paris eating place: they range from besuited politicians to film-producers, from students to photographers, who appreciate the excellent exposure afforded by La Coupole's open plan with its long, broad aisles. Intelligently refurbished in 1989 by Jean-Paul Bucher for the **Flo** group of restaurants, La Coupole now offers good quality fare, and its 600 seats are as sought-after as ever.

Daru
19 Rue Daru, 8ᵉ ☎ 42-27-23-60. Map **2E4** 〔 〕 to 〔〕〕 ▬ *Last orders*

11pm. Closed Sun, Mon, Aug. Métro: Courcelles.
White Russians, many of them taxi-drivers, used to recall the "good old days" over a glass of vodka and a *zakouski* in this grocery/snack bar opposite the Russian Orthodox Church. Although most of them have since departed this world, the Daru remains a repository of Russian tradition, boasting a score of Russian and Polish vodkas. There is also tasty food for every purse, from *tarama* and *bortsch* to smoked salmon and caviar.

Delmonico
39 Av. de l'Opéra, 2ᵉ
☎ 42-61-44-26. Map **8F7** 〔〕〕 〔AE〕
〔CB〕 ▬ *Last orders 10pm. Closed Sat, Sun, Aug. Métro: Opéra.*
This is the restaurant of the Hôtel Edouard VII, superbly located a stone's throw from Pl. de l'Opéra. Outwardly the building retains its original splendid Belle Époque style, but the English monarch would no longer recognize the interior, which has been thoroughly modernized. The restaurant is quietly elegant and verdant with potted plants: a fine setting for a business lunch, but perhaps less so for an evening out. The chef, Claude Monteil, practises a cuisine that is broadly *nouvelle* in orientation.

Dodin Bouffant ✿
25 Rue Frédéric-Sauton, 5ᵉ
☎ 43-25-25-14. Map **15J9** 〔〕〕 ▬
🏠 〔CB〕 *Last orders midnight. Closed Sun, Aug, 10 days over Christmas and New Year. Métro: Maubert-Mutualité.*
Jacques Manière, among Paris' most iconoclastic, outspoken and warm-hearted chefs, made Dodin Bouffant one of the finest — and certainly cheapest for quality — restaurants in the capital. It was he who installed the saltwater tanks in the cellar, where oysters, mussels, clams, the rare *violet*, and other shellfish co-exist peacefully before expiring at your command.

Manière retired in 1981, and the chef for the last few years has been Philippe Valin, trained by Manière and lacking nothing of the master's skills. With Maurice Cartier, Valin has kept the Manière ensign flying, and the restaurant continues to offer those wonderful fish combinations, both as starters and as main courses, a sumptuous *plateau de fruits de mer* of utter freshness, unusual meat dishes, featherlight desserts, and wines that frankly are no less than a gift.

Restaurants

Le Duc
243 Bd. Raspail, 14^e
☎ 43-20-96-30. Map **14M7** ▥ to
▥ No cards ☎ Last orders
10.30pm. Closed Sat, Sun, Mon.
Métro: Denfert-Rochereau.
If, like Fats Waller, your favourite
dish is fish, make a point of eating at
Paul and Jean Minchelli's
establishment, which is regarded by
many as being the finest seafood-
only restaurant in town. Paul, who
has written an authoritative cookery
book on the subject, was one of the
first chefs to approach the
preparation of fish with a
completely fresh and inventive eye,
and, among other things, to take his
cue from the Japanese and explore
the possibilities of raw fish. In his
hot dishes, the fish is always cooked
to perfection (just a second or two
underdone), and never swathed in a
strong sauce of the kind that
destroys delicate flavours. Not a
cheapskate place to eat — but
worth every penny.

L'Écluse:
Branches at:
15 Quai des Grands-Augustins,
6e ☎ 46-33-58-74. Map **9I9**.
Métro: St-Michel.
64 Rue François-1er, 8^e
☎ 47-20-77-09. Map **7G4**. Métro:
George-V.
15 Pl. de la Madeleine, 8^e
☎ 42-65-34-69. Map **8F6**. Métro:
Madeleine.
4 Rue Halévy, 9e ☎ 47-42-62-33.
Map **8F7**. Métro: Opéra.
Rue Mondétour, 1er
☎ 47-03-30-73. Map **9H9**. Métro:
Châtelet-Les-Halles.
▱ at all branches. Last orders
1.30am.
Throughout this wine bar chain, the
good selection of vintage wines
available at reasonable prices can be
accompanied by excellent "super-
snacks": carpaccio, foie gras,
smoked salmon, saucisson sec, goat
cheese, and a superbly rich and
sticky chocolate cake that
connoisseurs travel far to sink their
teeth into.

L'Espadon △
15 Pl. Vendôme, 1er
☎ 42-60-38-30. Map **8G7** ▥ ▣
▣ ☎ ⌂ ⌐ Last orders 11pm.
Métro: Tuileries.
The wonderfully atmospheric
restaurant of the **Ritz** (see Hotels),
with its gentle lighting and trompe-
l'oeil, was presided over by Escoffier
at the turn of the century, and until
fairly recently, it maintained
standards worthy of the great man.

In the last few years, however, there
has been a slight decline, from
superlative to just plain good, and
the classic French menu has a strong
accent on fish. The à la carte costs
the expected fortune, but the fixed
menu is a bargain.

Esther Street
6 Rue de Jarente, 4^e
☎ 40-29-03-03 Map **11I9** ▱ Last
orders 10pm. Métro: St-Paul.
A small restaurant with a bright,
modern decor, in the heart of Paris'
Jewish quarter. Jewish cuisine can
be heavy. Here, as cooked by a
young woman of Polish-Jewish
descent, everything — even the
gefilte fish — is ethereally light.
There is also excellent cold bortsch,
stuffed chicken neck and some
more adventurous dishes, all with a
real Central European flavour.

La Fermette Marbeuf 1900
5 Rue Marbeuf, 8e ☎ 47-20-63-53
Map **7G4** ▥ ▣ ▣ Last orders
11.30pm. Métro: Alma-Marceau.
One of perhaps three of the finest
Art Nouveau restaurants in Paris
(see also **Bistro de la Gare** at
Montparnasse and **Julien**), this busy
and rather noisy restaurant offers
high-quality, fairly traditional food
with good meat and fish specialities
and plenty of seasonal changes. It
caters for a mixed bag of business
and media people. Very useful, as it
remains open all year round and
serves till late.

Aux Fins Gourmets
213 Bd. St-Germain, 7^e
☎ 42-22-06-57. Map **8I6** ▥ No
cards. Last orders 10pm. Closed
Sun, Aug, 1wk at Christmas.
Métro: Rue-du-Bac.
A cheerful little bistro that prides
itself in being unmodernized — one
of the few remaining bastions of
yellowing lincrusta wallpaper and
banquette seating, and where one
feels totally at home, sitting elbow-
to-elbow with the French, who are
out in force at this excellent outlet
for the country cuisine of the
southwest. Huge helpings of
cassoulet, filling desserts and a
generous cheeseboard made a
warm impression, as did the low
final price.

Gérard Besson ♥
5 Rue du Coq-Héron, 1er
☎ 42-33-14-74. Map **10G9** ▥ ▣
☎ Last orders 10pm. Closed
Sun, July and 1wk over
Christmas and New Year. Métro:
Les Halles.

The lunchtime menu served by Gérard Besson, owner-chef of easily the best restaurant in the Les Halles area, is such good value it verges on the philanthropic. Besson, whose career took in a period at **Jamin**, has a classical yet very personal style that contrasts refreshingly with the striving-after-effect of which some *nouvelle cuisine* chefs are guilty. He also lays down his own wines (45,000 bottles), then offers them at bargain prices.

Le Grand Café
4 Bd. des Capucines, 9ᵉ
☎ 47-42-75-77. Map **4F8** ⅢⅡⅢ AE
ⓞ 🚇 Open 24hrs. Métro: Quatre-Septembre.
This is the best of the handful of Paris brasseries that serve full-blown meals 24hrs a day. Its late-night clientele are hungry local shift- and night-workers (mainly journalists), topping up with solid or liquid nourishment. By day, the place is forever crowded with shoppers from the nearby *grands magasins*, and the turn-of-the-century decor is still much appreciated.

Le Grand Véfour ⌂
17 Rue de Beaujolais, 1ᵉʳ
☎ 42-96-56-27. Map **9G8** ⅢⅢ AE
ⓞ ▭ Last orders 10.15pm. Closed Sat lunch, Sun, Aug. Métro: Pyramides.
If you walk out of the Palais-Royal at its N end, you will pass, under the arcade, a dimly-lit restaurant that looks like a rare fossil from another age. This is the world-famous Le Grand Véfour, formerly home ground of much-travelled author and cook Raymond Oliver, now the property of M. Taittinger, of champagne fame. Its decor, which dates from the Directoire, is one of the oldest extant restaurant interiors in Paris (it is classified as a historical monument). The excellent food, created by chef Jean-Claude Lhonneur, pupil of the great Robuchon, is classical, and has won great acclaim in recent years.

Hawai ✿
87 Av. d'Ivry, 13ᵉ ☎ 45-86-91-90.
ⅢⅡ Last orders 9.30pm. Closed Thurs. Métro: Porte d'Ivry.
No booking at this bustling and inexpensive Vietnamese restaurant in the heart of Paris' new Chinatown in the 13ᵉ, so get there early if you don't like being kept waiting. The cuisine is copious, particularly the soups, beautifully seasoned, and genuine: witness its popularity with the Vietnamese themselves.

La Hulotte ✿
29 Rue Dauphine, 6ᵉ
☎ 46-33-75-92. Map **9/8** ⅢⅡ AE
Last orders 10.30pm. Closed Sun, Mon, Aug. Métro: Mabillon.
This restaurant's snug little upstairs dining-room is a haven of reliability in the shark-infested waters of Latin Quarter catering. A basket of brown bread served, unusually for Paris, with a little dish of butter and a jug of good cheap wine will keep your hunger and thirst at bay while you wait for a very reasonable *filet d'agneau à l'estragon*. Follow that with one of their excellent desserts and you'll leave contented.

Le Restaurant de l'Institut du Monde Arabe
1 Rue des Fossés-St-Bernard, 5ᵉ
☎ 46-33-47-70. Map **16K11** ⅢⅡ to
ⅢⅢ AE ⓞ Last orders 10pm. Closed Sun eve, Mon. Métro: Cardinal Lemoine, Sully-Morland.
Architect Jean Nouvel's widely acclaimed new building fronting the Quai St-Bernard has attracted international attention. The s facade overlooking the visitor entrance is composed of geometric shapes that open and close according to the light.
The 9th-floor restaurant, by contrast, is set within a sweeping terrace that views the river through walls of glass and metal. This is the supreme example of a contemporary restaurant whose design owes nothing to any other influence, past or present. The view equals that at La Tour d'Argent, but at half the price. The food, mainly good Arab specialities, forms part of an overall experience that can only be described in superlatives.

Jamin   See **Robuchon**.

Le Jardin
100 Rue du Bac, 7ᵉ
☎ 42-22-17-91. Map **8I6** ⅢⅡ Last orders 10.30pm. Closed Sun. Métro: Rue-du-Bac.
Even in Paris, vegetarian cooking is becoming increasingly popular, as is proved by this well-patronized vegetarian restaurant on the Left Bank. You have to pass through a shop selling books and health foods and down a corridor into a serene, skylit courtyard dining room decorated with stone sculptures, a fountain and an abundance of plants. The cuisine at this restaurant is sophisticated and creative, marrying the best of health food with the imaginativeness of the

nouvelle style, as evidenced by dishes such as *salade orientale*, which features saffron rice, avocado, mushrooms, green beans and delicate strands of Japanese hiziki seaweed, all in a light vinaigrette dressing.

The menu is by no means spartan — fish, "biological" wine, teas and tempting desserts are also on offer. Dieters have the added comfort of calorie-counts listed alongside the prices.

Jules Verne

Tour Eiffel, 2e étage (2nd floor), 7e (access via S pillar)
☎ 45-55-61-44. Map **12H3** ▥▥▥ to ▥▥▥ AE ▣ ━ ✿ (private). Last orders 10pm. Métro: Bir-Hakeim.
Built on a 500sq.m platform, between the great wheels and the pulleys of the tower's lift mechanism, and 123m above the city, sits a restaurant that cannot fail to offer breathtaking views in every direction. Even the ceiling offers glimpses, through glass panels, of the metal structure up to the top of the tower, some 150m higher. The decor within is intentionally muted — the architect's intention likening it to the shadows in a theatre as the curtain rises on a stage spectacle. Two words of advice: first, book weeks ahead or you will not get in, and second, for the best of all views, ask for the intermediate room (*salle intermédiaire*) between the bar and the room facing the Palais de Chaillot. From here, the panorama extends from the Arc de Triomphe to the dome of Les Invalides, taking in Le Grand Palais, Montmartre and Notre-Dame. All that aside, the food, *nouvelle cuisine* under the direction of Louis Grondard, and the service are faultless. Even the coffee is worthy of note.

Julien

16 Rue du Faubourg-St-Denis, 10e ☎ 47-70-12-06. Map **5F10** ▥▥ AE ▣ Last orders 1.30am.
Métro: Strasbourg-St-Denis.
Jean-Paul Bucher, owner of six top Parisian eating places, has single-handedly done more than anyone to save authentic restaurant decors from the modernizer's axe. Although both **Brasserie Flo** and **Le Vaudeville** are splendid, the jewel in Bucher's crown must be Julien, which sports some of Paris' most fabulous Art Nouveau designs, including a number of murals by Alphonse Mucha — and is accordingly much favoured by extrovert admen and showbiz

154

people. The food is classical and straightforward, with a slight Alsatian bias.

Lapérouse

51 Quai des Grands-Augustins, 6e ☎ 43-26-68-04. Map **9I9** ▥▥▥ AE ▣ ━ Last orders 11pm. Closed Sun eve, Mon. Métro: Odéon.
The decor of this restaurant facing the Seine is that of a bourgeois interior of the 19thC, with its concealed doors, overladen woodwork and private rooms for four to eight diners, often frequented by politicians and writers. The cuisine is classic: *foie gras de canard, ris de veau à l'oseille, feuilleté aux poires*. A memorable place to dine.

Lasserre △

17 Av. Franklin-D-Roosevelt, 8e ☎ 43-59-53-43. Map **7F5** ▥▥▥ No cards. ━ Last orders 10.30pm. Closed Sun, Mon lunch, Aug. Métro: Franklin-D-Roosevelt.
The essence of Lasserre, like that of the equally famous **La Tour d'Argent**, is found particularly in the decor, tableware and superlative service. Built just after World War II, the white Directoire-style house, just opposite the Grand Palais, is a feast for the eyes. The ceiling of the first-floor restaurant opens, in fine weather, to allow the sun to bless the meal. The food is excellent and deeply traditional. It is a haven for the extremely rich, old-fashioned gourmets who almost seem to use it as their canteen.

Laurent △

41 Av. Gabriel, 8e ☎ 42-25-00-39. Map **8G6** ▥▥▥ AE ▣ ━ ▥ ▥ Last orders 11pm. Closed Sat, Sun. Métro: Concorde.
Well-bred opulence is the keynote of this distinguished establishment, occupying a delectable pavilion in the parkland setting off Av. des Champs-Élysées — all white and gold stucco on the outside, Second-Empire elegance inside, with a garden at the back where one can feast under the chestnut trees on a summer day. The menu is mostly *nouvelle cuisine*, with some traditional elements. Philippe Bourguignon, one of the top *sommeliers* in France, will offer discreet advice on choosing from the 600-strong wine list. Service is exceptionally good. In the evening, candlelight and a pianist add to the festive atmosphere. Prices are commensurately high, but in relative terms the value is good.

Lipp
*151 Bd. St-Germain, 6e*
☎ 45-48-53-91 (telephone reservations not accepted). Map 8I7 III□ AE ◫ 🚗 Open 8am (for breakfast) to 12.45am (main meals from noon). Closed over Christmas and New Year. Métro: St-Germain-des-Prés.
This delightfully intact turn-of-the-century brasserie attracts the capital's intellectual, political and showbiz élite in far greater swarms than any other Parisian restaurant, however chic. The previous owner, Roger Cazes, died in 1987, and the Lipp is now run by his niece, Mme Perrochon. She has followed the tradition of her uncle and is no doubt as careful as he was in seating clients. The unknowns usually get sent up to the first floor (where the occasional celebrity is to be spotted), but beware — it is perfectly possible to be turned away, even if the place is not full. Dogs are allowed — providing they have the right owners. Impeccable service by long-aproned and long-serving waiters, reliable *plats du jour*, and the herd instinct explain Lipp's phenomenal success.

Le Lord Gourmand
*9 Rue Lord-Byron, 8e*
☎ 43-59-07-27. Map 6F3 III□ to IIII AE Last orders 2am. Métro: George-V.
This intimate, dressy restaurant offers some of the best food to be had in the vicinity of Av. des Champs-Élysées. Owner-chef Roland Borne maintains a well-balanced menu, rich in creation. The fish dishes are recommended and the desserts are extremely good. One of the best places in the capital to go for a tête-à-tête celebration. But book in advance. Intimate means small, and the tables are sought after.

Le Maquis
*69 Rue Caulaincourt, 18e*
☎ 42-59-76-07. Map 4C8 II□ to III□ ⛟ Last orders 10pm. Closed Sun, Mon. Métro: Lamarck-Caulaincourt.
Montmartre — and in particular the streets bordering that centre of kitsch art, Pl. du Tertre — is not a good area for eating, as some of the bad habits of picture-vendors seem to have rubbed off on restaurant owners. A 10min walk down the Butte, however, reveals this attractively decorated bistro, which offers an inexpensive set lunch and interesting *à la carte* food — unfussy, up-to-date, colourful and light. The only other exception to the rule about the quality of food in Montmartre is **A. Beauvilliers**, although it's in a different price band altogether.

La Marcande
*52 Rue Miromesnil, 8e*
☎ 42-65-19-14. Map 7F5 IIII AE ◫ ⛟ Last orders 10pm. Closed Sat, Sun, three weeks in Aug. Métro: Miromesnil.
This elegantly appointed restaurant affords diners a view not only over a delightful courtyard garden, but also over part of the kitchens. Behind the glass partitions, a smart team of chefs prepares some of the most imaginative food to be had in this part of town, such as *papillote de Saint-Jacques au foie gras, galette de pigeonneau aux truffes*, and *ragoût de champignons des bois.* The walls are hung with a changing exhibition of modern paintings.

Maxim's ⏏
3 Rue Royale, 8e ☎ 42-65-27-94. Map 8G6 IIII AE ◫ 🚗 Last orders 1am. Closed Sun in July, Aug only. Métro: Concorde.
The reputation of this world-famous restaurant revived when it was taken over a few years ago, in the face of much scepticism, by fashion designer Pierre Cardin. In the event, those who said that a cobbler should stick to his last were proved wrong. Cardin has kept Maxim's essential character as a top-class restaurant (with top-class prices), and has maintained and renovated its marvellous Art Nouveau decor. The food is an artful combination of *nouvelle* and *classique*, with the simplest food being often the most exquisite. The *navarin d'agneau* is a delight, the duck with peaches most exciting. Reservations are essential.

La Méditerranée
*2 Pl. de l'Odéon, 6e*
☎ 43-26-46-75. Map 15J8 IIII to IIII AE ◫ 🚗 ⛟ Last orders 1am. Métro: Odéon.
Fish dishes from the South of France are lavishly served at this venerable restaurant, which has carried a reputation since the heady days of the early 1960s when Jean Cocteau and Orson Welles were regulars. Menus and crockery all bear the familiar Cocteau logo. All manner of crustaceans live in tanks, awaiting sacrifice, and the excellence of the menu is witnessed by many nationalities, including a number of

Japanese, who seek out good fish. The front opens up to become a terrace in summer and overlooks a pleasant and none-too-busy square.

Morot-Gaudry
8 Rue de la Cavalerie, 15^e
☎ 45-67-06-85. Map **12J3** ▥ ▭ ☛ ☀ Last orders 10.30pm. Closed Sat, Sun. Métro: La Motte-Piquet-Grenelle.

As majestically located as **La Tour d'Argent**, on the top floor of a ship-like 1920s building with a wonderful view of the nearby Eiffel Tower, this restaurant is much favoured by bigwigs from UNESCO (also nearby). French food gurus can't seem to decide whether Jean-Pierre Morot-Gaudry's cuisine is *nouvelle* or not. No matter: his concoctions have the stamp of true originality (calf's liver with raspberries, crab *boudin*, red mullet with *chanterelles*). There is an excellent and reasonably priced set luncheon menu that is roundly popular with businesspeople.

Le Moulin du Village
Cité Berryer, 25 Rue Royale, 8^e
☎ 42-65-08-47. Map **8G6** ▥ ▤ ☀ Last orders 11pm. Métro: Madeleine.

Probably the largest selection of little-known wines in Paris is to be found here, and owner Mark Williamson of **Willi's** is at least partly responsible for the growth of wine bars in Paris. The restaurant is in a mews, almost invisibly tucked away off Rue Royale, the courtyard a marvellously calm and unpolluted spot for outdoor eating in summer. Le Moulin du Village offers *nouvelle cuisine* of some distinction — try the veal kidneys in mustard.

Le Muniche
27 Rue de Buci, 6^e
☎ 46-33-62-09. Map **918** ▥ ▨ ☼ Last orders 3am. Métro: Mabillon.

This large, bustling, noisy and cramped restaurant is the canteen of Left Bank literati — a truly Parisian sort of place, where seafood predominates and the only German note, apart from the name, is the sauerkraut. The Layrac brothers also run the neighbouring **Le Petit Zinc** as well as the live jazz club below, **Le Furstemberg**, which is well air-conditioned and where the music starts at 10pm.

Au Pactole
44 Bd. St-Germain, 5^e
☎ 46-33-31-31. Map **16J10** ▥ to

▥ ▤ ☛ ▨ Last orders 10.45pm. Closed Sat lunch, Sun. Métro: Maubert-Mutualité.

Lunch is the best time to eat here, because, with luck, the sun will be streaming through the windows of the attractive covered terrace. The decor has bright tones of orange and yellow.

Roland Magne is an inventive yet unfussy cook with a penchant for unusual combinations (kid with mint, lamb with violets). His set menu is a wonderful bargain.

Le Pavillon Montsouris ✿
20 Rue Gazan, 14e ☎ 45-88-38-52
▥ to ▥ ▤ ▣ ☛ ▨ Last orders 10.30pm. Métro: Cité-Universitaire.

This restaurant, decorated in Belle Époque style, is set in a peaceful pavilion in the Parc Montsouris. A shady veranda and a summer terrace facing banks of flowers in the park, are pleasant settings for what is becoming recognized as masterful *nouvelle cuisine* with an extremely wide choice of dishes. Excellent value.

Au Petit Montmorency
5 Rue Rabelais, 8^e
☎ 42-25-11-19. Map **7F5** ▥ to
▥ ▤ Last orders 10.30pm. Closed Sat, Sun, Aug. Métro: Miromesnil.

Chef Daniel Bouché follows no school of cooking but his own. Discover this restaurant while you still can at such reasonable prices. A faithful and rather chic clientele comes back again and again for such inventive delights as rabbit with sea-urchins, beef cheek with calf's foot, or coffee and whisky ice-cream.

The decor is pleasantly old-fashioned — plants everywhere, ancient kitchen utensils and engravings on the walls.

Au Petit Riche
25 Rue Le Peletier, 9^e
☎ 47-70-68-68. Map **4E8** ▥ ▤
▣ ▨ Last orders 12.15am. Closed Sun. Métro: Le Peletier.

A quite exceptional decor, which, with its decorated frosted windows, large mirrors and brass luggage-racks, is somewhat more Edwardian than Belle Époque. Still divided into a number of small dining rooms, this fine bistro accommodates the after-theatre crowd at night. Good, solid *cuisine bourgeoise* without pretension is served here, and a commendable selection of Loire wines.

Le Petit Zinc
25 Rue de Buci, 6^e
☎ 46-33-51-66. Map 9J8 ⅢⅡ AE
⊡ 🍴 Last orders 3am. Métro:
Mabillon.
Probably the best restaurant in town
open until 3am, the ground-floor
bar of Le Petit Zinc has a pleasant,
old-fashioned bistro atmosphere, a
short menu of *plats bourgeois*, and
some unpretentious wines. The
first-floor dining room offers a
sparkling environment in which to
sample a wide range of seafood
dishes. Here you can eat the lightest
apple pie in Paris. Moustachioed
waiters in traditional long white
aprons give warmly efficient service.

La Petite Chaise
36 Rue de Grenelle, 7^e
☎ 42-22-13-35. Map 8I7 ⅢⅡ to ⅢⅡ
Last orders 11pm. Métro: Rue-
du-Bac.
The patina of 300yrs shines in this
quaint old inn, especially in the dark
and intimate bar. The decor within
the dining room is more stark,
perhaps a little Puritan, but it has its
appeal, particularly for American
visitors who come back again and
again. The fixed-menu-only policy
pays dividends and gives plenty of
choice. The cuisine is modest, and
the prices too.

Au Pied de Cochon
6 Rue Coquillière, 1er
☎ 42-36-11-75. Map 9G9 ⅢⅡ AE
⊡ 🍴 Open 24hrs. Métro: Les
Halles.
This old landmark of Les Halles has,
alas, succumbed to the winds of
change, adopting a strange, gaudy
Italian style in recent years. The
departure of the crowds of manual
workers for pastures new has meant
that this restaurant no longer retains
the authentic atmosphere of the old
Les Halles for which it was once
justly famed. Still open day in, day
out, Au Pied de Cochon customers
eat their way through a tonne of
shellfish every day and 80,000 pigs'
trotters a year. The restaurant's
popularity is undiminished.

Pharamond
24 Rue de la Grande-Truanderie,
1er ☎ 42-33-06-72. Map 10H9 ⅢⅡ
AE ⊡ 🍴 Last orders 10.30pm.
Closed Sun, Mon lunch, July 15-
Aug 15. Métro: Les Halles.
This gem of a restaurant, with its Art
Nouveau mirrors and *faïence*
created for the 1900 World's Fair, is
the last-remaining vestige of the
heart of Les Halles market. It's now
surrounded by the plethora of

trendy shops that have proliferated
in and around the Forum des Halles.
Pharamond was always famed for its
succulent tripe, *andouillette* and
pig's trotters, but it now features
some more modern dishes too.

Pierre Traiteur
10 Rue de Richelieu, 1er
☎ 42-96-09-17. Map 9F8 ⅢⅡ
🍴 AE ⊡ 🍴 Last orders 10pm.
Closed Sat, Sun, Aug. Métro:
Richelieu-Drouot.
A rather noisy, upmarket bistro that
offers a tempting choice between
Auvergnat food (such as the rare
estofinado, made from wind-dried
cod) and more sophisticated fare
(raw sea-bass with chives). There is
a commendable selection of lesser-
known wines.

Pierre Vedel ✿
19 Rue Duranton, 15^e
☎ 45-58-43-17 ⅢⅡ Last orders
10.15pm. Closed Sat, Sun, last
2wks July, week of Christmas
and New Year. Métro: Boucicaut.
Genuine Mediterranean restaurants
do not lie thick on the ground in
Paris, so all the more reason to be
thankful for the existence of this
welcoming bistro. Vedel himself,
who comes from the fishing port of
Sète, naturally feels most at home
with seafood (excellent garlicky
lobster soup, fillet of *rascasse* in
saffron-flavoured aspic), but he also
has a talent for inventive vegetable
dishes, for example, stuffed cabbage
and a gamut of combined vegetable
mousses. Extremely good value for
such quality.

Polidor 🍴 ✿
41 Rue Monsieur-le-Prince, 6^e
☎ 43-26-95-34. No advance
booking. Map 15J8 ⅢⅡ Last
orders 1am (Sun 10pm). Métro:
Odéon.
Price has little to do with fashion,
and the fact that Polidor gives away
a 3-course set meal for a ludicrously
low price does not deter the famous
from bestowing their custom on the
place. Little has changed in this
150yr-old *bouillon* since the time of
previous habitués such as Verlaine,
Valéry and Joyce: there are still lace
curtains, numbered serviette lockers
(some in use), a spiral staircase, and
even waitresses in turn-of-the-
century dress. Good *cuisine
bourgeoise, ragoûts, blanquettes*
and the rest.

Le Pouilly
96 Rue Daguerre, 14^e
☎ 43-22-60-18. Map 14M7 ⅢⅡ

Restaurants

Last orders 9pm. Closed Sat, Sun, Aug. Métro: Denfert-Rochereau.

One of the places to which the people working in the 195m Tour Montparnasse escape at lunchtime in order to restore their sanity and sate their appetites, is this quiet, almost provincial bistro. Located at the Montparnasse end of the equally provincial Rue Daguerre, it serves good, uncomplicated food.

Le Pré Catelan △
Route de Suresnes, Bois de Boulogne, 16ᵉ ☎ 45-24-55-58 ▥▥▥ AE ▣ 🚗 ➡ *Last orders 10.30pm. Closed Sun eve, Mon, one week in Feb.*

Many well-heeled Parisians who hanker after tip-top food in an accessible pastoral setting make for this establishment in the Bois de Boulogne. It was transformed a few years ago from an ailing eating place into a palatial summerhouse of a restaurant by the well-known caterer and pastry cook, Gaston Lenôtre.

The cuisine is stylish and decorative — mirroring the clientele. In winter you can dine in front of logs blazing in the vast black marble fireplace, or in the orangery, surrounded by the splendid gardens.

Les Princes △
31 Av. George-V, 8ᵉ ☎ 47-23-54-00. Map 7F4 ▥▥▥ AE ▣ ➡ *Last orders 10.30pm (11.30pm in summer). Closed mid-July to mid-Aug. Métro: George-V.*

Les Princes, in the luxury **Hôtel George-V** (see *Hotels*), is the epitome of dining in the grand manner, although the clientele here includes admen and film-producers as well as the wealthy patrons of the hotel.

The cuisine is a pleasing combination of the aristocratic (*tournedos de poisson au poivre noir, foie gras de canard au torchon*), the peasant (salt pork with lentils), and, for France, the exotic (angels on horseback). In summer you can eat in the George-V's delightful flower-filled, statue-lined courtyard.

Le Procope
13 Rue de l'Ancienne-Comédie, 6ᵉ ☎ 43-26-99-20. Map 9I8 ▥▥ to ▥▥▥ AE ▣ *Last orders 2am. Closed July. Métro: Odéon.*

No other restaurant in Paris has been going as long as Le Procope,

which opened as a café in 1686. Previous customers include La Fontaine, Voltaire, Benjamin Franklin, Jean-Jacques Rousseau, Robespierre, Napoléon, Balzac, George Sand and Huysmans. Its two floors have retained their warm, original atmosphere. The fare is traditional *cuisine bourgeoise* with a good selection of sea food. Live jazz groups grace the foyer from Wed-Sat 11pm-2am.

Régence-Plaza △
25 Av. Montaigne, 8ᵉ ☎ 47-23-78-33. Map 7G4 ▥▥▥ AE ▣ 🚗 ➡ *Last orders 10.15pm. Closed Aug. Métro: Franklin-D-Roosevelt.*

People go to the Régence-Plaza, the more expensive of the two restaurants at the **Hôtel Plaza-Athénée** (see *Hotels*), to savour the glittering company as much as the food. In summer, the inner courtyard is a marvellous, ivy-festooned haven of coolness. The cuisine is a mixture of classical and new styles, and the wine list is superb.

Au Relais Pereire
30 Rue du Printemps, 17ᵉ ☎ 42-27-26-97. Map 2C5 ▥▥ 🚗 ➡ *Last orders 9.30pm. Closed Sat, Sun, public holidays, Aug. Métro: Malesherbes, Wagram.*

This bistro is as classy and elegant as its *patronne*, the friendly Aline Perdrix. She has created a smart decor with a strong, warm blue mood, candlelit tables and a frequently changing array of modern paintings on the walls. Carefully executed cuisine with a southwest accent (*foie gras, cassoulet*, excellent *brebis des Pyrénées* cheese and superb game when in season). The 4-course set menu is very good value, and you can dine on a tranquil terrace when the weather is fine.

Relais Saint-Germain ✿
190 Bd. St-Germain, 7ᵉ ☎ 42-22-21-35. Map 8I7 ▥▥ ▣ *Last orders 11pm. Métro: Rue-du-Bac.*

The covered terrace of this restaurant is a good vantage point from which to observe the exotic parade that roves between the Café Flore at St-Germain-des-Prés and l'Escurial at Rue du Bac. The cuisine is good, with the emphasis on fish, especially home-made smoked salmon, and excellent value for money; and the chef makes excellent *charlotte au chocolat*.

Robuchon *(Jamin)*
32 Rue de Longchamp, 16ᵉ
☎ 47-27-12-27. Map **6**G2 ▥ ▧
*Last orders 10.15pm. Closed Sat,
Sun, July. Métro: Trocadéro.*
Booking weeks, perhaps even
months, ahead at Jamin, the altar at
which the great chef Joël Robuchon
is worshipped, is quite normal.
Awarded the Michelin 3-star rating
and the Gault-Millau 19.5/20
commendation, the fame of this
master chef is justified beyond
measure. The illusion of simplicity
in his cooking is deceptive, for he is
known as the master of detail, and
the thoughtful and controlled
accumulation of detail is what goes
to create the subtlest of dishes. Nor
does he produce just one or two
chefs d'oeuvre a year — the list is
almost endless. Go there — if you
can afford either the wait or the final
account. It is the gastronomic
experience of a lifetime.

Le Sancerrois ☕
12 Rue du Champ-de-Mars, 7ᵉ
☎ 45-55-13-47. Map **13**I4 ▯ ▧
▣ *Last orders 9pm. Closed Sat
evening, Sun, Aug. Métro:
École-Militaire.*
People from the nearby TV studios
appreciate the quiet atmosphere of
this friendly, unpretentious café-
restaurant. The food is Auvergnat,
and the handful of wines (some
available by the glass in the café
section) mainly Loire and
Beaujolais, all impeccably chosen.

Taillevent △
15 Rue Lamennais, 8ᵉ
☎ 45-63-39-94. Map **7**F4 ▥ ▧
*Last orders 10pm. Closed Sat,
Sun, Aug. Métro: Charles-de-
Gaulle-Etoile.*
Taillevent, named after one of the
first great French cooks who lived in
the 14thC, is run by Jean-Claude
Vrinat, who has made it one of the
capital's top five restaurants. He
follows new cooking trends and is
also always on the look-out for
excellent lesser-known wines to fill
out his vast wine list. He buys some
of his cheeses direct from the farm,
which is most unusual for this class
of establishment. Taillevent is much
frequented by politicians and top
businessmen. The decor in this
lovely mid-19thC mansion is
suitably discreet. Reserve weeks
— even months — ahead.

La Taverne du Sergent
Recruteur ✿
41 Rue St Louis-en-l'Île, 4ᵉ
☎ 43-54-75-42. Map **10**J10 ▯ ▪
*Open for dinner only. Last
orders 2am. Closed Sun. Métro:
Pont-Marie.*
In the 18thC, when the French army
was short of men, it would employ a
sergent recruteur (recruiting
sergeant), a sly character who
would ply his victims with food and
drink until they were so befuddled
that they signed his enlistment
papers without objection. At this
restaurant, on the romantic Île St-
Louis, you get similar lavish
treatment but without the penalty. If
you come here, make sure that you
have a big appetite. There is no *à la
carte*, only a fixed-price menu of
remarkably good value. You start
with a generous salad, a basket of
sausage and a crock of pâté. Then
comes a choice of main dishes,
followed by a cheese board and
finally a dessert.
This tourists' haven is just the sort
of place where you can imagine the
recruiting sergeant at work: leaded
windows, stone-flagged floor,
heavy wooden beams and stone
arches.

La Taverne des Templiers
106 Rue Vieille-du-Temple, 3ᵉ
☎ 42-78-74-67. Map **11**H11 ▥ to
▥ ▣ *Last orders 10pm. Closed
Sat, Sun, Aug. Métro: Filles-du-
Calvaire.*
Curiously, this part of the old and
picturesque Marais quarter contains
almost no restaurants of any quality.
But here is the exception. The
Taverne des Templiers occupies a
building dating from 1229 and
restored in 1500. It was therefore
originally put up not long after the
Marais was drained by the Knights
Templar. You can dine in a
wonderfully atmospheric room,
beneath a superb, beamed ceiling.
The food, scrupulously prepared
under the supervision of the patron,
Guy Bertrand, is mainly traditional
in style, with strong leanings
towards the Charente/Bordeaux
region. Try the *fricassée de chevreau
charentaise* or the *anguilles en
persillade*.

Le Télégraphe
41 Rue de Lille, 7ᵉ
☎ 40-15-06-65. Map **8**H7 ▥ to
▥ ▣ ▧ ▦ *Last orders
12.45am. Closed Sun. Métro:
Solférino.*
Only a stone's throw from the
Musée d'Orsay, Le Télégraphe's
astonishing popularity continues.
Publishers, journalists and
politicians foregather to talk shop,
and in the evenings (when

reservations are essential)
fashionable young Parisians flock
here.

The superb décor, by
François-Joseph Graf, is the main
reason, although he started with an
enviable advantage: for this room,
the astonishing refectory of a former
dormitory for female Post Office
workers, came equipped with
arches, arcades, stained-glass
windows and Art Nouveau
woodwork. A pleasant veranda
overlooks a small garden, and the
food is light and *nouvelle*, if
somewhat expensive.

Terminus Nord
23 Rue de Dunkerque, 10ᵉ
☎ 42-85-05-15. Map 5D10 ⅢⅢ AE
▣ *Last orders 12.30pm. Métro:
Gare-du-Nord.*
Cafés and restaurants near stations
tend to treat their irregular, hurried
and captive clientele in less than
gentlemanly fashion. A notable
exception is the Terminus Nord,
another restaurant in the stable of
Jean-Paul Bucher (see **Brasserie
Flo**, **La Coupole**, **Julien** and **Le
Vaudeville**). An ideal place at
which to eat before taking a train
from the station opposite, this
brasserie offers food that is good
enough to attract swarms of
gourmets who have no intention of
leaving town.

La Terrasse Fleurie ✿
*Hôtel Inter-Continental Paris, 3
Rue de Castiglione. 1ᵉʳ*
☎ 42-60-37-80. Map 8G7 ⅢⅢ AE
▣ ⇌ 🏠 🚗 *Last orders 11pm.
Métro: Tuileries.*
This all-year-round terrace
restaurant is unusual for a luxury
hotel (it's part of the **Hôtel Inter-
Continental**: see *Hotels*) in that it
offers a set menu, which, in view of
its copiousness and high quality, is
very good value indeed. Chef
Jean-Jacques Barbier shows a
refreshing interest in the kitchen
garden, and his two *plats du jour*,
themselves traditional rather than
inventive, are imaginatively served.

Thoumieux
79 Rue St-Dominique, 7ᵉ
☎ 47-05-49-75. Map 13H5 ⅠⅢ
*Last orders 11.30pm. Métro:
Latour-Maubourg.*
This spacious, vaguely Art Deco
brasserie, attached to a hotel of the
same name and not far from the
Tour Eiffel, has been in the same
family for three generations, serving
good traditional food from the
southwest region: country

charcuteries, an excellent *cassoulet*,
tête de veau vinaigrette, and a very
good fixed menu.

La Tour d'Argent ⌂
15 Quai de la Tournelle, 5ᵉ
☎ 43-54-23-31. Map 16J0 ⅢⅢ AE
▣ ⇌ *Last orders 10pm.
Closed Mon, Feb. Métro:
Maubert-Mutualité.*
This penthouse restaurant is world
famous. Eccentric but shrewd ex-
playboy Claude Terrail has, over the
years, perfected the art of giving his
customers what they want: the
pleasure of a table overlooking the
illuminated Notre-Dame (but
reserve well ahead); of dealing with
a *sommelier* who looks delighted,
not petulant, if they choose the
cheapest wine on his list (the finest
classical cellar in Paris); and the
convenience and style of walking
out of the lift afterwards straight into
their proffered coats, then outside to
find their cars purring at the
kerbside. Service of this calibre and
the very high quality of La Tour
d'Argent's cuisine cost a great deal;
it is Paris' most expensive
restaurant, although the fixed-price
lunch menu brings it more within
reach.

Au Trou Gascon
40 Rue Taine, 12ᵉ ☎ 43-44-34-26
ⅢⅢ *to* ⅢⅢ ⇌ 🚗 *Last orders
10pm. Closed Sat, Sun. Métro:
Daumesnil.*
The acclaimed chef Alain
Dutournier, creator of this
restaurant, has turned it over to his
wife, who has continued in the
same style. The restaurant offers a
most unusual blend of new ideas
and provincial (Gascon) tradition,
and an equally rare selection of
wines (some 450), ranging from
prestigious Bordeaux to humble,
little-known *crus*, all annotated in
detail on the city's most
compulsively readable wine list.
Throw in the amazing collection of
Armagnacs, and the restaurant's
turn-of-the-century decor (a riot of
mirrors and mouldings), and you
have the makings of a memorable
meal.

Le Val d'Or ✿
28 Av. Franklin-D-Roosevelt, 8ᵉ
☎ 43-59-95-81. Map 7F5 ⅠⅢ ⇌
*Restaurant closed for dinner;
snacks only served in evening
till 9pm. Closed Sun, 1wk over
Christmas. Métro: St-Philippe-
du-Roule.*
Youthful Géraud Rongier moved
several years ago from his tiny **La**

Cloche des Halles to this larger café near St-Philippe-du-Roule. On the ground floor he provides cold snacks (including, in many people's opinion, the very best sandwiches in town), and in the mirror-filled basement, hot lunches of exceptional value are served. At both levels, a small but very reliable selection of wines is available (mainly Beaujolais and Burgundy).

Le Vaudeville
29 Rue Vivienne, 2^e
☎ 42-33-39-31. Map 9F8 ▥▯ to ▥▥ ▦ Last orders 2am.
Métro: Bourse.
Once upon a time this was a dreary, half-empty Art Deco brasserie, haunted by tired journalists working nearby. In stepped Jean-Paul Bucher (see **Brasserie Flo, La Coupole**, **Julien** and **Terminus Nord**) with his magic wand, to restore the establishment's Egyptian-style walls and opaque fittings to their former glory, and put professionals in charge of the kitchens. It now offers very good classical cuisine at highly competitive prices — and, being open until 2am, it is a boon for people wanting a bite after a show.

Au Vieux Berlin
32 Av. George-V, 8^e
☎ 47-20-88-96. Map 7F4 ▥▯ to ▥▥ ▦ ▣ Last orders 11pm.
Closed Sat, Sun. Métro: George-V.
Film and showbiz people (Serge Gainsbourg, Jacques Dutronc) appreciate the discretion and attentive service available at this accurate reproduction of a prewar Berlin eating house (complete with pianist and candles in the evening). The food, although mainly German (plenty of game in season, pumpkin soup with bacon, knuckle of pork with pease pudding), has an attractively light and — dare one say it? — French touch.

Le Vivarois ⌂
192 Av. Victor-Hugo, 16^e
☎ 45-04-04-31. Map 6F2 ▥▥ ▦ ▣ ▭ Last orders 10pm.
Closed Sat, Sun, Aug. Métro: Av. Henri Martin.
This is the most unusual of the city of Paris' pantheon of first-class restaurants, frequented by well-heeled gourmands and run by a true eccentric, chef-patron Claude Peyrot, who likes nothing better than to discuss philosophy with his customers. Peyrot is no disciple of *nouvelle cuisine*, rather a past-master at dishes that defy categorization. His aim is not flashy inventiveness but utter perfection of both raw materials and the end-product. By reputation, he succeeds every time.

Willi's
13 Rue des Petits-Champs, 1er
☎ 42-61-05-09. Map 9G8 ▥▯ ▤ Open 11am-11pm. Closed Sun. Métro: Bourse.
Willi's (named after owner Mark Williamson) is a fairly faithful copy of a typical London wine bar, except that the large number of wines (many available by the glass) and the quality of the food served (Anglo-French) are much higher than one would normally expect in Britain. It is crowded with English expatriates and tweedy French Anglophiles.

Cafés

The café is one of the most civilized institutions ever invented. It is a living stage, a forum for debate, a club, a home from home. Paris was among the earliest cities to establish a café society, and it remains one of the few where traditional café life still thrives; in fact the French capital without its cafés would be unthinkable. In them revolutions have been plotted, poems written, philosophies born. As literary and artistic circles have migrated from one district to another, so different cafés have had their spells as fashionable meeting places. Some of the famous ones have disappeared, others have been ruined by modernization, but many are still virtually intact.

There are more than 10,000 cafés in Paris, catering, between them, for almost every need a Parisian might have. An often staggering range of alcoholic, soft and hot drinks is available;

solid fare includes *croissants*, hard-boiled eggs and sandwiches, and sometimes hot snacks and even sit-down meals, especially at lunchtime. You can make local and sometimes long-distance (*inter*) calls, although both will cost much more than from a public phone box. The main brands of French cigarettes can be found in most cafés, but *cafés-tabacs* (recognizable by their red lozenge sign) sell a wide range of cigarettes, cigars, pipe- and even chewing-tobacco, snuff, stamps, envelopes, postcards, pens, and state lottery tickets. If the letters PMU are displayed outside, it means the *café-tabac* turns into a betting shop on certain days, and you can have a flutter on the horses via the state tote system. Other café amusements may include pinball machines (known as *flippers*), electronic games, juke-boxes, miniature soccer, American pool and French billiards. You can even use them for their public conveniences, the standard of which these days is much improved. Leave 1-2f in the dish that is usually positioned in the toilet lobby, or at the counter as you leave, if you are not using the café.

There are free attractions, too. You can read, write, work or just while away the time with or without friends for as long as you like (except in one or two cafés on Bd. St-Michel, where notices fiercely warn you that your order will be automatically renewed every hour!). Cafés with terraces are good vantage points from which to observe the passers-by on, say, the Champs-Élysées or one of the busy boulevards (such as Haussmann, Clichy, des Italiens, des Capucines, St-Germain, St-Michel and du Montparnasse). But expect to be asked to pay a stiffer price here: you're paying also for the prime location.

If you simply want to rest your feet or appease the children, look for a side-street café, which will be quieter and cheaper, as well as providing friendlier and more personal service.

Remember that most cafés have a two-tiered price system, depending on whether you drink at the bar or occupy a table. Usually, the price difference is not enormous. However, at some more expensive establishments, the cement-stained building workers knocking back their *pastis* at the bar will pay up to 50 percent less than the well-heeled customers sitting on the terrace — cafés are democratic, too. Watch out for the price of certain drinks — non-French beer, bottled mineral water, Coca Cola, whisky and vodka, to name but a few.

A word about the different types of café you're likely to encounter. *Buvettes*, which are getting rarer every day, are grocery shops or wine merchants with a counter (*zinc*) but usually no tables; here, and at the almost extinct *bougnats* (tiny, Spartan cafés run by coal-and-wood merchants), you will find the authentic flavour of prewar Paris.

The already-mentioned *cafés-tabacs* differ from other cafés in that their prices may be fractionally lower and their atmosphere a little livelier. Brasseries, "drugstores" and "pubs" (the last two bear little relation to the American or British originals) are large and generally serve hot meals throughout the day.

Lastly, at the more elegant end of the spectrum, there are *salons de thé*. When they double up as *pâtisseries* they tend to cater for maiden aunts and usually do not serve alcoholic drinks. Sometimes, however, run-of-the-mill cafés with social ambitions arrogate the title *salon de thé*. Genuine *salons de thé*, if you can afford them, are the best places for a good Continental breakfast.

As in restaurants, tipping in cafés is no longer a problem: at the tables, the tip is clearly included on the ticket the waiter gives you, or else he will add it on himself.

There are far too many interesting cafés in this city to list exhaustively, but here, arranged according to area, are a few favourites.

Left Bank
Montparnasse

This is still the centre of Bohemian life in Paris, although many of the café decors have been ruined. Genuine artists, intellectuals, writers, movie people and hangers-on of every description gather in **La Coupole** (see *Restaurants*) or **Le Select Montparnasse** (*99 Bd. du Montparnasse*), which has hardly changed since it was frequented by Erik Satie, Francis Poulenc, Robert Desnos and Foujita. Across the way, **Le Dôme** (*108 Bd. du Montparnasse*) is still cashing in on its reputation as a favourite watering-hole of Modigliani, Stravinsky, Picasso and Hemingway. Unfortunately, its hybrid 1920s decoration has destroyed the charm of its former atmosphere. A further five minutes' walk along the boulevard is the still-lively **Closerie des Lilas** (see *Restaurants*). And behind Montparnasse station is **Les Mousquetaires** (*77 Av. du Maine*), a marvellous, cavernous café-cum-billiard hall.

St-Germain-des-Prés

Two of the most famous of all cafés, **Les Deux Magots** (a *magot*, by the way, is a Chinese miniature figure and not what you might think) and **Le Flore** (*6 Pl. St-Germain-des-Prés and 172 Bd. St-Germain respectively*), are to be found, side by side, right in the heart of this district. The list of their customers past and present reads like a roll call of French *vie intellectuelle* over the last century: Huysmans, Jarry, Barrès, Giraudoux, Sartre, de Beauvoir, Breton, Camus, and the Prévert brothers, to name but a few. The Existentialist movement was born in one or other of them, or both, as were many of Sartre's philosophical and literary works — he preferred to write at a café table rather than at a desk. Nowadays, however, times have changed, and only the wealthier literati can afford to hold court regularly at the two renowned cafés.

On the other side of the boulevard there is still plenty of action at **Lipp** (see *Restaurants*), where getting in is not as easy as one might expect. It can all depend on who you are — or what you seem. The high priests of modern French intellectual life, such as *nouveau philosophe* Bernard-Henri Lévy and novelist Philippe Sollers, have retreated to the quieter waters of the English "pub" around the corner, **The Twickenham** (*70 Rue des Sts-Pères*). Another "pub" in the area is the vast **Pub St-Germain** (*17 Rue de l'Ancienne-Comédie*), which boasts an unrivaled range of draught and bottled beers, teas and whiskies, and is open all day and all night. Two doors away is the famous **Le Procope**, the first-ever café in Paris, which opened its doors to the public in 1686. Although its prime function is now as a restaurant (see *Restaurants*), you can still take coffee and tea there throughout the day.

The man regarded by many as the finest *pâtissier* in Paris, **Christian Constant** (*26 Rue du Bac*), has a *salon de thé* in his shop that is worth a visit.

St-Michel

The cafés on Bd. St-Michel itself are no longer as interesting as they used to be, and two of them have been turned into McDonald's, although there are several around Pl. St-Michel that are popular with the Latin Quarter crowd. However, you can take refuge nearby at **L'Écluse**, **Le Balzar** or **Bistrot de la Nouvelle**

Mairie (see *Restaurants*). There are also two afternoon-only *salons de thé* within easy reach: **La Bûcherie** (see *Restaurants*) and **The Tea Caddy** (*14 Rue St-Julien-le-Pauvre*), where you'll enjoy first-class scones, muffins and cinnamon toast.

Right Bank
Av. des Champs-Élysées

There are only two cafés of any real interest actually on Av. des Champs-Élysées: **Fouquet's** (*no.99*) and **L'Alsace** (*no.39*). At the first, you pay withering prices for the privilege of joining starlets on its terrace; the real movie stars can be found in the hushed and old-fashioned (no unaccompanied ladies) bar within. L'Alsace is a brasserie that has the merit of serving genuine Alsatian beer, wine and food 24hrs a day. The **Drugstore Publicis** (see *Shopping*) near Pl. Charles de Gaulle is a bright and breezy source of quick food, or a place just to sit and chat.

Not far from the Champs-Élysées there are several good establishments serving refreshments and snacks outside meal times, notably **Le Val d'Or**, the bar of **Au Vieux Berlin**, **L'Écluse** and **Boulangerie St-Philippe**. **La Boutique aux Sandwichs** offers excellent take-away snacks (for addresses see *Restaurants*).

Opéra/Boulevard Haussmann

Once the hub of café society, this is now mainly a business quarter, and becomes quiet after the early evening. But with French office-workers being as demanding as they are, most cafés are reliable, particularly those that are tucked away down side-streets.

One of the most celebrated establishments in Paris is, of course, the **Café de la Paix** (*12 Bd. des Capucines*). It emerged from meticulous restoration a few years ago with its deliciously ornate green and gold decor, designed by Charles Garnier, architect of the Opéra opposite, and with its clientele (wealthy tourists for the most part) unscathed. Some of the best coffee, home-made *croissants* and other pastries are to be found at the smart but stark *salon de thé* of **Fauchon** (*26 Pl. de la Madeleine*), Paris' most famous food shop. Here you proceed as in Italy; you decide whether you want a pastry or not, pay for it and/or for a coffee at the cash desk, hand over your ticket at the counter, collect your order and eat it standing up at one of the pedestal tables. After a day's shopping in *Rue du Faubourg-St-Honoré*, treat yourself to tea at **Angélina** (*226 Rue de Rivoli*), where the *pâtisseries* are delectable concoctions of cream, chocolate and meringue.

A number of cafés serve good wines and snacks: as well as **Au Rubis** (*10 Rue du Marché St-Honoré*), **Ma Bourgogne** (*133 Bd. Haussmann*), frequented by French executives, and **Le St-Amour** (*4 Rue de Rome*), a friendly and rollicking café usefully located near the big department stores on Bd. Haussmann. An excellent **Brasserie Flo** (see also *Restaurants*) can be found on the top floor of **Le Printemps** (see *Department stores* in *Shopping*).

Les Halles

The transformation of this small area, spoiled for so many years by massive redevelopment work, is now almost complete. A mixture of new and refurbished buildings, it sports a reasonable number of places to sit, or to grab a quick bite. One of the most stylish terraces in town is at **Café Costes** (*Rue des Innocents*). It's worth a detour, if only to admire the decor created by superstar designer Philippe Starck. Opposite the excellent wine-bar **La**

Cloche des Halles (*28 Rue Coquillière*) is a pleasant, traditional café with nothing extraordinary about it except its name, **La Promenade de Vénus** (*44 Rue du Louvre*). This resulted in its being selected by André Breton as the meeting place for fellow Surrealists. Around the corner, the best-known Les Halles restaurant, **Au Pied de Cochon** (see *Restaurants*), functions as a café on its terrace, spilling over onto the pavement in fine weather. Although the restaurant is open 24hrs a day every day of the year, you can get coffee and snacks there only in the afternoon.

Le Marais

If you wander around this fascinating old quarter, which has retained an almost provincial calm, you're bound to find several small cafés, rich in character and filled with regulars. On the beautifully intact 17thC Pl. des Vosges, there is the cosy and altogether trendier **Ma Bourgogne** (*no.19*), which serves reasonably good wines. But for a really wide and reliable selection of vintages, try **La Tartine** (*24 Rue de Rivoli*) on the southern edge of Le Marais; this bustling, smoke-filled café has not changed much since Lenin and Trotsky drank there.

Montmartre/Pigalle

All self-respecting painters have long since fled Pl. du Tertre in Montmartre, which is now crammed with terrible paintings of sad-eyed children and dogs. Pigalle seems to have become a sex-shop jungle haunted by tough Brazilian transvestites. In both areas, cafés have turned the exploitation of tourists into a fine art, but as soon as you move away from the bright lights you may find a genuine Montmartre café.

One such establishment is the delightful **Aux Négociants** (*27 Rue Lambert*), where excellent and inexpensive wines flow freely as regulars converse, conveniently gathered around the tiny, horseshoe-shaped bar.

Nightlife & the performing arts

From the panhandling mimes in the piazza at Beaubourg to the idolized divas at the new *Opéra Bastille*, Paris remains a compelling magnet for performers and their followers from every French-speaking country, and much of the rest of Europe as well. The centres of established culture are the monumental *Opéra Garnier*, now liberated from the need to accommodate grand opera and at last providing a performance centre able to satisfy Paris' need for **contemporary and classical dance and concerts**, and the *Opéra Bastille*, the new, and still blossoming, hub of **operatic life**.

The French take their cinema-going very seriously, and this is witnessed by the crowds that attend the large number of grand **cinemas** along Av. des Champs-Élysées, as well as the host of avant-garde and revival cinemas to be found on the Left Bank, and the hundreds of neighbourhood cinemas too.

Café-théâtres, mainly offering the alternative humour that is beyond the grasp of most foreign visitors, have undoubtedly gone from strength to strength with the Parisian theatregoing population. **Theatre** attendances continue to improve as the waves of fashion cause interest to increase.

If visiting in summer, remember that many theatres and performance centres close for a month or more. Many theatres need reservations a week or two in advance, but **SOS Théâtres**

Nightlife and the performing arts

(☎ 42-25-67-07) or **Chèque-Théâtre** (☎ 42-46-72-40) provide last-minute assistance. For music bookings contact **FNAC** (*Rue de Rennes, 6ᵉ* ☎ 45-44-39-12 *or Rue Pierre-Lescot, Forum des Halles, 1er* ☎ 42-61-81-18). It is a good idea to reserve ahead wherever possible. There is a ticket booth next to *La Madeleine* church, where tickets can be purchased for half price on the day of the performance.

As for less serious nightlife, "Gay Paree" still conjures up visions of cancan dancers, champagne, and a level of cosmopolitan sophistication unique to the French capital. Ever since the Belle Époque, the combination of Bohemian artists, international café society and madcap expatriates has given Paris a slightly naughty but very glamorous after-dark reputation.

Although the favoured form of nightlife among certain natives nowadays is eating out rather than indulging in other forms of slumming, Paris is still very lively indeed by night. At the most expensive end of the scale, the spectacular **revues** with feathered and sequined scantily-clad beauties continue to flourish. The chief (and cheapest) visitor spectator-sport — people-watching — can be accomplished in many cafés, particularly on the Left Bank (see *Cafés*).

Parisians have always loved dancing, so **clubs and discos** are crowded and colourful. Like revues and cabarets, they tend to charge by the drink (*consommation*) rather than by the combination of admission fee plus drink. Prices can range from inexpensive at the more popular discos to vastly expensive at the most lavish nightclubs. Bar-hopping is not really a Parisian diversion, although many good **bars** welcome customers for the apéritif hour, or for a late-night drink. Wine bars continue to grow in popularity, especially with the under 35s.

Jazz clubs, with their echoes of the postwar era, have remained largely unchanged since the 1950s and they consequently offer both nostalgia and entertainment. Paris has always been *the* centre for jazz in Europe, however, and there are a number of excellent clubs hosting performers from all over the world.

Whatever your taste in entertainment, indispensable publications, giving performance times, telephone numbers, and lots more suggestions, are *Pariscope* and *l'Officiel des Spectacles*, published every Wed, or the monthly English magazine *Passion*.

The performing arts

Ballet and contemporary dance
In recent years, great efforts have been made to broaden the understanding and appreciation of dance. More informal space is offered to foreign and touring companies of every kind, who mainly visit the **Palais des Congrès** at Porte Maillot, or the **Palais des Sports** at Porte de Versailles, as well as those listed below.

Opéra-Garnier   Pl. de l'Opéra, 9ᵉ ☎ 47-42-57-50. Map **8**F7.
Métro: Opéra. Home of ballet and contemporary dance, both French and foreign. Magnificent setting: see entry in *Sights and places of interest*.

Théâtre Musical de Paris   See *Opera*.
Théâtre des Champs-Élysées   See *Concerts*.

Cafés-théâtres
Alternative comedy follows the same pattern in Paris as elsewhere. The great comedians of tomorrow are cutting their

teeth in the 100-seat *café-théâtres* of today. At some you eat, at others you can drink. If you are lucky, the show may turn out to be almost as good as the food — you never can tell.

Blancs-Manteaux   15 Rue des Blancs-Manteaux, 4ᵉ
☎48-87-15-84. Map **10**H10. Métro: Rambuteau.
Café d'Edgar   58 Bd. Edgar-Quinet, 14ᵉ ☎43-20-85-11. Map
14L7. Métro: Edgar-Quinet.
Café de la Gare   41 Rue du Temple, 3ᵉ ☎42-78-52-51. Map
10H10. Métro: Hôtel-de-Ville.
Petit Casino   17 Rue Chapon, 3ᵉ ☎42-78-36-50. Map **10**H10.
Métro: Arts-et-Métiers.
Point Virgule   7 Rue Sainte-Croix-de-la-Bretonnerie, 4ᵉ
☎42-78-67-03. Map **10**H10. Métro: Hôtel-de-Ville.

Cinema

Foreign movies are either dubbed in French (VF = *version français*) or presented in the original version, with sub-titles (VO = *version original*). The large cinemas along Av. des Champs-Élysées and Bd. des Italiens, near the *Opéra*, are the best cinemas for new films, while the numerous independents on the Left Bank present an extraordinary selection of revivals from every continent.

In recent years, smoking has become universally forbidden in French cinemas.

Les 14-Juillet Bastille   4 Bd. Beaumarchais, 11ᵉ
☎43-57-90-81. Map **11**I12. Métro: Bastille. Four screens, offering a programme that represents the conscience of French independent cinema.
3 Luxembourg   67 Rue Monsieur-Le-Prince, 6ᵉ ☎46-33-97-77.
Map **15**J8. Métro: Luxembourg. Regular late-night showings — a boon for insomniacs, shift-workers or those who dislike rush-hour travel. Deservedly popular.
Cinémathèque Française   Musée du Cinéma, Palais de Chaillot, Av. Albert-de-Mun, 16ᵉ ☎47-04-24-24. Map **12**H2.
Métro: Trocadéro. Closed Mon. See *Cinémathèque Française* in *Sights and places of interest*. This and **Salle Garance** (see below) are France's two national film theatres: sometimes obscure, always fascinating.
Centre Georges Pompidou: Salle Garance (see **Cinémathèque Française** above), Rue St-Merri, 4ᵉ
☎42-78-37-29. Métro: Rambuteau.
Gaumont Les Halles   1-3 Rue Pierre-Lescot, Forum des Halles (Level 3), 1ᵉʳ ☎40-26-12-12. Map **10**H9. Métro: Châtelet-Les-Halles. Six screens in the new Forum, most modern and convenient of the commercial cinemas.
Le Grand Rex   1 Bd. Poissonnière, 2ᵉ ☎42-36-83-93. Map
4F9. Métro: Bonne-Nouvelle. Giant theatre for big, spectacular films.
Kinopanorama   60 Av. De La Motte-Picquet, 15ᵉ
☎43-06-50-50. Map **12**J3. Métro: La Motte-Picquet-Grenelle. One of the most elegant of Parisian cinemas.
La Pagode   57bis Rue de Babylone, 7ᵉ ☎47-05-12-15. Map
13J5. Métro: St-François-Xavier. In an impressive Chinese pavilion, this is unquestionably the most beautiful cinema in the city of Paris.
Vendôme-Opéra   32 Av. de l'Opéra, 2ᵉ ☎47-42-97-52. Map
9G8. Métro: Opéra. Specializes in operatic films.
Vidéothèque de Paris   2 Grande Galerie, Porte St-Eustache,
Forum des Halles, 1ᵉʳ ☎40-26-34-30. Map **10**H9. Métro: Châtelet-les-Halles.

Concerts

The range of music is almost matched by the spread of its habitat. Conventional *salles* vie with theatres, museums, gardens, grand houses and, best of all, the old churches of Paris, including **La Madeleine**, **St-Germain-des-Prés**, **St-Julien-le-Pauvre** and **St-Roch**.

As for pop concerts, with both French and foreign performers, the biggest are held at **L'Olympia**, **Bercy Palais des Omnisports** and **Zénith**. For listings see *l'Officiel des Spectacles* or *Pariscope*.

Auditorium du Châtelet   Porte St-Eustache, Forum des Halles, 1ᵉʳ ☎ 40-28-28-40. Map **9**H9. Métro: Les Halles.

Auditorium du Louvre   Musée du Louvre, 1ᵉʳ ☎ 40-20-52-99. Map **9**H8. Métro: Palais-Royal.

Maison de Radio-France   116 Av. du Président-Kennedy, 16ᵉ ☎ 42-30-23-08. Métro: Ranelagh.

Salle Pleyel   252 Rue du Faubourg-St-Honoré, 8ᵉ ☎ 45-63-88-73. Map **7**E4. Métro: Ternes. Home of the Orchestre de Paris.

Théâtre des Champs-Élysées   15 Av. Montaigne, 8ᵉ ☎ 47-20-36-37. Map **7**G4. Métro: Franklin-D-Roosevelt. Concerts, dance and opera.

Théâtre Musical de Paris   1 Pl. du Châtelet, 1ᵉʳ ☎ 40-28-28-40. Map **10**I9. Métro: Châtelet. Musical theatre, dance and opera.

Jazz clubs

Once the refuge of American jazz musicians between the wars, and after World War II, Paris still retains its love for jazz. Clubs and bars abound. Consult the listings magazines for the full range; the following are some of the best known.

Bar Lionel Hampton   Hôtel Méridien, 81 Bd. Gouvion-St-Cyr, 17ᵉ ☎ 40-68-34-34. Map **6**D2. Métro: Porte-Maillot. Top jazz musicians and laid-back atmosphere.

Le Bilboquet   13 Rue St Benoît, 6ᵉ ☎ 45-48-81-84. Map **8**I7. Métro: St-Germain-des-Prés. A jazz hot-spot and an institution, with blues predominating.

Le Cambridge   17 Av. de Wagram, 17ᵉ ☎ 43-80-34-12. Map **6**E3. Métro: Charles-de-Gaulle-Étoile. Mainly traditional jazz.

Caveau de la Huchette   5 Rue de la Huchette, 5ᵉ ☎ 43-26-65-05. Map **15**J9. Métro: St-Michel. Very popular, excellent live music, dancing.

Le Montgolfier   8-12 Rue Louis-Armand, 15ᵉ ☎ 45-54-95-00. Métro: Porte de Versailles. Jazz and vertigo combined on the 23rd floor of this modern hotel.

New Morning   7 Rue des Petites-Écuries, 10ᵉ ☎ 45-23-51-41. Map **5**F10. Métro: Château d'Eau. Leading venue for visiting American musicians guesting with top French bands.

Le Petit Journal   71 Bd. St-Michel, 5ᵉ ☎ 43-26-28-59. Map **15**J8. Métro: Luxembourg. New Orleans jazz.

Opera

The most opulent of the performing arts has a new setting in the *Opéra Bastille*, and few other theatres in Paris have the facilities to deal with the scope of a full-scale opera production. Be advised to book ahead.

Opéra Bastille   2bis Pl. de la Bastille, 12ᵉ ☎ 40-01-16-16. Map **17**J12. Métro: Bastille.

Salle Favart (Opéra Comique)   5 Rue Favart, 2ᵉ ☎ 42-86-88-83. Map **9**F8. Métro: Richelieu-Drouot. Home of the

Opéra Comique company; also dance performances and concerts.
Théâtre des Champs-Élysées   See *Concerts*.
Théâtre Musical de Paris   See *Concerts*.

Theatres

More than a hundred theatres offer great variety, although the quality of production is inevitably variable. Subsidized theatres have increased steadily in number, and, for visitors with good spoken French, there is a wide choice of contemporary and period drama. Commercial theatres offer the expected international spectacular hits, such as *Cats* or *Les Misérables*, but in the main, people still do not visit Paris for its dramatic presentations. Reservations can often be made only 2wks ahead.
Théâtre de l'Atelier   1 Pl. Charles-Dullin, 18ᵉ ☎ 46-06-49-24. Map **4**D9. Métro: Anvers. Lovely building. Big productions, including musical spectaculars.
Les Bouffes du Nord   209 Rue du Faubourg-St-Denis, 10ᵉ ☎ 42-39-34-50. Map **5**D11. Métro: La Chapelle. Home to director Peter Brook's French company. Receiving house for international contemporary theatre.
La Cartoucherie   Route du Champs-de-Manoeuvre, Bois de Vincennes, 12ᵉ ☎ 43-74-24-08. Métro: Château-de-Vincennes, then bus no. 306. Avant-garde company repertory theatre, in idyllic setting.
Théâtre National de Chaillot   1 Pl. du Trocadéro, 16ᵉ ☎ 47-27-81-15. Map **12**H2. Métro: Trocadéro. Large-scale performances or classical works, from Molière to Shakespeare.
Théâtre National de la Colline   15 Rue Malte-Brun, 20ᵉ ☎ 43-66-43-60. Métro: Gambetta. Subsidized theatre with large and small auditoriums.
La Comédie Française   2 Rue de Richelieu, 1ᵉʳ ☎ 40-15-00-15. Map **9**H8. Métro: Palais-Royal. Respectable seat of the French classics; Molière, Racine and other classical playwrights are performed. See also entry in *Sights and places of interest*.
Marigny   Carré Marigny, 8ᵉ ☎ 42-56-04-41. Map **7**G5. Métro: Champs-Élysées-Clemenceau. Big, commercial theatre with first-class productions.
Théâtre National de l'Odéon   1 Pl. Paul Claudel 6ᵉ ☎ 43-25-70-32. Map **15**J8. Métro: Odéon.
Palais-Royal   38 Rue de Montpensier, 1ᵉʳ ☎ 42-97-59-81. Map **9**G8. Métro: Palais-Royal. Farces — and other spectacles.
Théâtre du Rond-Point (Renaud-Barrault)   2bis Av. Franklin-D-Roosevelt, 8ᵉ ☎ 42-56-60-70. Map **7**G5. Métro: Champs-Élysées-Clemenceau. Founded by the legendary couple of French theatre, Jean-Louis Barrault and Madeleine Renaud; presents powerful 20thC drama.

Nightlife

Bars

A night out in a bar is not a Parisian habit. Bars are almost always crowded before dinner for an apéritif, or very late after everything else has closed. They tend to open around 5pm, and some stay open till dawn. Unlike many other cities, Paris has no legal closing hours.

  Some of the most sophisticated bars are found in the smart hotels, notably **L'Hôtel**, the bar of which resembles an indoor garden, the **Plaza-Athénée**, the **Crillon**, the **Ritz** and the **George-V** (see *Hotels*).

Nightlife and the performing arts

Prices are high for spirits or champagne, considerably less for *pastis* or a wine-based drink such as *kir*. Non-alcoholic drinks, such as the refreshing *citron pressé*, are just as popular.

Bar du Lenox   9 Rue de l'Université, 7ᵉ ☎ 42-96-10-95. Map **8**I7. Métro: Rue-du-Bac. 1930s décor: agreeable setting for a quiet rendezvous.

La Closerie des Lilas   171 Bd. du Montparnasse, 6ᵉ ☎ 43-26-70-50. Map **15**L8. Métro: Vavin. The haunt of Hemingway still attracts assorted artists and literati. Good brasserie. (See also *Restaurants.*)

La Coupole   102 Bd. du Montparnasse, 14ᵉ ☎ 43-20-14-20. Map **14**K7. Métro: Vavin. Cultural landmark for generations of artists. (See also *Restaurants.*)

L'Entre-pots   14 Rue de Charonne, 11ᵉ ☎ 48-06-57-04. Map **17**J13. Métro: Ledru-Rollin. Cocktails and snacks, close to the *Opéra Bastille.*

Fouquet's   99 Av. des Champs-Élysées, 8ᵉ ☎ 47-23-70-60. Map **6**F3. Métro: George-V. Liveliest bar on the Champs-Élysées; friendly mix of regulars and tourists. (See also *Cafés.*)

Harry's New York Bar   5 Rue Daunou, 2ᵉ ☎ 42-61-71-14. Map **8**F7. Métro: Opéra. "Sank Roo Doe Noo": an all-American institution. Popular with Parisians too. Stocks 160 kinds of whiskey. Good piano bar in the basement. Closes only on Christmas Day.

Kitty O'Shea's   10 Rue des Capucines, 2ᵉ ☎ 40-15-08-08. Map **8**F7. Métro: Opéra. Parisian sister of Dublin's famous pub.

Polly Magoo   11 Rue St-Jacques, 5ᵉ ☎ 46-33-33-64. Map**15**J9. Métro: St-Michel. Chess... and a true Bohemian atmosphere.

Mayflower   49 Rue Descartes, 5ᵉ ☎ 43-54-56-47. Map **15**K9. Métro: Cardinal-Lemoine. Dutch-bar ambience; cocktails.

Rosebud   11bis Rue Delambre, 14ᵉ ☎ 43-35-38-54. Map **16**L7. Métro: Vavin. Former rendezvous for the likes of Sartre and de Beauvoir: a classic Montparnasse meeting-place.

Le Sous Bock   49 Rue St-Honoré, 1ᵉʳ ☎ 40-26-46-61. Map **10**H9. Métro: Les Halles. Beer, beer and more beer. 400 different kinds, including raspberry beer in a champagne flute.

La Villa   29 Rue Jacob, 6ᵉ ☎ 43-26-60-00. Map **9**I8. Métro: St-Germain-des-Prés. Ultra-designer flair in this daringly modern hotel (see *Hotels*). Split-level salons: cocktails, piano bar.

Cabarets and revues

Parisian revues blend nudity with entertainment and unabashed glamour. The formula varies, but establishments usually require customers to spend generously on drinks or dinner. The clientele tends to be made up of expense-account executives entertained by Parisian businessmen, or, perhaps, tourists gawking at the feathers, the sequins and skin.

Crazy Horse Saloon   12 Av. George-V, 8ᵉ ☎ 47-23-32-32. Map **7**F4. Métro: George-V. Strip show without the strip: dancers are already *déshabillée.* Artistic lighting and risqué costumes. Excellent entertainment with magicians too. But it's crowded, and very expensive.

Éléphant Bleu   49 Rue de Ponthieu, 8ᵉ ☎ 43-59-58-64. Map **7**F5. Métro: Franklin-D-Roosevelt. Glamorous Thai dancers and spectacle, with dinner.

Folies Bergères   32 Rue Richer, 9ᵉ ☎ 42-46-77-11. Map **4**E9. Métro: Cadet, Le Peletier. Strictly a theatre: no dinner or drinks required. You simply pay for your seat. Glorious history of Maurice Chevalier, Mistinguett and other old-time stars.

Au Lapin Agile ♣   22 Rue des Saules, 18ᵉ ☎ 46-06-85-87. Map

4C8. Métro: Lamarck-Caulaincourt. Old haunt of Renoir and Picasso, now devoted to tourists, offering song, humour and poetry. Good value for money.

Le Milliardaire 68 Rue Pierre-Charron, 8ᵉ ☎ 42-25-25-17. Map **7**F4. Métro: Franklin-D-Roosevelt. The sexiest strip, after the **Crazy Horse**.

Lido 116bis Av. des Champs-Élysées, 8ᵉ ☎ 45-63-11-61. Map **6**F3. Métro: George-V. Paris' most lavish revue: dancers, acrobats and magician. Very expensive.

Moulin Rouge Pl. Blanche, 9ᵉ ☎ 46-06-00-19. Map **4**D7. Métro: Blanche. Immortalized by Toulouse-Lautrec. The same management as the **Lido**, but less expensive.

Paradis Latin 28 Rue du Cardinal-Lemoine, 5ᵉ ☎ 43-25-28-28. Map **16**K10. Métro: Cardinal-Lemoine. Wonderful architecture in an old Eiffel warehouse; spectacle devised by old-time master of ceremonies.

Café-théâtres   See *The performing arts* on page 166.

Casinos
Except for a few exclusive and very private gaming clubs, it is not possible to gamble in Paris. The nearest good casino is at **Enghien** (☎ *34-12-90-00*), 16km (10 miles) NW of the city.

Dancing
The last tango in Paris still lives on. Dancing with strangers is viewed as a simple, entertaining diversion, just like taking tea in a café. A number of dance-halls and discotheques offer afternoon tea-dances (*thé-dancing*), as well as evening dances of the more traditional kind. Not an expensive pastime.

Chez Félix 23 Rue Mouffetard, 5ᵉ ☎ 47-07-68-78. Map **16**K10. Métro: Monge. Samba all night. Brazilian orchestra.

Club 79 79 Av. des Champs-Élysées, 8ᵉ ☎ 47-23-68-75. Map **6**F3. Métro: George-V. Large basement dance hall in chic location; daily tea-dances.

La Coupole 102 Bd. du Montparnasse, 14ᵉ ☎ 43-20-14-20. Map **14**K7. Métro: Montparnasse-Bienvenue. Dancing to old-fashioned tangos and waltzes; select clientele.

Madeleine Plaza 8 Bd. de la Madeleine, 9ᵉ ☎ 42-66-60-68. Map **8**F7. Nostalgia sessions and daily tea-dances.

Retro République 23 Rue du Faubourg-du-Temple, 11ᵉ ☎ 42-08-54-06. Map **11**G12. Métro: République. Tea-dances throughout the week; Retro orchestra at weekends.

Discos
The very word *discothèque* is, of course, French. Paris' discos tend to be wonderfully flashy affairs, with glittery decor and glittery people, throbbing lights and pulsating music. See also *Nightclubs* below. A few suggestions for various ages:

La Main Jaune Pl. de la Porte-Champerret, 17ᵉ ☎ 47-63-26-47. Métro: Porte-de-Champerret. Roller disco on the edge of the autoroute.

Là Scala de Paris 188bis Rue de Rivoli, 1ᵉ ☎ 42-61-64-00. Map **9**H9. Métro: Palais-Royal. Spacious disco with all the latest electronic gadgetry and stunning lighting.

"W" Salle Wagram 39 Av. de Wagram, 17ᵉ ☎ 43-80-30-03. Map **6**E3. Métro: Ternes. Huge former *salle de spectacles*, now transformed into one of the city's most chic discos.

Jazz clubs   See *The performing arts* on page 168.

Nightclubs

In Paris, as elsewhere, a nightclub is normally "private," although there are varying degrees of privacy, particularly for visitors. However, if you are young, or pretty, or well-dressed (or ideally all three), the chances increase of being given entry. Hotel *concièrges* are often knowledgeable about what is "in" for foreign visitors.

Private clubs are stuffy about male dress, and ties are expected. Women, however, can be as outrageous as they like. If you must go, and want to spend 120f on a drink, ask about **Castel-Princesse**, **Olivia Valère** and **Régine's**. These are the big names on today's club scene, as they have been for years.

Shopping

Paris gave the world the boutique, the small specialist shop that still embodies the intimate character of Parisian shopping. Entire *quartiers* are blanketed with boutiques, the specialities of which range from antiques to zippers. There are good department stores, but it is the boutiques that exhibit the individuality, variety and flair that makes Paris Europe's most seductive city for shopping.

Fine tailoring, luxurious fabrics and the indefinable chic of Parisian clothing is epitomized by the haute couture and designers' ready-to-wear. But Paris fashion is also translated into reasonably-priced clothing found in hundreds of small boutiques. Everything to do with fashion is a good buy, provided it is of French origin, mainly because you cannot get the same thing elsewhere at the same price. French perfume, cosmetics, home accessories and lingeries make Paris the woman's ultimate shop window, while men's and children's wear take a distinct second place.

Food and everything related to it — kitchen gadgets, cookbooks, herbs, linens — are especially close to the French heart, with a huge variety available in even the smallest neighbourhood shops.

Much of the 8e is devoted to expensive fashion, primarily Av. Montaigne, Rue du Faubourg-St-Honoré, Av. Victor-Hugo and Av. des Champs-Élysées. Rue du Faubourg-St-Honoré combines luxury shopping with small boutiques in a highly concentrated area. Around the Opéra cluster jewellers, shoe shops and perfumeries.

Trendier and less expensive is the area that has blossomed around Les Halles. The *Forum des Halles*, an underground shopping centre, combines designer boutiques with colourful, avant-garde fashion, plus furniture, *batterie de cuisine* and interesting home accessories. Adjacent streets are jammed with a collection of original shops with offbeat merchandise. The *Marais* quarter too is full of youthful life with its fashion boutiques, décor and giftware shops.

The area surrounding the newly opened *Opéra Bastille* is still in a state of flux, although its new status is already reflected in the number of art galleries that have opened up. Still on the Right Bank, the bustling Rue de Passy is worth a look, as it offers a choice of both classic and up-to-the-minute ready-to-wear fashions at considerably lower prices.

On the Left Bank, the *St-Germain* quarter is fairly bursting with designer fashion boutiques for those who dress young.

Department stores remain open from 9.30am-6.30pm Mon-Sat, and some are open until 8pm on Wed. Smaller boutiques generally open Mon-Sat 10am-7pm, although they may close for an hour at lunch. While neighbourhood shops often observe the traditional Mon closing, shops in the centre stay open. And, while Aug was once the universal holiday month, most of the larger shops now stay open throughout the summer.

Foreign visitors should ask for the *détaxe*, a refund of the French excise tax, returnable upon leaving the country with the purchases. Remember that you will need your passport for this. (See *Customs* in **Basic information**.) Also, many shops advertise "duty-free" goods, meaning this tax is deducted from the price on the spot. Be wary of this, for the basic price may be raised. Comparison-shopping is useful, particularly when buying perfumes and choosing designer accessories.

The French themselves are careful shoppers, unhurried by high-pressure sales techniques. Although Parisian sales personnel have a reputation for indifferent service, things have improved markedly in recent years.

Clothing and accessories

Bargains
Couturiers and ready-to-wear designers often sell last season's styles, with or without the labels (*dégriffé*), at half-price. Rue St-Placide, 6ᵉ (*Métro: Sèvres-Babylone*) and Rue d'Alésia, 14ᵉ (*Métro: Alésia*) are lined with discount shops for men, women and children.

Bab's ✿
89bis Av. des Ternes, 17ᵉ. Map 6D2. Métro: Porte-Maillot. 29 Av. Marceau, 16ᵉ. Map 6G3. Métro: Alma-Marceau.
Designer-wear by Nina Ricci, Guy Laroche and others. Gorgeous silk blouses.

Bidermann ✿
114 Rue de Turenne, 3ᵉ. Map 11H11. Métro: Filles-du-Calvaire.
Suits for men by St-Laurent and others.

Gigi's Soldes ✿
30 Pl. du Marché-St-Honoré, 1ᵉʳ. Map 8G7. Métro: Tuileries
French and Italian shoes, superb boots for men and women.

MicMac ✿
13 Rue Laugier, 17ᵉ. Map 6D3. Métro: Ternes.
Last year's collection at knock-down prices.

Le Mouton à 5 Pattes ✿
8-10 and 48 Rue St-Placide, 6ᵉ. Map 14J6&7. Métro: St-Placide.
All sorts of bargains are to be found in this shop, from last year's shoes and boots to imperceptibly flawed suits and dresses.

La Solderie
85 Rue de la Boëtie, 8ᵉ. Map 7F4. Métro: St-Augustin.
Goods by high-class couturiers, such as St-Laurent and Chanel, at cut prices.

Women's clothing
Paris is renowned for its fashion shops, which are liberally scattered in every corner of the city. A selection of recommended boutiques is listed below, but you will certainly make your own discoveries. Refer to the introduction on page 172 for a breakdown of areas.

Agnes B
3 Rue du Jour, 1ᵉʳ. Map 9G9. Métro: Les Halles.
Smart quilted coats, sportswear in wild colours.

Anastasia
18 Rue de l'Ancienne-Comédie, 6ᵉ. Map 8I8. Métro: Odéon.
Capes, romantic country clothes with a Russian flair.

Shopping

Armani
6 Pl. Vendôme, 8e. Map **8**G7.
Métro: Opéra.

Soft, classical elegance, with a fitting price tag.

Autour du Monde
12 Rue des Francs-Bourgeois,
8e. Map **11**I11. Métro: Saint-Paul.

Fashionable sportswear for the younger generation.

Dorothée Bis
17 Rue de Sèvres, 6e. Map **14**J7.
Métro: Sèvres-Babylone. 10 Rue
Tronchet, 9e. Map **8**F7. Métro:
Madeleine. Forum des Halles,
1er. Map **10**H9. Métro: Châtelet-
Les-Halles.

Young, inventive clothes in bright colours and avant-garde styles.

Boutique Lacoste
Galerie du Claridge, 74 Av. des
Champs-Élysées, 8e and
branches. Map **7**F4. Métro:
George-V.

The entire range of Lacoste clothes and luggage is available here, all emblazoned with the ubiquitous and instantly recognizable crocodile motif.

Cacharel
165 Rue de Rennes, 6e. Map
14J7. Métro: St-Sulpice. 34 Rue
Tronchet, 9e. Map **8**F7. Métro:
Madeleine. 7 Rue de Passy, 16e.
Map **6**I2. Métro: Passy.

Young, classical clothes, never quite in or out of style.

Chantal Thomass
5 Rue du Vieux Colombier, 6e.
Map **14**J7. Métro: St-Sulpice.

Revival of very sexy and feminine styles for women of every generation.

Comme des Garçons
40 Rue Étienne Marcel, 2e. Map
10G9. Métro: Étienne Marcel.

This is Japan's most strikingly original fashion house, with beautifully made clothes. The cutting edge of avant-garde fashion, like the pages of *Vogue* come to life.

Coulountjios ✿
3 Rue du Cygne, 1er. Map **9**H9.
Métro: Les Halles.

Exciting furs with hand-painted linings.

France Faver
79 Rue des Sts-Pères, 6e. Map
8I7. Métro: Sèvres-Babylone.

Semi-made-to-measure clothing, elegant and refined. Lovely hats.

France Rive Droite
Galerie du Claridge, 74 Av. des
Champs-Élysées, 8e. Map **7**F4.
Métro: George-V.

Ready-to-wear clothes and accessories bearing designer labels are among the choice goods available in this exclusive shopping precinct.

Jean Paul Gaultier
6 Rue Vivienne, 2e. Map **9**F8.
Métro: Bourse.

Provocative fashions for up-to-the-minute ladies.

Irié
8 Rue du Pré-aux-Clercs, 7e. Map
8I7. Métro: St-Germain-des-Prés.

Flowing materials and printed silks, Japanese-style.

Kenzo
3 Pl. des Victoires, 2e. Map **9**G8.
Métro: Bourse.

Considered to be one of Paris's most innovative designers, Kenzo introduces offbeat styles, sometimes later adopted by the stuffier couturiers.

Laïmoun ✿
2 Rue de Tournon, 6e. Map **15**J8.
Métro: Odéon.

Everything here is designed in Lebanon and is finely crafted from beautiful, hand-woven fabrics. Casually elegant day wear, sumptuous caftan-style gowns and an extensive range of unusual accessories.

Thierry Mugler
10 Pl. des Victoires, 2e. Map
9G8. Métro: Bourse.

Tough chic.

Maud Perl
47 Quai des Grands Augustins,
6e. Map **9**I8. Métro: Odéon,
Saint-Michel.

If you are saving your money for a Paris creation that is both elegant and versatile, this is it. Designed by Maud Perl, all the clothes are fashioned out of hand-dyed silk in every texture and colour imaginable. Every item a well-made classic, suitable for nearly any occasion.

Georges Rech ✿
54 Rue Bonaparte, 6e. Map **14**J7.
Métro: St-Germain-des-Prés. 23
Av. Victor-Hugo, 16e. Map **6**F2.
Métro: Charles-de-Gaulle-Etoile.

Smart, wearable clothes co-ordinated in chic, elegant ensembles.

Sonia Rykiel
4 and 6 Rue de Grenelle, 6ᵉ. Map 8I7. Métro: St-Sulpice. 70 Rue du Faubourg-St-Honoré, 8ᵉ. Map 8G6. Métro: Concorde.

Sleek, unlined knits and accessories, plus feathered and sequined evening wear. Original and amusing.

Ventilo
25 Rue du Louvre, 2ᵉ. Map 10G9. Métro: Sentier.

Handsome dresses and separates in unusual fabrics.

Giani Versace
67 Rue des Sts-Pères, 6ᵉ. Map 8I7. Métro: Sèvres-Babylone.

Highly tailored ready-to-wear, with a strong "Left Bank" accent.

Victoire
12 Pl. des Victoires, 1ᵉʳ. Map 9G8. Métro: Bourse.

Top designers, very chic with relaxed sales personnel. Co-ordinated accessories. A favourite with fashion-writers and editors.

Couturier boutiques

Designers' clothing, ready-to-wear and at much lower prices than the haute couture, is still expensive but stunning, with high-quality styling and fabrics and an excellent standard of workmanship. Today, couturier designs are aimed at every generation. Our comprehensive list below shows all the top names.

Pierre Balmain
44 Rue François-1ᵉʳ, 8ᵉ. Map 7G4. Métro: Franklin-D-Roosevelt.

Attractively simple and always a safe investment.

Pierre Cardin
27 Av. Victor-Hugo, 16ᵉ. Map 6F2. Métro: Charles-de-Gaulle-Étoile.

Eccentric women's fashions; men's clothing as well.

Chanel
31 Rue Cambon, 1ᵉʳ. Map 8G7. Métro: Concorde.

Inimitable little suits, quilted handbags, jewellery.

Christian Dior
26-32 Av. Montaigne, 8ᵉ. Map 7G4. Métro: Alma-Marceau.

Discreet daytime dresses, glamorous evening wear; sportswear in the boutique **Tricots**.

Louis Féraud
2 Pl. Porte Maillot, 17ᵉ. Map 6E2. Métro: Porte-Maillot. 88 Rue du Faubourg-St-Honoré, 1ᵉʳ. Map 8F5. Métro: Champs-Élysées-Clemenceau.

Noted for a good selection of long gowns and glittering evening wear, Féraud is a favourite of showbiz clients.

Givenchy
3 Av. George-V, 8ᵉ. Map 7G4. Métro: Alma-Marceau. 66 Av. Victor-Hugo, 8ᵉ. Map 6F2. Métro: Victor-Hugo.

Wide selection of classic styles.

Lanvin
22 Rue du Faubourg-St-Honoré, 1ᵉʳ. Map 8G6. Métro: Concorde.

Attractive cocktail wear and evening dresses.

Ted Lapidus
35 Rue François-1ᵉʳ, 8ᵉ. Map 7G4. Métro: Franklin-D-Roosevelt.

Good casualwear, especially coats, and lovely fabrics. Classic and fanciful designs in a variety of colours. Five other branches.

Guy Laroche ♣
27 Av. Montaigne, 8ᵉ. Map 7G4. Métro: Alma-Marceau.

The least expensive designers' ready-to-wear; nothing too way out, but everything very wearable if you like a "good", timeless look. Four other boutiques.

Hanae Mori
62 Rue du Faubourg-St-Honoré, 8ᵉ. Map 8F6. Métro: Concorde.

Sumptuous silks, interpreted through a Japanese-inspired design.

Nina Ricci
39 Av. Montaigne, 8ᵉ, Map 7G4. Métro: Franklin-D-Roosevelt.

Safe fashions in beautiful fabrics. Irresistible evening accessories.

St-Laurent Rive Gauche
6 Pl. St-Sulpice, 6ᵉ. Map 14J7. Métro: St-Sulpice.

Still supreme after more than 30yrs. Elegant and classic, with dash and versatility. Collectible fashions that can be built on each season. Four other branches.

Shopping

Haute couture
Opulent, made-to-measure clothing is the speciality that made
the Paris fashion industry the best and most famous in the
world. Each couturier has a distinct style, which can be seen
during the fashion shows, normally in Jan (for summer) and
July (for winter clothing) when the new collections are
modelled for prospective clients. Tickets for these fashion
shows can be obtained through hotel *concièrges*, or directly
from the couture houses, and for this purpose, telephone
numbers are given below. *Concièrges* can also arrange a
private video presentation of any of the main current
collections.

Pierre Balmain   44 Rue François-1er, 8e ☎ 47-20-35-34.
Map **7**F4. Métro: Franklin-D-Roosevelt.
Pierre Cardin   27 Av. Victor Hugo, 16e ☎ 45-01-69-53. Map
6F2. Métro: Charles-de-Gaulle-Étoile.
Chanel   31 Rue Cambon, 1er ☎ 42-61-54-55. Map **8**G7.
Métro: Madeleine, Opéra.
Christian Dior   30 Av. Montaigne, 8e ☎ 47-23-54-55. Map
7G4. Métro: Alma-Marceau.
Louis Féraud   88 Rue du Faubourg-St-Honoré, 8e
☎ 42-65-27-29. Map **8**F6. Métro: Madeleine.
Christian Lacroix   73 Rue du Faubourg-St-Honoré, 8e
☎ 42-65-79-08. Map **8**F6. Métro: Concorde.
Ted Lapidus   35 Rue François-1er, 8e ☎ 47-20-56-14. Map
7G4. Métro: Franklin-D-Roosevelt.
Guy Laroche   29 Av. Montaigne, 8e ☎ 47-23-78-72. Map
7G4. Métro: Alma-Marceau.
Hanae Mori   17 Av. Montaigne, 8e ☎ 47-23-52-03. Map
7G4. Métro: Alma-Marceau.
Nina Ricci   39 Av. Montaigne, 8e ☎ 47-23-78-88. Map **7**G4.
Métro: Franklin-D-Roosevelt.
Yves St-Laurent   5 Av. Marceau, 16e ☎ 47-23-72-71. Map
6G3. Métro: Alma-Marceau.
Jean-Louis Scherrer   51 Av. Montaigne, 8e ☎ 43-59-55-39.
Map **7**G4. Métro: Alma-Marceau.
Torrente   9 Rue du Faubourg-St-Honoré, 1er
☎ 42-66-14-14. Map **8**G6. Métro: Concorde.
Emmanuel Ungaro   2 Av. Montaigne, 8e ☎ 47-23-61-94.
Map **7**G4. Métro: Alma-Marceau.

Men's clothing
French styling combines English conservatism with Italian
flair. Many couturiers design men's lines (see women's
Couturier boutiques). But with a few exceptions, men's
clothing is not such a good buy in France.

Arnys
14 Rue de Sèvres, 7e. Map 14J6.
Métro: Sèvres-Babylone.
Impeccably elegant outfits of the
highest quality.

Cerruti 181
27 Rue Royale, 8e. Map 8G6.
Métro: Madeleine.
Traditional Italian suits in quality
materials.

Charvet
28 Pl. Vendôme, 1er. Map 8G7.
Métro: Opéra.

Highly celebrated gentlemen's tailor
offering a range of cravats and
kerchiefs as well as suits and shirts.

Façonnable
25 Rue Royale, 8e. Map 8G6.
Métro: Madeleine.
Well-cut sportswear in an excellent
range of materials and colours.

Marcel Lassance
17 Rue du Vieux Colombier, 6e.
Map 8J7. Métro: St-Sulpice.
Wide choice of tasteful styles at
reasonable prices.

Thierry Mugler
49 Av. Montaigne, 8ᵉ. Map 7G4.
Métro: Alma-Marceau.

The height of fashion, stated simply and without superfluous details.

Children's clothing

Paris is renowned for its stylish and chic children's clothes. Exquisite layettes and hand-embroidered gowns can still be found in Paris, but children's fashions are extremely expensive. Many designers (Dior, Hechter and others) make a children's line. The best selection is in department stores.

Baby Dior
28 Av. Montaigne, 8ᵉ. Map 7G4.
Métro: Franklin-D-Roosevelt.
Luxurious and pricey christening outfits, as well as a wider range of baby clothes.

Chipie
49 Rue Bonaparte, 6ᵉ. Map 8I7.
Métro: St-Germain-des-Prés.
Casual styles, jeans, label-smothered jackets and T-shirts. Superb, but not cheap.

Bonpoint
67 Rue de l'Université, 7ᵉ. Map 8H6. Métro: Solférino.
Classic children's wear with a demure, traditional feel.

Jacadi
60 Bd. de Courcelles, 17ᵉ. Map 2D4. Métro: Monceau.
Competitively priced, smart outfits with the accent on fashion.

Unisex and junior fashion

Autour du Monde
12 Rue des Francs-Bourgeois, 3ᵉ.Map 11I11. Métro: St-Paul.
Casuals with an African flavour.

Castelbajac
5 Rue des Petits-Champs, 1ᵉ. Map 9G8. Métro: Palais-Royal.
Comfortable clothes, presented with flair. For young adults too.

Chevignon
5 Pl. des Victoires, 2ᵉ. Map 9G8. Métro: Palais-Royal.
Leather clothing, often badge-encrusted. Recognizably *Chevignon* and rather expensive.

Kenzo
3 Pl. des Victoires, 2ᵉ. Map 9G8.
Métro: Palais-Royal.
Lastingly popular for his own blend of fabrics. Readily distinguishable.

Lacoste
2 Rue de Sèvres, 6ᵉ. Map 14J7.
Métro: Sèvres-Babylone.
Classic and rather sober sportswear, all bearing the famous Lacoste crocodile.

Jewellery

As in fashion, Paris has the haute couture of jewellery (*haute joaillerie*) and the ready-to-wear. Both are extremely stylish, a wide and interesting range is offered and, compared with the rest of the world, items are competitively priced. The "hautes" are mostly clustered together around Pl. Vendôme.

Boucheron   26 Pl. Vendôme, 1ᵉʳ. Map 8G7. Métro: Opéra, Concorde.

Cartier   13 Rue de la Paix, 1ᵉʳ. Map 8F7. Métro: Opéra.

Ilias Lalaounis   364 Rue St-Honoré, 1ᵉʳ. Map 8G7. Métro: Opéra, Madeleine.

Van Cleef et Arpels   22 Pl. Vendôme, 1ᵉʳ. Map 8G7. Métro: Opéra, Pyramides.

Zolotas   370 Rue St-Honoré, 1ᵉʳ. Map 8G7. Métro: Madeleine, Concorde.

Jewellery boutiques

Agatha   97 Rue de Rennes, 6ᵉ. Map 14K7. Métro: Rennes.

Fabrice   54 Rue Bonaparte, 6ᵉ. Map 9I8. Métro: St-Germain-des-Prés.

Impertinence   20 Rue du Bac, 7ᵉ. Map 8I7. Métro: Rue-du-Bac.

Mademoiselle Zaza   29 Boulevard Raspail, 7ᵉ. Map **14**J7.
Métro: Sèvres-Babylone.
Pulcinella   10 Rue Vignon, 9ᵉ. Map **8**F7. Métro:
Madeleine.
Reminiscence   22 Rue du Four, 6ᵉ. Map **14**J7. Métro:
St-Germain-des-Prés.
Utility-Bibi   27 Rue du Four, 6ᵉ. Map **14**J7. Métro:
St-Germain-des-Prés.
Leather goods

La Bagagerie ✿   41 Rue du Four, 6ᵉ. Map **15**J8. Métro:
St-Germain-des-Prés. 12 Rue Tronchet, 8ᵉ. Map **8**F7. Métro:
Madeleine. 74 Rue de Passy, 16ᵉ. Métro: Muette.
Hermès   24 Rue du Faubourg-St-Honoré, 1ᵉʳ. Map 8F6.
Métro: Madeleine.
Hervé Chapelier   13 Rue Gustave Courbet, 16ᵉ. Métro:
Trocadéro.
Lancel   43 Rue de Rennes, 6ᵉ. Map **14**J7. Métro:
St-Germain-des-Prés. 4 Rond-Point des Champs-Élysées, 8ᵉ.
Map **14**J7. Métro: Franklin-D-Roosevelt.
Louis Vuitton   79 Av. Montaigne, 8ᵉ. Map **7**G4. Métro:
Franklin-D-Roosevelt.
Lingerie

Beautiful French underwear is considered nearly as important
as outerwear, and men's underwear is sexy as well. Prices are
generally high. Lingerie shops often sell swimsuits.
Chantal Thomass   11 Rue Madame, 6ᵉ. Map **14**J7. Métro:
St-Sulpice.
Erès   2 Rue Tronchet, 8ᵉ. Map **8**F7. Métro: Madeleine.
Les Nuits d'Élodie   1bis Av. MacMahon, 17ᵉ. Map **6**E3.
Métro: Charles-de-Gaulle-Étoile.
Sabbia Rosa   71 Rue des Sts-Pères, 7ᵉ. Map **8**I7. Métro:
Sèvres-Babylone.

Clothing sizes

When shops give clothing sizes in inches or centimetres, use
the following conversion scale to determine the correct size

12 in	16	20	24	28	32	36	40	44	48
30 cm	40	50	60	70	80	90	100	110	120

When standardized codes are used, although these may be found
to vary considerably, the following provides a useful guide.

Women's clothing sizes

UK/US sizes	8/6	10/8	12/10	14/12	16/14	18/16
French sizes	38/34N	40/36N	42/38N	44/40N	46/42N	48/44N
Bust in/cm	31/80	32/81	34/86	36/91	38/97	40/102

Men's clothing sizes

European code (suits)	44	46	48	50	52	54	56
Chest in/cm	34/86	36/91	38/97	40/102	42/107	44/112	46/117
Collar in/cm	13½/34	14/36	14½/37	15/38	15½/39	16/41	16½/42
Waist in/cm	28/71	30/76	32/81	34/86	36/91	38/97	40/102
Inside leg in/cm	28/71	29/74	30/76	31/79	32/81	33/84	34/86

Men's and women's shoe sizes

UK/US sizes	3/4½	4/5½	5/6½	6/7½	7/8½	8/9½	9/10½	10/11½	11/12½
European	36	37	38	39	40	41	42	43	44

Shoes

Most shoe shops carry goods for men and women, and many stock handbags and luggage. The well-known labels are expensive, but Paris is still a wonderful place for shoes.

Bally   11 Bd. de la Madeleine, 1er. Map **8**F7. Métro: Madeleine. 35 Bd. des Capucines, 9e. Map **8**F7. Métro: Opéra. 20 other branches.

Carel   4 Rue Tronchet, 8e. Map **8**F7. Métro: Madeleine. Various other branches.

Céline   58 Rue de Rennes, 6e. Map **14**J7. Métro: St-Germain-des-Prés; 24 Rue François-1er, 8e. Map **7**G4. Métro: Franklin-D-Roosevelt; 3 Av. Victor-Hugo, 16e. Map **6**F2. Métro: Charles-de-Gaulle-Étoile.

Robert Clergerie   5 Rue du Cherche Midi, 6e. Map **14**J7. Métro: St-Placide.

Jocelyn   Arcades du Lido, 76-78 Av. des Champs-Élysées, 8e. Map **7**F4. Métro: George-V.

Charles Kamer   14 Rue de Grenelle, 6e. Map **14**J7. Métro: St-Sulpice.

Maud Frizon   7 Rue de Grenelle, 6e. Map **14**J7. Métro: Sèvres-Babylone; 83 Rue des Sts-Pères, 6e. Map **8**I7. Métro: St-Germain-des-Prés.

Charles Jourdan   12 Rue du Faubourg-St-Honoré, 8e. Map **8**G6. Métro: Concorde; 5 Bd. de la Madeleine, 1er. Map **8**F7. Métro: Madeleine; 86 Av. des Champs-Élysées, 8e. Map **7**F4. Métro: Franklin-D-Roosevelt.

Stephane Kélian   62 Rue des Sts-Pères, 6e. Map **8**I7. Métro: St-Germain-des-Prés; Forum des Halles, 1er. Map **9**H4. Métro: Châtelet-Les-Halles; 6 Pl. des Victoires, 1er. Map **9**G8. Métro: Palais-Royal.

Tokio Kumagai   52 Rue Croix-des-Petits-Champs, 1er. Map **9**G9. Métro: Palais-Royal.

Mancini   72 Av. Victor-Hugo, 16e. Map **6**F2. Métro: Victor-Hugo. Ready-made and made-to-measure shoes (allow at least 2wks).

Andrea Pfister   4 Rue Cambon, 1er. Map **8**G7. Métro: Concorde; 56 Rue du Four, 6e. Map **15**J8. Métro: Mabillon.

Sacha   15 Rue de Turbigo, 1er. Map **10**G9. Métro: Étienne-Marcel; 24 Rue de Buci, 6e. Map **9**I8. Métro: St-Germain-des-Prés; 43 Bd. Haussmann, 9e. Map **8**F7. Métro: Havre-Caumartin.

St-Laurent   See *Couturier boutiques*.

Cookware

Paris is a cook's heaven. No other city can compete with the array of food-related objects, often cheaper than and sometimes simply unobtainable elsewhere. Department stores all have large cookware departments, but it is more fun to go directly to the major specialists. Be prepared to pay cash, and ask for shipping and *détaxe* information.

Dehillerin ✿
*18 Rue Coquillière, 1er. Map **9**G9. Métro: Étienne-Marcel.*
Perhaps the best restaurant supply house in the world, but also sells happily on a smaller scale. Outstanding buys in copper, carbon steel knives, casseroles. Free catalogue in English. Excellent shipping service.

MORA
*13 Rue Montmartre, 1er. Map **9**G9. Métro: Étienne-Marcel, Les Halles.*
Smaller selection is offered than at the Dehillerin supply house, but this is still a shop for true professionals. You may find the cool, even casual service difficult to take, but be persistent.

179

Shopping

A. Simon
36 Rue Étienne-Marcel, 2ᵉ. Map 9G9. Métro: Étienne-Marcel, Les Halles.
Divided into two shops: one with metalware, electrical appliances and knives, the other devoted to pottery, glassware and a reasonable selection of porcelain. Good colourful displays and helpful personnel make shopping here a pleasure.

Department stores

Bazar de l'Hôtel de Ville ✿
55 Rue de la Verrerie, 4ᵉ. Map 10I10. Métro: Hôtel-de-Ville.
Excellent sporting goods, garden tools, books, records, and a dazzling array of hardware.

Bon Marché
38 Rue de Sèvres, 7ᵉ. Map 14J6. Métro: Sèvres-Babylone.
A true department store comprising fresh foods along with clothing, home furnishings and a wide selection of linens.

FNAC ✿
Forum des Halles, 1ᵉʳ. Map 10H9. Métro: Châtelet-Les-Halles; 136 Rue de Rennes, 14ᵉ. Map 14K6. Métro: Montparnasse-Bienvenue; 26 Av. Wagram, 8ᵉ. Map 6E3. Métro: Ternes.
This shop sells discount records, books, small appliances, sports goods and photo equipment. The Forum shop specializes in records, audiovisual supplies, photo goods and sports goods; Montparnasse concentrates on video and books; and Av. Wagram stocks the largest selection of audiovisual goods to be found in Paris.

Galeries Lafayette
40 Bd. Haussmann, 9ᵉ. Map 8F7. Métro: Chaussée-d'Antin-Lafayette, Auber; Maine-Montparnasse Centre, 14ᵉ. Map 14K6. Métro: Montparnasse-Bienvenue.
A serious attempt to update its fashion image has succeeded in turning both branches of this shop into trendy fashion spots, with vast home furnishings departments and a wide selection of porcelain, glassware and cookware. A variety of good, slick ideas, and an abundance of colour.

Le Printemps
64 Bd. Haussmann, 9ᵉ. Map 8F7. Métro: Havre-Caumartin, Auber.
Elegant, with deluxe ready-to-wear on the *Rue de La Mode*, and a magnificent stained-glass cupola that is a historical monument. Wide range of lingerie, gourmet boutiques, and a top-floor restaurant, **Brasserie Flo** (see *Restaurants*), renowned for its Art Nouveau decor. Weekly fashion shows.

Samaritaine ✿
Pont Neuf, 1ᵉʳ. Map 9H9. Métro: Pont-Neuf.
An old-fashioned shop noted for its uniforms (chefs' clothes and bartenders' outfits), sports goods and household items. The 10th storey of Magasin 2 offers an unparalleled panoramic view over the city.

Aux Trois Quartiers
17 Bd. de la Madeleine, 8ᵉ. Map 8F7. Métro: Madeleine.
In 1990, this traditional store was lavishly renovated and now aims at the deluxe market. A wide selection of gifts, accessories and linens. Worldwide shipping service.

Drugstores

These have nothing to do with American-style drugstores, although they all have chemists. The **Drugstores Publicis** are mini-shopping centres, meeting places and classy emergency shops, which often include cinemas and restaurants among their distractions. Open daily 9am-2am, they have counters devoted to books, perfume, food, gifts, toys and tobacco. Excellent selection of newspapers and periodicals in foreign languages. Branches at: 149 Bd. St-Germain 6ᵉ, map **8**I7, Métro: St-Germain-des-Prés; 133 Av. des Champs-Élysées 8ᵉ, map **6**F3, Métro: George-V; 1 Av. Matignon 8ᵉ, map **7**F5, Métro: Franklin-D-Roosevelt.

Food and drink

Every neighbourhood has its *charcuteries*, selling pork products, prepared foods and a bit of everything, and its *fromageries*, *caves* and *pâtisseries*. The area around Pl. de la Madeleine is particularly exciting.

Androuet
41 Rue d'Amsterdam, 8ᵉ. Map 3E7. Métro: St-Lazare.
Owned by Pierre Androuet, this shop is a temple to cheese. Special boxes for travelling.

Battendier
8 Rue Coquillière, 1ᵉʳ. Map 9G9. Métro: Étienne-Marcel.
A chic *charcuterie* known for its sausages, ham and pâtés.

Bertillon
31 Rue St-Louis-en-l'Île, 4ᵉ. Map 10J10. Métro: Pont-Marie.
Superb ice-cream and sorbets, made from the freshest fruits, which change with the seasons.

Cantin Marie-Anne
12 Rue de Champ-de-Mars, 7ᵉ. Map 13I4. Métro: École-Militaire.
The place to come for traditional cheeses. Mouthwatering selection.

Caves de la Madeleine
Passage Berryer, 24 Rue Boissy d'Anglas, 8ᵉ. Map 8G6. Métro: Madeleine.
This shop is nestled in a delightful mews and run by Englishman Steven Spurrier. A wide selection of wines and spirits. Gift-wrapping and a delivery service.

Fauchon
28 Pl. de la Madeleine, 8ᵉ. Map 8F6. Métro: Madeleine.
One of the world's most celebrated food shops, with three large boutiques, including one with a restaurant, Fauchon carries more than 20,000 products. Wonderful gift service; will ship anywhere.

La Ferme St-Hubert
21 Rue Vignon, 8ᵉ. Map 8F7. Métro: Madeleine.
Superb cheeses; helpful service.

Hédiard
21 Pl. de la Madeleine, 8ᵉ. Map 8F6. Métro: Madeleine.
A smaller Fauchon, with exotic products and spices, rare fruits and an outstanding wine selection. Five Paris branches.

Labeyrie
6 Rue Montmartre, 2ᵉ. Map 9G9. Métro: Étienne-Marcel.
Foie gras, truffles, *confits* of duck and goose, and all the wonderful foods of the Landes region.

Legrand ✿
1 Rue de la Banque, 2ᵉ. Map 9G8. Métro: Bourse.
Reasonably priced wines and alcohol, and interesting culinary products.

Lenôtre
44 Rue d'Auteuil, 16ᵉ. Métro: Michelange-Auteuil.
Now a famous chef, Lenôtre was first a caterer and then became a really outstanding *pâtissier*. Excellent chocolates, ice-cream and prepared food.

Maison du Miel
24 Rue Vignon, 8ᵉ. Map 8F7. Métro: Madeleine.
Fragrant and flavoursome honeys from every French province.

Maison de la Truffe
19 Pl. de la Madeleine, 8ᵉ. Map 8F6. Métro: Madeleine.
Truffles, of course, and an astounding selection of *charcuterie*.

Le Petit Bacchus
13, Rue du Cherche Midi, 6ᵉ. Map 14J7. Métro: St-Sulpice.
150 different wines, selected by Steven Spurrier.

Pétrossian
18 Bd. de LaTour-Maubourg, 7ᵉ. Map 13H5. Métro: Latour-Maubourg.
Finest caviars, smoked fish... and Russian vodka.

Piètrement
10 Rue Montmartre, 1ᵉʳ. Map 9G9. Métro: Étienne-Marcel, Les Halles.
Foie gras, truffles, dried mushrooms.

Poilâne
8 Rue du Cherche Midi, 6ᵉ. Map 14J7. Métro: St-Sulpice; 49 Bd. de Grenelle, 16ᵉ. Map 12I2. Métro: Bir-Hakeim; Forum des Halles, 1ᵉʳ. Map 10H9. Métro: Châtelet-Les Halles.
Baked in wood-fuelled ovens and containing no preservatives, Lionel Poilâne's crusty loaves are the best in Paris.

Shopping

Soleil de Provence
*6 Rue du Cherche Midi, 6ᵉ. Map
14J7. Métro: St-Sulpice.*
Sunny merchandise, indeed: fruity olive oil, honeys and olive oil soap.

Food markets

Every neighbourhood has its street market selling mainly food. Straw baskets and kitchen gadgets can also be good buys. In addition there are several streets known for outdoor food shops, primarily **Rue Mouffetard** (*5ᵉ, map 16 K10, Métro: Censier-Daubenton*) and **Rue Cler** (*7ᵉ, map 13 I4, Métro: École-Militaire*).

The following are some of the better, more central markets:
Av. President-Wilson (*16ᵉ, map 6 G3, Métro: Alma-Marceau*); **Av. de Saxe** (*7ᵉ, map 13 J4, Métro: École-Militaire*); **Bd. de Grenelle** (*15ᵉ, map 12 J3, Métro: La Motte-Picquet-Grenelle*); **Cité Berryer** (*26 Rue Royale, 8ᵉ, map 8 G6, Métro: Madeleine*).

Gifts

Allure
*17 Rue de Tournon, 6ᵉ. Map
15J8. Métro: Odéon.*
Goods across the household range, in any colour as long as it's white.

Au Chat Dormant
*13 Rue du Cherche Midi, 6ᵉ. Map
14J7. Métro: St-Placide.*
A cats-only boutique, selling everything feline, from pillows to postcards. A collector's dream.

Axis
*18 Rue Guénégaud, 6ᵉ. Map 9I8.
Métro: Odéon.*
Traditional and futuristic gadgetry.

L'Entrepôt
*50 Rue de Passy, 16ᵉ. Map 12I2.
Métro: Passy.*
A vast shop offering a choice of gifts of every kind: confectionery,

posters, toys, tableware, fashion accessories.

H G Thomas
*36 Bd. St-Germain, 5ᵉ. Map
16J10. Métro: Maubert Mutualité.*
Every kind of gift for men.

Jardins Imaginaires
*9 Rue d'Arras, 6ᵉ. Map 14J7.
Métro: Sèvres-Babylone.*
Anything to do with the garden, plus paintings, vases, potpourri.

Territoire
*30 Rue Boissy d'Anglas, 8ᵉ. Map
8F6. Métro: Madeleine.*
Stocks change according to the seasons, so look for ideas for the home and the garden. The children's department sports a wonderful collection of old, refurbished toys.

Household accessories, china, glass and silver

Au Bain Marie
*12 Rue Boissy d'Anglas 8ᵉ. Map
8G6. Métro: Concorde.*
Charming, old-fashioned objects and linens.

Baccarat
*30bis Rue de Paradis, 10ᵉ. Map
5E10. Métro: Château-d'Eau.*
World-renowned crystal, beautiful gifts. Also a fascinating museum of the history of crystal.

Christofle
*12 Rue Royale, 8ᵉ. Map 8G6.
Métro: Madeleine.*
Magnificent silver flatware in modern and retro patterns.

Daum
*4 Rue de la Paix, 2ᵉ. Map 8G7.
Métro: Opéra.*
Creations by contemporary artists in coloured glass.

Lalique
*11 Rue Royale, 8ᵉ. Map 8G6.
Métro: Madeleine.*
Collection of crystal, particularly frosted Art Nouveau and Deco patterns.

Limoges-Unic ✿
*12 and 58 Rue de Paradis, 10ᵉ.
Map 5E10. Métro: Château-d'Eau.*
Outlet for France's famed porcelain, at bargain prices.

Peter
191 Rue du Faubourg-St-
Honoré, 8ᵉ. Map 7E4. Métro:
Ternes.
Exclusive table settings. Specialist
for 200yrs.

Puiforcat
2 Av. Matignon, 8ᵉ. Map 7F5.
Métro: Franklin-D-Roosevelt.
World-famous silversmith noted for
well-designed silver and silver plate.

Quartz
12 Rue des Quatres-Vents, 6ᵉ.
Map 15J8. Métro: Odéon.
Contemporary glassware of the best
quality.

Xanadou
10 Rue St-Sulpice, 6ᵉ. Map 15J8.
Métro: Odéon.
A selection of household items —
teapots, glasses, ashtrays etc. —
designed by famous 20thC architects.

Markets

Each weekend Paris blossoms with flea markets on the
periphery, selling mainly antiques of varying quality, old
clothes, books, and just plain junk. Open Sat, Sun and
sometimes Mon, they invite bargaining.

Most vendors will not accept credit cards, but many will
gladly ship their merchandise worldwide.

The most famous flea market is the *Marché aux Puces* at
Porte de Clignancourt, where major antique dealers can be
found alongside more humble dealers in second-hand items
and bric-a-brac stalls. But Paris can offer other open-air
shopping experiences too, notably its *bouquinistes* on the Left
Bank. Some markets are for spending money in; others offer
superb photographic opportunities, or are worth visiting
simply for the sights and sounds.

For further ideas, see *Food and drink* on page 181 and
Textiles on page 184.

Animals
Quai du Louvre and **Quai de la Mégisserie**   1ᵉʳ. Map 9H8
and I9. Métro: Palais-Royal, Pont-Neuf.
Birds
Pl. Louis-Lépine   4ᵉ. Map 9I9. Métro: Cité. Sun only.
Booksellers (bouquinistes)
Quais des Grands-Augustins, **Conti** and **Malaquais**
6ᵉ. Map 9I8. Métro: St-Michel.
Quai du Louvre and **Quai de la Mégisserie**   1ᵉʳ. Map 9H8
and I9. Métro: Palais-Royal, Pont-Neuf.
Quai Voltaire   6ᵉ. Map 8H7. Métro: Rue-du-Bac.
Flea Markets
Marché d'Aligre   Pl. d'Aligre, 12ᵉ. Métro: Ledru-Rollin.
Open daily. A small and rather expensive market.
Puces de Didot   Av. Georges Lafenêstre, 14ᵉ. Métro:
Porte-de-Vanves.
Puces de Montreuil   Porte de Montreuil, 20ᵉ. Métro:
Porte-de-Montreuil. Second-hand goods and curios.
Puces de St-Ouen   18ᵉ. Métro: Porte de Clignancourt.
Puces de Vanves   14ᵉ. Métro: Porte de Vanves. Better
bargains to be found here. Open Sat, Sun, Mon, but primarily
Sat morning for bric-a-brac.
Flowers
Pl. Louis-Lépine   Quai de la Corse, 4ᵉ. Map 9I9. Métro:
Cité.
Pl. de la Madeleine   1ᵉʳ. Map 8F6. Métro: Madeleine.
Pl. des Ternes   8ᵉ. Map 6E3. Métro: Ternes.
Stamps and postcards
Av. Gabriel   1ᵉʳ. Map 7F5. Métro: Franklin-D-Roosevelt.
Open Thurs, Sat, Sun from 10am.

Perfume and cosmetics

Many shops offer "duty-free" perfumes, meaning that the price is lowered by the excise tax; others just offer discounts. Comparison-shopping is useful, since the best prices are at the duty-free airport shop, although the selection there is certainly more limited.

Dozens of shops surround the Opéra, all selling the major brands of cosmetics and perfumes. The following indicates where the slightly more unusual shops are to be found.

L'Artisan Parfumeur   84bis Rue de Grenelle, 6ᵉ. Map **8**I6. Métro: Rue-du-Bac. Charming, unusual scents such as grapefruit and cinnamon, lovely potpourris and gifts for men and women.

Caron   34 Av. Montaigne, 8ᵉ. Map **7**G4. Métro: Franklin-D-Roosevelt.

Dans un Jardin   71 Rue la Boëtie, 8ᵉ. Map **7**F5. Métro: St-Philippe-du-Roule. Custom-made perfumes and unusual gifts.

Guerlain   68 Av. des Champs-Élysées, 8ᵉ. Map **6**F3. Métro: George-V; 2 Pl. Vendôme, 1ᵉʳ. Map **8**G7. Métro: Tuileries; 29 Rue de Sèvres, 6ᵉ. Map **14**J7. Métro: Sèvres-Babylone.

Sur la Place   12 Pl. St-Sulpice, 6ᵉ. Map **14**J7. Métro: St-Sulpice. Old-fashioned bath jellies, algae from Brittany, natural beauty products.

Michel Swiss ✿   16 Rue de la Paix, 1ᵉʳ. Map **8**F7. Métro: Opéra.

Textiles

The backbone of the fashion industry, French textiles are sumptuous, beautifully designed and often very reasonably priced.

Alexandra   95 Rue du Faubourg-St-Honoré, 8ᵉ. Map **8**G6. Métro: Concorde.

Bouchara ✿   54 Bd. Haussmann, 9ᵉ. Map **8**F7. Métro: Havre-Caumartin. Five other branches also.

Marché St-Pierre (open-air market)   Pl. St-Pierre, 18ᵉ. Map **4**D9. Métro: Anvers.

Max   70 Av. des Champs-Élysées, 8ᵉ. Map **7**F4. Métro: George-V.

Rodin   36 Av. des Champs-Élysées, 8ᵉ. Map **7**F4. Métro: Franklin-D-Roosevelt.

Toys

French toys can be sophisticated, well designed and expensive. Internationally-known toys, such as Lego, cost considerably more than at home.

Ali-Baba
29 Av. de Tourville, 7ᵉ. Map 14I4. Métro: École Militaire.
A huge choice of toys for all ages. Specialist in lead soldiers.

Le Ciel est à Tout le Monde
10 Rue Gay-Lussac, 5ᵉ. Map 15K8. Métro: St-Michel.
Everything that can fly: saucers, aeroplanes, kites.

Farandole
48 Av. Victor-Hugo, 16ᵉ. Map 6F2. Métro: Victor-Hugo.
Two floors of scientific and classic toys plus some astonishing petrol-engine cars for older children.

Jouets et Compagnie
11 Bd. de Sébastopol, 1ᵉʳ. Map 10H9. Métro: Châtelet.
The nearest thing to a hypermarket, where you can find almost everything — and pay less for it.

Au Nain Bleu
406 Rue St-Honoré, 8ᵉ. Map 8G7. Métro: Madeleine.
Famous outlet for high-quality toys.

Paris for children

Paris is a city of adult pleasures where the world of childhood innocence is a restricted domain — and perhaps all the more cherished on that account. The needs of children are catered for in many imaginative ways, and Paris can be a rich and exciting place for the young. But it can also be frustrating, especially for active youngsters.

The perfect illustration is the Parisian park. Although the city has a large amount of green space per inhabitant, much of it is in the form of small, well-tailored public gardens bristling with signs telling visitors to keep off the grass. The inevitable children's play area, with its sandbox, slide and swings, is a welcome feature, but no substitute for an open space where children can kick a ball or roll in the grass. On the positive side, the larger parks offer more exciting distractions such as donkey rides and miniature farms, and there are many fun places for young visitors: zoos, museums, theatres and circuses.

Having children with you in Paris means careful planning if they are to get the best out of their stay. A good way to keep abreast of children's events is to consult the section *Pour les jeunes* in the weekly guides *l'Officiel des Spectacles* and *Pariscope*.

Parks and zoos

Top of the list is the **Jardin d'Acclimatation** (📞 ✇), which is a veritable children's paradise on the edge of the *Bois de Boulogne*. It offers enough distractions to please the most demanding youngster, including a puppet show, distorting mirrors, an archery range, miniature golf, a dolphinarium and a small zoo. Kids will enjoy riding to it, on a miniature train from Porte Maillot. The rest of the Bois is not really ideal for children, but there is a boating lake.

The Bois de *Vincennes* also has boating lakes, and the best zoo in the city. Another but less exciting zoo is to be found in the *Jardin des Plantes*. Other parks to take children to are:

- The *Buttes Chaumont*: dramatic scenery, grass you can walk on, roller-skating, boating and donkey rides
- The *Champ-de-Mars*, which has a playground for skate-boards and roller-skating; and there are also donkey-rides and puppet shows
- The excellent *Luxembourg* gardens: donkey rides, a pond for toy boats, sailing boats for hire, and a large marionette theatre
- The *Palais de Chaillot* gardens, E side, for an underground aquarium and small playground
- The *Parc de Monceau*, where there's a tremendous playground and merry-go-round
- The *Parc de Montsouris*: remember to take bread for the waiting ducks
- **Ranelagh Gardens** (*Av. Raphael, 16ᵉ*), for a playground, cycling and roller-skating track, donkey rides, merry-go-round and puppet shows
- The highly imaginative **Jardin d'Enfants** in the park near *Les Halles*
- Also in the centre of Paris, the *Tuileries* gardens, where there are small play areas, donkey rides, puppet shows and two ponds for toy boats
- Whether or not you plan to go into the **Cité des Sciences** (see below), the *Parc de la Villette* is a pleasant place to go, and has a good playground outside the main entrance

Paris for children

Museums and workshops

The main museums that give special emphasis to children and offer supervised activities are the **en Herbe** museum in the **Jardin d'Acclimatation** of the *Bois de Boulogne*, the **Musée des Enfants** (part of the *Art Moderne de la Ville de Paris* museum), the *Arts Décoratifs* museum and the *Pompidou Centre*. But for sheer old-fashioned fun, there is no museum that can beat the *Grévin*, with its waxworks and conjuring show. There's now a smaller but equally fascinating branch at the *Forum des Halles*.

Other museums that children enjoy visiting are: the *Arts et Traditions Populaires* museum, which shows everyday French objects, including toys, from past centuries; the *Palais de la Découverte*, a science museum with a planetarium; the **Army Museum** at *Les Invalides*; the *Marine* museum; and the technical museum (*Musée des Techniques*), with its push-button working models of machines.

Best of all, for those with even the slightest leanings towards the sciences, is a day at *Parc de la Villette*, where the **Cité des Sciences et de l'Industrie** is based. Don't be put off by the rather dry-sounding name: there's an **Inventorium** (a discovery-through-play environment), a **planetarium**, and **Explora**, which offers hands-on experience of all kinds of things, including computers.

Theatres, films, circuses and other events

Apart from the puppet shows in the parks, there are many theatres that stage special performances for children. A list of these, along with other children's events such as children's films and circuses, can be found in the *Pour les jeunes* section of *l'Officiel des Spectacles*.

Other ideas

Most older children enjoy climbing up to the high **vantage points** (*Tour Eiffel*, *Tour Montparnasse*, *Arc de Triomphe*, *Notre-Dame*, *Sacré-Coeur*) or, by contrast, plunging underground into the *Égouts* (sewers) and the *Catacombs* — but the latter is not for the squeamish. The new *Centre International de l'Automobile*, in Pantin to the E of Paris, is well worth a trip for any child old enough to handle a simulator. The *Parc Océanique Jacques Cousteau* will thrill most children, with its giant images... and the chance to step inside a whale.

The Sunday **bird market** on the *Île de la Cité* is always crowded, and **river and canal trips** are also popular with the young (see *Useful addresses* on page 18). And if you go up to *Montmartre* you can take them on the **funicular railway**. There are also **annual events** that are great attractions for kids, such as the Fête du Pont-Neuf, Marais Festival and Feux de St-Jean (see *Calendar of events* on page 36 for a fuller list).

For information about **sports**, including roller-skating and skate-boarding, see *Activities and sports*, particularly for details of the superb new **Aquaboulevard** leisure centre, where you might spend a whole day. For **toys** and **clothes**, see *Shopping* on pages 184 and 177.

And finally, if a visit to Disneyland has just seemed like a dream, why, that dream could become reality.... For in spring 1992, **EuroDisneyland** opens its doors at Marne La Vallée, which is only about 15km NE of Paris. 15 million visitors a year are predicted.

Activities and sports

In a city as devoted to urban pleasures as Paris, it is perhaps surprising to find that there is a rich choice of sports both for those who want to take part and for those who prefer to watch. Within the city boundaries, where space is at a premium, it is easier to pursue indoor than outdoor sports, but on the periphery a full range of open-air sports is available.

Pursuing a sport in Paris can be an expensive business, but is not necessarily so. Many facilities, often in the form of multi-purpose leisure complexes, are provided by the City of Paris, and these can be used by the public at relatively low cost. For details on all aspects of sporting activity for visitors, including information on major spectator events, contact **Allô Sports** (☎ *42-76-54-54 Mon-Fri daytime only*). Some sporting facilities are also listed in the weekly magazines *L'Officiel des Spectacles* and *Pariscope* and in the monthly English magazine *Passion*. The best way to keep abreast of events is to read the daily sports newspaper *L'Équipe*.

Conveniently, the 16ᵉ contains the major tennis and football stadiums **Roland Garros** and **Parc des Princes**, as well as **Longchamp** and **Auteuil** racecourse, both located in the Bois de Boulogne. The main arena for spectator sport is the **Palais Omnisports de Bercy** near the Gare de Lyon, where you can see anything from basketball and judo to motorcycle racing and show jumping.

For a leisure centre to end all leisure centres, make a day at **Aquaboulevard de Paris** (*4 Rue Louis-Armand, 15ᵉ* ☎ *40-60-10-00; Métro: Balard*). Here you will find an aquatic park with wave machine, water cannon, giant slides and special water games for children, as well as aerobics, bowling, billiards, golf, gymnasium, health club and massage, solarium, squash, tennis and yoga. You could even play Scrabble, chess or bridge, watch horse-racing — or just eat and drink.

As a starting point, the following section is an A-Z guide to the main sports, games and other leisure activities in and around Paris.

Athletics

There are numerous centres in Paris where you can practise athletics. Contact the **Ligue de l'Île de France de l'Athlétisme** (*39 Rue de Palestro, 75002 Paris* ☎ *42-33-23-50*).

Bicycling

Cycle-racing is a French passion, culminating in the annual Tour de France, which finishes in Paris in July. A good idea is to make use of the *Train plus vélo* scheme offered by the French National Railways (SNCF), which gives you a day's excursion with bicycle rental thrown in. Information on hiring bicycles is in *Basic information*. Remember the possible dangers of cycling in Paris traffic.

For general inquiries get in touch with the **Fédération Française du Cyclisme** (*43 Rue de Dunkerque, 75010 Paris* ☎ *42-85-41-20*).

Ballooning

Montgolfier first flew his balloon over Paris in the 18thC. Nowadays, for a 3hr round-trip in a balloon, contact **Espace Plus** (*14 Rue de Sèvres, 92100 Boulogne Billancourt* ☎ *46-05-91-25; trips all year round, weather permitting*). It's hardly cheap, at

1350f each, but must be the experience of a lifetime. Advance booking is essential: allow one week.

Boating
Pleasure boats (*barques*) can be rented at the following parks:
Bois de Boulogne   Métro: Porte-Dauphine.
Bois de Vincennes   Métro: Château-de-Vincennes.
Parc des Buttes-Chaumont   Métro: Buttes-Chaumont.

Boules
This game, and its close relative, *pétanque*, are national obsessions in France. Walk into almost any park in Paris on a Sat or Sun afternoon, and you will find a series of amateur matches in progress on any convenient patch of earth or gravel. To find out more, contact the **Ligue de l'Île de France de la Fédération Française de Pétanque et de Jeux Provençales** (*9 Rue Duperré, 75009 Paris* ☎ 48-74-61-63).

Bowling
The largest alley is the **Bowling de Paris** (*Jardin d'Acclimatation, Bois de Boulogne* ☎ 40-67-94-00). Other "bowlings" are advertised in *L'Officiel des Spectacles* and *Pariscope*.

Bridge
There are several good bridge clubs in Paris where you can also play backgammon and gin rummy. Try **Bridge Club de Paris** (*68 Bd. de Courcelles, 17ᵉ* ☎ 47-63-68-31) or **Bridge Club Étoile** (*99 Rue de la Pompe, 16ᵉ* ☎ 45-53-54-40). For further information get in touch with the **Fédération Française de Bridge** (*73 Av. Charles de Gaulle, 92200 Neuilly* ☎ 47-38-24-40).

Chess
You will find that chess is played in many Paris cafés as well as in special clubs. The **Ligue de l'Île de France d'Échecs** (*33-37 Quai de Grenelle, 15ᵉ* ☎ 45-78-98-43) can provide information.

Dance
Whether your bent is towards classical ballet, flamenco, rock or folk, there is sure to be a dance centre in Paris to suit you. Ask at the **Fédération Française de la Danse** (*12 Rue St-Germain-l'Auxerrois, 75001 Paris* ☎ 42-36-12-61).

Fishing
Twenty different types of fish can be caught nowadays in Paris waters. An annual permit costs about 130f from **Fédération Interdépartementale des Associations de Pêche et de Pisciculture** (*83 Rue Léon Frot, 11ᵉ* ☎ 43-48-36-34), who will give information on the many lakes, canals and quays.

Football (soccer)
The main Paris stadium is the **Parc des Princes** (*Porte de St-Cloud, 16ᵉ*) near the s end of the Bois de Boulogne, where such events as the French Cup Final (either May or June) take place.

For more details contact the **Fédération Française de Football** (*60bis Av. d'Iéna, 75016 Paris* ☎ 47-20-65-40) or the **Ligue Parisienne de Football** (*5 Pl. de Valois, 75001 Paris* ☎ 42-61-56-47).

Gardens

There are floral gardens in the **Bois de Vincennes** and the **Bois de Boulogne** (see *Sights and places of interest*). Also worthy of a visit are the **Jardin des Plantes**, and the **Jardin Fleuriste** (*Porte d'Auteuil*), where all the capital's flowers are grown. There is also a glasshouse with exotic and tropical plants, as well as a palm house.

Worth a short journey are the **Albert Kahn Gardens**, on the banks of the Seine in Boulogne-Billancourt, and the rose museum at **L'Häy-les-Roses**.

Golf

Most of the best golf courses belong to clubs, which will admit players on payment of a green fee and where you can also hire clubs and other golfing equipment. Public golf courses also welcome visitors.

For further details about golfing facilities contact the **Fédération Française de Golf** (*69 Av. Victor-Hugo, 75016 Paris* ☎ *43-02-13-55*).

Gymnastics

There are plenty of gymnasiums in Paris. List available from **Allô Sports** (☎ *42-76-54-54*) or the **Fédération Française d'Éducation Physique et de Gymnastique Volontaire** (*41 Rue de Reuilly, 75012 Paris* ☎ *43-41-86-10*).

Health clubs

Although there are many health clubs in Paris, most are open to members only. Many hotels now have saunas and other health facilities for residents. For exercise classes, including aerobics and "dancersize", go to **Espace Vit'Halles** (*48 Rue Rambuteau, 4ᵉ* ☎ *42-77-21-71*). For the whole lot, and much more, try the **Aquaboulevard de Paris** leisure centre (see page 187).

Helicopter rides

Pleasure trips in a helicopter are run by a number of companies operating from the **Héliport de Paris** in the 15ᵉ (☎ *45-54-04-44*).

Horse-racing

The principal racecourses are **Longchamp** (*Bois de Boulogne*) and **St-Cloud** (*12km/8 miles w of Paris*) for flat-racing, and **Auteuil** (*Bois de Boulogne, Métro: Porte d'Auteuil*) for steeple-chasing. Other courses in or comfortably near Paris are to be found at **Chantilly**, **Enghien**, **Evry**, **Maisons-Laffitte** and **Vincennes**.

Longchamp is a superb racecourse, and has a restaurant overlooking the track. The biggest racing event, the *Prix de l'Arc de Triomphe*, is held there on the first Sun in Oct.

Ice-skating

There are several ice-rinks in Paris where skates can also be hired. One is the **Patinoire des Buttes-Chaumont** (*30 Rue Edouard Pailleron, 19ᵉ* ☎ *42-08-72-26*). For a list of other rinks and for more specific information, try the **Fédération Française des Sports de Glace** (*42 Rue du Louvre, 75001 Paris* ☎ *40-26-51-38*).

Language courses

Courses can be booked before you leave home. Your French

Activities and sports

Consulate will have general information as well as details of how to apply.

Courses for all ages and all levels are organized by **Alliance Française** (*101 Bd. Raspail, 75006 Paris* ☎ *45-44-38-28*) and **Eurocentre de Paris** (*13 Passage Dauphine, 75006 Paris* ☎ *43-25-81-40*).

Motor-racing

One of the world's great motor-racing circuits is at **Le Mans**, about 184km (115 miles) sw of Paris, where the 24hr road race takes place every year in mid-June.

For information contact the **Fédération Française de Sport Automobile** (*136 Rue de Longchamp, 75016 Paris* ☎ *47-27-97-39*).

Parachuting

If you want to risk life and limb while you're abroad, parachuting is one exhilarating possibility. Contact the school for parachuting at **Le Centre de Parachutisme Sportif de Paris Île de France** (*L'Aérodrome, 77320 La Ferté-Gaucher* ☎ *64-04-01-73, open Fri, Sat, Sun and holidays*).

Riding

There are many riding stables in the Paris region, although they tend to be in the outlying areas, such as the Bois de Boulogne and the Bois de Vincennes. Contact the **Ligue Équestre de Paris** (*22 Rue de Penthièvre, 75008 Paris* ☎ *42-25-97-73 afternoons only*) for details of horse shows and clubs offering temporary membership.

Roller-skating

It's as much fun to watch the skills of others as it is to participate at a number of outdoor roller-skating and skate-boarding pistes such as the big concourse at the **Palais de Chaillot**. Or try a roller-skating discotheque like **La Main Jaune** (*Pl. de la Porte-de-Champerret, 17e* ☎ *47-63-26-47*), where you can hire skates. Telephone to check which evenings; it's open to children during the day.

Rugby

For rugby union contact the **Fédération Française de Rugby** (*7 Cité d'Antin, 75009 Paris* ☎ *48-74-84-75*). Important rugby (as well as football) fixtures are held at the **Parc des Princes** (*Métro: Porte de St-Cloud*).

Squash

Although squash is an increasingly popular sport in France, there are still relatively few courts in the centre of Paris, and they usually require membership. There are excellent courts at **Tour Montparnasse** (*37 Av. du Maine, 15e* ☎ *45-38-66-20*) and at **Le Squash Front de Seine** (*21 Rue Gaston-de-Caillavet, 15e* ☎ *45-75-35-37*). At both you will pay a small monthly membership fee.

Swimming

There are many municipal pools, details of which can be obtained from **Allô Sports** (☎ *42-76-54-54*) or by looking in the telephone directory under *Piscines*. The excellent new leisure centre **Aquaboulevard** offers much more than just swimming (see p187), and the *Forum des Halles* now has a first-class pool.

Tennis

Both municipal courts (for example in the Luxembourg gardens) and many private ones are available. Information from **Allô Sports** (☎ *42-76-54-54*). The **Stade Français** club (*Porte de St-Cloud, 2 Rue du Commandant-Guilbaud, 16* ☎ *46-51-66-53*) is open to visitors.

Walking and rambling

Historical and cultural guided walks around Paris take place all year round. See *Randonnées Pedestres* in *L'Officiel des Spectacles*, or *Pariscope*. For general information, contact the **Fédération Française de Randonnées Pédestres** (*8 Av. Marceau 75008* ☎ *47-23-62-32*).

Zoos

Zoos are found at **Bois de Vincennes**, **Jardin d'Acclimatation, Bois de Boulogne** and **Jardin des Plantes**. See *Paris for children* on page 185 for locations, and separate entries in *Sights and places of interest*.

Excursions

Paris has always been the centre of power, politics and the arts in France, and over the centuries, great châteaux have grown up within easy striking distance of the city. Several important cathedral towns are also close at hand, as well as pretty villages and many magnificent forests, a famous feature of the Île de France. All these sights make easy one-day excursions from Paris. Four of the best-known sightseeing towns near Paris — Chartres, Fontainebleau, Reims and Versailles — are described in full. Here is a taste of some of the other options:

Barbizon
58km (35 miles) SE of Paris. By train: from Gare de Lyon; by car: on A6 or N7.
Small village close to Fontainebleau, famed for its artistic associations in the 19thC when several Romantic painters settled there. They included Rousseau and Corot, whose studios are open to the public. The inn where they gathered, Pierre Ganne's, also stands.

Beauvais
76km (45 miles) N of Paris. By train: from Gare du Nord; by car: on N1.
Although the centre of Beauvais was destroyed in a 1940 air raid, the Gothic cathedral miraculously survived.

Chantilly
50km (30 miles) N of Paris. By train: from Gare du Nord; by car: on N16.
Famed for its cream, its hand-worked lace, and its racecourse, but most of all for its elegant château.

Compiègne
82km (50 miles) NE of Paris. By train: from Gare du Nord; by car: on A1.
The impressive palace here was a favourite royal hunting residence, and is surrounded by the majestic Compiègne Forest, where in 1918 and 1940 two very different armistices were signed.

Giverny
87km (54 miles) NW of Paris. By train: from Gare St-Lazare to

*Vernon, then short taxi-ride. **By car**: on A13, to Vernon exit (D181), then D5.*

The exquisite and idyllic home and studios of Impressionist painter Claude Monet, with its water garden, is the scene of many touristic pilgrimages. The gardens are open all year round, but the house is closed Nov-Mar (☎ *(16) 32-51-28-21*).

Malmaison

*6km (4 miles) w of Paris. **By Métro/RER**: to Rueil-Malmaison; **by car**: N13 via La Défense.*

The château of the Empress Joséphine, now a fascinating museum.

Rouen

*140km (87 miles) NW of Paris. **By train**: from Gare St-Lazare; **by car**: on A13, N14 or N15.*

An important city since the Middle Ages, Rouen witnessed the trial and execution of Joan of Arc in 1431. The last bridging point on the Seine, it has suffered numerous sieges over the centuries, and severe bombing during World War II, yet it has retained an intimate domestic atmosphere, some superb church and secular architecture including a splendid cathedral, fine museums, and a bustling shopping centre. It is an ideal city for walking.

St-Germain-en-Laye

*21km (12 miles) w of Paris. **By Métro/RER**: to St-Germain-en-Laye; **by car**: on N13.*

Smart suburb of Paris; old streets, château, museum of French national antiquities, museum of Symbolist art.

Senlis

*51km (30 miles) NE of Paris. **By train**: from Gare du Nord; **by car**: on A1.*

Old town with narrow streets, a ruined royal castle and a lovely 12thC cathedral.

Vaux-le-Vicomte

*60km (35 miles) SE of Paris. **By train**: from Gare de Lyon; **by car**: on N5.*

Fabulous château — still privately owned — and spacious grounds designed by Le Vau, Le Brun and Le Nôtre.

Chartres

*88km (55 miles) SW of Paris. Population: 41,250. **By train**: from Gare Montparnasse; **by car**: N10 or A11; **by bus**: tours from Cityrama, 4 Pl. des Pyramides, 1ᵉʳ ☎ 42-60-30-14 and Paris-Vision, 214 Rue de Rivoli, 1ᵉʳ ☎ 42-60-31-25. Tourist information: Pl. de la Cathédrale ☎ (16) 37-21-50-00.*

The old district along the banks of the River Eure is beautiful and unspoiled. Here you can wander past old stone bridges, half-timbered houses and gardens reflected in the water, with the cathedral visible at every turn above the jumble of rooftops.

Chartres Cathedral

✗ (compulsory in crypt). Cathedral open daily Apr-Sept 7am-7.30pm, Oct-Mar 7.30am-7pm. Opening hours of crypt, tower and treasury can vary according to season.

No one who has seen the cathedral of Notre-Dame at Chartres will ever forget the experience, for it is a building of potent beauty, a representation of the New Jerusalem on earth, as well as a shrine to the Virgin Mary. The building as it now stands was erected on the site of an earlier church. This burned down in 1194, leaving only the crypt with its precious relic, the **Sancta Camisia** (now in the treasury), said to be the garment which the Virgin was wearing when she gave birth to Jesus. The fire and the survival of the relic were taken to be a sign from the Virgin that she wanted a more impressive shrine. Accordingly, enormous donations poured in from all over Christendom, and a huge army of craftsmen set to work, completing the basic structure of the cathedral in the extraordinarily short span of about 25yrs. This rapidity explains the unique unity of the building as an architectural and aesthetic whole.

The cathedral overflows with visual riches, but one of its most famous features is the abundant **stained glass** (★), which includes three staggering rose windows. The imagery of the stained glass, its graceful tracery depicting legends of saints, could by itself occupy many hours of study. Another attraction is the curious **maze** set into the floor of the nave near the W door, to which many people attribute an esoteric significance. The rich sculpture around the **portals** should also not be missed, nor the intricately worked **screen** separating the choir from the ambulatory. If you have time, climb up to the roof (≼) via a stairway on the N side, for a dizzying view to the N and W through the flying buttresses. It is worthwhile taking one of the excellent English lecture-tours of the cathedral.

Other buildings worth visiting include the churches of **St-Pierre, St-André, St-Martin-au-Val** and **St-Aignan** and the Bishops' Palace, now the **Musée des Beaux-Arts** (▩ *open 10am-noon, 2-6pm; closed Tues*), which contains many fine works of art from medieval ivories to 18thC paintings.

≈ **Le Grand Monarque** (*22 Pl. des Épars, 28000 Chartres* ☎ *(16) 37-21-00-72*▥), grand and sedate; **L'Ouest** (*3 Pl. Pierre-Semard, 28000 Chartres* ☎ *(16) 37-21-43-27*▥).

══ **Le Buisson Ardent** (*10 Rue au Lait* ☎ *(16) 37-34-04-66*▥ *to* ▥▥▥), delicious and interesting food in an old Chartres house; book in advance for the restaurant of **Le Grand Monarque** (*see hotel address above* ☎ *(16) 37-21-00-72*▥▥▥), which serves exceptionally good *nouvelle cuisine*.

▣ **Le Moulin** (*21 Rue de la Tannerie*), by the river; **Salon de Thé Bergamote** (*opposite N door of cathedral*).

Fontainebleau ★
65km (40 miles) SE of Paris. Population: 19,500. By train: from Gare de Lyon to Fontainebleau station, then bus to the palace; by car: on A6 or N7; by bus: tours with Cityrama, 4 Pl. des Pyramides, 1ᵉʳ ☎ *42-60-30-14 or Paris-Vision, 214 Rue de Rivoli, 1ᵉʳ* ☎ *42-60-31-25. Tourist information: 31 Pl. Napoléon Bonaparte* ☎ *64-22-25-68.*

Ideally your visit to Fontainebleau should be a 2-day affair, one to visit the **palace and town**, another to explore the **forest**. This great expanse of woodland is a remarkable natural phenomenon. Over the millennia, a strange alchemy of glacial action and erosion has produced a surreal terrain of hills, ravines and extraordinary rock formations. Giant boulders with organic-looking contours lie everywhere, some resembling stranded whales, others sculptures by Henry Moore. No wonder the forest has been used as a setting for more than 100 films, in which it has served to represent, among other things, the terrain of the Holy Land, the Wild West and the Switzerland of William Tell.

The palace
☎ *64-22-34-39* ▩ ✗ *Open Mon, Wed-Sun 9.30am-12.30pm, 2-5pm. Closed Tues.*

As a former royal residence, the palace of Fontainebleau is just as interesting as Versailles and possesses a much more subtle beauty; even the name has a magical quality, deriving from a fountain in the grounds of the palace, *fontaine belle eau* (fountain of beautiful water). The town also has its charm, a place of well-heeled grace and elegance, with leafy avenues and large, quietly prosperous houses. All around it lies the lovely Fontainebleau forest.

If you have time to spare before visiting the palace, take a walk (allow 45-50mins) through the thickly wooded park, and approach the palace through the **formal garden** with its carp pond, its great *parterres* designed by Le Nôtre in 1664, and its curious statues, which include a pair of sphinxes.

A royal residence from the 12thC, Fontainebleau saw the birth of two French Kings, Philippe le Bel and Louis XIII. But the palace is linked particularly with the colourful François I (1494-1547), rake, military adventurer, friend of Leonardo da Vinci and one of the greatest royal patrons of the arts in French history. In 1528 he knocked down most of the existing medieval edifice and began to build a new château according to the Renaissance principles that had influenced him during his Italian campaigns. All over the building, carved in stonework and panelling, you will see the fire-breathing salamander that was his emblem. Henry II, Catherine de Medici and Henry IV added to the palace.

Most of the French sovereigns lived for a time at Fontainebleau, and the palace has witnessed a rich pageant of history: Louis XIV's decision to revoke the Edict of Nantes was made there; Pope Pius VII lived as a virtual prisoner in the palace from June 1812-Jan 1814; Napoleon I made it his favourite residence after the *Tuileries*, and it was here that he came when he abdicated in 1814, before departing for Elba.

Fontainebleau has been described as a "rendezvous of châteaux", for it is really a sprawling conglomeration of buildings of different periods, built around five courtyards. Before entering, take a walk around the palace. On the N side is the charming **Garden of Diana**, with its fountain decorated with a statue of the goddess. Travelling anti-clockwise, pass into the White Horse Courtyard, or **Courtyard of Farewells**, which was the scene of Napoleon's farewell to his guard. Note the graceful double-horseshoe staircase with its hermetic *caduceuses* carved in the stonework of the balustrade.

To the right of the stairway is an arch leading into the **Fountain Courtyard** looking onto the carp pond. Notice on the right the two stone statues of fierce-looking Fô dogs, guarding the entrance to the Empress Eugénie's Chinese salons.

Through another archway to the W is the **gilded door** that is one of the most famous features of the palace. This huge gateway, with its three superimposed loggias, was the first structure to be completed when rebuilding began in 1528.

From here, the way leads NE along the facade of the ballroom. Turn left to stand between the **Oval Courtyard** to the SW, with its domed gateway, and the **Courtyard of the Kitchens** to the NE. The gateway to the latter is decorated by two huge **Hermes heads** in stone.

Arguably the most remarkable room in the palace is the **François I Gallery (★)**, which was decorated in the years 1534-37 by a team of Italian artists and craftsmen. The walls are adorned with 14 frescoes surrounded by rich decorative stucco work and illustrating events or allegorical subjects connected with the reign of François I. One shows an elephant decorated with the fleur-de-lys — an allegory of the king's wisdom;

another, symbolizing the unity of the state, depicts François I presenting a pomegranate, symbol of concord, to representatives of different classes. Another splendid Renaissance-style room is the vast **ballroom**, which was designed by Philibert Delorme under Henry II. It has deep, arched bays, frescoes of mythological scenes, and a coffered ceiling, the design of which is reflected in the woodwork of the floor.

The rooms known as the **apartments of the King and Queen** are a rich confection of different periods, much of the decoration being in the overblown 19thC style of King Louis-Philippe.

Equally ornate is the series of **Napoleonic rooms**, including the Emperor's Throne Room, bedroom and council chamber. Notice that the Napoleonic bee emblem of industry and discipline figure prominently in the decoration.

Those interested in Napoleon and in militaria should visit the **Musée Napoléonien d'Art et d'Histoire Militaires** (*88 Rue St-Honoré; open Tues-Sat 2-5pm*), which has a splendid collection of military paraphernalia.

Aigle Noir 🏨 (*27 Pl. Napoléon-Bonaparte, 77300 Fontainebleau* ☎ *64-22-32-65* ▮▮▮); **Napoléon** (*9 Rue Grande, 77300 Fontainebleau* ☎ *64-22-20-39* ▮▮).

Aigle Noir (▮▮▮ *to* ▮▮ *see hotel address above*); **François 1er** (*3 Rue Royale* ☎ *64-22-24-68* ▮ *to* ▮▮).

Reims

143km (89 miles) NE *of Paris. Population: 183,500.* **By train:** *from Gare de l'Est;* **by car:** *on A4;* **by bus:** *tours with Cityrama, 4 Pl. des Pyramides, 1er* ☎ *42-60-30-14 and Paris-Vision, 214 Rue de Rivoli, 1er* ☎ *42-60-31-25. Tourist information: 2 Rue Guillaume de Machault* ☎ *(16) 26-47-25-69.*

Reims is famous for two main reasons: its **Gothic cathedral** and the fact that it is the **capital of the Champagne Country** and the place where many of the big producers have their cellars. On a day excursion from Paris, try to arrive early, as the town has much to offer. Try to avoid going Mon-Tues, when the most interesting museums are closed.

Despite the heavy damage suffered in World War I, Reims has remained a gracious place, with quietly elegant streets, solid houses, wide boulevards, fashionable shops and a lively air. Particularly fine is the 18thC **Place Royale**, which was built with Classical simplicity as one unit.

Reims was an important city in Roman times, and some fine monuments of that era remain; the most striking is the **Mars Gate** near the station. This three-arched edifice is thought to have been the largest of its kind in the Roman Empire. The mythological themes carved on it include the story of Romulus and Remus, and local etymology has it that the latter was the founder of the city — hence the name. The Roman forum also survives, in the centre of the **Place du Forum**, and includes among other things an imposing vaulted colonnade, which has been beautifully restored.

Notre-Dame Cathedral (★ *open 8am-7pm, high sections closed in winter*), begun in 1211, is one of the chain of great Gothic churches that includes Chartres, Amiens and Notre-Dame de Paris. Its special importance lies in the fact that all but three kings of France were crowned there. It was one of Joan of Arc's triumphs to take the Dauphin to Reims in 1429, escorting him with an army of 12,000 men through English-held territory, for his coronation as Charles VII.

The cathedral is not as overwhelming as that at Chartres, but it has a graceful splendour. The **w facade**, with its three portals and its sculpture, has eroded over the centuries, but some fine statues still survive, notably the angel to the right of the centre door, whose face bears a curiously mischievous smile.

Inside, the cathedral has the typical majesty and grace of its era, with the characteristic soaring **ribbed ceiling**. The large **rose window** at the w end retains its original 13thC stained glass; most of the original glass was destroyed in World War I, but some of the modern glass is of a very high standard, most notably the three **windows by Chagall** at the E end, and the intriguing windows in the s transept depicting aspects of the Champagne industry.

The **Palais du Tau** (☎ 26-47-74-39 ▨ *open daily 10am-noon, 2-6pm*) is a museum containing the cathedral treasury. It was once a royal residence, and dates from the 12thC. It was damaged in World War I and has been extensively restored. Other churches include the 11thC **Basilica of St-Remi** and the small 20thC **Chapelle Foujita**, in Rue du Champ-de-Mars, which was designed and decorated by the Japanese artist Léonard Foujita, who lived in France.

A delightful museum is the **Hôtel Le Vergeur** (*36 Pl. du Forum* ☎ (16) 26-47-20-75 ▨ *open Tues-Sun 2-6pm*), in a lovely rambling house, parts of which date from the 13thC. The museum was formerly the residence of the art collector and traveller Hugues Krafft, and the contents range from antique furniture and works of art to a priceless collection of original Dürer engravings of the *Apocalypse* and the *Passion of Christ*. The museum also illustrates the history of Reims, and the garden contains a fascinating collection of old facades and doorways.

There are other interesting museums too. The **Musée St-Denis** (*8 Rue Chanzy* ☎ (16) 26-47-28-44 ▨ *open daily 10.30am-noon, 2-6pm; closed Tues*) is a museum of fine arts with a collection of sculpture, furniture, *objets d'art* and French paintings from the 17th-20thC. It contains works by most of the great French painters. The **Ancien Collège des Jésuites** (*1 Pl. Museux* ▨ *open Mon, Wed, Thurs, Fri 10am-noon, 2-6pm*) is a 17thC building with some magnificent rooms, a fine art and furniture collection, and a planetarium (▨ *✕ on weekend afternoons only*).

Champagne cellars and vineyards

If you are interested in champagne, a prime focus of a visit to Reims must be the cellars of one or more of the producers dotted around the suburbs of the town. At the premises of **Piper-Heidsieck**, for example, you descend 18m (54ft) below ground and then proceed, in wagons pulled by an electric car, through catacombs flanked by stacks of bottles. An audiovisual programme on champagne production is also shown.

The easiest way to visit the cellars and vineyards of Reims and also of **Épernay**, 24km (15 miles) to the s, is to take a day trip by bus from Paris. These are arranged by Cityrama, Paris-Vision and other tour operators. If you have your own car, a brochure, obtainable from the Tourist Office in Reims, gives details to enable you to choose your route.

The following champagne cellars in Reims and Épernay welcome visitors. Asterisks indicate that appointments are required.

Reims **Abel Lepitre*** (*2 Av. du Gl-Giraud*); **Besserat de Bellefon***
(*Allée du Vignoble*); **Charles Heidsieck*** (*46 Rue de la Justice*); **Veuve
Clicquot-Ponsardin** (*1 Pl. des Droits-de-l'Homme*); **George Goulet*** (*4
Av. du Gl-Giraud*); **Heidsieck & Co Monopole** (*83 Rue Coquebert*);
Henriot & Co* (*3 Pl. des Droits-de-l'Homme*); **Krug*** (*5 Rue Coquebert*);
Lanson Père & Fils* (*12 Bd. Lundy*); **Louis Roederer*** (*21 Bd. Lundy*);
G.H. Mumm & Co (*34 Rue du Champ-de-Mars*); **Piper-Heidsieck** (*51 Bd.
Henri-Vasnier*); **Pommery & Greno** (*5 Pl. Gl-Gouraud*); **Ruinart Père &
Fils*** (*4 Rue des Crayères*); **Taittinger** (*9 Pl. St-Nicaise*).
Épernay **De Castellane*** (*57 Rue du Verdun*); **G.H. Martel & Co*** (*46
Av. Champagne*); **Mercier** (*75 Av. Champagne*); **Moët & Chandon** (*20
Av. Champagne*); **Perriet-Jouët** (*26 Av. Champagne*); **Pol Roger*** (*1 Rue
Henri-Lelarge*).

☙ **Altea Champagne** (*31 Bd. P-Doumer, 51100 Reims* ☎ *(16)
26-88-53-54* ▥), a stylish modern hotel with above-average service; **La
Paix** (*9 Rue Buirette, 51100 Reims* ☎ *(16) 26-40-04-08* ▢), quiet,
comfortable and modern, good restaurant; **Boyer "Les Crayères"** (*64 Bd.
Vasnier* ☎ *(16) 26-82-80-80* ▦) an elegant hotel with a delightful garden
and one of the best-regarded restaurants in France, offering superb *nouvelle
cuisine*.

═ **Le Chardonnay** (*184 Av. d'Épernay* ☎ *(16) 26-06-08-60* ▥ to ▦);
Les Ombrages (▢ to ▥ *see hotel Altea Champagne above*).

Versailles ★

*24km (15 miles) sw of Paris. Map 24. Population: 97,150. By
train/RER: from Gare St-Lazare or Gare Montparnasse/RER
line C; by car: on N10; by bus: tours with Cityrama, 4 Pl.
des Pyramides, 1ᵉʳ ☎ 42-60-30-14 and Paris-Vision, 214 Rue
de Rivoli, 1ᵉʳ ☎ 42-60-31-25. Tourist information: 7 Rue des
Réservoirs ☎ 39-50-36-22.*

The name of Versailles is so closely linked with the palace that
the town itself tends to be neglected by tourists. It is worth
knowing, however, that Versailles is one of the earliest examples
of what we now call town planning. It was built by royal
command in the 17thC following a carefully designed layout. Its
regular, grid-like pattern of streets and squares (exemplified in
the elegant Pl. Hoche) inspired the designers of such cities as St
Petersburg, Karlsruhe and Washington, DC. Today it preserves a
wealth of domestic architecture dating from the time of Louis XV
and XVI. Two churches worth visiting are **Notre-Dame**, built by
J.H. Mansart in the 1680s, and **St-Louis**, built by Mansart de
Sagonne in the mid-18thC.

Musée Lambinet
54 Bd. de la Reine ☎ *39-50-30-32* ▨ ✗ *Open Tues-Sun 2-6pm.
Closed Mon, public holidays.*

This museum fulfills two objectives: to give an insight into 18thC
life, and to cover the history of the town of Versailles. One room
is dedicated to Charlotte Corday, and others to 19th and 20thC
paintings by artists such as Corot and Boilly.

Le Château de Versailles
*For information on opening times, programmes, group visits
☎ 30-84-74-00* ▨ *but various discounts for children, students and
over-60s, depending on day of week and type of entry (e.g., if not
taking guided tour, under-18s always* ▨*; over-⁻18 and under-26, or
over-60, reduced rate Tues-Sat; everyone, reduced rate on Sun)*
✗ *in English, compulsory* ✗ *in some parts of building. For guided
tours, go to entrance 1; for non-guided tours, go to entrance 2.
Audio-guides available* ═ ▥ ⎾ ⬥ *State apartments open
Tues-Sun 9.45am-5pm; Grand Trianon (separate* ▨*) open
9.45am-noon, 2-5pm; Petit Trianon (separate* ▨ *or cheaper if*

combined with Grand Trianon) open 2-5pm; gardens open daily dawn to dusk. Palace closed Mon, public holidays.

The palace of Versailles is perhaps the greatest monument to absolute monarchy ever built. It is overwhelming, fascinating, unforgettable, but to many people not exactly beautiful. Louis XIV, the Sun King who built it, was extremely vain, and his palace is an expression of egomania in stone, plaster and gold leaf.

The site was first occupied by a hunting lodge and then by a small brick-and-stone château, built by Louis XIII and enlarged by his son Louis XIV, the work continuing from 1661 for about 50yrs. The architects were first Le Vau, then Jules Hardouin-Mansart. The decoration was supervised by Le Brun, and the gardens were planned by Le Nôtre, creator of the **Tuileries** gardens. At the height of the building work, 36,000 men and 6,000 horses were employed.

In 1682 Louis decided to make Versailles the court residence and seat of government, and it retained this function until the Revolution. Thus Versailles was the capital of France for more than 100yrs. It was the scene of a glittering court, which in its heyday included a thousand nobles, who lived in the palace along with a vast retinue of servants.

Approaching the palace from the station and Av. de Paris, the grand **stables** are to the right and left of the vast **Place d'Armes** in front of the palace. Passing through the great wrought-iron gates, the visitor enters the enormous courtyard, with its equestrian statue of Louis XIV, erected by King Louis-Philippe, in the middle. Enter by the doorway on the right of the courtyard, and follow the stairway to the upper chapel vestibule, from where the **chapel** can be seen. Dedicated to St-Louis (King Louis IX of France), it is a frothy confection in white and gold, with a sumptuously painted ceiling.

From here you pass into the series of **State apartments** leading into the astonishing **Hall of Mirrors**, where the 17 windows that overlook the gardens are matched on the opposite wall by a row of arches filled with reflecting glass.

Beside the Hall of Mirrors are the sumptuous **King's apartments**, with the bed where each morning and night the monarch's *levée* and *couchée* took place in front of the assembled courtiers. Louis XIV died of gangrene on this bed on Sept 1, 1715.

At the opposite end of the Hall of Mirrors are the **Queen's apartments**, followed by the **Coronation Room** and then the s wing. Its first floor is taken up almost entirely by the **Hall of Battles**, built by Louis-Philippe, and containing 33 paintings of war scenes. Also on the first floor are several rooms, including the **private apartments of the King and Queen**.

The **Royal Opera**, which occupies the end of the N wing, can also be visited only on a guided tour. Its interior is entirely of wood, ornately carved and painted in gold, blue and pink.

The gardens

🔲 *Open daily, dawn-dusk. Picnics not allowed.*

To understand Versailles fully, it is necessary to appreciate that the whole complex, palace and gardens, is a kind of symbolic Utopia in which one theme is constantly emphasized: that of a solar deity around which everything revolves, just as the state revolves around the king.

This comes across particularly clearly in the **gardens**, which were laid out by Le Nôtre in a series of highly formal terraces adorned with *parterres*, statues, vases and fountains. Nature is subdued, as a demonstration of the power of the Sun King, who is represented here as Apollo.

Bear this in mind as you approach the main focus of the garden, the **fountain of Apollo**, down a long avenue flanked by statues and with a carpet of lawn stretching away into the distance. The figure of Apollo in his chariot emerges out of the water, just as in legend the sun rose out of the sea at daybreak. You can also witness the amazing spectacle of the **illuminated fountains**, by night, and the **Grandes Eaux Musicales** by day (☎ 39-50-36-22 *(Office de Tourisme) for details of times and tickets)*.

Beyond the fountain of Apollo stretches the **Grand Canal**, on which there once sailed a flotilla of small-scale ships and gondolas. Today you can rent a boat to row on the canal, in more modest style. The waterway forms a cross, the northern arm of which leads to the **Grand Trianon** and **Petit Trianon**. These are well worth a visit, the former with its pink marble colonnade and lavish interior, the latter more elegant and restrained, with its exquisite theatre in which Marie-Antoinette used to act. Close by is the **Hameau de la Reine** (Queen's hamlet), a collection of mock-rustic buildings where the same queen used to play at leading the simple life.

Recognizing that some of these attractions are some 15-20mins walk from the château, the management has introduced glass-sided trains (▨ ☎ 39-50-55-12 *for information and reservations*), which offer a running commentary in several languages, and interludes of classical music. These either make a driving circuit, slowing down but not stopping, or allow passengers to descend and be collected again 1½hrs later.

☜ **St-Louis** (*28 Rue St-Louis, 78000 Versailles* ☎ 39-50-23-55 ▮▯ *to* ▮▮▯ ▨).

⇌ **Le Champfagou** (*3 Rue des Deux-Portes* ☎ 39-50-64-04 ▮▮▯ *to* ▮▮▮▯), set in a pedestrianized street and serving the recipes of yesteryear; **La Flotille** (*Parc du Château* ☎ 39-51-41-58 ▮▯), a delightful little restaurant near the E end of the canal, in the palace gardens.

A guide to French

This glossary covers the basic language needs of the traveller: for pronunciation, essential vocabulary and simple conversation, finding accommodation, visiting the bank, shopping, using public transport or a car, and provides a detailed menu decoder, to help when eating out.

Pronunciation

It is plainly impossible to give a summary of the subtlety and richness of the French language, but there are some general tips about pronunciation that it will be helpful to remember once you have decided to communicate with the French in their own language.

French tends to be pronounced in individual syllables rather than in rhythmic feet. For example, the word *institution* has four stresses in French but only two in English. In French the voice usually rises at the ends of words and sentences, whereas it drops in English. French vowels and consonants are shorter, softer and generally more rounded than their English counterparts.

The French language is full of characteristic sounds — the r, the u, the frequent *eau* sound and the nasal sounds (e.g., an, en, ien, in, ain, on, un). These are not as difficult as they may seem: the key is to have confidence. The best way is to speak English while mimicking a strong French accent. The poet Verlaine used this method with his English pupils.

Reference words

Monday	lundi	Friday	vendredi
Tuesday	mardi	Saturday	samedi
Wednesday	mercredi	Sunday	dimanche
Thursday	jeudi	Public holiday	jour férié (m)

January	janvier	July	juillet
February	février	August	août
March	mars	September	septembre
April	avril	October	octobre
May	mai	November	novembre
June	juin	December	décembre

0	zéro	11	onze	22	vingt-deux
1	un	12	douze	30	trente
2	deux	13	treize	40	quarante
3	trois	14	quatorze	50	cinquante
4	quatre	15	quinze	60	soixante
5	cinq	16	seize	70	soixante-dix
6	six	17	dix-sept	80	quatre-vingts
7	sept	18	dix-huit	90	quatre-vingt-dix
8	huit	19	dix-neuf	100	cent
9	neuf	20	vingt	500	cinq cent
10	dix	21	vingt-et-un	1,000	mille

1991/92/93	mil neuf cent quatre-vingt-onze/douze/treize

First	premier, -ière	Quarter-past....	....et quart
Second	second, -e	Half past....	....et demie
Third	troisième	Quarter to....	....moins le/un quart
Fourth	quatrième	Quarter to six	six heures moins le
....o'clock	....heures		quart

Mr	monsieur/M.	Ladies	dames
Mrs	madame/Mme.	Men	hommes
Miss	mademoiselle/Mlle.	Gentlemen	messieurs

Words and phrases

Basic communication

Yes oui (si, for emphatic contradiction)
No non
Please s'il vous plaît
Thank you merci
I'm very sorry je suis désolé/pardon, excusez-moi
Excuse me pardon/excusez-moi
Not at all/you're welcome de rien
Hello bonjour, salut (familiar), allô (on telephone)
Good morning bonjour
Good afternoon bonjour
Good evening bonsoir
Good night bonsoir/bonne nuit
Goodbye au revoir
Morning matin (m)
Afternoon après-midi (m/f)
Evening soir (m)
Night nuit (f)
Yesterday hier
Today aujourd'hui
Tomorrow demain
Next week la semaine prochaine
Last week la semaine dernière
....days ago il y a....jours
Month mois (m)
Year an (m)/année (f)
Here ici
There là
Over there là-bas
Big grand, -e
Small petit, -e
Hot chaud, -e
Cold froid, -e
Good bon, bonne
Bad mauvais, -e
Well bien
Badly mal
With avec
And et
But mais
Very très
All tout, -e
Open ouvert, -e

Closed fermé, -e
Left gauche
Right droite
Straight on tout droit
Near près/proche
Far loin
Up en haut
Down en bas
Early tôt
Late tard
Quickly vite
Pleased to meet you. Enchanté.
How are you? Comment ça va? (Formal: comment allez vous?)
Very well, thank you. Très bien, merci.
Do you speak English? Parlez-vous anglais?
I don't understand. Je ne comprends pas.
I don't know. Je ne sais pas.
Please explain. Pourriez-vous m'expliquer?
Please speak more slowly. Parlez plus lentement, s'il vous plaît.
My name is.... Je m'appelle....
I am English/American. Je suis anglais, -e/americain, -e.
Where is/are? Où est/sont....?
Is there a....? Y a-t-il un, une....?
What? Comment?
How much? Combien?
That's too much. C'est trop.
Expensive cher/chère
Cheap pas cher/bon marché
I would like.... je voudrais....
Do you have....? Avez-vous....?
Just a minute. Attendez une minute. (On telephone: ne quittez pas!)
That's fine/OK. Ça va/OK/ça y est/d'accord.
What time is it? Quelle heure est-il?
I don't feel well. Je ne me sens pas bien/j'ai mal.

Accommodation

Making a reservation by letter

> Dear Sir or Madam, *Monsieur, Madame,*
> I would like to reserve one double room *Je voudrais réserver une chambre pour deux personnes* (with bathroom), *(avec salle de bain),* one twin-bedded room *une chambre avec deux lits* and one single room (with shower) *et une chambre pour une personne (avec douche)* for 7 nights from 12th August. *pour 7 nuits à partir du 12 août.*
> We would like bed and breakfast/half board/full board, *Nous désirons le petit déjeuner/la demi-pension/pension,* and would prefer quiet rooms *et préférerions des chambres tranquilles* with a sea view. *qui donnent sur la mer.*
> Please send me details of your terms with the confirmation. *Je vous serais obligé de m'envoyer vos conditions et tarifs avec la confirmation.*
> Yours sincerely,
> *Veuillez agréer l'expression de mes sentiments distingués.*

Words and phrases

Arriving at the hotel

I have a reservation. My name is....
J'ai une réservation. Je m'appelle....

A quiet room with bath/shower/toilet/wash basin
Une chambre tranquille avec bain/douche/toilette/lavabo

....overlooking the sea/park/street/back.
....qui donne sur la mer/le parc/la rue/la cour.

Does the price include breakfast/service/tax?
Ce prix comprend-il le petit déjeuner/le service/les taxes?

This room is too large/small/cold/hot/noisy.
Cette chambre est trop grande/petite/froide/chaude/
  bruyante.

That's too expensive. Have you anything cheaper?
C'est trop cher. Avez-vous quelque chose de moins cher?

Where can I park my car?
Où puis-je garer ma voiture?

Is it safe to leave the car on the street?
Est-ce qu'on peut laisser la voiture dans la rue?

Floor/storey   étage (m)
Dining room/restaurant   salle à manger (f)/restaurant (m)
Lounge   salon (m)
Porter   portier/concierge(m) porteur (station)
Manager   directeur (m)
Do you have a room?   Avez-vous une chambre?
What time is breakfast/dinner?   À quelle heure est le petit déjeuner/
  dîner?
Can I drink the tap water?   L'eau du robinet est-elle potable?
Is there a laundry service?   Y a-t-il un service de blanchisserie?
What time does the hotel close?   À quelle heure ferme l'hôtel?
Will I need a key?   Aurai-je besoin d'une clé?
Is there a night porter?   Y a-t-il un portier de nuit?
I'll be leaving tomorrow morning.   Je partirai demain matin.
Please give me at call at....   Voulez-vous m'appeler à....
Come in!   Entrez!

Shopping

Where is the nearest/a good....?
Où est le....le plus proche?/Où y a-t-il un bon....?

Can you help me/show me....?
Pouvez-vous m'aider/voulez-vous me montrer....?

I'm just looking.
Je regarde.

Do you accept credit cards/travellers cheques?
Est-ce que vous acceptez les cartes de crédit/chèques de voyage?

Can you deliver it to....?
Pouvez-vous me le livrer à....?

I'll take it.
Je le prends.

I'll leave it.
Je ne le prends pas.

Can I have it tax-free for export?
Puis-je l'avoir hors taxe pour exportation?

This is faulty. Can I have a replacement/refund?
Celui-ci ne va pas. Voulez-vous me l'échanger?

I don't want to spend more than....
Je ne veux pas mettre plus de....

I'll give....for it.
Je vous donne....

Can I have a stamp for....?
Donnez-moi un timbre pour....s'il vous plaît.

Shops

Antique shop antiquaire (m/f)	Bookshop librairie (f)
Art gallery galerie d'art (f)	Butcher boucherie (f)
Bakery boulangerie (f)	Horse butcher boucherie
Bank banque (f)	chevaline (f)
Beauty parlour salon de	Pork butcher charcuterie (f)
beauté (m)	Tripe butcher triperie (f)

202

Cake shop   pâtisserie (f)
Chemist/pharmacy   pharmacie(f) /drugstore (m)
Clothes shop   magasin de vêtements/de mode (m)
Dairy   crèmerie (f)
Delicatessen   épicerie fine (f) charcuterie (f)
Department store   grand magasin (m)
Fishmonger   marchand de poisson/poissonnier (m)
Florist   fleuriste (m/f)
Greengrocer   marchand de légumes (m)
Grocer   épicier (m)
Haberdasher   mercier (m)
Hairdresser   coiffeur (m)
Hardware store   droguerie (f)
Jeweller   bijouterie/joaillerie (f)

Market   marché (m)
Newsagent   marchand de journaux (m)
Optician   opticien (m/f)
Perfumery   parfumerie (f)
Photographic shop   magasin de photographie (m)
Post office   bureau de poste (m)
Shoe shop   magasin de chaussures (m)
Souvenir shop   magasin de cadeaux/souvenirs (m)
Stationer   papeterie (f)
Supermarket   supermarché (m)
Tailor   tailleur (m)
Tobacconist   bureau de tabac (m)
Tourist office   syndicat d'initiative (m)
Toy shop   magasin de jouets (m)
Travel agent   agence de voyage (f)

At the bank
I would like to change some pounds/dollars/travellers cheques.
Je voudrais changer des livres/dollars/chèques de voyage.
What is the exchange rate?
Quel est le cours du change?
Can you cash a personal cheque?
Pouvez-vous encaisser un chèque personnel?
Can I obtain cash with this credit card?
Puis-je obtenir de l'argent avec cette carte de crédit?
Do you need to see my passport?
Voulez-vous voir mon passeport?

Some useful goods
From the chemist:
Antiseptic cream   crème antiseptique (f)
Aspirin   aspirine (f)
Bandages   pansements (m) bandes (f)
Cotton wool   coton hydrophile (m)
Diarrhea/upset stomach pills   comprimés (m) pour la diarrhée/ l'estomac dérangé
Indigestion tablets   comprimés pour l'indigestion
Insect repellant   anti-insecte (m)
Laxative   laxatif (m)
Sanitary towels   serviettes hygiéniques (f)
Shampoo   shampooing (m)
Shaving cream   crème à raser (f)
Soap   savon (m)
Sticking plaster   sparadrap (m)
String   ficelle (f)
Sunburn cream   crème écran solaire (f)

Suntan cream/oil   crème solaire (f)/huile bronzante (f)
Tampons   tampons (m)
Tissues   mouchoirs en papier (m)
Toothbrush   brosse à dents (f)
Toothpaste   (pâte) dentifrice (f)
Travel sickness pills   comprimés pour les maladies de transport

Clothing:
Bra   soutien-gorge (m)
Coat   manteau (m)
Dress   robe (f)
Jacket   veste/jaquette (f)
Pants   slip (m)
Pullover   pull (m)
Shirt   chemise (f)
Shoes   chaussures (f)
Skirt   jupe (f)
Socks   chaussettes (f)
Stockings/tights   bas/collants (m)
Sunglasses   lunettes de soleil (f)
Swimsuit   maillot de bain (m)
Trousers   pantalon (m)

Miscellaneous:
Film   film (m)/pellicule (f)
Letter   lettre (f)
Money order   mandat (m)

Postcard   carte postale (f)
Stamp   timbre (m)
Telegram   télégramme (m)

Motoring
Service station   station-service (f)
Fill it up.   Le plein, s'il vous plaît.
Give me....francs worth.   Donnez m'en pour....francs.

Words and phrases

I would like....litres of petrol. Je voudrais....litres d'essence.
Can you check the....? Voulez-vous vérifier....?
There is something wrong with the.... Il y a quelque chose qui ne va pas dans le....

Battery batterie (f)
Brakes freins (m)
Exhaust échappement (m)
Lights phares (m)

Oil huile (f)
Tyres pneus (m)
Water eau (f)
Windscreen pare-brise (m)

My car won't start. Ma voiture ne veut pas démarrer.
My car has broken down/had a flat tyre. Je suis tombé en panne/J'ai eu une crevaison.
The engine is overheating. Le moteur chauffe.
How long will it take to repair? Il faudra combien de temps pour la réparer?

Car rental

Is full/comprehensive insurance included? Est-ce que l'assurance tous-risques est comprise?
Is it insured for another driver? Est-elle assurée pour un autre conducteur?
Unlimited mileage kilométrage illimité
Deposit caution (f)
By what time must I return it? À quelle heure devrais-je la ramener?
Can I return it to another depot? Puis-je la ramener à une autre agence?
Is the petrol tank full? Est-ce que le réservoir est plein?

Road signs

Aire (de repos) motorway layby
Autres directions other directions
Centre ville town centre
Chaussée deformée irregular surface
Déviation diversion
Passage à niveau level crossing
Passage protégé priority for vehicles on main road
Péage toll point

Priorité à droite priority for vehicles coming from the right
Ralentir slow down
Rappel remember that a previous sign still applies
Route barrée road blocked
Sortie de secours emergency exit
Stationnement interdit no parking
Stationnement toléré literally, parking tolerated
Toutes directions all directions
Verglas (black) ice on road

Other methods of transport

Aircraft avion (m)
Airport aéroport (m)
Bus autobus (m)
Bus stop arrêt d'autobus (m)
Coach car (m)
Ferry/boat ferry/bâteau/bac (m)
Ferry port port du ferry/bâteau/bac (m)
Hovercraft hovercraft/ aéroglisseur (m)

Station gare (m)
Train train (m)
Ticket billet (m)
Ticket office guichet (m)
Single billet simple
Return billet aller-retour
Half fare demi-tarif
First/second class première/ seconde classe
Sleeper/couchette wagon-lit (m)

When is the next....for....? À quelle heure est le prochain.... pour....?
What time does it arrive? À quelle heure arrive-t-il?
What time does the last....for....leave? À quelle heure part le dernier....pour....?
Which platform/quay/gate? Quel quai/port?
Is this the....for....? Est-ce que c'est bien le....pour....?
Is it direct? Where does it stop? C'est direct? Où est-ce qu'il s'arrête?
Do I need to change anywhere? Est-ce que je dois changer?
Please tell me where to get off? Pourrez-vous me dire ou je dois descendre?
Take me to.... Conduisez-moi à....
Is there a buffet car? Y a-t-il un wagon-restaurant?

Food and drink

Have you a table for....? Avez-vous une table pour....?
I want to reserve a table. Je voudrais réserver une table.
A quiet table. Une table bien tranquille.
A table near the window. Une table près de la fenêtre.
Could we have another table? Est-ce que nous pourrions avoir une autre table?

204

Set menu   Menu prix-fixe
I did not order this   Je n'ai pas commandé cela
Bring me another....   Apportez-moi encore un....
The bill please   L'addition, s'il vous plaît
Is service included?   Le service, est-il compris?

Breakfast   petit déjeuner(m)
Lunch   déjeuner(m)
Dinner   dîner(m)
Hot   chaud
Cold   froid
Glass   verre(m)
Bottle   bouteille(f)
Half-bottle   demi-bouteille
Beer/lager   bière(f)/lager(m)
Draught beer   bière pression
Orange/lemon squash   sirop
   d'orange/de citron(m)
Mineral water   eau
   minérale(f)
Fizzy   gazeuse
Still   non-gazeuse
Fruit juice   jus de fruit(m)
Red wine   vin rouge(m)
White wine   vin blanc
Rosé wine   vin rosé
Vintage   année(f)

Dry   sec
Sweet   doux(of wine)
   sucré(of food)
Salt   sel(m)
Pepper   poivre(m)
Mustard   moutarde(f)
Oil   huile(m)
Vinegar   vinaigre(m)
Bread   pain(m)
Butter   beurre(m)
Cheese   fromage(m)
Milk   lait(m)
Coffee   café(m)
Tea   thé(m)
Chocolate   chocolat(m)
Sugar   sucre(m)
Steak   biftek(m)
   well done   bien cuit
   medium   cuit à point
   rare   saignant
   very rare   bleu

Menu decoder

Agneau   lamb
Agneau de pré salé   young lamb
   grazed in fields bordering the sea
Aiglefin   haddock
Aigre-doux   sweet and sour
Aiguillettes   thin slices
Ail   garlic
Ailerons   chicken wings
Aïoli   garlic mayonnaise
Allumettes   puff pastry strips
   garnished or filled
Alouette   lark
Ananas   pineapple
Anchoïade   anchovy paste, usually
   served on crispy bread
Anchois   anchovies
Andouillette   chitterling sausage
Anguille   eel
Arachides   peanuts
Artichaut   artichoke
Asperges   asparagus
Assiette assortie   mixture of cold
   hors d'oeuvre
Baguette   long bread loaf
Banane   banana
Barbue   brill
Barquette   pastry boat
Basilic   basil
Baudroie   monkfish
Belons   flat shelled oysters
Betterave   beetroot
Beurre   butter
Biftek   beefsteak
Bignorneaux   winkles
Bisque   shellfish soup
Blanchailles   whitebait
Blanquette   "white" stew thickened
   with egg yolk
Bombe   elaborate ice cream
Bouchée   tiny vol-au-vent

Boudin (noir ou blanc)   (black or
   white) sausage pudding
Bouillabaisse   Mediterranean fish
   soup with fresh fish and saffron
Bouillon   broth
Bourride   Provençal soup of mixed
   fish with aïoli
Brandade de morue   purée of salt
   cod, milk and garlic
Brioche   soft bread
(à la) Broche   spit-roasted
Brochet   pike
Brochette   meat or fish on a
   skewer
Cabillaud   cod
Calmar   squid
Canard   duck
Carré (d'agneau)   loin (of lamb)
Cassis   blackcurrant
Cassoulet   casserole from
Languedoc   with beans, preserved
   goose and pork
Cèpes   prized wild, dark brown
   mushrooms
Cervelles   brains
Champignon   mushroom
Chanterelle, girolle   apricot-
   coloured mushroom
Chantilly   whipped cream with
   sugar
Chicorée   curly endive/chicory
Chou   light puff pastry/cabbage
Choucroute   pickled white
   cabbage/sauerkraut
Chou-fleur   cauliflower
Citron   lemon
Citron vert   lime
Civet de lièvre   jugged hare
Colin   hake
Concombre   cucumber

Words and phrases

Confit meat covered in its own fat, cooked and preserved
Confit d'oie preserved goose
Confiture jam
Contre-filet sirloin steak
Coquillages shellfish
Coquilles St-Jacques scallops, usually cooked in wine
Côte, côtelette chop, cutlet
Coupe ice-cream dessert
Crabe crab
Crème cream
Crêpe thin pancake
Cresson watercress
Crevettes grises shrimps
Crevettes roses prawns
Croque-monsieur toasted cheese-and-ham sandwich
Croustade small bread or pastry mould with savoury filling
(en) Croûte cooked in a pastry case
Cru raw
Crudités selection of raw sliced vegetables
Cuisses (de grenouilles) (frogs') legs
Cuit cooked
Culotte de boeuf rump of beef
Darne thick slice, usually of fish
Daube meat slowly braised in a rich wine stock
Daurade sea bream
Dindon turkey
Écrevisses freshwater crayfish
Émincé thinly sliced
Endive endive
Épaule (d'agneau) shoulder (of lamb)
Éperlans smelts
Épices spices
Épinards spinach
Escabèche various fish, fried, marinated and served cold
Escargots snails
Estouffade a stew marinated and fried then slowly braised
Estragon tarragon
Faisan pheasant
Farci stuffed
Faux filet sirloin steak
Fenouil fennel
Feuilleté light flaky pastry
Filet fillet
Flageolets fava beans
Flétan halibut
Foie liver
Foie gras goose liver
(au) Four cooked in the oven
Fourré stuffed
Frais, fraîche fresh
Fraises strawberries
Framboises raspberries
Frappé surrounded by crushed ice
Fricadelle kind of meat ball
Frit fried
Frites chips/French fries

Fritots fritters
Fruits de mer seafood
Fumé smoked
Galantine cooked meat, fish or vegetables served cold in a jelly
Galette flaky pastry case
Gambas large prawns
Garbure very thick soup
Garni garnished
Gâteau cake
Gibier game
Gigot (d'agneau) leg (of lamb)
Glace ice-cream
Glacé iced, frozen, glazed
(au) Gratin crisp browned topping of cheese
Grenouilles frogs
Grillé grilled
Grive thrush
Hachis minced
Harengs herrings
Haricot stew with vegetables/beans
Haricots verts green beans
Homard lobster
Huile (d'olive) (olive) oil
Huîtres oysters
Jambon ham
Laitue lettuce
Langouste spiny lobster or crayfish
Langoustines Dublin bay prawns
Langue (de boeuf) (ox) tongue
Lapin rabbit
Légumes vegetables
Lièvre hare
Loup de mer sea bass
Magret (de canard) breast (of duck)
Maïs sweetcorn
Maquereaux mackerel
Marcassin young wild boar
Marrons chestnuts
Matelote freshwater fish stew
Merlin whiting
Morilles edible dark-brown fungi
Morue cod
Moules mussels
Moules marinière mussels cooked with white wine and shallots
Museau de porc pig's snout
Navarin stew of lamb and young root vegetables
Noix nuts, usually walnuts
Noix de veau rump of veal
Oeufs eggs
Oie goose
Oignons onions
Oseille sorrel
Oursins sea urchins
Palourdes clams
Pamplemousse grapefruit
(en) Papillote cooked in oiled or buttered paper
Pâte pastry
Paupiette thin slices of meat or fish rolled up and filled
Pêche peach
Perdreau partridge

Persil   parsley
Petit salé   salted pork
Petits fours   tiny cakes and sweets
Petits pois   peas
Pieds de porc   pigs' trotters
Pignons   pine nuts
Piments doux   sweet peppers
Pintade   guinea fowl
Pissaladière   bread dough or pizza
   covered with tomatoes
Pissenlits   dandelion leaves, used
   in salads
Pistou   vegetable soup with a paste
   of garlic, basil and oil
Poché   poached
Pochouse   fish stew
Poire   pear
Poireaux   leeks
Poisson   fish
Poitrine de porc   belly of pork
Pomme   apple
Pomme de terre   potato
Porc   pork
Poularde   capon
Poulet   young spring chicken
Poulpe   octopus
Poussin   very small baby chicken
Primeurs   young vegetables or
   wines
(à la) Provençale   with tomatoes,
   garlic, olive oil, etc
Quenelles   light dumplings of fish
   or poultry
Queue de boeuf   oxtail
Quiche   egg- and milk-based open
   pie
Radis   radishes
Raie   skate
Raifort   horseradish
Ris (de veau)   (calf's) sweetbreads
Riz   rice
Rognons   kidneys

Romarin   rosemary
Rôti   roast
Rouget   red mullet
Rouille   garlic and chili sauce
   usually served with fish soups
Safran   saffron
Saint Pierre   John Dory
Salade Niçoise   salad including
   tomatoes, beans, potatoes, black
   olives and tuna
Sanglier   wild boar
Saucisses   fresh wet sausage
Saucisson   dry sausage
   (salami-type)
Sauge   sage
Saumon   salmon
Selle (d'agneau)   saddle (of
   lamb)
Suprême de volaille   chicken
   breast and wing fillet
Tapenade   purée of black olives
   and olive oil
Tête (de veau)   (calf's) head
Thon   tuna fish
Thym   thyme
Timbale   dome-shaped mould or
   the pie cooked within it
Tournedos   small thick round slices
   of beef fillet
Tourte   covered tart
Tranche   slice
Truffes   truffles
Truite   trout
Truite saumonée   salmon trout
(à la) Vapeur   steamed
Veau   veal
Viande   meat
Vinaigrette   oil-and-vinegar
   dressing
Volaille   poultry
Vol-au-vent   puff pastry
   case

Index

With the exception of a few of the most notable, such as the café Les Deux Magots and the Hôtel de Crillon, individual hotels, restaurants, cafés and shops have not been indexed, because they appear in alphabetical order within their appropriate sections. However, the sections themselves are indexed. Similarly, although most streets are given in the list of street names on page 220 and not in the index, a few exceptions, such as the Av. des Champs-Élysées, are indexed as well.

Page numbers in **bold** type indicate the main entry. *Italic* page numbers refer to the illustrations and plans.

Index

Index

Index

Index

214

Index

Index

List of street names

All streets mentioned in the book that fall within the area covered by our maps are listed here. Each street name is followed by a map reference to one or more of the maps that follow this list. Map numbers are printed in **bold** type.

It was not possible to label every street drawn on the maps, although of course all major streets and most smaller ones are named. Those streets that are not named on the maps are still given map references in this list, because this serves as an approximate location that will nearly always be sufficient for you to find your way.

A

Aguesseau, Rue d', **8**F6
Albert-de-Mun, Av., **12**H2
Alésia, Rue d', **7**H5
Alger, Rue d', **8**G7
Aligre, Pl. d', **17**J13
Alma, Pont de l', **7**G4
Alphonse-Laveran, Pl., **15**L9
Amsterdam, Rue d', **3**E7
Anatole-France, Quai, **8**H6-7
Ancienne-Comédie, Rue de l', **9**I8
André Malraux, Pl., **9**H8
Anjou, Rue d', **11**J11
Antoine-Bourdelle, Rue, **14**K6
Arago, Bd., **15**M8
Archevêché, Pont de l', **10**J10
Archives, Rues des, **11**H11
Arrivée, Rue de l', **14**K6
Arsenal, Rue de l', **16**J11-**17**J12
Arts, Pont des, **9**H8
Assas, Rue d', **14**J-K7
Athènes, Rue d', **3**E7
Auber, Rue, **8**F7
Aubriot, Rue, **10**H10
Auguste-Vacquerie, Rue, **6**F3

B

Babylone, Rue de, **13**J5
Bac, Rue du, **8**H7-J6
Barbès, Rue, **18**C3
Barbet-de-Jouy, Rue, **13**J6
Barres, Rue des, **10**I10
Barye, Sq., **11**J11
Bastille, Bd. de la, **11**J-K12
Bastille, Pl. de la, **17**J12
Bayard, Rue, **7**G4
Beaubourg, Plateau, **10**H10
Beaubourg, Rue, **10**H10
Beaujolais, Pge. de, **9**G8
Beaujolais, Rue de, **9**G8
Beaumarchais, Bd., **11**I12
Beauregard, Rue, **10**F9

Beaux-Arts, Rue des, **9**I8
Bellechasse, Rue de, **8**H6
Belleville, Bd. de, **19**C5
Belleville, Rue de, **19**C5
Belzunce, Rue de, **5**E10
Bercy, Quai de, **17**L13-M14
Berri, Rue de, **7**E4
Berryer, Cité, **8**G6
Béthune, Quai de, **16**J10-11
Bichat, Rue, **11**F12
Birague, Rue de, **11**I11
Blanche, Pl., **4**D7
Blanche, Rue de, **3**D-E7
Blancs-Manteaux, Rue des, **10**H10
Boëtie, Rue de la, **7**F4
Boissy d'Anglas, Rue, **8**G6
Bonaparte, Rue, **9**I8
Bonne-Nouvelle, Bd. de, **5**F10
Boul'Mich *see* St-Michel, Bd.
Bourdonnais, Rue des, **9**H8
Bourg-l'Abbé, Pge. du, **10**G10
Bourg-l'Abbé, Rue du, **10**G10
Bourgogne, Rue de, **8**H6
Bourse, Pl. de la, **9**F8
Branly, Quai, **12**I2
Bûcherie, Rue de la, **10**J9
Buci, Rue de, **9**I8

C

Cadet, Rue, **4**E9
Caire, Pge. du, **10**G10
Cambon, Rue, **8**G7
Canettes, Rue des, **15**J8
Capucines, Bd. des, **8**F7&**9**F8
Cardinal-Lemoine, Rue du, **16**K10
Carmes, Rue des, **10**J9
Carnot, Av., **6**E3
Carrousel, Pl. du, **8**H7
Carrousel, Pont du, **8**H7
Cassette, Rue, **14**J7
Castiglione, Rue de, **8**G7
Caulaincourt, Rue, **4**C8
Cavalerie, Rue de la, **12**J3

Cdt-Mouchotte, Rue du, **14**L6
Celestins, Quai des, **11**J11
Chaligny, Rue, **17**K14
Champ-de-Mars, Rue du, **13**I4
Champerret, Porte de, **18**C3
Champs-Élysées, Av. des, **6**E1-**7**G6
Champs-Élysées, Rond-point des, **7**F-G5
Chanoinesse, Rue, **10**I10
Chapon, Rue, **10**H10
Chaptal, Rue, **4**D8
Charles-de-Gaulle, Pl., **6**F3
Charles-Dullin, Pl., **4**D9
Charonne, Rue de, **17**J13
Chat-qui-Pêche, Rue du, **10**I9
Châteaubriand, Rue de, **7**F4
Chemin-Vert, Rue du, **11**I12
Cherche-Midi, Rue du, **14**K6-J7
Chevalier-de-la-Barre, Rue du, **4**C9
Choiseul, Pge., **9**F8
Choiseul, Rue de, **9**F8
Christine, Rue, **9**I8
Ciseaux, Rue des, **15**I8
Clément, Rue, **15**J8
Cler, Rue, **13**H4
Cléry, Pge. de, **9**G9
Clichy, Bd. de, **3**D7&**4**D8
Colisée, Rue du, **7**F4-5
Colombe, Rue de la, **10**I10
Commerce-St-André, Cours du, **11**H11
Concorde, Pl. de la, **8**G6
Concorde, Pont de la, **8**H6
Conférence, Port de la, **7**G4
Constantine, Rue, **13**H5
Conti, Quai de, **9**I8
Contrescarpe, Pl. de la, **15**K9
Copernic, Rue, **6**F2
Coq-Héron, Rue du, **10**G9

Street names

L

Lamarck, Rue, **4**C8
Lambert, Rue, **4**C9
Lamennais, Rue, **7**F4
Lavandières-Ste-
    Opportune, Rue des,
    9H9
Lappe, Rue de, **11**I12
La Tour-Maubourg,
    Bd. de, **7**H-I5
Laugier, Rue, **6**D3
Léonard-de-Vinci, Rue,
    6F2
Lille, Rue de, **8**H7
Linné, Rue, **16**K10
Longchamp, Rue de, **6**G2
Lord-Byron, Rue, **6**F3
Louis XVI, Sq., **8**F6
Louis-Boilly, Rue, **18**D4
Louis-Lépine, Pl., **9**I9
Louvois, Sq., **9**G8
Louvre, Pl. du, **9**H9
Louvre, Quai du, **9**H8
Louvre, Rue du, **10**G-H9
Lyon, Rue de, **11**J-K12

M

MacMahon, Av., **6**E3
Madame, Rue, **14**J7
Madeleine, Bd. de la, **8**F7
Madeleine, Pl. de la, **8**F6
Madrid, Rue de, **3**E6
Maine, Av. du, **14**L6
Maître-Albert, Rue, **16**J10
Malaquais, Quai, **9**I8
Manin, Rue, **19**C5
Marbeuf, Rue, **7**F-G4
Marceau, Av., **6**G3
Marcellin-Berthelot, Pl.,
    15J9
Marché-St-Honoré, Pl.
    du, **8**G7
Marché-St-Honoré, Rue
    du, **8**G7
Mare, Rue de la, **4**E8
Marigny, Carré, **7**G5
Martyrs, Rue des, **4**D-E8
Matignon, Av., **7**F5
Mazarine, Rue, **9**I8
Mégisserie, Quai de la,
    9I9
Ménilmontant, Bd. de,
    7F5
Miromesnil, Rue, **7**E-F5
Molière, Rue, **9**H9
Monceau, Rue de, **7**E5
Mondétour, Rue, **9**H9
Monge, Rue, **16**J-L10
Monsieur-le-Prince, Rue,
    15J8
Montreuil, Pte. de, **19**D5
Mont-Thabor, Rue du,
    8G7
Montagne Ste-
    Geneviève, Rue de la,
    10J-K9

Montaigne, Av., **7**G4
Montalembert, Rue, **8**I7
Montebello, Quai, **9**J9
Montmartre, Bd., **9**F9
Montmartre, Rue, **9**G9
Montmorency, Rue de,
    10H10
Montorgueil, Rue, **10**G9
Montparnasse, Bd. du,
    14K6-**15**L8
Montparnasse, Rue, **14**K7
Montpensier, Rue de, **9**G8
Morillons, Rue des, **19**D4
Motte-Picquet, Av. de la,
    12J3
Mouffetard, Rue, **16**K10

N

Nation, Pl. de la, **19**D5
Navarre, Rue de, **16**K10
New York, Av. de, **12**H2-3
Nollet, Rue, **3**C6
Notre-Dame-des-Champs,
    Rue, **14**K7

O

Oberkampf, Rue,
    11G-H12
Observatoire, Av. de l',
    15K-L8
Odéon, Carrefour de l',
    15J8
Odéon, Pl. de l', **15**J8
Odéon, Rue de l', **15**J8
Opéra, Av. de l', **9**G8
Opéra, Pl. de l', **8**F7
Orfèvres, Quai des, **9**I6
Orléans, Quai d', **10**J10
Orsay, Quai d', **7**H4-6

P

Paix, Rue de la, **8**F7
Palais, Bd. du, **10**I9
Palais-Royal, Pl. du, **9**H8
Palestro, Rue de, **10**G10
Panoramas, Pge. des, **9**F9
Panthéon, Pl. du, **15**K9
Paradis, Rue de, **5**E10
Parcheminerie, Rue de la,
    10J9
Parc-Royal, Rue du,
    11H11
Parvis-du-Sacré-Coeur,
    Pl. du, **4**C9
Parvis-Notre-Dame, Pl.
    du, **16**J10
Passy, Rue de, **6**I2
Patriarches, Pge. des,
    16L10
Paul-Chatrousse, Rue,
    15J8
Paul-Claudel, Pl., **15**J8
Paul-Painlevé, Pl., **10**J9
Pavée, Rue, **11**I11
Payenne, Rue, **11**I11
Peletier, Rue Le, **4**E8

Penthièvre, Rue de, **7**F5-6
Pereire, Bd., **2**C4-5
Pergolèse, Rue, **6**E2
Perle, Rue de la, **11**H11
Petits-Champs, Rue des,
    9G8
Petites-Écuries, Cour des,
    5F10
Pierre 1er-de-Serbie, Av.,
    6G3
Pierre-Charron, Rue, **7**F4
Pierre-Demours, Rue,
    6D3
Pierre-Lescot, Rue, **10**H9
Pigalle, Pl., **4**D8
Plâtre, Rue du, **10**H10
Poissonnière, Bd., **4**F9
Poissonnière, Rue, **9**F9
Pompe, Rue de la, **6**F1
Ponceau, Pge., **10**G10
Pont Louis-Philippe, Rue
    du, **10**I10
Pont-Neuf, **9**H9
Ponthieu, Rue, **7**F5
Pontoise, Rue de, **10**J10
Pont-Royal, **8**H7
Porte-Maillot, Pl. de la,
    6E1
Postes, Pge. des, **16**L10
Potier, Pge. de, **9**G8
Poulbot, Rue, **4**C8
Pré-aux-Clercs, Rue du,
    8I7
Président-Kennedy, Av.
    du, **12**I1-2
Président-Wilson, Av. du,
    12G3
Prêtres St-Séverin, Rue
    des, **10**J9
Princes, Pge. des, **9**F8
Princesse, Rue, **15**J8
Printemps, Rue du **2**C5
Puits-de-l'Ermite, Pl. du,
    16L10
Pyramides, Pl. des, **8**G7
Pyrénées, Rue des, **8**G7

Q

Quatre-Vents, Rue des,
    15J8

R

Rabelais, Rue, **7**F5
Rambuteau, Rue, **10**H10
Raphael, Av., **14**M7
Raspail, Bd., **14**I-M7
Raynouard, Rue, **12**I1
Reine-de-Hongrie, Pge.
    de la, **10**G-H9
Renard, Rue du, **10**H10
René Viviani, Sq., **10**J9
Rennes, Rue de, **14**K6
République, Pl. de la,
    11G11
Résistance, Pl. de la, **7**H4
Richelieu, Pge. de, **9**G8
Richelieu, Rue de, **9**F-G8

PARIS

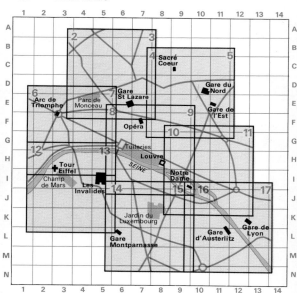

LEGEND

City Maps

| 0 | 100 | 200 | 300 | 400 | 500 m. |

- Major Place of Interest
- Other Important Building
- Built-up Area
- Park
- Cemetery
- Named church, church
- ☾ Mosque
- ✡ Synagogue
- ✚ Hospital
- ✚ Emergency Hospital
- *ℓ* Information Office
- ⊠ Post Office
- ✋ Police Station
- ⬤ Car Park
- Ⓜ Métro/R.E.R. Station
- → One-way Street
- Stepped Street
- No Entry
- Arrondissement Boundary
- **10** Adjoining Page No.

Area Maps

- ■ Place of Interest
- Built-up Area (Paris centre)
- Surrounding built-up area
- Wood or Park
- Cemetery
- Motorway (with access point)
- Motorway under construction
- Main Road-Dual Carriageway
- Other Main Road
- Secondary Road
- Railway
- R.E.R.
- ✈ Airport

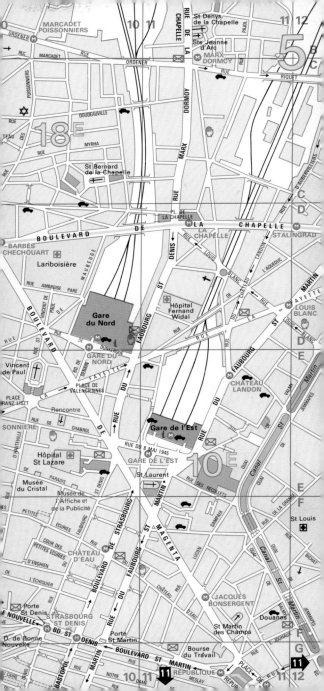

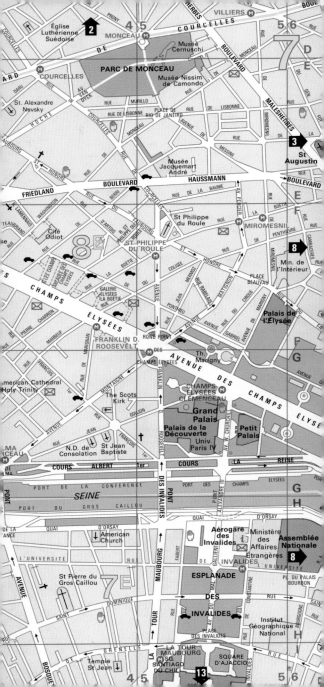

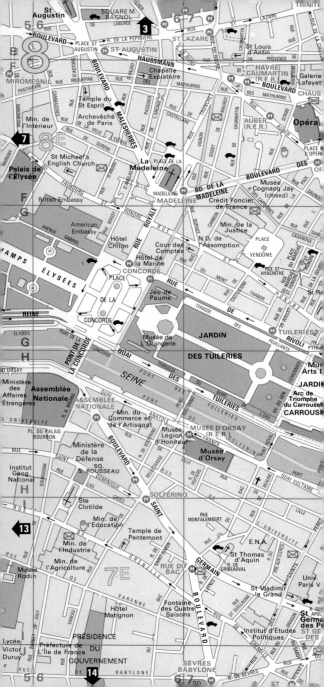

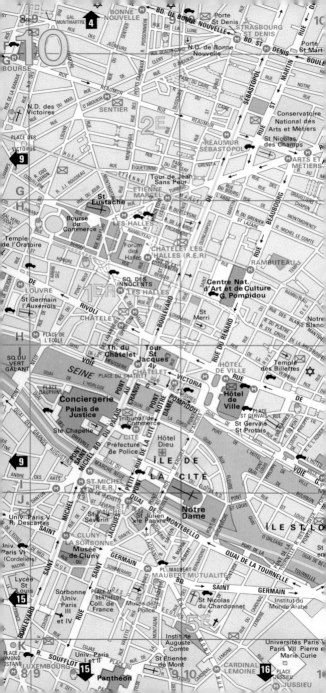

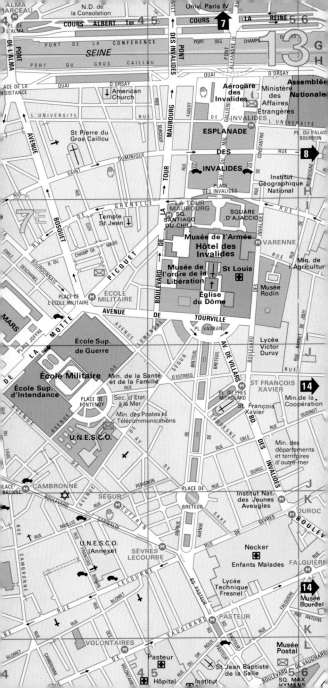

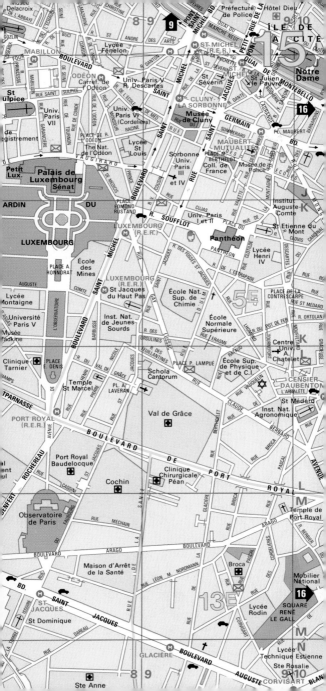

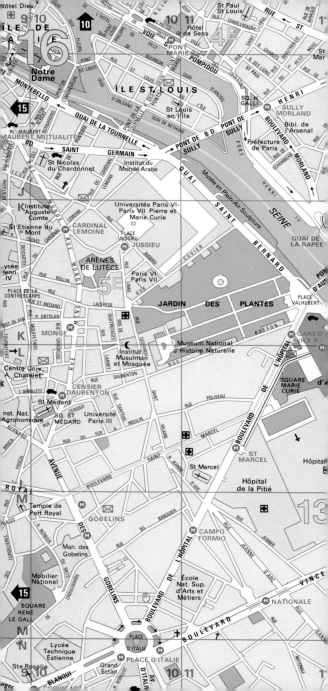

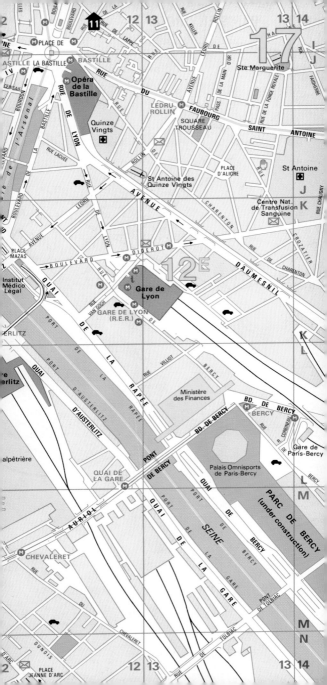

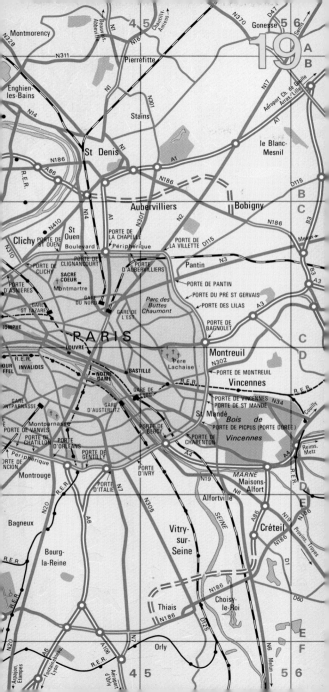

PARIS MÉTRO/R.E.R.

*Chambre des Députés is now called Assemblée Nationale.
◆Liége and Rennes stations are closed after 8pm, and on Sundays and public holidays.

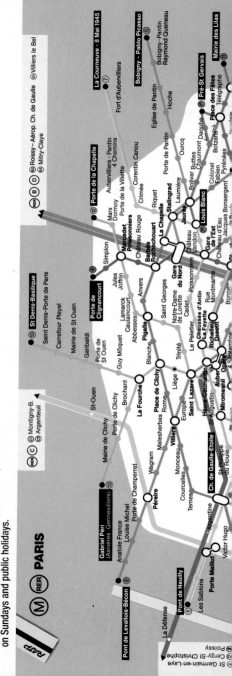

PARIS AUTOBUS

BUS Paris

RATP

La Défense 73

Neuilly
Hôp. Américain 82

Neuilly
Pl. de Bagatelle 43

Levallois
Libération 93

Levallois-Marie 94

Levallois
Gustave Eiffel 53

Pte de Champerret 84 92

Ch. de Gaulle-Etoile 83

Victor Hugo

Pte Maillot

Pte de Clichy

Asnières-Genneviliers
Gabriel Péri 54

Pte d'Asnières

Pont
Cardinet

Brochant

Guy
Môquet

Clichy-Hôp. Beaujon 54

Clichy-Victor Hugo 81

Pte de St Ouen 66

St Ouen-Marie 85

Pte de Clichy

Pl. de Clichy 68

Gare St Lazare
20 21 26
27 28 29

St Augustin

Madeleine

Rd-Point des
Champs Elysées

Friedland
Haussmann 84 83

Pte de Montmartre 60 95

Marie du XVIII 56

Pte de Clignancourt
42 43 45
47 48 49

Pte de la Chapelle

Pte de la Villette

Aubervilliers-Marie 65

Roissy-Aérop. Ch. de Gaulle 350

Marx Dormoy

Pte de Pantin

Pré St Gervais
Jean Jaurès 61

Bobigny-Pantin
Raymond Queneau 151

Bagnolet-Malassis

Pte des Lilas 48

Gambetta 60 69

Gare du Nord

Gare de l'Est
30 31
32 38
39 350

République 54

Strasbourg
St Denis

Richelieu-Drouot

Carrefour de
Châteaudun

Trinité

Pigalle 67

Montmartrobus

Opéra
22 32
24 53
66

Colonel Fabien

Mairie du XIX

Jaurès

Marie du XVIII

Pte de la Chapelle
350 65